Oxford AQA History

A LEVEL AND AS

Component 1

The Tudors: England 1485–1603

Michael Tillbrook

SERIES EDITOR
Sally Waller

OXFORD

OXFORD
UNIVERSITY PRESS

Great Clarendon Street, Oxford, OX2 6DP, United Kingdom

Oxford University Press is a department of the University of Oxford. It furthers the University's objective of excellence in research, scholarship, and education by publishing worldwide. Oxford is a registered trade mark of Oxford University Press in the UK and in certain other countries

First published in 2015

British Library Cataloguing in Publication Data
Data available

978-019-835460-4

Kindle edition: 978-019-836398-9

10 9 8 7 6 5 4

Paper used in the production of this book is a natural, recyclable product made from wood grown in sustainable forests.
The manufacturing process conforms to the environmental regulations of the country of origin.

Printed in India by Multivista Global Pvt. Ltd

Approval message from AQA

This textbook has been approved by AQA for use with our qualification. This means that we have checked that it broadly covers the specification and we are satisfied with the overall quality. Full details of our approval process can be found on our website.

We approve textbooks because we know how important it is for teachers and students to have the right resources to support their teaching and learning. However, the publisher is ultimately responsible for the editorial control and quality of this book.

Please note that when teaching the AQA A Level History course, you must refer to AQA's specification as your definitive source of information. While this book has been written to match the specification, it does not provide complete coverage of every aspect of the course.

A wide range of other useful resources can be found on the relevant subject pages of our website: www.aqa.org.uk.

The Practice Questions in this book allow students a genuine attempt at practising exam skills, but they are not intended to replicate exam questions in every respect.

Contents

Contents (continued)

Introduction to features

The *Oxford AQA History* series has been developed by a team of expert history teachers and authors with examining experience. Written to match the new AQA specification, these new editions cover AS and A Level content together in each book.

How to use this book

The features in this book include:

TIMELINE

Key events are outlined at the beginning of the book to give you an overview of the chronology of this topic. Events are colour-coded so you can clearly see the categories of change.

LEARNING OBJECTIVES

At the beginning of each chapter, you will find a list of learning objectives linked to the requirements of the specification.

SOURCE **EXTRACT**

Sources introduce you to material that is primary or contemporary to the period, and **Extracts** provides you with historical interpretations and the debate among historians on particular issues and developments. The accompanying activity questions support you in evaluating sources and extracts, analysing and assessing their value, and making judgements.

KEY QUESTION

The six key thematic questions in the specification for this topic are highlighted to help you understand and make connections between the themes.

A LEVEL AS LEVEL PRACTICE QUESTION

Focused questions to help you practise your history skills for both AS and A Level, including evaluating sources and extracts, and essay writing.

STUDY TIP

Hints to highlight key parts of **Practice Questions** or **Activities**.

ACTIVITY

Various activity types to provide you with opportunities to demonstrate both the content and skills you are learning. Some activities are designed to aid revision or to prompt further discussion; others are to stretch and challenge both your AS and A Level studies.

CROSS-REFERENCE

Links to related content within the book to offer you more detail on the subject in question.

A CLOSER LOOK

An in-depth look at a theme, event or development to deepen your understanding, or information to put further context around the subject under discussion.

KEY CHRONOLOGY

A short list of dates identifying key events to help you understand underlying developments.

KEY PROFILE

Details of a key person to extend your understanding and awareness of the individuals that have helped shape the period in question.

KEY TERM

A term that you will need to understand. The terms appear in bold, and they are also defined in the glossary.

AQA History specification overview

AS exam

Part One content

Consolidation of the Tudor Dynasty: England, 1485–1547

1 Henry VII, 1485–1509
2 Henry VIII, 1509–1547

Part Two content

England: Turmoil and Triumph, 1547–1603

3 Instability and consolidation: 'the mid-Tudor crisis', 1547–1563
4 The triumph of Elizabeth, 1563–1603

A Level exam

AS examination papers will cover content from Part One only (you will only need to know the content in the blue box). A Level examination papers will cover content from both Part One and Part Two.

The examination papers

The grade you receive at the end of your AQA AS History course is based entirely on your performance in two examination papers, covering Breadth (Paper 1) and Depth (Paper 2). For your AQA A Level History course, you will also have to complete an Historical Investigation (Non-examined assessment).

Paper 1 Breadth Study

This book covers the content of a Breadth Study (Paper 1). You are assessed on the study of significant historical developments over a period of around 100 years, and associated interpretations or extracts.

Exam paper	Questions and marks	Assessment Objective (AO)*	Timing	Marks
AS Paper 1: Breadth Study	**Section A: Evaluating historical extracts** One compulsory question linked to two historical interpretations (25 marks) • The compulsory question will ask you: *'with reference to these extracts and your understanding of the historical context, which of these extracts provides the more convincing interpretation of…'*	AO3	Written exam: 1 hour 30 minutes	50 marks (50% of AS)
	Section B: Essay writing One from a choice of two essay questions (25 marks) • The essay questions will contain a quotation advancing a judgement, and could be followed by: *'explain why you agree or disagree with this view'*.	AO1		
A Level Paper 1: Breadth Study	**Section A: Evaluating historical extracts** One compulsory question linked to three historical interpretations with different views (30 marks) • The compulsory question will ask you: *'using your understanding of the historical context, assess how convincing the arguments in these three extracts are, in relation to…'*	AO3	Written exam: 2 hours 30 minutes	80 marks (40% of A Level)
	Section B: Essay writing Two from a choice of three essay questions (2 x 25 marks) • The essay questions require analysis and judgement, and could include: *'How successful…'* or *'To what extent…'* or *'How far…'* or a quotation offering a judgement followed by *'Assess the validity of this view'*.	AO1		

*AQA History examinations will test your ability to:

AO1: Demonstrate, organise and communicate **knowledge and understanding** to analyse and evaluate the key features related to the periods studied, **making substantiated judgements and exploring concepts**, as relevant, of cause, consequence, change, continuity, similarity, difference and significance.

AO2: **Analyse and evaluate** appropriate source material, primary and/or contemporary to the period, within the historical context.

AO3: **Analyse and evaluate**, in relation to the historical context, different ways in which aspects of the past have been interpreted.

Visit **www.aqa.org.uk** to help you prepare for your examinations. The website includes specimen examination papers and mark schemes.

Introduction to the *Oxford AQA History* series

Breadth Studies

The study of history concerns the study of change and continuity over time. Sometimes it is easy for you to over-concentrate on the former and forget that, for long periods throughout history, much remained the same. In undertaking a historical breadth study covering approximately 100 years of history, you will have the opportunity to reflect on the processes of change and continuity and, in so doing, come to appreciate what drives and hinders change and how historical development is a multi-faceted process.

The course of history brings together many different strands or themes, so, in order to understand any broad period as a whole, it is helpful to divide it into its various aspects or perspectives. This book reflects the AQA **Key Questions** which address a range of perspectives. These Key Questions are given at the beginning of the book and regularly through the text of the chapters. The most common themes in all the questions relate to the differing political, economic and social developments, but sometimes they highlight the place of religion, ideology or cultural movements across time.

Sometimes specific individuals colour history, changing the course of events or affecting others for good or ill, and the **Key Profile** features in this book will help you to identify the major influences on the period you are studying.

Practice Questions help familiarise you with the new exam-style questions, while **Study Tips** highlight key parts of the Practice Questions and words to look out for

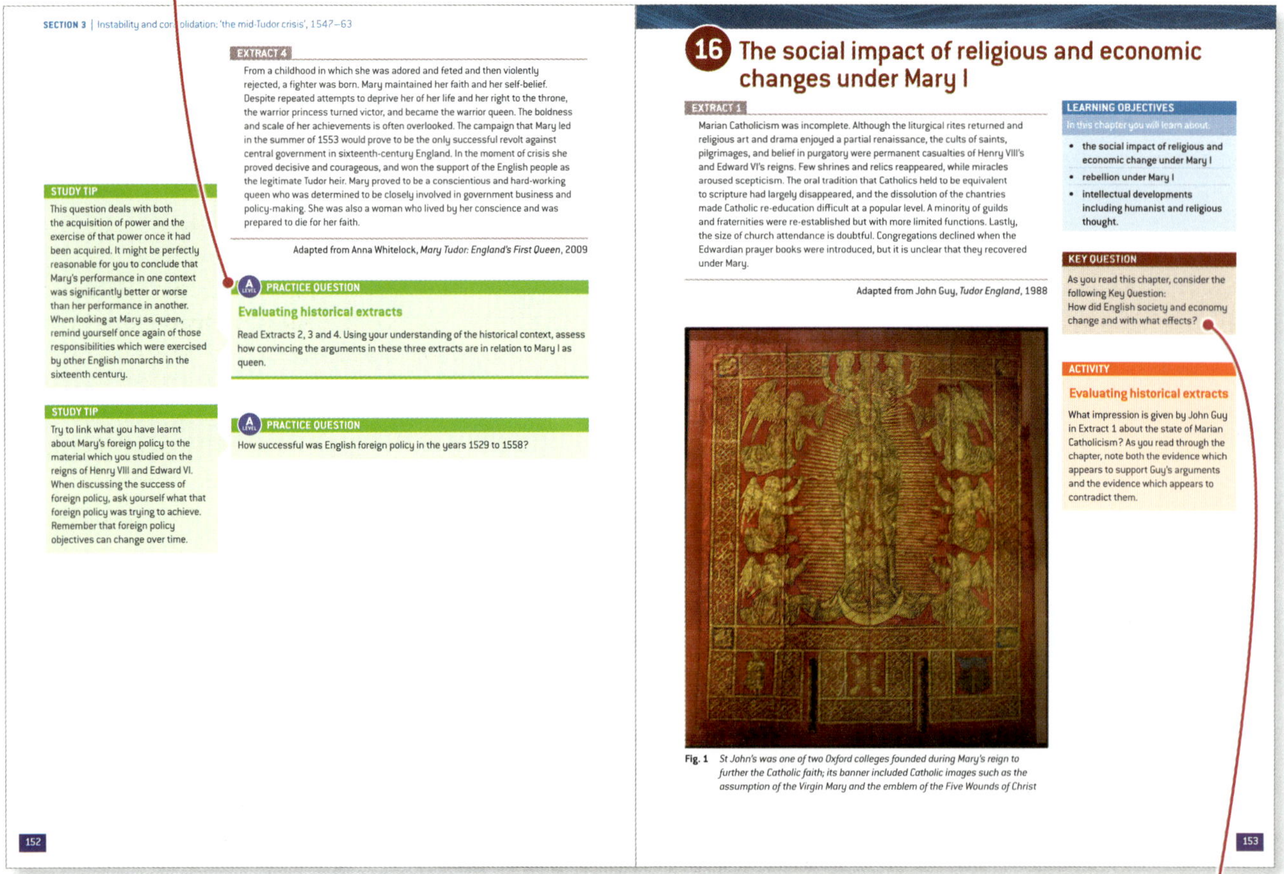
SECTION 3 | Instability and consolidation: 'the mid-Tudor crisis', 1547–63

EXTRACT 4

From a childhood in which she was adored and feted and then violently rejected, a fighter was born. Mary maintained her faith and her self-belief. Despite repeated attempts to deprive her of her life and her right to the throne, the warrior princess turned victor, and became the warrior queen. The boldness and scale of her achievements is often overlooked. The campaign that Mary led in the summer of 1553 would prove to be the only successful revolt against central government in sixteenth-century England. In the moment of crisis she proved decisive and courageous, and won the support of the English people as the legitimate Tudor heir. Mary proved to be a conscientious and hard-working queen who was determined to be closely involved in government business and policy-making. She was also a woman who lived by her conscience and was prepared to die for her faith.

Adapted from Anna Whitelock, *Mary Tudor: England's First Queen*, 2009

STUDY TIP

This question deals with both the acquisition of power and the exercise of that power once it had been acquired. It might be perfectly reasonable for you to conclude that Mary's performance in one context was significantly better or worse than her performance in another. When looking at Mary as queen, remind yourself once again of those responsibilities which were exercised by other English monarchs in the sixteenth century.

A LEVEL PRACTICE QUESTION

Evaluating historical extracts

Read Extracts 2, 3 and 4. Using your understanding of the historical context, assess how convincing the arguments in these three extracts are in relation to Mary I as queen.

STUDY TIP

Try to link what you have learnt about Mary's foreign policy to the material which you studied on the reigns of Henry VIII and Edward VI. When discussing the success of foreign policy, ask yourself what that foreign policy was trying to achieve. Remember that foreign policy objectives can change over time.

A LEVEL PRACTICE QUESTION

How successful was English foreign policy in the years 1529 to 1558?

152

16 The social impact of religious and economic changes under Mary I

EXTRACT 1

Marian Catholicism was incomplete. Although the liturgical rites returned and religious art and drama enjoyed a partial renaissance, the cults of saints, pilgrimages, and belief in purgatory were permanent casualties of Henry VIII's and Edward VI's reigns. Few shrines and relics reappeared, while miracles aroused scepticism. The oral tradition that Catholics held to be equivalent to scripture had largely disappeared, and the dissolution of the chantries made Catholic re-education difficult at a popular level. A minority of guilds and fraternities were re-established but with more limited functions. Lastly, the size of church attendance is doubtful. Congregations declined when the Edwardian prayer books were introduced, but it is unclear that they recovered under Mary.

Adapted from John Guy, *Tudor England*, 1988

LEARNING OBJECTIVES

In this chapter you will learn about:

- the social impact of religious and economic change under Mary I
- rebellion under Mary I
- intellectual developments including humanist and religious thought.

KEY QUESTION

As you read this chapter, consider the following Key Question:
How did English society and economy change and with what effects?

ACTIVITY

Evaluating historical extracts

What impression is given by John Guy in Extract 1 about the state of Marian Catholicism? As you read through the chapter, note both the evidence which appears to support Guy's arguments and the evidence which appears to contradict them.

Fig. 1 St John's was one of two Oxford colleges founded during Mary's reign to further the Catholic faith; its banner included Catholic images such as the assumption of the Virgin Mary and the emblem of the Five Wounds of Christ

153

▲ The Tudors: England 1485–1603

Key Questions in each Breadth Study help you to understand and make connections between the key themes

While this book is designed to impart a full and lively awareness of a significant period in the history of one or more countries, far more is on offer from the pages that follow. With the help of the text and activities in this book, you will be encouraged to analyse past events, rather than merely learn to describe them. You will thus build up key historical skills that will increase your curiosity and prepare you, not only for A Level History examinations, but for any future study.

This book also incorporates passages of historical interpretation. These **Extract** features will encourage you to reflect on the way in which the past may be seen in different ways by academic historians and how the same factual evidence may support a variety of conclusions. The accompanying **Activity** features pose questions that are designed to stimulate debate on these interpretations. Suggestions for research also encourage you to read further and understand for yourself how history is a 'living' discipline and subject to constant revision.

The chapters which follow are laid out according to the content of the AQA specification, in four sections. Obviously, a secure chronological awareness and understanding of each section of content will be the first step in appreciating the historical period covered in this book. However, on reaching the end of each section, you should pause to reflect on the key questions posed and consider the 'big picture' which has emerged by that point, and the interpretations that have accompanied this. In this way, a broad and satisfying appreciation of history and historical processes will emerge.

Developing your study skills

You will need to be equipped with a paper file or electronic means of storing notes. Organised notes help to produce organised essays and sensible filing provides for efficient use of time. This book uses **Cross-References** to indicate where material in one chapter has relevance to that in another. By employing the same technique, you should find it easier to make the final leap towards piecing together your material to produce a broad historical picture. The exercises and research activities in this book are intended to guide you towards making selective and relevant notes with a specific purpose. Copying out sections of the book is to be discouraged, but selecting material with a particular theme or question in mind will considerably aid your understanding.

For students preparing for the AQA A Level examination, the essay questions posed in the examination will cover around 20–25 years of history or more. AS questions will also be broad, although there is no specific minimum timeframe for these. There are plenty of examples of such 'breadth' **Practice Questions** in these books, both at AS in Part One and A Level in Parts One and Two of this book, as well as **Study Tips** and activities to encourage you to think about change, continuity, historical perspectives and interpretations. You should also develop timelines, make charts and diagrams, for example, to illustrate causation and consequence, analyse interpretations of key events, dissect broader developments thematically and identify the significance of major issues.

It is particularly important for you to have opinions on and be able to make informed judgements about the material you have studied. Some of the activities in this book encourage pair discussion or class debate, and you should make the most of such opportunities to voice and refine your own ideas. The beauty of history is that there is rarely a right or wrong answer, so this supplementary oral work should enable you to share your own opinions.

Writing and planning your essays

At both AS and A Level, you will be required to write essays and, although A Level questions are likely to be more complex, the basic qualities of good essay writing remain the same:

- **read the question carefully** to identify the key words and dates
- **plan out a logical and organised answer** with a clear judgement or view (several views if there are a number of issues to consider). Your essay should advance this judgement in the introduction, while also acknowledging alternative views and clarifying terms of reference, including the time span
- use the opening sentences of your paragraphs as stepping stones to take an argument forward, which allows you to **develop an evolving and balanced argument** throughout the essay and also makes for good style
- **support your comment or analysis** with precise detail; using dates, where appropriate, helps logical organisation
- **write a conclusion** which matches the view of the introduction and flows naturally from what has gone before.

While these suggestions will help you develop a good style, essays should never be too rigid or mechanical. This book will have fulfilled its purposes if it produces, as intended, students who think for themselves!

Sally Waller

Series Editor

Timeline

The colours represent different types of event as follows:

- Blue: economic events
- Red: political events
- Green: religious events
- Yellow: social and cultural
- Black: international events (including foreign policy)

Note that during this period these factors were very much interlinked.

1485
- Henry VII takes throne following victory at Battle of Bosworth
- Henry's first parliament

1486
- Henry marries Elizabeth of York
- Lovell rebellion
- Birth of Prince Arthur

1487
- Imposture of Lambert Simnel
- Defeat of the Earl of Lincoln at the Battle of Stoke
- Export of unfinished cloth by foreign merchants banned

1489
- Murder of Earl of Northumberland and Yorkshire rising
- Treaty of Redon
- Treaty of Medina del Campo

1496
- Intercursus Magnus treaty signed

1497
- Cornish Rebellion
- Surrender of Warbeck

1499
- Execution of the Earl of Warwick and of Warbeck

1501
- Marriage of Prince Arthur and Catherine of Aragon

1510
- Abolition of Council Learned in the Law
- Empson and Dudley executed
- Thomas Wolsey appointed to Council

1512
- War against France
- Re-foundation of St Paul's School

1513
- Battle of Flodden
- Capture of Tournai and Thérouanne

1514
- Wolsey emerges as chief minister
- Wolsey appointed archbishop of York
- Princess Mary marries Louis XI of France

1520
- Field of the Cloth of Gold

1521
- Execution of Duke of Buckingham
- Treaty of Bruges

1523
- War against France

1525
- Opposition to imposition of Amicable Grant

1533
- Henry marries Anne Boleyn
- Birth of Princess Elizabeth
- Princess Mary declared illegitimate
- Act in Restraint of Appeals

1534
- Act of Supremacy

1535
- Execution of Thomas More

1536
- Execution of Anne Boleyn
- Marriage of Henry VIII and Jane Seymour
- Princess Elizabeth declared illegitimate
- Beginning of dissolution of the monasteries
- First set of royal injunctions issued
- Ten Articles issued
- Pilgrimage of Grace

1542
- Execution of Catherine Howard
- Battle of Solway Moss

1543
- Treaty of Greenwich

1544
- Mary and Elizabeth reinstated to succession
- Invasion of France
- Capture of Boulogne
- Currency debasement begins

1545
- Battle of Ancrum Moor

1491
- Beginning of imposture of Perkin Warbeck
- Birth of Prince Henry
- War against France

1492
- Treaty of Etaples

1494
- Poynings appointed Lord Deputy of Ireland

1495
- Execution of Sir William Stanley
- Introduction of the Council Learned in the Law under the leadership of Sir Reginald Bray
- Creation of Privy Chamber

1502
- Death of Prince Arthur

1503
- Death of Sir Reginald Bray
- Marriage of Princess Margaret to James IV of Scotland

1506
- Treaty of Windsor
- Intercursus Malus treaty agreed

1509
- Death of Henry VII and accession of Henry VIII
- Empson and Dudley arrested
- Henry VIII's coronation
- Marriage of Henry VIII and Catherine of Aragon

1515
- Wolsey appointed Lord Chancellor
- Princess Mary marries the Duke of Suffolk
- Wolsey appointed cardinal
- Wolsey begins building Hampton Court

1516
- Birth of Princess Mary
- Publication of Thomas More's *Utopia*

1517
- Completion of Torrigiano's funeral effigies of Henry VII and Elizabeth of York

1518
- Treaty of London

1526
- Eltham Ordinances issued
- League of Cognac

1528
- Legatine court enquiring into the validity of the king's marriage

1529
- Fall of Wolsey
- Sir Thomas More appointed Lord Chancellor
- Treaty of Cambrai

1532
- Resignation of More
- Thomas Cromwell emerges as chief minister
- Thomas Cranmer appointed Archbishop of Canterbury

1537
- Birth of Prince Edward

1538
- Second set of royal injunctions issued

1539
- Six Articles Act
- First edition of the *Great Bible* published

1540
- Marriage of Henry and Anne of Cleves; quickly dissolved
- Execution of Cromwell
- Marriage of Henry and Catherine Howard

1547
- Death of Henry VIII
- Marquis of Hertford (later Duke of Somerset) appointed Protector
- Third set of royal injunctions issued
- Invasion of Scotland

1548
- Enclosure commission

1549
- Execution of Thomas Seymour
- Fall of Somerset
- Earl of Warwick takes over leadership of government
- Act of Uniformity and issue of first Book of Common Prayer
- Western Rebellion
- Kett's Rebellion

1550
- Warwick becomes Lord President of the Council, and Duke of Northumberland

1552
- Execution of Somerset
- Act of Uniformity and issue of second Book of Common Prayer

1553
- Death of Edward VI, who is succeeded temporarily by Lady Jane Grey
- Mary I proclaimed queen
- Execution of Northumberland
- Forty-Two Articles of Religion
- Pole appointed papal legate to England

1554
- Wyatt's Rebellion
- Execution of Lady Jane Grey
- Marriage of Mary and Philip of Spain

1555
- Restoration of heresy law
- Burnings for heresy resume
- Harvest failure

1560
- Treaty of Edinburgh signed

1561
- Undebased currency completely restored

1562
- Elizabeth seriously ill with smallpox
- Military support for French Huguenots

1563
- Elizabeth urged to marry
- Thirty-Nine Articles issued
- Publication of Foxe's 'Book of Martyrs'
- Statute of Artificers

1569
- Northern Rebellion

1570
- Elizabeth excommunicated by Pope Pius V

1571
- Ridolfi Plot
- Cecil raised to the peerage as Lord Burghley

1572
- Duke of Norfolk executed
- Cartwright and Field begin campaign for reform of organisation of English Church
- Treaty of Blois signed

1579
- Marriage negotiations between Elizabeth and the Duke of Anjou

1580
- Arrival of first Jesuit missionaries

1581
- Tightening of anti-Catholic laws

1583
- Throckmorton Plot
- John Whitgift appointed Archbishop of Canterbury
- Whitgift's Articles issued

1588
- Death of Earl of Leicester
- First 'Marprelate' tracts published
- Defeat of Spanish Armada

1590
- Death of Walsingham

1591
- Death of Sir Christopher Hatton
- Robert Cecil promoted to Privy Council

1593
- Execution of separatists

1598
- Death of Lord Burghley
- Defeat of English force in Ireland at Battle of Yellow Ford
- Poor law enacted

1599
- Cecil appointed Master of Wards
- Essex returns from Ireland

1601
- 'Rebellion' and execution of Earl of Essex
- Agitation in Parliament over monopolies
- Poor law revised

1603
- Death of Elizabeth I and accession of James I

1556

- Execution of Cranmer
- Harvest failure

1557

- Paul IV revokes Pole's papal legateship
- War against France
- Influenza epidemic

1558

- Death of Mary I and accession of Elizabeth I
- Sir William Cecil appointed secretary
- Loss of Calais
- Influenza epidemic continues

1559

- Coronation of Elizabeth I
- Acts of Supremacy and Uniformity
- Fourth set of royal injunctions issued
- Matthew Parker appointed Archbishop of Canterbury
- Treaty of Câteau-Cambrésis signed
- Elizabeth aids the Lords of the Congregation in Scotland

1564

- Treaty of Troyes signed

1566

- Elizabeth again pressed to marry
- Parker's Advertisements

1567

- Mary, Queen of Scots forced to abdicate

1568

- Mary, Queen of Scots flees to England
- Clash between Spanish fleet and English fleet under John Hawkins
- Elizabeth impounds Spanish bullion

1573

- Sir Francis Walsingham appointed secretary of state

1574

- Arrival of first Catholic missionary priests

1575

- Edmund Grindal appointed Archbishop of Canterbury

1577

- Suspension of Grindal
- Execution of first Catholic priest, Cuthbert Mayne

1584

- Bond of Association
- Expulsion of Spanish ambassador
- Treaty of Joinville

1585

- Parry Plot
- Further tightening of anti-Catholic legislation
- Treaty of Nonsuch
- Start of war between England and Spain

1586

- Babington Plot
- Mary, Queen of Scots convicted of treason
- Treaty of Berwick

1587

- Mary, Queen of Scots executed
- Successful English attack on Spanish fleet in Cadiz

1594

- Start of Tyrone Rebellion in Ireland
- Harvest failure

1595

- Harvest failure

1596

- Cecil appointed secretary of state
- Harvest failure
- Food riots

1597

- Harvest failure
- Reports of starvation in parts of the north

Introduction to this book

The political context in 1485

England had experienced much political instability in the fifteenth century. The successful short reign of Henry V (1413–22) was followed by the disastrous rule of Henry VI. The shortcomings of his rule culminated in the outbreak of the so-called Wars of the Roses in 1455 between the royal houses of Lancaster and York. England was then subjected to intermittent civil war for over thirty years and five violent changes of monarch.

Table 1 Changes of monarch, 1422–85

Monarch*	Reign	The ending of the reign
Henry VI (L)	1422–61	Defeated in battle and overthrown by Edward, Earl of March who took the throne.
Edward IV (Y)	1461–70	Overthrown by Warwick 'the Kingmaker' and forced into exile.
Henry VI (L)	1470–71	Murdered after the defeat of his forces in the Battle of Tewkesbury. His son and heir, Edward Prince of Wales, was also killed.
Edward IV (Y)	1471–83	Died suddenly and unexpectedly, leaving as his heir the 13-year-old Edward V.
Edward V (Y)	1483	Disappeared in the Tower of London and probably murdered, along with his brother Richard, on the orders of his uncle and protector, Richard, Duke of Gloucester, who succeeded him on the throne.
Richard III (Y)	1483–85	Defeated and killed at the Battle of Bosworth. Succeeded on the throne by his successful adversary Henry Tudor, Earl of Richmond.

* (L) = Lancaster (Y) = York

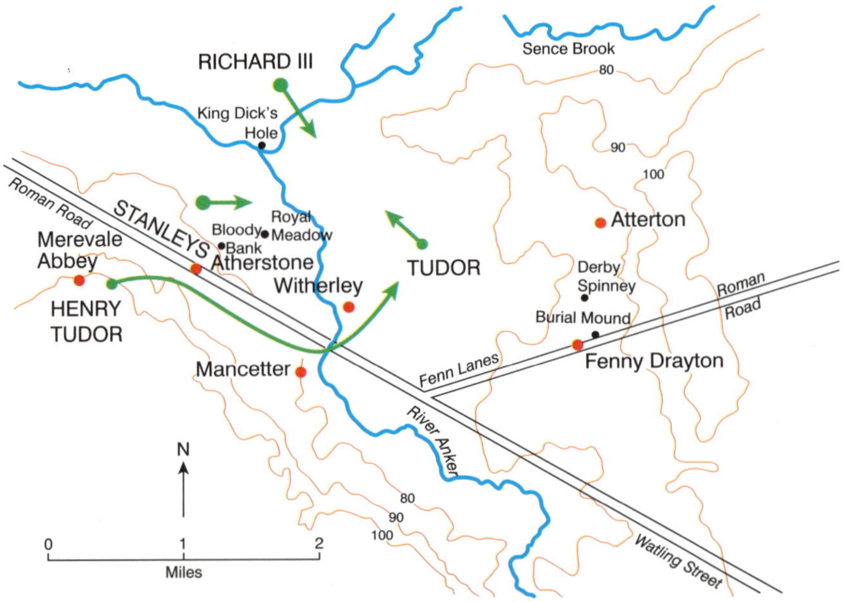

Fig. 1 *This map illustrates an interpretation of the Battle of Bosworth, suggesting where the fighting took place*

Richard III's usurpation in 1483 destroyed the unity of the House of York, and prompted within a few months an unsuccessful rebellion by disaffected Yorkists led by the Duke of Buckingham. Richard III's unpopularity grew and his rule was increasingly seen as lacking legitimacy. These factors created the opportunity for Henry Tudor, Earl of Richmond, to make what proved to be a successful attempt to gain the throne at the Battle of Bosworth in August 1485.

Richmond was successful in gaining the throne, but there was no guarantee that he would keep it. As can be seen in Figure 2, with his descent through the female line deriving from Edward III's third son, John of Gaunt, his claim to the throne was weak and the early years of Henry VII's reign were beset by feelings of insecurity. He was always fearful of a possible Yorkist threat to the throne, and such fears did not die with him in 1509, for Henry VIII continued to fret about possible Yorkist conspiracies until the final years of his reign and remained obsessed with fear about the instability which would ensue should he be unable to pass on the throne to a male heir.

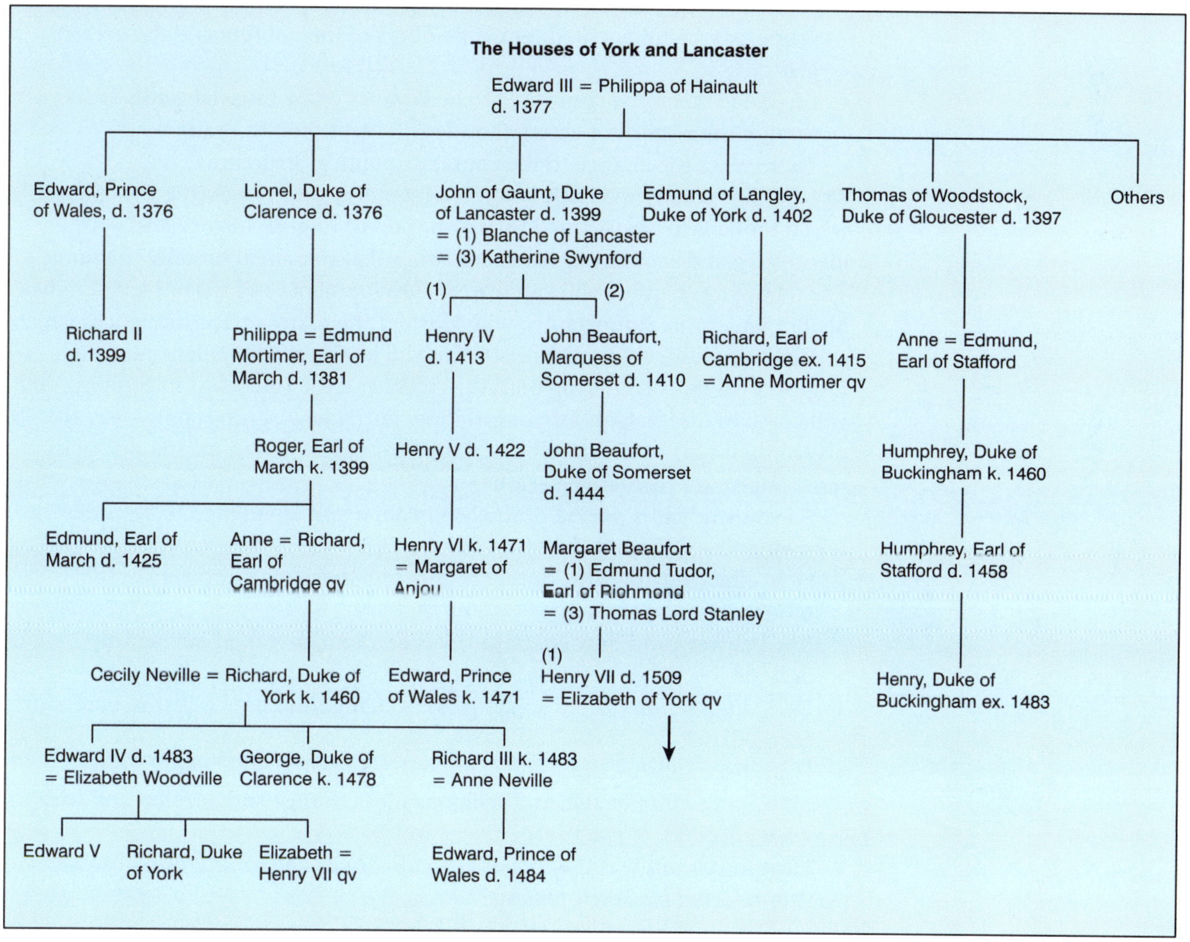

Fig. 2 *The rival royal houses of York and Lancaster*

Continuity and change 1485–1603

All periods of history embrace both continuity and change. Tudor England, which lasted from 1485 to 1603, was no exception to this rule. Three changes above all would have surprised any Englishman or Englishwoman alive in 1485:

- The Catholic Church, which was a huge part of the lives of almost the entire nation in 1485, had all but disappeared by 1603, taking with it many of the social and charitable institutions which were such an important feature of late-medieval England.

- England, which in political terms had been a small player in Europe in 1485, was by 1603 acknowledged as a major European power and had begun the process which would lead it to become the world's dominant power.
- England was becoming a much more ordered society, as exemplified by the flight of the nobility from draughty and uncomfortable but secure medieval castles to country houses where the emphasis was on ease and comfort.

Other developments, while less surprising, were, nevertheless, significant. Most importantly, the monarchy, which had changed hands by force on no fewer than five occasions during the fifteenth century, recovered under the Tudors the power and prestige which it had once enjoyed during the reigns of Edward I and Edward III.

On the other hand, some aspects of the England of 1603 would have seemed familiar to anyone who had been alive in 1485:

- Differences between rich and poor remained immense, which was particularly noticeable as a result of the increase in income from landed property which benefited many members of the nobility and the greater gentry.
- England's economy continued to be dominated by internal trade, even though the pattern of external trade was beginning to change.
- There was little change to the country's political structures.

This book is concerned both with understanding and explaining the changes which took place across this 118-year period of English history and with identifying and accounting for those issues that remained broadly the same. The following chapters will explore the developments and narrative of English history and, more importantly, will consider the many varied influences which shaped the country's development. You will be taken on a journey through English history, considering both the rulers and the ruled and in so doing you will come to understand for yourself how individuals, groups and ideas all played their part in the development of the English nation during one of its most important formative periods.

As you study this period of English history, you are invited to consider the following Key Questions:

- How effectively did the Tudors restore and develop the powers of the monarchy?
- In what ways and how effectively was England governed during this period?
- How did relations with foreign powers change and how was the succession secured?
- How did English society and economy change and with what effects?
- How far did intellectual and religious ideas change and develop and with what effects?
- How important was the role of key individuals and groups and how were they affected by developments?

Try to keep these questions in mind as you work your way through this book; you will find them highlighted in the text too. These are the 'big' questions which have occupied historians studying the 1485 to 1603 period and by reflecting on them you will come to appreciate the development of the English State over this period more fully. Remember too that political, economic, social and cultural developments go hand in hand, and to build up a full picture you will need to explore the links between them.

There is plenty to learn and much to think about in the following pages. If you approach your studies in a spirit of enquiry, anxious to piece together past events to enrich your understanding of the whole, you will not only find much to enjoy in your study of Tudor England, you will also emerge the wiser from it.

1 Henry VII, 1485–1509

1 The consolidation of power

EXTRACT 1

Henry VII's attitude to ruling was, for the most part, similar to that of his predecessors. He believed in the imposition of strong and unquestioned royal leadership. This was particularly needed in England after an interval of instability in which the authority of the Crown had been badly damaged. However, Henry's own background also made demands on him. Henry Tudor was a stranger in England when he ascended the throne, having won that throne by conquest. Thrust in this position by the events of a single afternoon, Henry had to master the realm he now ruled. Henry had no immediate relations whose services he could employ nor a reliable body of nobles he could turn to. What he did, he had to do on his own.

Adapted from Wallace MacCaffrey, *The Oxford Illustrated History of Tudor and Stuart Britain*, 2000

Fig. 1 *Henry VII*

Henry Tudor, Earl of Richmond, became King Henry VII of England following his victory over Richard III's forces at the Battle of Bosworth on 22 August 1485. This victory terminated Plantagenet rule in England, and saw the establishment of a new dynasty, the Tudors. However, Henry VII's grasp of power was insecure; he had virtually no discernible claim to the throne and he had many enemies who were only too keen to see him experience the same fate as his immediate predecessor. It was therefore essential for him to consolidate his power by establishing his dynasty and ensuring that any rivals to the throne were dealt with firmly.

Henry's claim to the throne was weak in two respects. Firstly he was descended through the female line represented by his mother, Lady Margaret

LEARNING OBJECTIVES

In this chapter you will learn about:

- **Henry VII's seizure of the throne and consolidation of power**
- **Henry's character and aims in government**
- **the establishment of the Tudor dynasty**
- **Henry's treatment of claimants and pretenders to the throne.**

KEY QUESTION

As you read this chapter, consider the following Key Questions:

- How effectively did the Tudors restore and develop the powers of the monarchy?
- How important were the roles of key individuals and groups and how were they affected by developments?

ACTIVITY

What are the key points made in Extract 1? As you read this chapter, make notes that either confirm, or conflict with, Wallace MacCaffrey's interpretation. At the end of the chapter you will be asked to give your opinion on MacCaffrey's view.

CROSS-REFERENCE

To understand potential rival claims to the throne, study the family tree of the descendants of Edward III in the Introduction, page xv.

Beaufort (as illustrated by Figure 2, in the Introduction). More importantly, the line came from John of Gaunt's third wife: their son John Beaufort had been born before their marriage and was therefore seen as illegitimate. Henry became the Lancastrian claimant only because there was no one else who could fulfil the role. In reality, however, it was victory on the battlefield alone which had brought him to the throne.

Henry, who had lived abroad since he was 14, was proclaimed King of England on the battlefield by **Lord Stanley**. Following the battle, Henry made the short journey to Leicester, where the mortal remains of his enemy were interred, then to London where on 3 September 1485 Henry was met by the lord mayor of the city. The London public was wooed by pageantry and ceremony into cheering the new monarch. In truth, by this point Richard had become such an object of suspicion because of the disappearance of the princes in the Tower, along with other presumed crimes, that it mattered little who Henry was and how slender was his claim to the throne. That he was not Richard was enough for the public to accept him.

CROSS-REFERENCE

Richard's treatment of the princes in the Tower is covered in the Introduction, page 14.

Margaret Beaufort played a significant role in her son's reign. Her profile features in Chapter 2, page 10.

KEY PROFILE

Thomas, Lord Stanley (1435–1509)

Stanley, Henry VII's stepfather, initially stood aside from the battle. His intervention on behalf of Henry proved crucial, and he was rewarded with the title Earl of Derby. Derby was crucial to the exercise of royal power in the northwest of England and north Wales during Henry's reign.

Henry VII's character and aims

Henry VII had not been brought up to rule. In 1471, when Henry was 14, Edward IV regained power for the House of York in the Battle of Tewkesbury, in which many of Henry's relations, the Lancastrians, died or were executed. Henry fled to France, where he lived for most of the time as a fugitive in the Duchy of Brittany. To the historian Thomas Penn, Henry's ability to think like a fugitive proved to be useful political training for his future as a ruler.

CROSS-REFERENCE

Henry's attitudes to money are covered in Chapter 2, pages 15–17.

EXTRACT 2

Henry was undoubtedly shrewd, calculating and long-headed; he seems never to have been overcome by passion. Yet if he had even a touch of the temper, this exercise of self-restraint must have cost him a great deal. Probably the hard training of a youth spent in wars, danger of execution and long exile tamed him and taught him to hide his feelings and veil his purposes. That he was eager for money is certain. He was not, however, a miser; where it served his purpose money was spent freely, and he saved and extorted only in the interests of the Crown. To the establishment of peace, the preservation of law and order, the security of the realm he applied all his high intelligence and his determination, his shrewdness and his steady and daily interest in affairs.

Adapted from Geoffrey Elton, *England Under the Tudors*, 3rd edition, 1991

ACTIVITY

According to Extract 2, what kind of lessons in kingship did Henry learn from his experiences in exile?

From 1485, Henry's main purpose was to ensure that he kept his throne, mindful as he was that four monarchs from the previous hundred years had met untimely ends themselves. Therefore, his primary aim at the start of his reign was to consolidate his power, which he did by a number of political actions combined with military success.

CROSS-REFERENCE

Chapters 2 and 3 will discuss how Henry carried out his aim to consolidate power.

ACTIVITY

Research

Find out more about Henry VII as a character and family man. Good places to start your research would be the short biography of Henry VII by Steven Gunn in www.oxforddnb.com and *Winter King: the Dawn of Tudor England* by Thomas Penn. For a contemporary view you might use Polydore Vergil (see Chapter 4, page 39, for a Key Profile on Polydore Vergil).

KEY PROFILE

Edward, Earl of Warwick (1475–99)

The son of Edward IV's brother, the Duke of Clarence, he was placed in the Tower of London in 1485. There he remained except for occasional public appearances. He was alleged to have plotted with Perkin Warbeck against Henry VII in 1499 and was beheaded for doing so.

KEY TERM

parliamentary sanction: an official confirmation or ratification of a law given by Parliament as the acclaimed body of the State; by the laws of the time, King Henry VII's tenuous claims to the throne would normally have had to be fortified by a parliamentary sanction

Act of Attainder: this declared a landowner guilty of rebelling against a monarch; the attainted noble lost his title, lands and sometimes his head; his heirs were disinherited

tonnage and poundage: the right to raise revenue for the whole reign from imports and exports

Henry immediately consolidated his power in a number of ways:

- He dated his reign from 21 August 1485, the day before the Battle of Bosworth, thereby ensuring that anyone who had fought on the Yorkist side could be designated a traitor.
- He publicly rewarded many of his key supporters, for example by conferring 11 knighthoods.
- He arranged for supporters to detain Elizabeth of York, daughter of Edward IV, and the **Earl of Warwick**, Edward IV's nephew, each of whom could be seen as having a much greater claim to the throne than Henry himself.
- He made key appointments to his Council and household, for example making Sir Reginald Bray Chancellor of the Duchy of Lancaster and **Sir William Stanley** Chamberlain of the Household.

KEY PROFILE

Sir William Stanley (c1435–95)

Stanley, the brother of Thomas Stanley, the Earl of Derby, and Henry VII's step-uncle, was rewarded with the post of Lord Chamberlain following Bosworth. This not only gave him considerable political influence, it also enabled him to develop his landed estate in Cheshire and North Wales. It was therefore a shock when he was accused of treason.

CROSS-REFERENCE

Henry's Council, including the roles of the Chancellor of the Duchy of Lancaster and the Lord Chamberlain, will be discussed in Chapter 2, pages 9–11.

To read more about the king's household, turn to Chapter 2, pages 11–13.

For the role of Parliament in Henry VII's reign, see Chapter 2, pages 13–14.

- He arranged his coronation to take place on 30 October before the meeting of his first Parliament on 7 November, thereby demonstrating that his right to the throne was based on hereditary right and not only because Parliament had **sanctioned** it.
- Parliamentary **Acts of Attainder** against Yorkists who had fought at Bosworth ensured that their property was forfeit to the Crown, thereby increasing royal income. This was further enhanced when Parliament granted Henry the customs revenues of **tonnage and poundage** for life.
- Having had her detained the previous year, in January 1486 Henry married Elizabeth of York, the daughter of King Edward IV. By waiting until the other steps towards consolidation of power had been completed, Henry was able to ensure that his assumption of the Crown was not brought about by his wife's own claim to the throne. However, he was able to exploit in royal propaganda the union of the two houses of Lancaster and York. For example, the emblem of the Tudor rose combined the red rose of Lancaster with the white rose of York.
- A vital step in the securing of the dynasty took place in September 1489 with the birth of an heir to the throne, Prince Arthur.

Fig. 2 *The Tudor Rose, combining both the red rose of Lancaster and the white rose of York*

ACTIVITY

Pair discussion

In pairs, consider the main problems which Henry might have faced on coming to the throne and how he might have sought to deal with them. Compare your answers with the information in the next section of this chapter.

KEY CHRONOLOGY

Henry VII's consolidation of power

1485	Henry seizes power at Battle of Bosworth (Aug); crowned king (Oct)
1486	Lovell rebellion fails
1486	Prince Arthur born
1487	Lambert Simnel conspiracy; defeated at Battle of Stoke Field
1495	Warbeck lands in Kent but is quickly defeated; arrives at the court of James IV of Scotland
1496	A small Scottish force crosses the border in support of Warbeck but soon returns
1497	Warbeck fails to exploit a Cornish rebellion and is eventually captured
1499	Warbeck executed

CROSS-REFERENCE

To familiarise yourself with all the potential claimants to the throne, refer to the York family tree on page xv.

The murder of the two princes is outlined in the Introduction, page xiv.

KEY PROFILE

Lambert Simnel

Simnel was a boy from Oxford who was tutored in courtly manners by a priest, Richard Symonds, with the intention initially of impersonating Richard, Duke of York, the younger of the two princes in the Tower, though he soon switched to impersonating the Earl of Warwick. Captured at the Battle of Stoke, Simnel was spared by Henry VII, who gave him a job in the royal kitchens.

Establishing the Tudor dynasty

Henry's position was extremely insecure. Many Yorkists, not satisfied by his marriage to Elizabeth, still regarded him as a usurper. There were several potential Yorkist claimants to the throne, such as the earls of Warwick and Lincoln, Edward IV's nephews. Moreover, the situation was complicated by the appearance of pretenders to the throne who were allegedly either Edward V or his younger brother Richard, the two murdered 'princes in the Tower'. However, what Henry had to fear most was the influence of Margaret of Burgundy, the sister of Edward IV and Richard III. Margaret was never reconciled to the Tudor takeover and, as the dowager duchess of Burgundy, she had access to funds which enabled her to encourage the ambitions of Yorkist claimants.

Viscount Lovell and the Staffords, 1486

The first (rather minor) rising against Henry occurred at Easter, 1486. It was led by Francis, Viscount Lovell – who had prospered as a key supporter of Richard III – and Humphrey Stafford. Lovell tried to raise a rebellion in Richard III's heartland of support in the North Riding of Yorkshire. Simultaneously, Stafford tried to raise forces against Henry, drawing upon another area of Yorkist support in the Midlands. Lovell managed to escape from the king's forces, but Humphrey Stafford was captured and executed, though his younger brother and accomplice, Thomas, was pardoned. What seems significant about this rising is how little enthusiasm there was at this stage for a Yorkist rising in their traditional heartlands. It was easily suppressed, but later rebellions, promoted by Margaret of Burgundy, would prove rather more problematic.

Lambert Simnel and the rebellion of the Earl of Lincoln

Following the Lovell rebellion, leading Yorkists realised that a change in strategy was needed if they were to be successful in their attempts to get rid of Henry VII. There were two key aspects to this. Firstly, they needed a figurehead who could claim to be a Yorkist prince and, secondly, they needed the financial support to generate a significant military threat to Henry. Their figurehead was **Lambert Simnel**. Simnel was being passed off as the **Earl of Warwick**, who had been imprisoned by Henry, and was even crowned as King Edward in Ireland in May 1487. The conspiracy was put together by **John de la Pole, the Earl of Lincoln**, himself a potential Yorkist claimant. In response to this hoax, Henry now had the real Earl of Warwick exhibited in London for all to see. Lincoln subsequently fled from Henry VII's court and had joined the failed plotter Lord Lovell at the court of Margaret of Burgundy in the Netherlands. They persuaded Margaret to support Simnel's bogus claim and to pay for a force of **mercenaries** to invade England.

Henry had plenty of notice that a rebellious conspiracy was being planned, and thus he had ample opportunity to plan his response. Given that Richard III's main power base was in the north of England, Henry took the gamble of reinstating the rather untrustworthy Earl of Northumberland, who led a major portion of Richard III's army at the Battle of Bosworth, to power in the north. This helped to neutralise Richard's old power base and also ensured that the traditionally Yorkist Howard family had no intention of joining the conspiracy, as Northumberland was one of their descendants. He also reinforced coastal defences in East Anglia. However, the rebels landed on the northwest coast of England in Cumberland, and crossed the Pennines in order to drum up support in Richard III's old heartland in the North Riding of Yorkshire. In actual fact the Yorkist gentry of the North Riding were reluctant to commit themselves wholeheartedly to the cause, presumably waiting to see who was likely to win.

Battle of Stoke Field, 1487

Henry gathered a group of advisors, which included the close relatives of former Yorkists who had been victims of Richard III, in the south and Midlands. The two armies met at East Stoke near Newark in Nottinghamshire. Henry himself was not confident. He could remember only too vividly how Richard had been double-crossed at Bosworth and feared that he himself might suffer the same fate. However, his army, led effectively by the Earl of Oxford, held firm and the Earl of Lincoln was killed in the battle, having crucially been unable to add sufficient followers to the army of mercenaries with which he had landed in England.

Fig. 3 *The Battle of Stoke Field*

Henry's victory at the Battle of Stoke Field was very significant. It was this battle rather than Bosworth which really brought an end to the Wars of the Roses, and Henry's position became safer though by no means completely secure. Henry had been faced with a crisis which he had overcome by a combination of his own shrewdness and hard work, the organisational skills and military leadership of his key supporters and the willingness of landowners in many parts of the country to support his cause. He was relatively mild in his treatment of many of those who had rebelled, in the process weakening the resolve of many Yorkists to oppose him. He also began to develop the policy of using **bonds of good behaviour** to ensure well-behaved landowners who might otherwise face financial ruin.

ACTIVITY

Using the information from the Introduction and this chapter, produce a report in the style of a newspaper article to explain why Henry VII's rebellion against Richard III succeeded while the Earl of Lincoln's similar rebellion against Henry VII failed.

KEY PROFILE

John de la Pole, Earl of Lincoln (c1460–87)

Lincoln, a nephew of Edward IV and Richard III, was the latter's designated successor. As such, he was regarded as the Yorkist leader in the immediate aftermath of Bosworth.

KEY TERM

mercenaries: hired soldiers who work simply for pay and have no specific commitment to the cause for which they are fighting

A CLOSER LOOK

Bonds of good behaviour

When giving bonds to the landowners, Henry recognised himself as owing the lump sum stated. The sum did not have to be paid back provided the condition (usually good behaviour) was observed. If the condition was broken, the sum had to be paid in penalty. You can read more about bonds in Chapter 2, page 15.

CROSS-REFERENCE

Return to the Introduction to familiarise yourself with the War of the Roses.

CROSS-REFERENCE

Henry's weakness in international matters will be discussed in Chapter 3, pages 21–28.

Fig. 4 *There are no surviving contemporary images of Perkin Warbeck admitting to his imposture. This is a later interpretation of the dramatic climax*

CROSS-REFERENCE

The role of Margaret of Burgundy is discussed in Chapter 3, pages 24–25.

For details of Henry's marriage negotiations with James IV of Scotland, look ahead to page 30.

For the implications of Henry's methods of government, see Chapter 2.

The Cornish Rebellion of 1497 is described on pages 27 and 40–41.

KEY TERM

household government: medieval system of governance where the head of a household, invariably an adult male, had authority over the property, labour, and mobility of everyone living on his land

The Perkin Warbeck imposture

Perkin Warbeck, a cloth trader from Tournai in Flanders, was a persistent irritant to Henry VII over a period of eight years, during which he claimed to be Richard, Duke of York. Had his activities been confined to England he might have been dismissed as a deluded pest. However, it was his ability to attract patronage from foreign rulers which transformed him from an irritant to a potentially serious threat. It also demonstrated how fragile Henry's position was considered to be by other rulers.

In 1491 Warbeck began to impersonate Richard, Duke of York in Ireland. After a brief appearance at the court of Charles VIII of France, the following year, he was forced to flee from France, to the court of Margaret of Burgundy, where he was trained as a potential Yorkist prince and began to draw English courtiers into his conspiracies.

Several years after the Battle of Stoke in 1487, Warbeck's first attempt to land in England in 1495 proved to be a fiasco. Henry had been informed of Warbeck's intentions by one of his royal agents, Sir Robert Clifford, who had infiltrated Warbeck's retinue. Warbeck was quickly defeated, and fled to the court of **James IV** of Scotland.

However, it would be a mistake to write off this event simply as a farce which had no chance of success. In actual fact, it could have proved very costly for Henry because the conspirators had an accomplice in the heart of Henry's government, Sir William Stanley. Stanley, Henry's step-uncle and potential traitor, was Lord Chamberlain and headed the royal household at a time when **household government** was still the normal model of political operation. The modern historian Christine Carpenter believes it was therefore striking that this conspiracy actually revealed Henry at his most vulnerable in the very place where he should have been most secure.

In 1496, a small Scottish force crossed the border on Warbeck's behalf but quickly retreated. Warbeck's interests were soon sacrificed when James gave in to Henry's offer of marriage to his daughter, Margaret. Having failed to successfully invade England from Scotland in 1496, Warbeck made a final attempt to seek the English throne by trying to exploit the uncertainties created by the Cornish Rebellion in 1497, but his forces were crushed and Warbeck eventually surrendered to the king. Henry, remarkably lenient at first, allowed Warbeck to stay at court, but confined him to the Tower after he tried to abscond. This time there was to be no mercy. Having allegedly tried to escape with the Earl of Warwick, he was accused of treason, and they were both tried and executed.

The Earl of Warwick

It was highly convenient for Henry that Warbeck's final attempts at conspiracy enabled him to get rid of the Earl of Warwick, potentially the most obvious Yorkist claimant to the throne. Warwick was in many respects an innocent victim of the political manoeuvrings of the period. Aged only ten at the time of the Battle of Bosworth, he spent most of his life in confinement before he met his fate in 1499; having been accused of plotting with Perkin Warbeck against Henry VII, he was beheaded.

ACTIVITY

Thinking point

How successful was Henry VII in dealing with the challenges he faced from Perkin Warbeck and why?

Edmund de la Pole, Earl of Suffolk and Richard de la Pole, 'The White Rose'

The final piece of dynastic security concerned Edmund de la Pole, Earl of Suffolk, and Richard de la Pole, younger brothers of the Earl of Lincoln. Suffolk had fled to Flanders in 1498. He was persuaded to return after a short exile, but once again fled in 1501, this time seeking refuge at the court of the Emperor Maximilian. For as long as Margaret of Burgundy was politically opposed to Henry VII, Suffolk was safe. However, with the Treaty of Windsor in 1506, more friendly relations were restored. One feature of this improvement in relations was that Maximilian agreed to give up Suffolk, who was duly imprisoned in the Tower of London. Henry VII took no further action against him. However, Henry VIII had him executed for treason in 1513. This still left Richard de la Pole, nicknamed the 'White Rose', at large during his time in exile, but he was killed fighting for the French forces at the Battle of Pavia in 1525.

CROSS-REFERENCE

For detail on the Treaty of Windsor in 1506, see page 26.

ACTIVITY

As a class, create your own picture gallery of all the rebellions and impostors from Henry VII's reign.

EXTRACT 3

> Henry's attempts to override local powers by means of his own servants, his use of spies, his institution of a personal bodyguard as soon as he became king, all point to a misguided policy, which was what he knew best. It would be surprising if local instability and Henry's deep mistrust of the nobles that bred mistrust towards the king had not raised some questions about his suitability to rule, and it is a fact that Henry was troubled by plots and rebellions for much longer than he should have been after the Battle of Stoke.

Adapted from Christine Carpenter, *The Wars of the Roses: Politics and the Constitution in England, c1437–1509,* 1997

CROSS-REFERENCE

More about Henry's use of spies is mentioned in Chapter 2, page 14.

Summary

Having consolidated his power in the short term, Henry was also concerned with ensuring long-term dynastic stability: he wanted English men and women to believe that the Tudors had a legitimate claim to the throne. He aimed to ensure the succession of his line to the throne, ensure law and order by keeping control over the nobility who had engaged in bitter power struggles, improve the Crown's financial position and stabilise the dynasty by securing the recognition of foreign powers.

It is clear that Henry enjoyed some success in consolidating his power and establishing his dynasty. How much of this was due to his own actions and qualities and how much was the consequence of the way in which the Yorkists had become demoralised even before the death of Richard III is open to debate. It should not be assumed that his victory at the Battle of Stoke left Henry in an unchallengeable position; Henry himself certainly did not think so. The immediate threat from the House of York might have been vanquished and many Yorkists had made their peace, albeit reluctantly in some cases, with the regime. The immediate threat from his own relative Sir William Stanley had not, however, been vanquished, as the crisis with Warbeck of 1497 made only too clear. There had certainly been royal leadership, though whether it was as 'unquestioned' as Wallace MacCaffrey and John Guy have suggested, is open to some doubt.

A LEVEL PRACTICE QUESTION

Using your understanding of the historical context, assess how convincing the arguments in Extracts 1, 2 and 3 are in relation to Henry VII's consolidation of power.

STUDY TIP

You should consider the ways in which each extract is both convincing and unconvincing by applying your own knowledge to support or challenge the points made by each author. Try to provide an overall conclusion in which you justify your decision as to which is the most convincing.

ACTIVITY

Using the information from this chapter, give your assessment on the different threats to Henry's throne during this period. Copy and complete the table below, giving evidence for your answers.

	How great was the threat to Henry VII?			Why was Henry able to overcome the threat?
	Foreign support	**Support within England**	**Quality of leadership**	
Lord Lovell and the Staffords				
Lambert Simnel and the Earl of Lincoln				
Perkin Warbeck				
Sir William Stanley				

ACTIVITY

Evaluating historical extracts

Look back at Wallace MacCaffrey's interpretation given at the beginning of the chapter (page 1). In small groups, consider whether you find his interpretation convincing. You will need to find specific evidence to support or refute his views.

STUDY TIP

In answering this question it is important that you consider Henry VII's personal strengths. You should weigh these against other reasons for the consolidation of power.

AS LEVEL PRACTICE QUESTION

'Henry VII's consolidation of power in the years 1485 to 1499 was the result of his own personal strengths.' Explain why you agree or disagree with this view.

2 Henry VII's government

EXTRACT 1

[Henry's] success as a ruler was achieved by a highly unusual style of rule which bypassed the **elites** and relied heavily on the exercise of royal power through official channels, backed by the intervention of the monarch. To the governing classes it was baffling. Henry was a king who held them, his natural councillors and servants, at a distance. Nor did they understand a king who was obsessed with accumulating income, not for the traditional purposes of war or to reward his servants, but to ensure his freedom from dependence on their goodwill. It is not surprising they greeted his death with relief.

Adapted from Wallace MacCaffrey, *The Oxford Illustrated History of Tudor and Stuart Britain*, 2000

ACTIVITY

Evaluating historical extracts

What view of Henry VII's style of rule is given in Extract 1? Can you summarise this view in one sentence?

LEARNING OBJECTIVES

In this chapter you will learn about:

- royal government and the use of councils under Henry VII
- Henry's use of Parliament
- Henry's domestic policies, including justice and royal finance.

KEY QUESTION

As you read this chapter, consider the following Key Questions:

- In what ways and how effectively was England governed during this period?
- How important was the role of key individuals and groups?

Councils and the court

The king ruled with a 'council' of advisers who supported him in making key decisions. Around 227 men are recorded as having attended the Council during his reign. In practice, however, Henry VII's actual working Council was a much smaller affair with around six or seven members.

KEY TERM

elites: select groups that are considered to be superior in terms of ability, birth or qualities to the rest of a group or society

The Council

The Council under Henry VII had three main functions:

- to advise the king
- to administer the realm on the king's behalf
- to make legal judgements.

A CLOSER LOOK

There were three main types of councillor:

1. Members of the nobility, such as Lords Daubeney and Dynham, though the working Council only rarely included the great **magnates** of the realm.
2. Churchmen such as **John Morton** and **Richard Fox**, who often had legal training and were excellent administrators.
3. Laymen, either gentry or lawyers, who were skilled administrators, such as **Sir Reginald Bray** and Edmund Dudley. This dependence on lawyers did not begin with Henry VII; they had also played a significant role in the 'second reign' of Edward IV from 1471, so Henry was continuing a trend which had become increasingly evident.

KEY TERM

magnate: in this context a member of the higher ranks of the nobility

CROSS-REFERENCE

For more detail on the role of Richard Fox as a churchman during Henry VII's reign, see his Key Profile in Chapter 4, page 36.

KEY PROFILE

John Morton (d. 1500)

A highly able churchman and lawyer, Morton began his public career as a passionate Lancastrian, but made his peace with the Yorkists to serve Edward IV, under whom he became the Bishop of Ely. However, he worked against Richard III and was promoted for his services by Henry to Archbishop of Canterbury in 1486. He also became a cardinal in 1493.

KEY TERM

Duchy of Lancaster: a significant body of property, mostly but not exclusively situated in Lancashire, which personally belonged to the king but was formally the territory of the duke; Henry VII's habit was to grant positions of authority within the duchy to his most trusted servants

KEY PROFILE

Sir Reginald Bray (d. 1503)

Bray had been a faithful servant of Henry Tudor for a long time. He had helped Henry to raise funds before the Battle of Bosworth. Under Henry's reign his influence was exercised through his role as Chancellor of the **Duchy of Lancaster**. He also led the Council Learned in Law. Thomas Penn described him as the 'king's chief executive'. As such he was 'more powerful than most nobles'.

Fig. 1 *Sir Reginald Bray*

KEY PROFILE

Margaret Beaufort (1443–1509) married Edmund Tudor in 1455 and gave birth to the future Henry VII when aged only 14. Her third husband was Thomas, Lord Stanley. She, in her turn, remained an important unofficial adviser to the king. Margaret was granted a large landed estate by Henry at Collyweston in Northamptonshire. She retained her political influence throughout her son's reign. However, her ability to intervene directly in political affairs was limited because she spent much of her time keeping her own lavish household.

During Henry VII's reign the Council had no established rules and procedures, though it was a permanent body with a core membership. Sometimes members also met separately, however, to deal with key administrative concerns when the king was not present, so it was possible for different members of the Council to meet in two places simultaneously. Those 'professional' councillors such as Bray and Dudley, who did not see themselves as courtiers, often met to deal with legal and administrative matters in London when other councillors were with the king elsewhere. The importance of the Council depended on its key members (particularly Bray) and its offshoot, the Council Learned.

It was not, however, essential for a man or woman to hold office as a councillor in order to advise the king. Indeed, the historian David Loades has argued that Henry's most influential adviser was someone who held no office, his formidable mother, **Lady Margaret Beaufort**.

CROSS-REFERENCE

The House of Commons and House of Lords are discussed later in this chapter.

A CLOSER LOOK

The Great Council

The Council should not be confused with the Great Council. The Great Council was a gathering of the **House of Lords**, meeting without the **House of Commons**. It had no clearly defined functions and was an occasional rather than a permanent body. It met only five times in total throughout Henry VII's reign. It usually concerned itself with issues relating to war or rebellion and was a means of binding the nobility to key decisions relating to national security.

KEY TERM

prerogative rights: describes those rights or powers which the monarch could exercise without requiring the consent of Parliament

CROSS-REFERENCE

Bonds and recognizances are described later in this chapter, page 15.

CROSS-REFERENCE

The financial control of Empson and Dudley in the final years of Henry VII's reign is covered on page 16.

The Council Learned

The Council's main offshoot was the Council Learned (or Council Learned in Law). This body developed during the second half of the reign, at first under Bray's leadership. It often met in the office of the Duchy of Lancaster, where it formed what the modern historian John Guy describes as a 'specialist board'. Its function was to maintain the king's revenue and to exploit his **prerogative rights**. It was the Council Learned which made the system of bonds and recognizances work so effectively and thus able to entrap many of the king's subjects. The workings of the Council Learned have often been seen as a rather 'shady' operation by historians. It was not a recognised court of law and those summoned before it had no chance to appeal. The modern historian Thomas Penn has argued that the Council Learned caused fear, frustration and anger, as it bypassed the normal legal system. It was, however, the expression of the king's will and was thus as important for the maintenance of his authority as it was for the raising of finances.

Bray's associate in the Council Learned was **Richard Empson**, a fiercely ambitious lawyer and **bureaucrat**, whose ruthless approach seemed increasingly to define the behaviour of the Council Learned. Following Bray's death in 1503, Empson was joined by **Edmund Dudley**. Together they formed a feared combination of able and conscientious bureaucrats who raised the extraction of money from the king's subjects to a fine art. Unsurprisingly, in the process they created enemies amongst some of the king's other key advisers, such as Bishop Fox and Sir Thomas Lovell, who removed them after Henry VII's death. The downfall of Empson and Dudley brought rejoicing on the streets. This is an indication of just how feared and unpopular their financial control became in the last years of Henry VII's reign.

KEY TERM

bureaucrat: an official in a government department, in particular one perceived as being concerned with procedural correctness at the expense of people's needs

KEY PROFILE

Sir Richard Empson (c1450–1510)

Empson was a member of the king's Council from 1494. He eventually chaired the Council Learned. Closely identified with the increasing ruthlessness of Henry VII's regime, Empson was arrested shortly after the death of the king, charged with treason and executed in the following year.

Edmund Dudley (c1462–1510)

Dudley came to prominence following the death of Bray. Steven Gunn argues that his role was to exploit financial opportunities, which gave him ample opportunity to make influential enemies. He therefore became vulnerable to counter-attack as soon as he lost the king's protection. Upon Henry Tudor's death he became accountable for what had been the king's demands.

Fig. 2 *Sir Richard Empson (left) with Henry VII (centre) and Edmund Dudley (right)*

Court and household

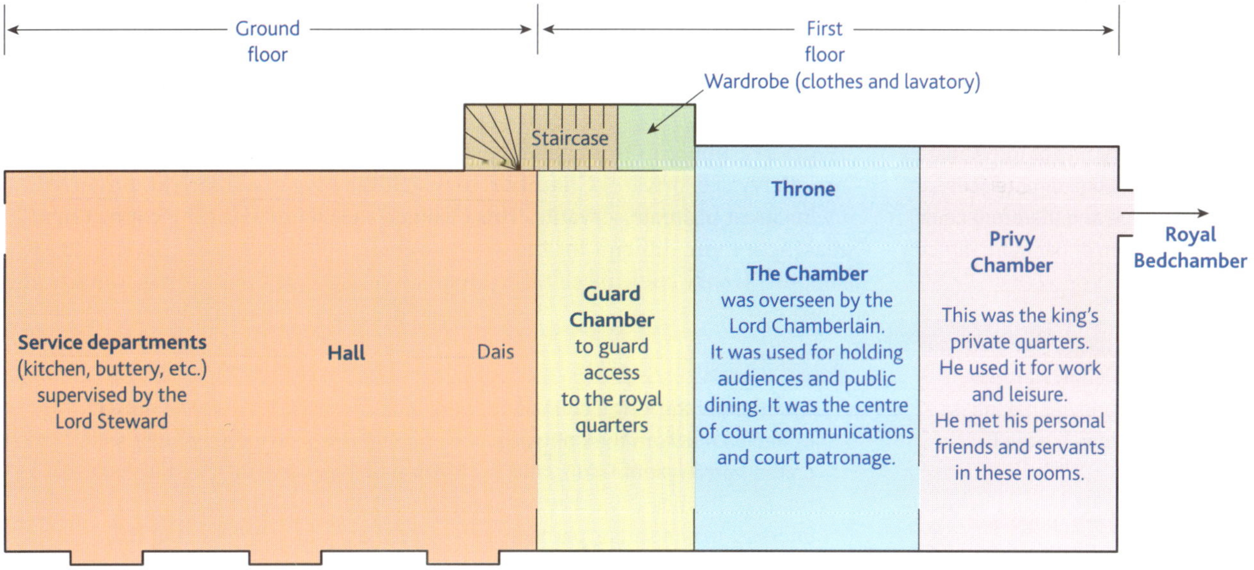

Fig. 3 *Henry VII's court after the creation of the Privy Chamber in 1495*

The Tudors, like their predecessors, relied heavily on the royal court. This was the centre of government. Since wealth was power, the royal court had to be magnificent and generous. In this, Henry VII was influenced by continental examples of royal courts, especially those in Burgundy and France. The royal court was always to be found wherever the king was at any given time. It was the focus of a personal monarchy and a place for royal ceremony, about which Henry VII was very enthusiastic. It was where the power of the monarch was demonstrated to all the **courtiers** in attendance. It was through the court that rewards and status were distributed to those who were deserving or, more likely, well connected.

Courtiers enjoyed paid positions or the right to receive free food. Not only was the court where advancement could be attained, it was also where the support of the king or other influential persons could be obtained, which might be useful in the event of legal problems.

KEY TERM

courtier: a person who attends a royal court as a companion or adviser to the monarch

A CLOSER LOOK

Personal monarchy

Medieval monarchy was personal. In any personal monarchy the political power and influence of an individual depended more on the relationship that person had with the monarch than on any specific office which they might have held. Access to the king, therefore, was the main determinant of power and it was through the royal court that access was controlled. This remained the case whatever a particular monarch's style of kingship was.

There were different levels to the court:

1. The household proper was responsible for looking after the king, the courtiers, guests and other 'hangers-on' who were being entertained. These personal and catering requirements were supervised by the Lord Steward.
2. The politically important part of the system was the **Chamber**, presided over by the **Lord Chamberlain**. The Lord Chamberlain and other senior household officials were influential courtiers. The position of Lord Chamberlain was both powerful and a matter of considerable trust. It was therefore a considerable blow to Henry VII to discover in 1495 that his Lord Chamberlain, **Sir William Stanley**, had been involved in a treasonable plot with the pretender **Perkin Warbeck**.

Henry's response to this challenge was to remodel the Chamber by creating a new **Privy** (i.e. private) **Chamber**, to which the king could retreat, protected by his most intimate servants. This changed the character of the court, thus making it more difficult for those who were out of favour to regain the king's support. Henry cut himself off from much of the king's traditional contacts at court.

KEY TERM

Chamber: the private areas of the court; also a key department for the efficient collection of royal revenues

The Lord Chamberlain: also known as the Chamberlain, an experienced nobleman and member of the king's council, and a personal friend of the king; he had administrative and political power, often speaking for the monarch in an official capacity, and was also responsible for organising court ceremonies

Privy Chamber: comprising the close personal servants of the monarch; its members had direct access to the monarch and therefore could influence him or her more directly

CROSS-REFERENCE

The attempt of Perkin Warbeck to claim the throne of England is outlined in Chapter 1, page 6.

There is a Key Profile of William Stanley in Chapter 1, page 3.

EXTRACT 2

A number of the king's councillors were also courtiers, men whose power rested as much on their physical and emotional proximity to the ruler as on their professional skills and administrative positions. Despite his legal training, Thomas Lovell began his career helping the king to dress and undress. In one sense, perhaps, every councillor was a courtier, but there does seem to have been a real distinction between Lovell and others such as Empson and the Chancellor of the Duchy of Lancaster, whose careers rested almost entirely on their legal skills, who showed little interest in the **chivalrous** culture of the court, and whose work may have tied them to London and Westminster while others were freer to travel with the king. There was no hard and fast division of roles.

Adapted from Steven J. Gunn, 'The courtiers of Henry VII' in *The Tudor Monarchy*, edited by John Guy, 1997

KEY TERM

chivalrous: to be gallant, or courteous; the chivalrous culture of the early Tudor court was a code of conduct associated historically with the dutiful behaviour of medieval knights

ACTIVITY

1. Working in groups, what conclusions can you draw from Extract 2 about courtiers and councillors during the reign of Henry VII?
2. Based on your historical knowledge and the information in this section, produce a diagram, with Henry VII at the top, indicating the relationships between king, court and council. Include the names of key figures in your diagram.

CROSS-REFERENCE

The chivalric ideal was recorded in literature and stories, which are discussed in Chapter 6, pages 59–60.

Parliament

Parliament, comprising the House of Commons and the House of Lords, had existed since the thirteenth century, but it only met occasionally and was not, therefore, central to the system of government. It had two main functions: to pass laws and to grant taxation to the Crown. It had a further subsidiary function as a means by which local issues and grievances could be passed on to the king's officials by local Members of Parliament (MPs).

A CLOSER LOOK

At this time the House of Lords, comprising the Lords Spiritual (bishops and abbots of major religious houses) and the Lords Temporal (the nobility), was the more important of the two houses. The House of Commons comprised two MPs for each county, two MPs for each borough, and representatives of the two universities (Oxford and Cambridge). The right to vote was largely restricted to men of property, 'forty shilling freeholders' in the counties, though the precise voting qualification varied in boroughs.

Table 1 *Henry VII's parliaments*

First parliament	Nov 1485 – Mar 1486
Second parliament	Nov 1487 – Dec 1487
Third parliament	Jan 1489 – Feb 1490
Fourth parliament	Oct 1491 – Mar 1492
Fifth parliament	Oct 1495 – Dec 1495
Sixth parliament	Jan 1497 – Mar 1497
Seventh parliament	Jan 1504 – Apr 1504

Only the king could call Parliament, and Henry demonstrated his right to rule by calling his first parliament early in his reign. Henry called a total of seven parliaments in his reign, though five of these met in the first ten years of the reign leaving only two to meet in the remaining fourteen years. Henry's early parliaments were largely concerned with issues of national security and the raising of revenue. For example, his first two parliaments passed numerous Acts of Attainder. These declared individuals guilty without having to go through the inconvenience of a trial if they were alive; if they were dead, their property would be forfeit to the Crown. His first parliament granted tonnage and poundage (customs revenues) for life; other parliaments granted **extraordinary revenue**, taxation granted to enable the king to wage war. The most usual form of extraordinary revenue was fifteenths and tenths, which were imposed upon the alleged value of a taxpayer's goods. Fractional taxes of **fifteenths and tenths** were made in 1487, 1489–90, 1491–92 and 1497, yielding £203,000. Henry's

KEY TERM

extraordinary revenue: money raised by the king from additional sources as one-off payments when he faced an emergency or an unforeseeable expense of government; this could be made up of parliamentary grants, loans, clerical taxes, for example

fifteenths and tenths: standard form of taxation, calculated in the fourteenth century, paid by towns and boroughs to the Crown

final parliament in 1504 did manage, however, to limit the demand for extraordinary revenue, and received an undertaking that the king would not seek more revenue by this means.

There is little surviving evidence of the parliamentary proceedings in Henry's reign. However, the research of historian Paul Cavill has shown that, on the whole, Parliament operated effectively, the king respected its decisions and there were a number of private acts passed in response to local demands for improvements. There is little evidence that the king tried to 'manage' Parliament through his ministers.

CROSS-REFERENCE

Acts of Attainder are introduced in Chapter 1, page 3.

For the consolidation of power in the early stages of the reign, see Chapter 1, pages 3–7.

Domestic policy: justice and the maintenance of order

A prime responsibility for the king was the maintenance of law and order. At worst, problems with law and order could lead to uprisings or rebellions and Henry was always concerned that potential enemies might exploit trouble to challenge his authority. As had been traditional throughout earlier centuries, the king relied on well-placed members of the nobility to exercise power on his behalf, although there was a delicate balance to strike to ensure that the more influential of these nobles did not themselves become so powerful that they could challenge the king's own authority.

Henry did not have the luxury enjoyed by Edward IV, who had divided the whole country into spheres of influence, each controlled by a great noble (or magnate). The number of magnates had been reduced in the last years of the Wars of the Roses and their lands had fallen into the hands of the Crown. Magnate control was largely confined to the north of England, to Henry's relatives the Stanleys in the northwest and to the Earl of Northumberland in the northeast and Yorkshire, though the murder of the latter in 1489 left Henry without a great magnate to exercise power on his behalf in that strategically important area. He solved this problem by releasing the Yorkist Earl of Surrey from the Tower, where he had been imprisoned since the Battle of Bosworth, to rule the north on his behalf. Sending a known supporter of Richard III to the area which had been his predecessor's centre of power was a high-risk strategy, but Surrey proved his loyalty through effective service in the north for ten years. In much of the rest of the country Henry had to rely on those whom he did trust, such as the Earl of Oxford and Lord Daubeney, but who lacked the resources of the great magnates. Elsewhere he had to rely on those in whom he had little real faith, such as the Marquis of Dorset. This lack of trust was demonstrated by Henry's employment of a spying network whose task was to report on magnate performance as well as with the imposition of **bonds** and **recognizances**.

KEY TERM

bond: a legal document which bound an individual to another to perform an action or forfeit a specified sum of money if they failed to do so

recognizance: a formal acknowledgement of a debt or other obligation which could be enforced by means of financial penalty

Justices of the peace (JPs)

At a local level, Henry relied increasingly on justices of the peace (JPs) to maintain law and order in the countryside. JPs were appointed on a county-by-county basis and met four times a year to administer justice through the quarter sessions. Though it was quite common for royal officials to be appointed as JPs in counties in which they had an interest, most JPs were local gentry who fulfilled their unpaid tasks either out of a sense of duty or because they perceived that doing so might open the path to greater advancement or local prestige. Various Acts of Parliament were passed to increase the powers and responsibilities of JPs who were responsible for routine administration such as: tax assessments, alehouse regulation, the investigation of complaints against local officials, and the maintenance of law and order. In that role they superseded the traditional authority of the county sheriff.

CROSS-REFERENCE

The social and political importance of the nobility is discussed in Chapter 4, pages 34–35.

The rebellions faced by Henry VII are discussed in Chapter 1, pages 4–7.

Bonds and recognizances

This was, however, only part of the picture, for Henry VII restored law and order largely through forcing many of his subjects to take out bonds and recognizances. Some of the bonds and recognizances were the result of genuine debts owed to the Crown. However, many of them were purely political. In the words of Edmund Dudley, the king wished 'to have many persons in danger at his pleasure'. This means that the king used bonds to enforce order and obedience, and defeat the law, a system which can be regarded as morally dubious.

ACTIVITY

Pair discussion

Based on the information in this chapter, discuss in pairs whether or not you think Henry's use of bonds and recognizances was 'morally dubious'. Share your thoughts with a partner.

A CLOSER LOOK

The judicial system

Type of court	Area(s) of jurisdiction
Church courts	Church administration Offences committed by the clergy Proving of wills Issues relating to marriage 'Moral' offences
Local courts: Manor courts	Landholding Rights and responsibilities of landlords and tenants Use of common land Responsibilities for drainage and land issues
Borough courts	Medieval trading standards Specific judicial rights granted by royal charter
King's courts at county level	Assizes: held twice a year to deal with major criminal and civil cases and presided over by senior Westminster judges Quarter sessions: held four times a year, presided over by JPs, to deal with less important criminal cases as well as civil and administrative affairs Special commissions: set up on an *ad hoc* basis to deal with major issues such as rebellion
King's common law courts	King's Bench: had superior criminal jurisdiction Common Pleas: dealt with major civil cases Exchequer: dealt with issues relating to royal revenues
Chancery and other equity courts	Exercised jurisdiction on the basis of equity (fairness) rather than on a strict reading of the common law

A CLOSER LOOK

The historiography of Henry VII's justice system

On balance Steven Gunn considers that the administration of justice broadly improved during Henry VII's reign, with limited but effective steps being taken to improve the law. Christine Carpenter is much more critical in her judgement, especially of Henry's mistrust of the nobility and local society.

Domestic policy: improving royal finances

There were a number of sources of royal income:

- Crown lands
- profits from feudal dues and the exercise of the royal prerogative
- customs revenue
- pensions from other powers
- profits of justice
- extraordinary revenue.

For many years two things were assumed about Henry VII and finance: that he was a miserly king who begrudged throwing money away like many other contemporary rulers, and that he had transformed the royal finances by leaving a vast amount of money to his son, Henry VIII. Each of these views can be traced to Francis Bacon's *History of the Reign of King Henry VII*, written in 1621. In recent years, however, there has been considerable research on Crown finances, often based on the interpretation of complex sources, such as Henry VII's own private accounts. As a consequence, a different picture of Henry's finances has emerged.

SOURCE 1

Henry VII's private accounts from 1497 include the following:

January 6	To Hugh Vaughan for two harpists, 13s 4d [67p]
January 7	To a little maiden that dances, £12
	To a welsh man that makes rhymes, 6s 8d [33p]
February 17	To the Queen's fiddler in reward, £1 6s 8d [£1.33]
	To the gardener at Sheen for grafts £2
May 31	Delivered to the Queens grace for jewels. £31 10s. [£31.50]

ACTIVITY

Evaluating primary sources

What is the value of Source 1 to a historian researching Henry VII's attitude towards finances?

EXTRACT 3

As for Empson and Dudley's tax mills, they did grind more than ever: so that it was a strange thing to see what golden showers poured down upon the king's treasury at once. And this is the more to be marvelled at, because the king had then no occasions at all of wars or troubles. He had now but one son, and one daughter unmarried. He was wise; he was of a high mind; he did not need to make riches his glory; he did excel in so many things else. Besides, he thought to leave his son such a kingdom, and such a mass of treasure, as he might choose his greatness where he would. It is no marvel that the king's treasure of state, that he left at his death, most of it in secret places under his own key and keeping, at Richmond, amounted to the sum of near eighteen hundred thousand pounds sterling [£1.8 million], a huge mass of money even for those times.

Adapted from Francis Bacon, *The History of the Reign of King Henry the Seventh*, 1621

EXTRACT 4

The idea is that Henry VII amassed treasure worth £1,800,000, but this is pure myth. Although his revenue from all sources averaged £104,800 per annum in 1502–05, reaching £113,000 per annum by 1509, Henry had been forced to borrow money, raise 'loans' under his signet, and was granted a benevolence by a Great Council in 1491. After his Chamber system of finance got into gear, he purchased jewellery, plate, cloth of gold etc., and he spent large sums on building.

John Guy, *Tudor England*, 1988

STUDY TIP

Try to comment on the overall interpretation of each extract and any subsidiary views. In applying your own contextual knowledge, you might find it helpful to think about comments on the amount collected, the efficiency of collection, the level of indebtedness and the distribution of spending. You should provide a judgement on which extract is the more convincing.

AS LEVEL PRACTICE QUESTION

Evaluating historical extracts

With reference to Extracts 3 and 4 and your understanding of the historical context, which of these two extracts provides the more convincing interpretation of Henry VII's attitude to royal finance?

A CLOSER LOOK

Henry VII's financial policies

There is some debate as to whether Henry's greed was a feature throughout his reign or whether he became much greedier in the later stages of the reign, as was suggested by the contemporary chronicler Polydore Vergil. Certainly, there is evidence that contemporaries were relieved at his death. Lord Mountjoy wrote that such extreme greed was now dead and Sir Thomas More wrote a Latin poem for Henry VIII which contained criticism of both Henry VII and his advisers. Henry VIII was not slow to take the hint and to achieve cheap popularity by executing Empson and Dudley.

Crown lands

Henry VII was by far the country's largest landowner and the rental income from his property was a very important part of the Crown's ordinary revenue. Income from Crown lands had significantly increased during the reign of Edward IV.

At the beginning of Henry's reign income had dropped to about £12,000 per year. This was because the income from lands was collected and administered through the inefficient Court of Exchequer, which exemplifies Henry's inexperience in such financial matters. It was probably in 1492 that Henry decided to revert to Edward's system of administration through the Chamber (in other words through the royal household rather than through an administrative department), where policies were formulated and decisions were made. Finances improved markedly and the income from land had increased by the end of the reign to around £42,000 per year. This was partly achieved by effective treasurers of the Chamber, such as Sir Thomas Lovell and Sir John Heron.

A CLOSER LOOK

The historiography of Henry VII

Even Christine Carpenter, who is very critical of many aspects of Henry's kingship, regards this growth of income from Crown lands as impressive.

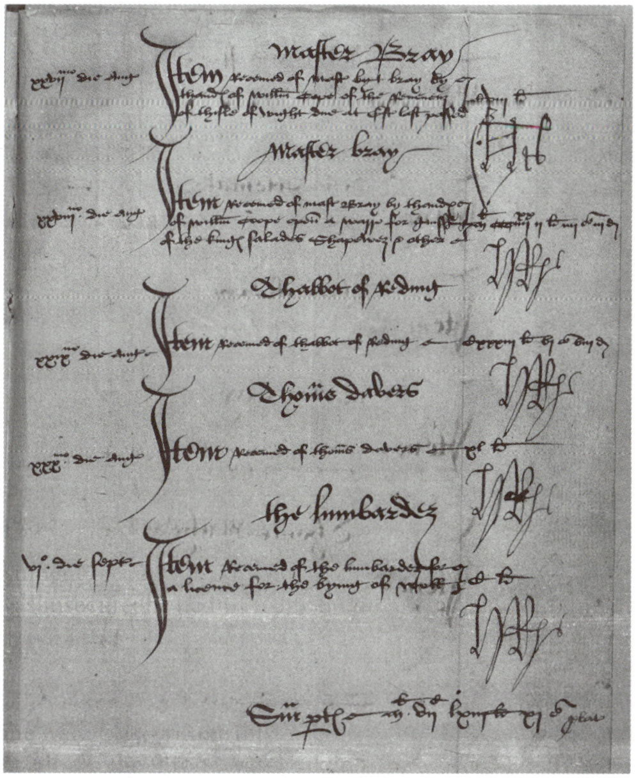

Fig. 4 *Royal accounts signed by Henry VII*

Profits from feudal dues and the exercise of the royal prerogative

The pursuit of the king's feudal rights was tightened. There were increased profits from **wardship** and Parliament granted a **feudal aid** in 1504. A thirteenth-century text, *Prerogativa Regis*, was examined by court lawyers anxious to find precedents for the levying of fees deriving from the king's prerogative, and from feudal powers. Obligations payable on the death of a feudal tenant-in-chief became a useful additional source of revenue which landowners found particularly irritating, especially when the **Statute of Uses** of 1489 cut out a potential loophole for avoidance of the charge.

KEY TERM

wardship: an aspect of the feudal system which enabled the Crown to gain the profits from property held by a minor

feudal aid: a right by which the Crown could impose a tax on their tenants for the knighting of the eldest son, the marriage of the eldest daughter or to ransom a lord; this was typical of the skilful way in which Henry revived old forms of raising revenue, much to the irritation of landowners

Statute of Uses: a law passed to prevent landed property from being turned into trusts which in modern terms were mechanisms for avoiding paying tax on a deceased person's estate

A CLOSER LOOK

Feudalism was the dominant social system in medieval Europe, in which the nobility held lands from the Crown in exchange for military service.

CROSS-REFERENCE

Prerogative powers are explained earlier in this chapter, page 10.

Other sources of revenue

- Customs revenue: tonnage and poundage had been granted for life by Henry's first parliament. Over the course of the reign there was a small increase in the annual revenue from this source from £34,000 to £38,000.
- Pensions from other powers: at the Treaty of Etaples in 1492 the French agreed to pay Henry a pension of £5000 per annum.
- Profits of justice: this included fines and income from bonds. Bonds represented a potential rather than an actual asset. For example, between 1504 and 1507 a total of at least £200,000 was promised to the king, though not all was collected.
- Extraordinary revenue: Henry received over £400,000 from extraordinary taxation. However, raising all this revenue came at a price and helped to provoke rebellions in 1489 and 1497. Henry had to promise the Parliament of 1504 not to raise any more money by this method. In 1489, when Parliament had granted Henry a subsidy of £75,000, the Convocation of Canterbury in addition offered £25,000 on behalf of the clergy.

In total, Henry left plate and jewels worth around £300,000 and £10,000 in cash. Although a substantial sum, this is a far cry from Bacon's estimate of £1,800,000.

Much energy was spent on improving Henry's revenues, but there was a political price to be paid. The main victims of Henry's policies were the nation's landowners, precisely the people whose support Henry would need if his throne was threatened. Yet Henry treated them in a way which might have made them threaten the Crown. Whenever earlier medieval monarchs had adopted this strategy, the outcome for the Crown's authority had been disastrous. Henry's policies were therefore quite dangerous ones.

CROSS-REFERENCE

Tonnage and poundage is defined in Chapter 1, page 3.

The Treaty of Etaples of 1492 is discussed in Chapter 3, page 24.

Henry's associations with the Church and the clergy are covered in Chapter 4, page 36.

CROSS-REFERENCE

Extraordinary revenue is explained in this chapter, page 13.

The relationship between Henry VII and the nobility is discussed in this chapter, page 14.

Summary

In 1874 John Richard Green put forward the argument that Edward IV and Henry VII together represented a 'new monarchy'. For a long time historians accepted that Henry was a 'new monarch', either by taking further Edward IV's innovations in government or by being himself the innovator. The latter view implies that the Tudors were not only a new dynasty but were a consciously modernising dynasty that had set aside the weaknesses of medieval and personal monarchy. On the other hand, Stanley Chrimes, in his biography of Henry published in 1972, claimed that he was no innovator, a view condemned by David Starkey, who has emphasised the originality involved in the establishment of the Privy Chamber.

Some recent views of Henry VII have revived notions of a new monarchy, though in rather different forms. Steven Gunn, for example, places Henry's reign in a century of governmental centralisation lasting from the reign of Edward IV to the accession of Elizabeth I. He regards the reign as having been broadly beneficial to both the monarchy and most of the people and believes that Henry's policies, though sometimes harsh, were a necessary response to the problems which he inherited as king. Moreover, Gunn sees the monarch as being deeply involved at a personal level in the business of government. In this respect, Gunn's views differ from those of John Watts, for whom Henry largely stood aside from the business of government, leaving the work to bureaucrats such as Morton, Bray and Empson who pursued their own interests as much as they pursued those of the king. Each of them arguably accords more substance to Henry than does Christine Carpenter; for Carpenter, Henry is a ruler of very modest ability who failed to understand the needs of the nation over which he had control.

ACTIVITY

Evaluating historical extracts

Look back at Wallace MacCaffrey's interpretation in Extract 1, at the beginning of this chapter (page 9). In small groups, consider whether you find his interpretation convincing. How far does the evidence presented in this chapter support the view that Henry VII's government was 'baffling' to the nobility? You will need to find specific evidence to support or refute MacCaffrey's views.

Most historians agree that Henry VII's rule was distinctive, though they might differ about its nature. John Watts, in particular, has played down Henry's role in the day-to-day management of government. After Henry's death the downfall of some of Henry's key courtiers was sudden. However, as Margaret Condon has argued, it was Henry himself who created the fragility in government, which brought about a division within the ruling elites.

ACTIVITY

Thinking point

Why do you think there has been so much debate about Henry VII's monarchy?

A LEVEL PRACTICE QUESTION

'Henry VII's reforms in government were limited both in scope and in success.' Assess the validity of this view.

STUDY TIP

It is important when answering questions such as this to address both parts of the quotation. In deciding whether or not reforms were limited in scope it is necessary to identify what the reforms were and how much change they brought about. In deciding whether or not they were successful it is important to establish what they were trying to achieve and the extent to which they achieved these aims.

3 England's relations with Scotland and other foreign powers, 1485–1509

Henry VII's relations with foreign powers

EXTRACT 1

Throughout his reign Henry VII's foreign policy was defensive: he reacted to external events in order to secure his Crown and dynasty. Initially in debt to Brittany and France, he had to neutralise the capacity of France, Spain, Burgundy and Scotland to profit from Yorkist claimants and safeguard his northern border with Scotland.

Adapted from John Guy, *Tudor England*, 1988

Henry's foreign policy aims were essentially straightforward. He had no grand plans to assert English power in Europe, and was therefore more concerned with maintaining good relations and defence. He certainly had no intention of restarting the **Hundred Years War** with France. Broadly speaking, he sought to maintain positive relations with foreign powers to ensure:

- national security
- recognition of the Tudor dynasty
- defence of English trading interests.

KEY CHRONOLOGY

Foreign relations during the reign of Henry VII

1487	French invasion of Brittany
1488	Anglo-French truce
1489	Treaty of Redon between England and Brittany
	Treaty of Medina del Campo between England and Spain
1492	England invades France
	Treaty of Etaples between England and France
1496	Magnus Intercursus
	Scotland invades England
1497	Truce of Ayton between England and Scotland
1501	Marriage of Prince Arthur and Catherine of Aragon
1502	Death of Prince Arthur
1503	Marriage of Princess Margaret and James IV of Scotland
1504	Death of Queen Isabella of Castile
1506	Philip of Burgundy and Juana of Castile in England (January)
	Malus Intercursus
	Death of Philip of Burgundy (September)

Brittany and France

Henry's first major foreign policy involvement came in Brittany, a **fiefdom** of the French Crown which had enjoyed effective independence.

LEARNING OBJECTIVES

In this chapter you will learn about:

- Henry VII's relations with European powers
- Henry's relations with Scotland
- ways that Henry VII set about securing the succession and marriage alliances.

KEY QUESTION

As you read this chapter, consider the following Key Questions:

- How did relations with foreign powers change and how was the succession secured?
- How important was the role of key individuals and groups and how were they affected by developments?

KEY TERM

Hundred Years War: conflict that lasted on and off from 1337 to 1453, and was fought between England and the country seen by many English people as the traditional enemy: France

ACTIVITY

Evaluating historical extracts

1. Make a list of Henry's foreign policy aims, as given in Extract 1.
2. As you read this chapter, consider whether you think that he had any other foreign policy aims.

Following an invasion in 1487 it looked as if the French would gain complete control of Brittany. This alarmed Henry who, in 1489, summoned Parliament to grant him extraordinary revenue to raise an army against the French. There were two main reasons for this:

- his sense of obligation to the Bretons
- his fear that direct French control of Brittany could increase a potential French threat to England.

KEY TERM

suzerainty: the feudal control of one territory by another

CROSS-REFERENCE

Extraordinary revenue is explained in Chapter 2, page 13.

A CLOSER LOOK

Brittany, fiefdom of the French Crown

A fiefdom denotes an area over which feudal overlordship is exercised. Brittany was a fief ruled over by Duke Francis II. He had no sons so his daughter, Duchess Anne, was his only heir. Had she been born a man she would have ruled Brittany as her father did, but she was born a woman in a time when women could not rule. The French were eager to use the opportunity afforded by the death of Francis and the lack of male heirs to claim Brittany and strip it of its independence.

KEY PROFILE

Maximilian I (1459–1519) was Holy Roman Emperor from 1493 to 1519, though he had taken over rule of the Empire in 1486. In 1477 he had married Mary of Burgundy and through her had gained control of the Netherlands, England's main trading partner.

England and Brittany agreed the Treaty of Redon in February 1489, according to which the Duchess Anne would pay for a small English army to defend Brittany from the French threat. At the same time Henry tried to strengthen his position by an alliance with **Maximilian**, the Holy Roman Emperor-elect. A widower, Maximilian had contracted a **marriage-by-proxy** with Anne and had no desire, therefore, for the Duchy of Brittany to fall into French hands.

KEY TERM

marriage-by-proxy: one or both of the individuals being united is not physically present, usually being represented instead by another person

KEY PROFILE

Fig. 1 *Charles VIII*

Charles VIII (1470–98) was King of France from 1483 to 1498. He ruled in his own right from 1491, and his main concern was to assert his claim to the throne of the kingdom of Naples in the Italian peninsula. This reduced any potential threat from Charles to Henry VII.

Fig. 2 *Anne of Brittany depicted with her patron saints Anne, Ursula and Catherine*

Scotland was the only country with which England shared a border, and where cross-border lawlessness was a way of life. Scotland often worked closely with France as part of the 'auld alliance', which was explicitly anti-English.

The most powerful European country, France was seeking to bring duchies like Brittany and Burgundy more directly under the control of the French Crown, which had important implications for wider European relations. France and England shared a long-standing hostility which included the Hundred Years War, 1337–1453.

The Holy Roman Empire was a loose federation of about 300 states, mostly situated in what is now Germany. The emperor was elected, though by the later fifteenth century the elected emperor was always a member of the Austrian Habsburg dynasty. Maximilian I was elected in 1486 and became emperor in 1493.

The position of Ireland at this time was something of an anomaly. There was no separate Irish state. The title of 'Lord of Ireland' had been granted by the Pope to the King of England in the twelfth century.

The medieval power of the Duchy of Burgundy had been broken with the death of Duke Charles the Bold in 1477, after which the lands of the duchy proper had been resumed by the French Crown. However, the title of Duke of Burgundy would pass to Maximilian, Holy Roman Emperor, and most of the Low Countries were under Maximilian's **suzerainty**.

The marriage of Ferdinand of Aragon and Isabella of Castile in 1469 helped to bring the two kingdoms together, giving them a façade of unity. However, the death of Isabella in 1504 weakened that perception and the next few years saw Ferdinand involved in conflict to reassert his control over Castile, which would have a significant effect on Henry VII's foreign policy.

Fig. 3 *European powers during the reign of Henry VII*

CROSS-REFERENCE

To recap Perkin Warbeck, and his attempts to undermine Henry's claim to the throne, look back to Chapter 1, page 6.

ACTIVITY

Produce a draft speech to Parliament in 1491 which might have been delivered by one of Henry's ministers to justify the seeking of extraordinary revenue to pay for the second invasion of France.

The English army went to Brittany but Anne, fearing the futility of prolonged resistance to the French, surrendered and reluctantly married **Charles VIII**. This left the English army marooned in Brittany, and also meant that Maximilian lost interest in the matter, which left Henry in a difficult position. The situation was made worse for Henry by **Perkin Warbeck** seeking French backing for his claim to the English throne. In his first foreign adventure Henry had suffered an immediate setback.

However, Henry did recover his position very skilfully. He launched an invasion of France in 1492, rather late in the campaigning season, and the French quickly sought a peace settlement. Though Henry's invasion might have appeared a gamble, he used information from his agents that Charles VIII was much more interested in launching an invasion of Italy and would therefore quickly seek a peace settlement with Henry. Henry showed enough flexibility in his approach to benefit from this change in French priorities.

At the signing of the Treaty of Etaples in November 1492, Charles VIII agreed to withdraw his support for Perkin Warbeck and to pay a pension to Henry to compensate him for the expense of having recruited an army of invasion. Henry's strategy had proved successful, and he had managed to defend national and dynastic interests. Moreover, he had improved his financial position and ensured a period of relative cordiality in Anglo-French relations.

Burgundy, the Netherlands and the Holy Roman Empire

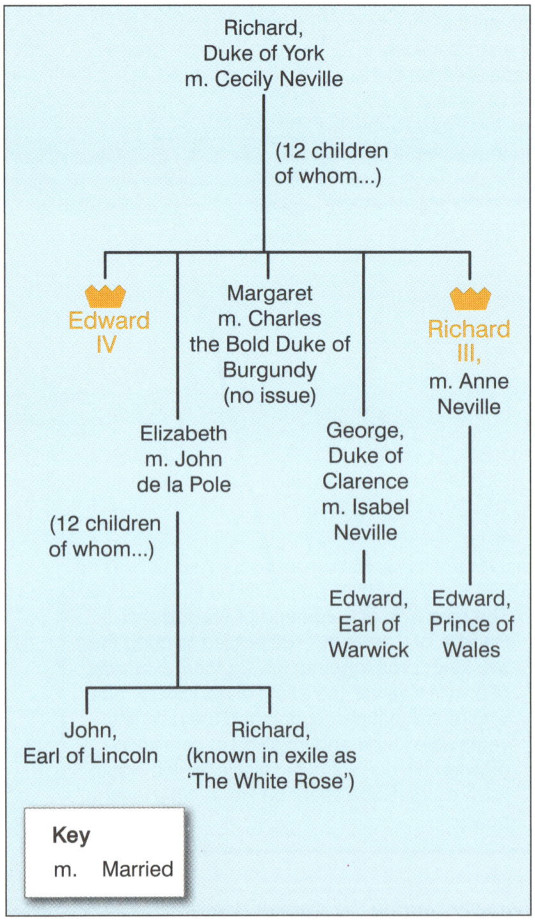

Fig. 4 *Margaret of Burgundy and the Yorkist interest*

The bulk of England's exports went through the ports of the Netherlands, such as Antwerp and Bruges, which came under Burgundy's jurisdiction. It was therefore important for commercial reasons for good relations to be maintained. The complicating factor was, however, the presence of Margaret, widowed Duchess of Burgundy in ownership of her late-husband's estate. She was the sister of Edward IV and Richard III, and the leading upholder of the Yorkist cause. Margaret also enlisted the support of her stepson-in-law, Maximilian, who became Holy Roman Emperor in 1493 and passed over jurisdiction in the Netherlands to his sixteen-year-old son Philip in the following year. Relations between England and Burgundy deteriorated as a result of the hospitality which Maximilian and Philip were offering to Perkin Warbeck, and Henry gambled that putting an embargo on English trade with Burgundy would ease the matter. The problem which this caused was that it brought two of Henry's foreign policy objectives – securing the dynasty and encouraging trade – into conflict with each other. In giving priority to his dynastic interests, Henry showed himself prepared to sacrifice the commercial interests of London and east-coast merchants, which did nothing for his popularity in those parts of the country. Relations did improve to an extent after Warbeck left Burgundy, and Henry and Philip were able to agree the **Intercursus Magnus** in 1496 which brought the **trade embargo** to an end.

Anglo-Burgundian relations again became central to Henry's foreign policy calculations in 1504 following the death of Isabella, Queen of Castile (see the map at the beginning of this chapter). One of the outcomes of the resulting Treaty of Windsor was a new trade agreement, the **Intercursus Malus**. In this, Henry showed the same forceful approach which by this time he was adopting in his domestic financial affairs: he demanded a trade deal which would have given a much stronger trading position to English merchants in the Netherlands had it ever been enforced (in the end, this trade deal was never put into practice). Another outcome was that Philip and Maximilian agreed to hand over their Yorkist fugitive, the Earl of Suffolk, whom Henry promptly imprisoned in the Tower. Henry appeared to have improved both England's trading position and also the security of the dynasty.

Spain

Fig. 5 *Ferdinand and Isabella of Spain*

KEY TERM

Intercursus Magnus: the major commercial treaty between England and the Duchy of Burgundy which restored normal trading links between the two

Intercursus Malus: trade agreement from 1506; this treaty never became fully operative and by the following year trading relationships had been restored on the basis of Intercursus Magnus

CROSS-REFERENCE

The trade embargo was one of a number of issues relating to trade and economic development, which will be discussed in Chapter 5, page 47.

CROSS-REFERENCE

More detail on the Intercursus Magnus and Intercursus Malus is in Chapter 5, pages 46–47.

CROSS-REFERENCE

Henry's treatment of The Earl of Suffolk is covered in Chapter 1, page 7.

The implications of Isabella's death for English foreign policy are discussed on page 22.

Ruled over by Ferdinand and his wife Isabella, Spain was a powerful state, with which Henry hoped to develop good relations. The Treaty of Medina del Campo in 1489 was an important development for Henry in that it gave him some of the international peace and security to which he aspired:

- the two monarchies offered mutual protection in the event of attack
- they agreed not to harbour rebels or pretenders
- the treaty arranged a marriage alliance between Arthur, Prince of Wales, and Catherine, Princess of Aragon, the daughter of Ferdinand and Isabella.

There were problems with the implementation of the treaty:

- arrangements for the royal marriage did not go smoothly
- Ferdinand proved reluctant to allow the marriage to go ahead as long as Henry's dynastic stability remained threatened by Perkin Warbeck
- the two monarchs argued over the size of Catherine's dowry.

The details of the marriage were finally agreed in 1499 and it took place in 1501. However, the death of Arthur in 1502 brought complications to Henry's relations with Ferdinand:

- Henry immediately suggested that Catherine should marry his second son, Prince Henry, but Ferdinand was reluctant to agree. He had little need for an English alliance and the proposed marriage would require a **papal dispensation** – which could be arranged but at a price.
- In 1504, Henry lost his enthusiasm for the marriage, when the death of Isabella made Ferdinand a less significant political figure. During the resultant succession struggle in Spain between Ferdinand and Juana (Catherine of Aragon's sister), Henry chose to support the latter.
- Juana and her husband Philip of Burgundy set sail for Spain in January 1506, but were forced to take refuge in England when their ship was wrecked at sea.

Henry was able to take advantage of his guests' situation. By the Treaty of Windsor (1506) Henry secured a stronger relationship with Juana and Philip with:

- the Intercursus Malus (restoring trade relations between England and Burgundy)
- the return of the Earl of Suffolk (further securing Henry's dynasty)
- a proposed marriage alliance for himself with Philip's sister, the Archduchess Margaret (aimed at strengthening Henry's rule after the death of his wife Elizabeth, but this marriage never happened)
- Henry's recognition of Juana and Philip as rulers of Castile (strengthening the couple's claim to the Spanish throne).

However, Philip of Burgundy's death, soon after the couple's arrival in Spain, proved disastrous for Henry:

- Juana, in her grief, was described by her father Ferdinand as having gone mad.
- This gave Ferdinand the opportunity once more to become regent of Castile.
- This left Henry diplomatically isolated as once again he had been diplomatically outsmarted by a major European monarch.
- Ferdinand ensured that the marriage between Prince Henry and Catherine would not take place in Henry VII's lifetime (though they did marry once Prince Henry had come to the throne as King Henry VIII).

KEY TERM

papal dispensation: permission was required from the Pope in order to be exempted from the laws or observances of the Church; it was considered only in special or unusual circumstances

STUDY TIP

It is possible to answer such questions either thematically or chronologically. If you adopt a chronological approach, you should ensure that you make considered judgements on each development which you discuss.

AS LEVEL PRACTICE QUESTION

'Henry VII showed himself to be a capable ruler in his dealings with Spain in the years 1485 to 1509.' Explain why you agree or disagree with this view.

Scotland

1485–95	Anglo-Scottish relations were often tense, though for the first few years of Henry's reign relationships remained relatively cordial.
1495–96 A turning point	Problems arose when **King James IV** came of age and in 1495 offered hospitality to Perkin Warbeck. Warbeck stayed for two years at the Scottish court, and received not only a pension from the king but also an aristocratic marriage – to the king's cousin Lady Catherine Gordon. This was already a potential threat to Henry but, to make matters worse, James encouraged Warbeck to cross the border in 1496 with an army. The army was small, spent little time in England, received no support from the people of Northumberland and quickly retreated back over the border when word was received that an English force was making its way north from Newcastle. However, this attempt at an invasion led Henry to raise a larger army to launch an invasion of Scotland. This decision had important political repercussions because it prompted a taxation rebellion the following year.
1497 The Cornish Rebellion	A large-scale rebellion in Cornwall shook Henry. It was evident that it was in the interests of both England and Scotland to secure an immediate truce, which took place at Ayton, a few miles north of the English border stronghold of Berwick-upon-Tweed.
1498 onwards	Anglo-Scottish relations significantly improved. Because of this improvement James no longer had any diplomatic use for Warbeck, who had become tiresome. Warbeck was executed in 1499.
1501–03	It was agreed that James should marry Henry's daughter, the Princess Margaret. In 1502 this was sanctioned by a formal peace treaty, the Treaty of Perpetual Peace, and the marriage took place in 1503. The improvement in relations with Scotland lasted until the end of Henry's reign. In terms of Anglo-Scottish relations it is evident that Henry had been successful in ensuring the security of the dynasty.

ACTIVITY

Write a letter from James to Margaret, explaining why relations with England have been variable but expressing your hope that your union will bring peace. Before you start writing, refer to the notes on Scotland in the map at the beginning of this chapter, and the situation with Perkin Warbeck, as detailed in Chapter 1, page 6.

Ireland

Henry VII's power in Ireland only extended as far as the 'Pale', the area of land which surrounded Dublin. Power in the rest of Ireland lay with the descendants of the Anglo-Norman barons who had settled there in the twelfth century, of whom the most important were the Fitzgeralds (or Geraldines) and the Butlers.

The dominant figure was the **Earl of Kildare** (the leader of the Geraldines), Lord Deputy of Ireland since 1477. He was feared by Henry because he had Yorkist sympathies. This suspicion was reinforced by Kildare's support for Lambert Simnel, whom he crowned king of Ireland in 1486. He compounded his suspicion in Henry's eyes by supporting Perkin Warbeck in 1491.

KEY PROFILE

Fig. 6 *James IV*

James IV (1473–1513) succeeded to the Scottish throne at the age of 15 in 1488. He was responsible for the invasion of England in 1496, but did not pursue the policy, making peace the following year. He married Henry VII's daughter, Margaret. He was killed at the Battle of Flodden in 1513.

CROSS-REFERENCE

The taxation rebellion in Cornwall of 1497 is discussed in Chapter 4, pages 40–41.

Perkin Warbeck had been a potential threat to Henry VII's throne. More detail about this can be found in Chapter 1, page 6.

CROSS-REFERENCE

Lambert Simnel's pretence to the throne of England is covered in Chapter 1, pages 4–5.

KEY PROFILE

Gerald Fitzgerald, 8th Earl of Kildare (c1456–1513), known as 'the uncrowned king of Ireland', was the leading member of the Irish nobility. Henry became dependent upon Kildare for the maintenance of law and order in Ireland.

Kildare's actions forced Henry into action:

- Instead of relying on the established Irish aristocracy, who were cheap but unreliable, he attempted the more costly approach of rule of the 'Pale' through an Englishman, backed by armed force.
- He appointed his infant son Prince Henry as Lieutenant of Ireland and appointed Sir Edward Poynings as his deputy.

Poynings was initially successful in establishing royal authority by means of the threat of force and the use of bribery. He reinforced this success by requiring the Irish parliament to pass 'Poynings' Law' in 1495, which laid down that the Irish parliament could pass no law without the prior approval of the English Crown. He also attempted to implement English law in Ireland.

This strategy proved too expensive for Henry's liking, and the financial problems were made worse when Warbeck returned to Ireland in 1495 and amassed a force which besieged the town of Waterford. Henry, who was short of money because of the threat of invasion by the Scots, was forced to recall Poynings and once again had to depend on the cheap option of using Kildare as his deputy.

By this stage in 1496 Kildare had decided that there was no benefit in supporting the Yorkist cause any longer and decided to serve Henry loyally, in the process securing the submission of the various Irish chieftains. By around 1500 Henry had eventually secured some level of peaceable – and cheap – authority over Ireland, though he was undoubtedly fortunate in that Kildare eventually proved so amenable. The fact that Kildare was able to use his office to rebuild his family's fortunes doubtless made him eager to support his former enemy.

ACTIVITY

Construct a timeline showing key developments in Henry VII's relations with Scotland on one side of the date line, and with Ireland on the other. Mark out the periods when Henry faced the greatest threat.

SOURCE 1

In 1507 Henry made the following claim to the City of London:

'This our realm is now environed, and, in manner, closed in every side with such mighty princes our good sons, friends, confederates and allies, that by the help of our Lord the same is and shall be perpetually established in rest and peace and wealthy condition.'

ACTIVITY

Evaluating primary sources

1. What evidence can be found in this chapter (a) to justify and (b) to weaken this claim?
2. What is the value of this source to a historian studying Henry's foreign policy?

ACTIVITY

Evaluating foreign policy

How successful was Henry VII in his conduct of foreign policy? Copy and complete the table, supporting your judgements with evidence for each category.

	Brittany/France	Burgundy/Holy Roman Empire	Spain	Scotland
National security				
Dynastic recognition				
Defence of trade				

CROSS-REFERENCE

The disappearance of the young Edward V and his brother Richard while in captivity in the Tower of London is outlined in the Introduction, page xiv.

The Earl of Suffolk's claim to the throne is outlined in Chapter 1, page 7.

Henry VII's victory at the Battle of Bosworth secured his succession as the next king of England. Read more about this in the Introduction, pages xiv–xv.

Securing the succession and marriage alliances

Before 1502 it seemed that there would be no problems with the succession to Henry VII. In 1486, his wife Elizabeth gave birth to a son, Prince Arthur, and in 1491, to another, Prince Henry. Arthur received the education which was deemed to be fitting for a prince and was set up with his own court at Ludlow in Shropshire.

A CLOSER LOOK

Henry VII's children

Henry VII had four children that survived childhood: Arthur, Henry, Margaret and Mary. In 1503, one year after Arthur died, Henry's wife Elizabeth of York died shortly after giving birth to their seventh child, Katherine, who also died.

Arthur's unexpected death in April 1502 increased the insecurity of the dynasty. The heir to the throne was now the young Prince Henry, which raised the issue of what might happen if the king himself were to die while Henry was still a child. The precedent of Edward V was not encouraging. Moreover, the issue was complicated by the fact that once again the Yorkist claimant the Earl of Suffolk seemed to be gaining influence.

ACTIVITY

Prince Arthur died in April 1502. Working in pairs, identify the potential threats to the Tudor succession, as they might have appeared at that time to Henry VII.

The dynasty thus depended on Henry VII's survival until his son was old enough to rule, and his deteriorating health was a continuous cause of concern to many of his key advisers. Henry also recognised the need to dispose of the threat from the Earl of Suffolk. In this he was lucky in that Juana and Philip of Burgundy were forced to take refuge in England in 1506 as it gave him the opportunity to press Philip of Burgundy and his father Maximilian to hand Suffolk over to him. Nevertheless, there was still uncertainty amongst Henry's key followers and much jockeying for position. What seems evident is that there was a growing split between those officials who were particularly associated with the Council Learned, especially Sir Richard Empson and Edmund Dudley, and some of Henry's other advisers, especially Bishop Fox and Sir Thomas Lovell, who were looking to position themselves effectively once Henry's health finally failed. There were still fears about Suffolk and his brother Richard de la Pole, and there were also fears that the Duke of Buckingham, a descendant of Edward III, might launch an attempt at seizing the throne.

CROSS-REFERENCE

Refresh your memory of Henry's various advisers by returning to Chapter 2, pages 9–11.

Henry's health deteriorated rapidly from February 1509 and he died on the evening of 21 April. No announcement was made at first of the king's death. Instead, Bishop Fox and his trusted friend within the Privy Chamber, Richard Weston, aided and abetted by Lady Margaret Beaufort, sought to manipulate the terms of the succession to their advantage and to position themselves around the new king. Most importantly, Empson and Dudley were excluded from their deliberations. The king's death was announced on 23 April, and on the following day the process of rounding up potential troublemakers began. Among those arrested were Empson and Dudley. There was a clear message, therefore, that the new regime would be different from the old.

Royal marriage alliances, foreign policy and the succession

Marriage alliances were an essential part of international diplomacy during this period. All monarchs sought marriage alliances in order to enhance their power and influence. In addition, it was important for Henry VII to seek appropriate marriage alliances in order to help bring about dynastic security. He planned to maintain an alliance with Spain by securing a marriage alliance between Catherine of Aragon and his eldest son and heir, Arthur. Although his plans were dashed when Arthur suddenly died, Henry VII quickly sought another marriage between Catherine and his younger son, Prince Henry, instead. He arranged for his oldest daughter, Margaret, to be married to James IV of Scotland, which strengthened alliances with Scotland during his reign and weakened Perkin Warbeck's threat to the Tudor throne. Henry's younger daughter Mary would later, during Henry VIII's reign, marry the much older King of France, Louis XII, in order to secure peaceful relations between the two countries. Henry VII tried also, albeit unsuccessfully, to re-enter the marriage market after the death of his wife, Elizabeth. Possible alliances with Castile, Aragon, France and the Holy Roman Empire were considered, but came to nothing partly because the princesses concerned proved reluctant to marry Henry and partly because Henry himself gradually lost enthusiasm for the prospect of remarriage.

CROSS-REFERENCE

Henry VII's relations with Spain are discussed earlier in this chapter, on page 26.

Henry VII's relations with Scotland are discussed earlier in this chapter, on page 27. Relations between the two countries would, however, change dramatically during Henry VIII's reign. Turn to Chapter 9, pages 91–92, to read more about this.

Princess Mary's marriage was secured by Thomas Wolsey, an important advisor to Henry VIII in the earlier years of his reign. You can read more about why this was an important marriage alliance with France in Chapter 7, page 87.

ACTIVITY

Create a poster showing Henry VII alongside his children and each of their spouses.

ACTIVITY

Would you consider Henry's negotiations of marriage alliances for his children a success or a failure?

Copy and complete the table below using your historical knowledge from this chapter.

Name	Suggested marriage	Actual marriage	When?	Foreign policy objectives	Success/ failure
Prince Arthur					
Prince Henry					
Princess Margare					
Princess Mary					

Summary

Foreign policy and the succession were inextricably linked. Royal marriage proposals were a normal part of diplomatic activity as monarchs attempted to use their family members as pawns in the game of diplomatic chess. It was a game in which Henry had mixed fortunes. As Christine Carpenter has pointed out, the death of Henry VII's own queen, Elizabeth, in 1503, after the loss of his first son Arthur, made Henry's dynastic security appear significantly weakened. He faced the need first to secure the dynasty, knowing full well that his hold on royal power was tenuous, and had to manipulate the international situation to enhance his security. At this he was largely successful. Having initially secured his dynasty, he became more ambitious and broadly successful in his foreign policy, in the main avoiding expensive foreign wars. It should not, however, be thought that his foreign policy was consistently successful. Henry, more than most monarchs, was aware of the influence that luck could play in diplomatic affairs. In that context, Henry was wrong-footed by the death of Isabella of Castile in 1504 and for a time he found himself dangerously isolated. On the whole, however, he responded skilfully to the changing circumstances in which he found himself.

ACTIVITY

Look back at the list of Henry VII's aims which you compiled at the beginning of this chapter. Make a chart to show the ways in which he fulfilled these aims – and the ways he failed to do so.

A LEVEL PRACTICE QUESTION

How successful was Henry VII in fulfilling his foreign policy objectives?

STUDY TIP

Use the chart you compiled in the activity on this page to help you to identify some of Henry's foreign policy objectives. Try to refer to both broad aims and specific objectives in different areas of foreign policy and comment on success or failure within those areas as well as overall.

EXTRACT 2

Henry's foreign policy failed in detail; neither the expedition to relieve Brittany, nor the attempts to isolate Ferdinand after 1507 were a success. His policy also proved expensive; between 1505 and 1509 he gave £342,000 in cash, plate or jewels to the Habsburgs. Yet when Henry died, he left his country and dynasty internationally secure. There was no threat of foreign military intervention in England's internal affairs. Henry's success can be judged by comparing his weakness in 1485 with his strength towards the end of his reign. This success was based on the firm foundation of domestic strength and realistic objectives in foreign policy.

Adapted from Susan Doran, *England and Europe, 1485–1603*, 1986

EXTRACT 3

The death of his queen in 1503, and of various other players in these domestic politics about the same time, led Henry into a number of grandiose marriage and alliance schemes in his last years, all of which proved abortive. Reluctance to tax a country which seemed all too ready to rebel when he did so may well have contributed to the relative failure of his foreign policy in these years. By 1509 England had become rather isolated in European politics, something which might have proved dangerous had Henry VIII's accession been challenged.

Christine Carpenter, *The Wars of the Roses: Politics and the Constitution in England c1437–1509*, 1997

AS LEVEL PRACTICE QUESTION

Evaluating historical extracts

With reference to Extracts 2 and 3 and your understanding of the historical context, which of these two extracts provides the more convincing interpretation of Henry VII's foreign policy?

STUDY TIP

Consider the overall interpretation put forward in each extract about Henry VII's foreign policy. You can comment on specific parts of the extract and should explain the views expressed with reference to your own knowledge. Make sure you answer which is the 'more convincing' and explain why.

4 English society at the end of the fifteenth century

The structure of society

EXTRACT 1

The nobility was defined in early Tudor England more clearly than any other element in society. But the English nobility was not a **caste** like that in most parts of the continent. Although knighthood had lost most of its military significance, it still retained its value. It was normally conferred on the heads of about a dozen of the leading noble families in each shire. For every early Tudor knight there were at least ten other landowners calling themselves gentlemen. Yeomen on the whole occupied larger farms and they also tended to be the farmers with the most secure tenure.

Adapted from Joyce Youings, *Sixteenth-Century England*, 1983

KEY QUESTION

As you read this chapter, consider the following Key Question:
How did English society change?

ACTIVITY

Read Extract 1 and try to identify all the groups of society mentioned. As you read through this chapter try and find out more about each group.

LEARNING OBJECTIVES

In this chapter you will learn about:

- the structure of English society, including churchmen, nobles and commoners
- regional divisions within England
- social discontent and rebellions.

KEY TERM

caste: a class or group of people who inherit exclusive privileges or are perceived as socially distinct

CROSS-REFERENCE

Yeomen were significant members of Tudor society. They are described later in this chapter on page 38.

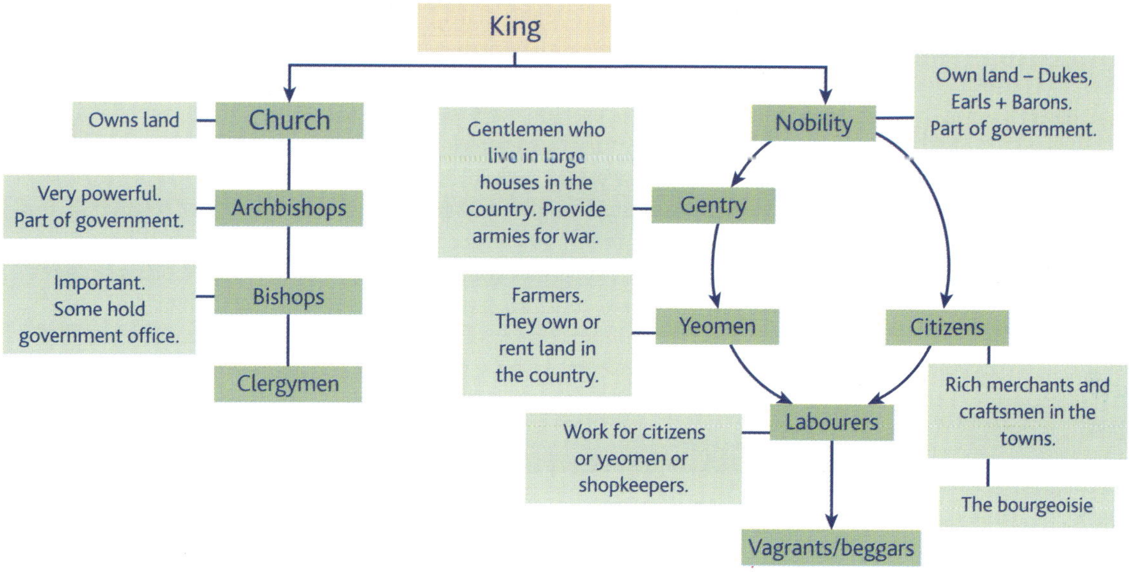

Fig. 1 *English society in the early Tudor period*

English society at the end of the fifteenth century, while not as rigidly hierarchical as that of France or Spain, was exceedingly stratified (i.e. layered). At one level society had changed little from that which had existed during the high point of the **feudal system**. The apex of the system under the monarch comprised the great landowners and senior churchmen; the base of the system comprised those who laboured on their behalf. In contrast, society also witnessed the growth of a professional and mercantile **bourgeoisie** who had become increasingly important in London and the major provincial cities such as Norwich and Bristol.

The remnants of the feudal system were still apparent in the law, social relationships and attitudes. However, economic pressures, especially since the **Black Death** of 1348 to 1349, had increased social mobility and had created alarm amongst more conservative-minded members of the upper classes who attempted vainly to uphold traditional values by passing **sumptuary laws** which proved unenforceable.

KEY TERM

feudal system: the medieval system by which society was structured depending on relationships in which land was held in return for some form of service; at the top end of the structure land was held of the monarch in return for military service, and at the bottom serfs were required to give labour services to their lord in return for the lord's protection

bourgeoisie: middle-class residents of towns and cities

sumptuary laws: laws that attempted to regulate how individuals should dress, depending on their social status

peerage: group of persons who held one of the five ranks of the aristocracy (duke, marquis, earl, viscount, baron); they were usually considerable landholders, exercised considerable power in their localities and were members of the House of Lords

A CLOSER LOOK

The **Black Death** reached England in August 1348. Between 20 and 40 per cent of the English population died of plague within 2 years. The plague returned in 1361, and there were further outbreaks in 1368 to 1369, 1374 to 1375 and 1378. These later outbreaks reduced the population of England by half, and it did not begin to recover until after 1450. These deaths caused a shortage of land usage and food.

Nobility

The nobility still dominated landownership. The **peerage** (i.e. the nobility) comprised no more than about 50 or 60 men. The peerage was not a closed caste. Peerage families died out on a regular basis but were replaced by others who had acquired or bought the king's favour. The Crown often relied on such families for the maintenance of order in the countryside. Henry VII, unlike Edward IV before him or Henry VIII after him, was reluctant to create new peerage titles. This is possibly because he was deeply distrustful of the nobility as a class. Only trusted Lancastrian military commanders such as the **Earl of Oxford** and **Lord Daubeney** had much political influence under Henry. He never really trusted the Earl of Northumberland, even though he had swung the Battle of Bosworth in Henry's favour by betraying Richard III. Nevertheless, Henry relied on Northumberland to control the northeast of England on behalf of the Crown.

Henry's most important method of controlling the nobility was through bonds and recognizances. However, the key to the nobles' power was the system which nineteenth-century historians labelled **bastard feudalism** (also known as 'retaining') by which wealthy magnates (the leading and most wealthy members of the nobility) recruited knights and gentlemen (also known as 'retainers') to serve them as administrators or accountants, or sometimes for military purposes. Potentially, noblemen could use their retained men to bring unlawful influence on others in a court case, or use them against the Crown, so Henry sought to limit the military power of the nobility through the use of legislation against retaining. However, at the same time he remained conscious of the fact that loyal retainers were essential to maintain the Crown's security.

KEY PROFILE

John de Vere, Earl of Oxford (1442–1513) was Henry's most trusted military commander and led his troops at the battles of Bosworth and Stoke.

Giles, Baron Daubeney (c1451–1508) was originally a Yorkist, but he rebelled against Richard III in 1483, fled to Brittany and transferred his loyalty to Henry, for whom he fought at Bosworth. He led the Crown's forces against the Cornish rebels in 1497. He succeeded Sir William Stanley as Lord Chamberlain in 1495.

A CLOSER LOOK

Bastard feudalism

This system implied a reciprocal relationship between the magnate and his retainers. In return for service, which could be military service if necessary, a retainer might receive rewards such as local office or grants of land as well as direct payment. The Victorian historians who invented and developed the use of the term 'bastard feudalism' saw the system as abusive and contributing largely to the violence associated with the Wars of the Roses. However, the influential historian of late-medieval England, Kenneth B. McFarlane, argued that the system should be seen in a positive light as a natural response to the changes of the period. It was only when the position of the monarch was insecure that the system could be seen as politically destabilising.

CROSS-REFERENCE

The use of bonds and recognizances as a means of improving Crown finances is covered in Chapter 2, pages 14–15.

Magnates are explained in Chapter 2, page 14.

Henry VII's response was to have Parliament pass Acts in 1487 and 1504 and to take strong action against individual nobles who were held to abuse the system, such as Lord Bergavenny in 1506. However, such action had to be balanced with the realisation that nobles were a powerful social force.

Fig. 2 *The funeral effigy of Lord and Lady Daubeney*

Fig. 3 *Lord Bergavenny, by Holbein*

A CLOSER LOOK

The 1504 Act stated that only the king could grant licences for retaining. However, this lasted only for the duration of the king's lifetime. The one significant victim of the Act was Lord Bergavenny, who was indicted for illegal retaining in 1507 and fined the enormous sum of £100,000. However, he probably paid no more than £1000 and was pardoned by Henry VIII shortly after he came to the throne.

There were a number of limits on retaining employed during Henry's reign:

- In 1486 peers and MPs were required to take an oath against illegal retaining or being illegally retained. However, what constituted illegality in this context remained conveniently undefined.
- In 1487 a law against retaining was established.
- The 1487 law was reinforced by an **Act passed in 1504**, under which licences for retaining could be sought.

ACTIVITY

In pairs identify the advantages and disadvantages to Henry VII of adopting a strict attitude towards retaining.

ACTIVITY

Explain the importance of the nobility in Tudor society. Jot down several ideas and share with a friend. Consider the role the nobles played in their own localities and their relationship to those beneath them.

ACTIVITY

Divide into groups. Each group should identify a peer who played a significant role during the reign of Henry VII, research the roles which he played in the Crown's service and find out where his power base was (for example, the land he owned, the office he held, or the affinity he had with the king).

Gentry

Immediately below the peerage in status came the greater gentry. By the late fifteenth century these were often great landowners in their own right. The most important members of the gentry, such as **Sir Reginald Bray**, sought knighthoods as confirmation of their social status. In 1490 there were about 375 knights. Originally, this status had imposed military obligations upon its holders. Though that was dying out as a specific obligation, it was, nevertheless, assumed that those holding the status would assist in the

CROSS-REFERENCE

More information on Sir Reginald Bray is in Chapter 2, page 10.

administration of their localities. According to John Guy, peers and knights together owned 15 to 20 per cent of the country's land and together they 'formed a homogeneous [of the same kind] elite with a common outlook derived from their substantial interest as landowners'.

Esquires and 'mere gentry' were far more numerous. At the end of the fifteenth century the status of 'esquire' could still be defined quite tightly: the eldest sons of knights, the younger sons of barons, men 'invested esquire', magistrates and others of wealth. Mere 'gentlemen' were harder to define. In practice, a 'gentleman' was anyone recognised as such by his neighbours.

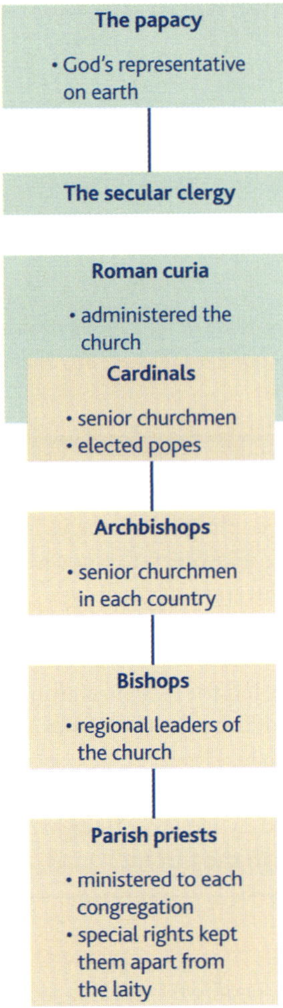

Fig. 4 *The hierarchy of the Church*

A CLOSER LOOK

Gentry

The gentry were not a fixed caste. However, the identity of the greater gentry could be established by a number of features: the possession of a knighthood, a coat of arms authenticated by the College of Arms, considerable income, and an imposing country residence or courtly connections. They possessed considerable social prestige, often, for example, dominating local office. On the other hand, the lesser gentry often had more in common with the local yeomanry, living far more modestly than the greater gentry, and with social horizons which were much more local than national.

Churchmen

The Church was hugely important, not merely for its spiritual role but also as a great landowner. The social status of the clergy varied enormously. At the lower parish level, curates and chantry priests were modestly rewarded for dealing with the spiritual needs of ordinary folk. On the other hand, bishops and the abbots of larger religious houses were important figures who were entitled to sit in the House of Lords and who often had political roles to undertake.

Martin V, Pope from 1417 to 1431, famously declared that the king of England rather than the Pope governed the Church in England. Henry VII tended to use that power to appoint as bishops only men who had legal training and whose administrative competence was valued more than their spirituality. The two most important clergymen of the reign, **John Morton** and **Richard Fox**, both came into this category. Moreover, the king was reluctant to appoint men whose social background was aristocratic. The higher clergy were thus becoming less socially exclusive than had once been the case.

CROSS-REFERENCE

For more information on chantries go to Chapter 6, page 54.

John Morton is profiled in Chapter 2, page 9.

To learn about the borough corporations and the importance of guilds and confraternities to the religious life of England, see page 58.

KEY PROFILE

Richard Fox (c1447–1528) began serving Henry VII when he was still in exile. In 1487 Fox became bishop of Exeter and Lord Keeper of the Great Seal. He became successively bishop of Bath and Wells, Durham and Winchester and, along with Morton, managed the Crown's transition to Henry VIII.

Fig. 5 *Richard Fox*

ACTIVITY

Based on your understanding of this section, why do you think Henry VII felt confident about appointing churchmen to senior roles within government?

Commoners

Below the nobility, gentry, and higher clergy were the commoners. At the top level of the commoner group were those known as the 'middling sort', the bourgeoisie. In towns and cities, the relatively small number of educated professionals, of whom the most numerous and influential group were lawyers, exercised considerable influence, often in collaboration with wealthier merchants. Lower down the social scale, but still considered respectable, came shopkeepers and skilled tradesmen. Such groups tended to dominate the borough corporations (town councils) and also played a key role in organisations such as guilds and lay confraternities which were a common feature of urban life in pre-**Reformation** England.

KEY TERM

Reformation: a sixteenth-century movement opposing the Catholic Church, which resulted in the establishment of Protestant and reformed churches

Fig. 6 *A contemporary illustration of peasant toil*

ACTIVITY

Divide into groups, representing each different social category in this chapter. Each group should argue for the worth of their social group to the country. Once each group has presented, take a vote to decide which group was the most valuable.

KEY TERM

peasant: a country dweller who farms directly land which can be either owned or rented; the term 'peasant' does not apply to town-dwellers

grazing rights: a legal term referring to the right of a user to allow their livestock to feed (graze) in a given area

In the countryside the middling sort comprised yeomen farmers who farmed substantial properties for an increasingly sophisticated market economy. The decline in population that had occurred as a result of the Black Death in 1348 to 1349 had reduced the demand for land and the resulting drop in land values had enabled the emergence of this group, which Joyce Youings termed a 'peasant aristocracy'. Below yeomen came husbandmen who typically kept smaller farms than yeomen and who supplemented their farming incomes through employment by yeomen or gentry. Together, the yeomanry and husbandmen can be described by the term **'peasant'**. Labourers were usually dependent for income on the sale of their labour, though in some cases they could supplement their irregular income through the planting of vegetables or the exercise of **grazing rights**. Their position was very insecure.

Regional divisions

Though both relatively small and politically relatively unified, England did demonstrate regional variations. Some of these derived from differences in agriculture. A line drawn roughly from the mouth of the Tees to Weymouth in Dorset would have revealed the extent of these contrasts, though even within the two areas distinctions could be made. Roughly three quarters of the population lived below this line, which divided the country into two basic agricultural areas. South and east of that line, mixed farming predominated in the more densely populated counties, especially Norfolk, Suffolk and Kent. In the more sparsely populated area to the north and west, pastoral farming predominated with the rearing of sheep, cattle and horses. There were exceptions to this rule: pastoral farming dominated in the Fens and in the wood pastures of the Kent and Sussex Weald, and grain farming and fruit growing in Herefordshire and the Welsh border counties. Contemporaries were certainly aware of regional differences. Londoners, in particular, tended to look down upon northerners for their perceived savagery, while northerners were envious of southern riches.

Regional identity was also reinforced by local government structures. Justice was increasingly administered at a county level and county towns often contained jails and major churches. On the other hand, areas of magnate influence often cut across county boundaries. Local identities were also reinforced by saints' cults which placed importance on centres of pilgrimage, such as Canterbury and Durham. Nevertheless, Derek Keene has argued that medieval England, 'was a country where ideas of language and nationhood conferred a stronger sense of a single identity than ever before'.

CROSS-REFERENCE

For more on the saints' cults that gave places and communities a sense of identity, look ahead to Chapter 6, page 55.

ACTIVITY

Extension

Research briefly *an* aspect of your own town or local area's history during the late-medieval period.

1. For example, what can you find out about the church and monasteries in your area?
2. Did your area have an important noble family resident in the vicinity? What can you find out about their importance?
3. If you live in a town which was a medieval borough, what can you find out about its local government?

Social discontent and rebellions

During much of the second half of the fifteenth century, living conditions for the poor appeared to be improving. **Real wages** seem to have increased, but towards the end of the fifteenth century inflationary pressures were becoming more evident. Though evidence points tentatively towards a further slight increase in real wages in the 1490s, by the following decade this situation seems to have reversed. Compared with later in the Tudor period, there does not seem to have been much social discontent. England also seems largely to have avoided the **subsistence crises** which every so often affected some other countries so that in John Guy's words, 'Tudor England's greatest success was its ability to feed itself'.

Two rebellions did take place in Henry VII's reign, in Yorkshire in 1489 and in Cornwall in 1497. In each case the main catalyst (or trigger) was taxation.

KEY TERM

real wages: the value of income in relation to prices of goods on the market, instead of actual money received

subsistence crises: when harvest failure raises food prices to such an extent that significant numbers of the poor die from starvation

Fig. 7 *Farming regions of England*

CROSS-REFERENCE

The Brittany campaign is discussed in Chapter 3, pages 23–24.

Northumberland was considered an untrustworthy character after the Battle of Bosworth. See Chapter 1, page 4.

The Yorkshire Rebellion, 1489

This rebellion was sparked off by resentment of the taxation granted by Parliament in 1489 in order to finance the involvement of English forces in the campaign in Brittany. It became particularly notorious because of the murder by the rebels of the Earl of Northumberland just outside Topcliffe near Thirsk in the North Riding of Yorkshire in April of that year.

The details on this rebellion are sparse. Northumberland was, according to **Polydore Vergil**, a victim of resentment against taxation. He was murdered by his tenants, but what enabled them to murder the earl was the fact that Northumberland's retainers allowed them to do so by deserting him in his hour of need – as punishment for his own desertion of Richard III at Bosworth.

KEY PROFILE

Polydore Vergil (c1470–1555) was an Italian humanist. Vergil came to England in 1502 in the employ of the Church. He was welcomed at the court of Henry VII and began writing his *History of England* in about 1505. The first edition was published in 1513, but a third edition published in 1555 covered the period up to 1537.

Fig. 8 *Warkworth Castle, the residence of the Earl of Northumberland*

The Cornish Rebellion, 1497

Just as the Yorkshire Rebellion was sparked off by the demand for extraordinary revenue to finance a far-away military campaign, so also was the Cornish Rebellion of 1497. In this case the revolt was triggered by the need for revenue to finance the campaign against Scotland.

CROSS-REFERENCE

The campaign against Scotland is covered in Chapter 3, page 27.

SOURCE 1

Polydore Vergil described the events in his *History of England* (first published in 1513):

The Cornishmen, who dwell in a part of the island as restricted in area as it is poor in resources, began to claim loudly that they could not bear the weight of tax imposed for the Scottish war. First, they accused the king, complaining of the cruelty and malice of his counsellors; then they began openly to get out of hand, threatening death to the authors of the great oppression and making bold to seek them out for punishment. While the people were this in an uproar, two men out of the dregs of the population, Thomas Flamank, a lawyer, and

ACTIVITY

Evaluating primary sources

1. What does the source reveal about the reasons for discontent amongst the Cornish?
2. What interpretation of the rebels and their actions is offered in this source?

Michael Joseph, a blacksmith, both daring scoundrels, put themselves at the head of the rebellion. When these two saw that the mob was aroused, they continually proclaimed it to be an infamous crime that the king should, for the purpose of making such a small expedition against the Scots, so grievously oppress with taxes the wretched Cornish. But they attributed the blame above all to John Morton Archbishop of Canterbury, to Reginald Bray and to many other counsellors.

Though the Cornish rebels did not murder a high-profile political figure like the Earl of Northumberland, their rebellion posed a much greater threat to the stability of Henry's rule. This was a reflection of three factors:

- the sheer numbers involved (15,000 according to some estimates)
- the attempt to exploit the rebellion made by Perkin Warbeck
- the fact that the rebels marched on London, only being halted at Blackheath.

Christine Carpenter considers the rebellion to have been 'alarming' for the king. It was certainly a cause for immense concern for the Crown that the rebels could have marched such a long distance without any serious attempt being made to stop them. It raises questions about just how effective were the Crown's systems for maintaining order in the countryside. Moreover, by reaching London they were in effect challenging the security of Henry VII's regime.

The rebellion created a problem for Henry in that in order to ensure its effective suppression he needed to withdraw Lord Daubeney and his troops from defending the Scottish border. In the end the rebellion was crushed easily enough by Daubeney. The rebel leaders, including the peer Lord Audley, were executed. However, Henry punished only the leaders, and treated the bulk of the rebels with conspicuous leniency. The rebellion shocked Henry into ensuring that Anglo-Scottish tensions were eased and made him particularly cautious about entering into any further foreign conflicts.

CROSS-REFERENCE

For Perkin Warbeck's attempts to exploit the rebellion and lay claim to the throne, look back to Chapter 3, page 28.

Summary

Socially, England remained broadly stable in this period, and this is mainly because the people at the bottom of the social scale remained reasonably well off, as they had been since the Black Death.

For most of Henry VII's reign, most English people remained peaceable most of the time, and the various pretenders and claimants were unable to attract much support.

The two rebellions of the reign, the Yorkshire Rebellion of 1489 and the Cornish Rebellion of 1497, were exceptional, and easily suppressed.

ACTIVITY

Look back at Joyce Youings's interpretation given at the beginning of the chapter (page 33). In small groups, consider whether you find her interpretation convincing. You will need to find specific evidence to support or refute her views.

EXTRACT 2

The nature of Henry VII's relations with the nobility has been examined in depth by T.B. Pugh. Pugh argued that bonds and recognizances were not unprecedented. The need to increase royal revenue in order to buy off the rulers of the Low Countries largely explains their increased frequency from 1502. Many noblemen found bounds and recognizances useful instruments as they arranged wardships and marriages. Between 1502 and 1509 only twenty-seven out of forty adult nobles were involved in any form of bonds and recognizances and only sixteen out of forty were involved as principals rather than as sureties. Only a few noblemen were listed in Edmund Dudley's petition, drawn up after the king's death and listing those whom he believed had been harshly treated by the king.

Adapted from George Bernard, 'Foreword', in Stanley B. Chrimes, *Henry VII,* 1999

EXTRACT 3

The use of bonds and recognizances was of a piece with other aspects of the king's relationship with the nobility. Though quite prepared to give responsibility and reward to noblemen he trusted, he gave less wholeheartedly than most previous kings. Those he trusted from the start, such as Oxford and Derby, never gained complete regional power. Those he grew to trust as they proved themselves, such as Thomas Howard, Earl of Surrey, grew in influence only little by little. Those he never trusted, such as Edward Stafford, Duke of Buckingham, he seemed to frustrate at every turn. These last were also prominent victims of his financial exactions. Meanwhile great offices which might have vehicles for noble ambition were often kept in the king's hands.

Adapted from Steven J. Gunn, 'Henry VII', in *Oxford Dictionary of National Biography*, 2004

STUDY TIP

Each extract makes judgements about the extent to which Henry was successful in foreign policy. In evaluating such judgements it is necessary to consider what Henry's objectives might have been and how close he came to realising those objectives.

AS LEVEL PRACTICE QUESTION

Evaluating historical extracts

With reference to Extracts 2 and 3 and your understanding of the historical context, which of these two extracts provides the more convincing interpretation of Henry VII's relationship with the nobility?

STUDY TIP

This type of question invites students to make a judgement. It is important, when coming to the conclusion of an essay such as this, to make sure that the conclusion emerges logically from the way in which you have framed your discussion. When planning answers it is often good practice to begin by outlining those arguments with which, ultimately, you are going to disagree.

AS LEVEL PRACTICE QUESTION

'The popular rebellions faced by Henry VII gave him more problems than the threats posed by pretenders to the throne.'
Explain why you agree or disagree with this view.

5 Economic development: trade, exploration, prosperity and depression

The economy: agriculture and trade

EXTRACT 1

Fifteenth-century England was much more regionalised than it is today. England was still overwhelmingly an agrarian [i.e. farming] country for nine tenths of the people lived more or less directly from the land. Probably no greater proportion of the population lived in towns than in Anglo-Saxon times. By 1500 the cloth industry, England's major industry, possibly employed 30,000 people, or about 1.3 per cent of the population, full-time. Although it provided part-time work for a great many more people to support peasant agriculture, it was still insignificant as compared with the contribution of agriculture to the national economy. The harvest was the harsh, fundamental fact of life. In a 'normal' decade about one harvest in every four would be, in some degree, deficient, one in six really bad. This caused price fluctuations so violent as to be almost inconceivable even these days.

Adapted from Jack Lander, *Government and Community: England, 1450–1509,* 1980

LEARNING OBJECTIVES

In this chapter you will learn about:

- the economy of England and the importance of trade
- early English exploration and its significance
- economic prosperity and depression.

ACTIVITY

What can we learn from Jack Lander about the English economy in the fifteenth century? Make a note of the key points raised in Extract 1.

KEY QUESTION

As you read this chapter, consider the following Key Question:
How did the English economy change and with what effects?

The population of England at the beginning of the fifteenth century was around 2.2 million. The majority of people at this time were living in the countryside and relying on some form of farming for a living. Most of the 10 per cent of the population who were actually urban dwellers lived in towns which were small by continental standards. London was the obvious exception, with a population which probably exceeded 50,000, but probably no more than 20 towns had as many as 3000 people. Amongst provincial towns only Norwich had a population exceeding 10,000, with Bristol, York and Coventry having populations in the range of 8000 to 10,000. In these urban areas wool and cloth were the main industries. Other industries included mining tin, lead and coal; metal working; leatherwork; shipbuilding; and papermaking.

Although Henry VII was interested in building up his personal wealth, he had no specific 'economic policy' as a modern leader would. The Acts of Parliament that dealt with economic matters were mainly the result of the private lobbying of merchants, who had a vested interest.

The agrarian economy

Income from land had declined in the aftermath of the Black Death of the 1300s and early 1400s, though it has been suggested that there was something of a recovery in the 1480s and 1490s, as the population began to increase again. There was much evidence of a greater move towards sheep farming in the 1480s and 1490s. This was a reflection not only of the depressed profitability of arable (crop) farming, but also the improved profitability of sheep farming brought about by the increasing demand for wool, as the population grew and trade overseas developed.

ACTIVITY

Pair discussion

In pairs, discuss the factors which might have contributed to the fluctuation in agricultural prices during the reign of Henry VII.

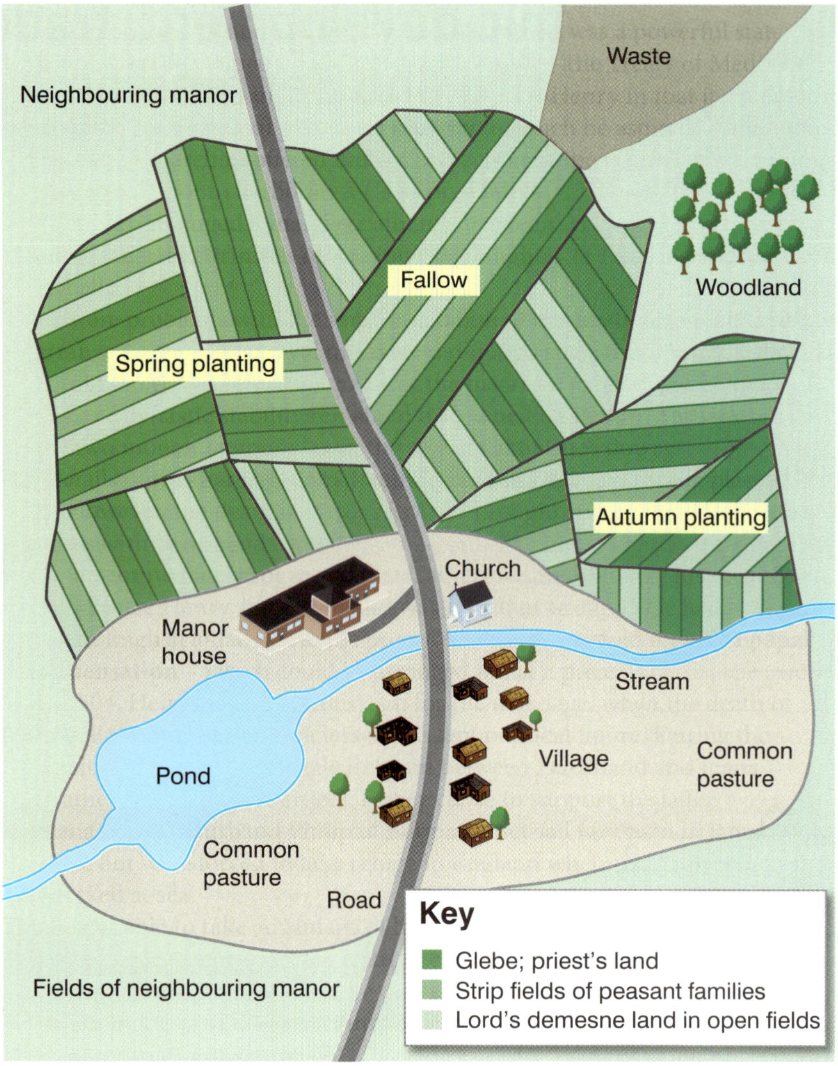

Fig. 1 *A general impression of an open-field village in lowland England*

CROSS-REFERENCE

For a detailed picture of the 'highland' and 'lowland' zones refer back to the map in Chapter 4, page 39.

KEY TERM

mixed farming: a system of farming which involves the growing of crops as well as the raising of animals as livestock

pastoral farming: farming involving the rearing of animals – either for animal by-products such as milk, eggs or wool, or for meat

common rights: denotes the legal right of tenants to use common land, for example for keeping animals; the exact nature of these rights varied from place to place

As a largely agricultural society, England could be divided into a 'lowland zone' to the south and east (a line drawn from the Tees estuary to Weymouth) and a 'highland zone' (roughly north and west of that line). **Mixed farming** was the most common form of farming found in the lowland zone, though **pastoral farming** predominated in woodland areas and there were specialisms such as horse breeding in the Fenlands. The traditional manorial system of **open-field husbandry** could be found in such areas and was concentrated mainly in the grain-growing areas of the southeast and the east Midlands.

A CLOSER LOOK

Open-field husbandry

The 'manorial system of open-field husbandry' (or open-field system) was the form of landholding which predominated in most of 'lowland' England. The manor was a specific landed estate whose tenants farmed strips of land found in open fields and who enjoyed **common rights,** particularly for keeping animals. This system came under increasing pressure by **enclosure** in some parts of the country as the sixteenth century unfolded.

However, some parts of this region were increasingly experiencing change, with the wool and cloth trades making sheep farming relatively more profitable. The efficiency gains in terms of improved production and profitability came at a price for **peasants** who lost their access to land and common rights, and were often left destitute by the process. In the late fifteenth century this was not a frequent occurrence. It became more widespread in the first half of the sixteenth century, when it created both a moral outcry and political pressures which proved difficult to contain. On the whole, however, it would be fair to say that English agriculture underwent no significant changes towards the end of the fifteenth, and beginning of the sixteenth, century.

CROSS-REFERENCE

The wider impact of enclosure is discussed on page 122.

Trade and industry

The cloth trade

The cloth trade was responsible for about 90 per cent of the value of English exports. The trade certainly flourished in the last quarter of the fifteenth century. Jack Lander has estimated that there was an increase of over 60 per cent in the volume of cloth exports during Henry VII's reign. In the earlier part of the century, the bulk of exports had comprised raw wool; this was shipped mainly from east-coast ports such as Boston, Lynn and Yarmouth and exported through Calais by the **Merchants of the Staple**. Increasingly, however, it was finished cloth which dominated the trade. This led to the development of weaving, usually done as a domestic process, and **fulling** and dyeing, which were commercial enterprises. As a result, the industry offered opportunities for rural employment to supplement agrarian incomes.

Fig. 2 *Women spinning woollen cloth*

Some cloth towns, such as Lavenham in Suffolk and Lewes in Sussex, were extremely prosperous. However, some historic cities such as Winchester and Lincoln had suffered significant decay as the cloth industry tended to move from older corporate boroughs to newer manufacturing centres in smaller market towns and villages in East Anglia, the West Riding of Yorkshire and parts of the West Country.

An increasing proportion of the finished cloth was exported from London through the **Merchant Adventurers**. This reinforced London's commercial dominance within the country and established a commercial axis with Antwerp which, during this period, according to the economic historian Donald Coleman, was the commercial metropolis of Europe and its main money market. From Antwerp, English cloth was transported all over Europe.

KEY TERM

Merchants of the Staple: incorporated by royal charter in 1319, they controlled the export of wool; the staple was based at Calais (an English possession) from 1363, but the eventual decline in the wool trade reduced the company's importance

fulling: a step in woollen cloth making which involves the cleansing of cloth (particularly wool) to eliminate oils, dirt, and other impurities, making it thicker in the process

CROSS-REFERENCE

The Intercursus Magnus and the Intercursus Malus were introduced in Chapter 4, page 25. They are outlined further in this chapter on page 47.

A CLOSER LOOK

The Merchant Adventurers

Founded in 1407 and dominated by members of the Mercers' Company, the wealthiest and most influential company of the City of London, the Merchant Adventurers were a trading organisation which came increasingly to dominate London's cloth trade with Antwerp. The Merchant Adventurers' domination of the cloth trade matched the dominance of the wool trade by the Merchants of the (Calais) Staple, whose economic position they increasingly supplanted. Their positive relationship with the Crown was immensely important. On the one hand, they could act as the voice of the industry when its commercial needs were subordinated to national policy; on the other hand, the king increasingly used their expertise in the negotiating of trade treaties such as the **Intercursus Magnus** and the **Intercursus Malus.** They had become the most powerful English business organisation of the age.

KEY TERM

Hanseatic League: a group of free cities originating in the thirteenth century, which came together to form a commercial union with the intention of controlling trade in the Baltic Sea; the league dominated commercial activity in northern Europe from the thirteenth to the fifteenth century

The Merchant Adventurers could not achieve complete domination of trade because they proved unable to overcome the trading privileges enjoyed by the **Hanseatic League** which had been reasserted by treaty in 1474 and again in 1504. Henry VII may have agreed to reassert this treaty because he needed to ensure that the Hanseatic League would offer no support to the Yorkist claimant to the throne, the Earl of Suffolk. However, this sacrifice of English commercial interests was, Jack Lander has asserted, 'out of all proportion to the feeble threat' posed by the de la Poles.

CROSS-REFERENCE

The Earl of Suffolk's claim to the throne and the threat posed by the de la Poles are discussed in Chapter 1, page 7. For the political repercussions of these events, see page 29.

ACTIVITY

Research

Research the origins of the Hanseatic League and find out which cities were members and where the bulk of their trading activities took place.

Other industries

England remained dependent, in trading terms, on the cloth industry, especially as other industries remained small and failed to compete effectively with their continental competitors. Germany and Bohemia, for example, were superior in mining and **metallurgy** and the Spanish, Portuguese and Dutch were superior in shipbuilding.

Most industrial activities, for example weaving or brewing, were small-scale craft operations which required little capital investment. Most such operations supplied the basic necessities of life, food and shelter. Mining required

Fig. 3 *A contemporary depiction of commercial activity*

KEY TERM

metallurgy: the scientific study of the extraction, refining, alloying and fabrication of metals, and of their structure and properties

rather more capital investment, but remained fairly small scale. Tin was mined in Cornwall, lead was mined in upland areas such as the high Pennines and the Mendips, and coal was mined in Durham and Northumberland. Iron ore was mined and smelted in the Weald of Sussex and Kent, where there was a blast furnace as early as 1496. Much of the coal from the northeast was shipped from Newcastle to meet the growing demand for domestic and industrial fuel in London, but there was also a small export trade to Germany and the Netherlands. The development of basic pumping technology, first recorded at Finchale in County Durham in 1486, enabled greater production.

Trade laws and treaties

The Crown's approach to trade during Henry VII's reign had little consistency. Henry was clearly interested in maximising customs revenue. However, it was equally clear that he was quite prepared to sacrifice revenue and trade in the interests of securing the dynasty, and he was also happy for Parliament to legislate in favour of **sectional interests**.

The biggest issue concerning trade in Henry's reign stemmed from his embargo (i.e. ban) on trade with the Netherlands. He imposed this in 1493 as a result of the fear and insecurity brought about by Margaret of Burgundy's support for Perkin Warbeck. Instead of trading directly with the Netherlands, merchants were required to direct their trade through Calais. This simply invited retaliation from the Netherlands. The embargo ended with the treaty known as the **Intercursus Magnus**, though the terms of the treaty were still being debated two years later.

A CLOSER LOOK

Intercursus Magnus ('Great Intercourse') and **Intercursus Malus** ('Evil Intercourse') were terms which were used in Francis Bacon's *History of the Reign of King Henry VII*, written in 1621. Intercursus Magnus set down that English merchants could export to any part of the Duke of Burgundy's lands apart from Flanders, that merchants would be granted swift and fair justice and that effective arrangements would be put in place for the resolution of disputes. Philip of Burgundy confirmed Intercursus Magnus in 1499 and it was to prove a solid basis for trading relationships from that point on. Intercursus Malus was in practice **extorted** from Philip as a result of his weakness in 1506. The treaty never became fully operative and by the following year trading relationships had been restored on the basis of Intercursus Magnus.

Henry appeared to panic once again in 1503 when the claim of the Earl of Suffolk was once again being taken seriously around Burgundy. Henry attempted to reimpose the embargo. In this instance he was fortunate that circumstances in 1506 allowed him to negotiate the Intercursus Malus, even if its full terms were never imposed.

Several trade treaties were concluded, though these were of minor importance and showed that Henry rated foreign policy and dynastic interests as greater priorities than the interests of English merchants. Trading restrictions, which had existed since Edward IV's reign, were removed in 1486. They were reimposed in the following year as a result of Henry's support for Brittany, but largely removed again by the Treaty of Etaples of 1492. This treaty, while not primarily a trade treaty, did try to encourage Anglo-French commercial relations. Most of the remaining trading restrictions were removed in 1497. Weaknesses in trading policy were shown when the attempt to make a significant breakthrough in Mediterranean trade proved a dismal failure, and the Hanseatic League was largely successful in limiting the development of English trading interests in the Baltic.

CROSS-REFERENCE

Henry's policies on customs revenue were to help him secure his dynasty. They are discussed in Chapter 2, page 18.

KEY TERM

sectional interests: the interests of a particular group within a community or country

CROSS-REFERENCE

Return to Chapter 1, page 6, to refresh your memory on Perkin Warbeck.

Henry VII's relationship with Burgundy is discussed in Chapter 3.

KEY TERM

extort: obtain (something) by force, threats, or other unfair means

CROSS-REFERENCE

Refer back to Chapter 3 for information on Henry's foreign policy and Anglo-French relations, including the Treaty of Etaples of 1492.

KEY CHRONOLOGY

Trading developments under Henry VII

1485	Navigation Act
1489	Navigation Act
1492	Treaty of Etaples
1493	Trading embargo with the Netherlands
1496	Intercursus Magnus
1506	Intercursus Malus

KEY QUESTION

How did English society and economy change and with what effects?

KEY PROFILE

John Cabot (c1451–98) was, like Christopher Columbus, a native of Genoa. He seems to have been a merchant involved in the Venetian spice trade before moving to Spain where his services were in demand as a harbour designer. He might have met Columbus in 1493 and his navigational intuition led him to believe that a more northerly course across the Atlantic would reach land more quickly.

Henry also passed the Navigation Acts of 1485 and 1489. The objective of these was to encourage English shipping by trying to ensure that only English ships should carry certain products to and from English ports. Such legislation had only limited usefulness, as foreign vessels continued to transport a substantial proportion of English exports.

Early English exploration

The fifteenth century had proved to be a great era of European exploration. Spanish and Portuguese explorers had opened up much of the world, and the Portuguese had particularly benefited from their domination of the spice trade. English sailors were much slower to engage in such activities. However, Bristol merchants and seamen were interested in the possibilities of transatlantic discovery; indeed, it was rumoured that such a discovery had been made some time before 1465 and there is evidence that Atlantic exploration was taking place from 1480, albeit on a small scale and unsuccessfully.

John Cabot appears to have arrived in Bristol in 1494 or 1495. This was a time when Bristol fish merchants were looking for alternative fishing grounds to exploit, having been excluded from Icelandic waters by the Hanseatic League. Cabot received authorisation from Henry VII to 'search out any isles, countries, regions or provinces of heathens and infidels whomsoever set in any part of the world soever, which have been before these times unknown to all Christians'. He sailed in 1497, located what became known as Newfoundland and reported the existence of extensive fishing grounds. He set off on a second voyage in the following year, from which he never returned. He was presumed lost at sea.

Cabot, however unrealistic his overall objectives, did establish, in the words of David Quinn, that 'a substantial land mass did exist within reasonable sailing from Europe' and laid the way for the Bristol fishery. Despite some claims to the contrary, it is almost certain that Cabot never set foot on the American mainland. However, it has recently been discovered that a Bristol merchant named William Weston might have done so in 1499 or 1500. Even if he did not do so he was certainly the first Englishman to lead an expedition to the New World.

Although John Cabot's son, Sebastian, received sponsorship from Henry VII and led an unsuccessful attempt to find the 'north-west passage' to Asia in 1508, English exploration of the north Atlantic tailed off with the accession of Henry VIII, who had little appetite for supporting such enterprises. The newly discovered fishing grounds became for a long time afterwards the preserve of seamen from Portugal and the Basque region of northern Spain.

SOURCE 1

In a letter dated 18 December 1497, Raimondo de Soncino, ambassador of the Duke of Milan, wrote to Ludovico Sforza, Duke of Milan:

And in the spring [John Cabot] says that his Majesty will arm some ships, and will give him all the criminals so that he may go to [Newfoundland] and plant a colony there. And in this way he hopes to make London a greater place for spices than Alexandria. And the principals of the business are the citizens of Bristol, great mariners that now know where to go. They say that the voyage will not take more than fifteen days, if fortune favours them after leaving Ireland. I have talked with a Burgundian who affirms the same, and who is willing to go, since the Admiral has given him an island. And I believe that some poor Italian friars will go on the voyage who have the promise of being bishops. And I, being a friend of the admiral, if I wished to go, could receive the office of archbishop, but I have thought the benefices which your Excellency has reserved for me a safer thing.

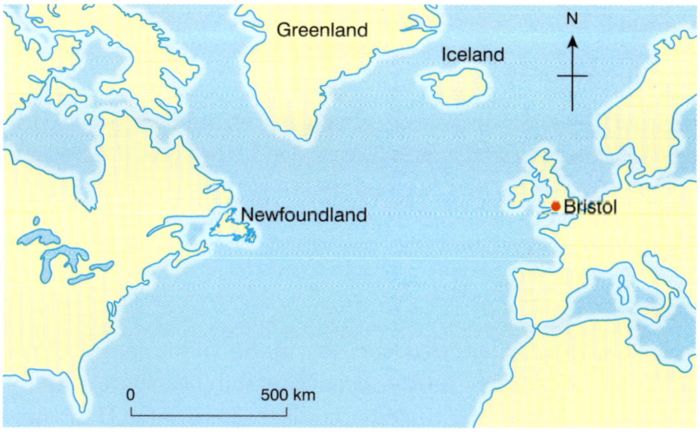

Fig. 4 *The North Atlantic, showing Newfoundland in modern Canada, where John Cabot landed in 1497*

Prosperity and depression

There is relatively little evidence from which to estimate the extent of prosperity and depression in the final years of the fifteenth century. Apart from a temporary rise in the 1480s, prices seem to have remained steady. The available evidence suggests that much the same happened to wages. On the other hand, there does appear to have been a decline in the export price of wool and in the price of grain and animal products in the 1490s. This might imply a reduction in farming profitability at this time but also rising real incomes for domestic consumers. Both building workers and agricultural labourers were, on the whole, better off during the 1490s than they would be at any other time during the Tudor period.

Table 1 *Price of consumables and wage rates in southern England, 1480–1609*

Decade	1 Price of consumables	2 Purchasing power of wage rate of a building craftsman	3 Purchasing power of wage rate of an agricultural labourer
1480–89	116	93	86
1490–99	101	103	104
1500–09	104	96	97
1510–19	111	88	89
1520–29	148	76	80
1530–39	155	68	80
1540–49	192	70	71
1550–59	289	51	59
1560–69	279	62	66
1570–79	315	64	69
1580–89	357	57	57
1590–99	472	47	49
1600–09	475	46	50

1. Price of consumables (1451–75 = 100)
2. Purchasing power of wage rate of a building craftsman (1450–99 = 100)
3. Purchasing power of wage rate of an agricultural labourer (1450–99 = 100)

ACTIVITY

Statistical analysis

On the basis of the statistical data in Table 1, can you identify in which decades of the Tudor period building craftsmen experienced (1) their greatest prosperity and (2) the greatest attack on their standards of living.

ACTIVITY

Evaluating historical extracts

Look back at Jack Lander's interpretation given at the beginning of this chapter (page 43). In small groups, consider whether you find this interpretation convincing. You will need to find specific evidence to support or refute his views.

Summary

In comparison with what was to occur later in the Tudor period, the reign of Henry VII was a period of relative economic stability, apart from the temporary disruptions to Anglo-Netherlands trade with the Hanseatic League. There was little to differentiate the reign economically from what had gone before, under Edward IV. The economy remained firmly based on agriculture, with a leavening of small-scale industrial enterprises. The king was associated with some attempts to encourage English trade, though how much influence these had is debatable. Dynastic interests always prevailed over commercial interests when the two appeared to clash.

ACTIVITY

Extension

What evidence is there of economic change during Henry VII's reign? Use information from this chapter and your own research to complete the table below.

	Positive	Negative
Trade (Netherlands)		
Trade (elsewhere)		
Industry		
Agriculture		
Living standards		

STUDY TIP

In answering a question such as this, it is important to place the cloth trade within a wider context of economic features, such as farming and industries.

AS LEVEL PRACTICE QUESTION

'The cloth trade was the most important contributor to the English economy during the reign of Henry VII.' Explain why you agree or disagree with this view.

STUDY TIP

In assessing significance you will need to balance the contribution of agriculture to the English economy against other contributors in industry and trade. Try to provide a well-supported judgement that looks at all aspects of agriculture.

A LEVEL PRACTICE QUESTION

How significant was the position of agriculture in the English economy in the years 1485 to 1509?

6 Religion, humanism, arts and learning

Religion in the reign of Henry VII

EXTRACT 1

Late-medieval Catholicism exerted an enormously strong, diverse and vigorous hold over the imagination and the loyalty of the people. Traditional religion had about it no particular marks of exhaustion and decay, and indeed in a whole host of ways, from the multiplication of religious books to adaptations of the saints, showed that it was well able to meet new needs and new conditions. The teachings of late-medieval Christianity were graphically represented, endlessly reiterated in sermons [and] saints' lives, enacted in the Corpus Christi and Miracle plays and carved and painted on the walls, screens, bench-ends and windows of the parish churches.

Adapted from Eamon Duffy, *The Stripping of the Altars: Traditional Religion in England, c1400–c1580*, 1992

ACTIVITY

Evaluating historical extracts

In Extract 1, Duffy is referring to the Catholic faith, under which Englishmen had lived for centuries. What does he say about the strength of that faith and its ritual?

The function of the Church and churchmen

During the reign of Henry VII all English people belonged, at least theoretically, to the Catholic Church and were under the jurisdiction of the Pope in Rome. Although prayers in the Mass were always said for the Pope, what really counted for ordinary people was their own religious experience, which was central to the lives of most people living in the fifteenth century.

Lives were lived and regulated according to the Church's major ceremonies. The parish church, of which there were over 8000, was the focus of religious experience. The church provided the focus of popular entertainment. Its festivals, which were closely linked to the agricultural year, provided much-needed enjoyment and its **guilds and confraternities** offered charity, good fellowship and the chance for ordinary people to contribute to the good of their local community.

The Church made it easier for the social and political elites to maintain social control through its encouragement of good behaviour, obedience and stress on the values of community. It also provided employment opportunities and, for a few like Cardinal Wolsey, the opportunity to advance themselves socially through the attainment of high office in Church and State.

EXTRACT 2

Henry VII changed the character of the bench of bishops to the extent that he weakened its religious leadership. His policy marked a real shift. Most of Henry's theologians, too, were administrators – this transformation of the bishops' bench was a deliberate strategy. Moreover, service to the State, even to the detriment of the Church, was required of his bishops.

Adapted from John Guy, *Tudor England*, 1988

The political role of the Church was significant, both in terms of international relations and in domestic matters. The highest position in the

LEARNING OBJECTIVES

In this chapter you will learn about:

- the place of religion in late fifteenth-century English society
- the role and influence of the Church in social life
- the influence of humanism on the arts and learning in England.

KEY QUESTION

As you read this chapter, consider the following Key Questions:

- How far did intellectual and religious ideas change and with what effects?
- How did intellectual ideas change and develop and with what effects?

CROSS-REFERENCE

Read more about the Corpus Christi and Miracle plays in this chapter, page 58.

KEY TERM

guilds and confraternities: voluntary associations of individuals created to promote works of Christian charity or devotion

CROSS-REFERENCE

The role of churchmen in society during the reign of Henry VII is covered in Chapter 4, page 36.

Cardinal Wolsey and his career are outlined in chapters 7 and 8.

Church was held by the Pope in Rome, who not only wielded considerable spiritual power but was also the head of a substantial state in northern Italy. It is typical both of Henry VII's carefulness and the Pope's influence that he sought, through Thomas Morton, a dispensation to marry Elizabeth of York. On the other hand, successive popes did little at this time to interfere directly with the running of the Church in England; the relationship between Church and State was **Erastian**. The king was firmly in control and popes were generally eager to grant the favours demanded by the king. The papacy had no objection to the way in which Henry used the wealth of the Church to reward those churchmen to whom he had given high political office.

KEY TERM

Erastian: the view that the State should have authority over the Church

diocese: an area under the pastoral care of a bishop in the Christian Church

The Church in England was administered through two provinces, Canterbury and York, each under the jurisdiction of an archbishop, and seventeen **dioceses**, each under the control of a bishop. Some of these dioceses, such as Winchester and Durham, enjoyed considerable wealth, and it was common in the late fifteenth century for senior churchmen to enjoy positions of significant influence and power within the kingdom.

Fig. 1 *The dioceses of the English and Welsh Churches before the Reformation*

It was common for senior clergy to participate at a high level in the political process. During much of the medieval period it was normal for the most senior figures within the Church in England to be drawn from the senior ranks of the aristocracy. Margaret Beaufort's great uncle, for example, had been a cardinal and bishop of Winchester. The two churchmen who exercised most power under Henry VII were **John Morton** and **Richard Fox**.

Some offices of State, especially that of the chancellor (the highest adviser to the king), were monopolised by clergymen. The most senior clergymen were, on the whole, highly competent and conscientious professionals, often with legal training, who performed their duties to both Church and State effectively. The abbots, who were heads of the wealthiest religious houses, shared membership of the House of Lords with the bishops. They also had to possess a range of management and administrative skills to keep their complex organisations running effectively, as well as demonstrating the spirituality necessary to maintain the reputation of their houses. Not all heads of house lived up to all of these demands, and criticisms of the monastic life were increasing.

CROSS-REFERENCE

The political role of John Morton and Richard Fox is discussed in Chapter 2 on page 9. A profile on Richard Fox is in Chapter 4, page 36.

Religious community, belief and services

The parish church was central to religious experience and this period was, according to Eamon Duffy, emphatically the age of the parish church and of those who worshipped there. The church provided the outward structures of community life. A late-medieval community was a religious one, which believed that the prayers made together, as part of the collective unit of the parish, were more powerful than those from the individual alone. The church provided a framework for controlling how an individual thought, reasoned and behaved. Its function was not only to spread and uphold Christian teaching, it also offered various ways by which an individual could acquire **grace** in order to reach heaven and minimise the time a soul would spend in **purgatory**.

KEY TERM

grace: the pure state a soul needed to be in to enter heaven

purgatory: in traditional Catholic thinking, purgatory was the state in which the souls of the dead were purged of their sins before they could enter the kingdom of heaven

To reach heaven, it was necessary to observe as many of the seven sacraments as possible:

- Baptism, which welcomed the newly born infant into the community.
- Confirmation, which marked the transition from childhood to adulthood.
- Marriage, in which the community could witness two individuals pledging themselves to each other.
- Anointing of the sick, which prepared the dying for their passage into the next world.
- Penance, during which the individual sought God's forgiveness for the sins which s/he had committed.
- Holy Orders, the process by which the priest himself became empowered to deliver the sacraments (rituals) to others.
- Eucharist, in which church members received Christ's body and blood in the form of bread and wine to be nourished physically and spiritually and brought closer to God.

The central religious experience of the Catholic Church came with the Mass, during which the priest would perform the sacrament of Holy Communion, also known as the Eucharist ('thanksgiving'). The climax of this ceremony was the point where the priest consecrated the bread and the wine (i.e. declared it to be sacred). Catholics believed that at the point of consecration, the bread and the wine were transformed figuratively and literally into the body and blood of Christ, a process known as **transubstantiation**. The priest consumed both the bread and the wine; lay members of the congregation took the bread only.

KEY TERM

transubstantiation: the Christian belief that the substance of bread and wine completely changed into the substance of Christ's body and blood by a validly ordained priest during the consecration at Mass

The Mass was important for two reasons:

- It was a sacrifice performed by the priest on behalf of the community.
- It was a sacred ritual in which the whole community participated.

The importance of the consecrated bread was emphasised at the feast of **Corpus Christi**, which was one of the important festivals of the fifteenth-century Church.

KEY TERM

Corpus Christi: literally meaning the 'body of Christ', Corpus Christi is a feast of the Catholic Church which celebrates the 'blessed sacrament' and whose importance developed from the thirteenth century with the increasing emphasis on transubstantiation

ACTIVITY

Pair discussion

1. Why do you think religion played such a major role in people's lives in the fifteenth century?
2. Identify a range of reasons which help to explain the popularity of the late-medieval Church in England.

The Church's social role

The communal aspects of late-medieval religion were emphasised by the investment which many lay people made into their parish churches. In addition to funding the lavish rebuilding of many churches, it was largely lay people who paid for the objects which accompanied services. The dying would often leave money to the parish church, which had a triple purpose: to enhance the beauty of worship, to ensure the remembrance of the **benefactor** and to reduce the time the benefactor would spend in purgatory.

Benefactors would leave money for the foundation of **chantries**. Usually chantries were financed from property bequeathed in someone's will for that purpose. According to Eamon Duffy, 'the central function of a chantry priest was **intercession** for the soul of his patron'. Benefactors saw their donations as a way of benefiting the religious experience of themselves and their community. This is important for understanding why the dissolution of the chantries by Henry VIII caused so much distress.

Another significant expression of communal religious influences was the confraternity (also known as a religious guild or lay brotherhood). These were groups of men (and sometimes women) who gathered together, usually in association with the parish church, to provide collectively for the funeral costs of members, to pay chaplains for Masses for their members, to help maintain church fabric, to make charitable donations and to socialise. Guilds were enormously popular (the small rural parish of Salle in Norfolk had seven). They also varied greatly in size and wealth. Wealthier guilds could be sources of local patronage and power. Some of them ran schools and almshouses, maintained bridges, highways and sea walls, or, as in Louth in Lincolnshire, paid for expensive projects such as the building of the spire at the parish church. Many parishes in the south and the south Midlands raised funds through church-ale festivals, which involved much drinking and a range of entertainments. Ale made and donated for the event was the chief drink.

KEY TERM

benefactor: a person who makes a charitable donation

chantries: chapels where Masses for the souls of the dead took place

intercession: the action of saying a prayer on behalf of another; in traditional Catholic thinking it was the role of the priest to intervene with God on behalf of an individual

CROSS-REFERENCE

The dissolution of the chantries is discussed in Chapter 14, page 135.

SOURCE 1

A well-informed Italian visitor, possibly the Venetian ambassador who was himself a bishop, to England in 1497 observed:

But above all are their riches displayed in the church treasures; for there is not a parish church in the kingdom so mean as not to possess crucifixes, candlesticks, censers [container for burning incense], patens [plate on which the communion bread is placed] and cups of silver, besides many other ornaments worthy of a cathedral church in the same metal.

ACTIVITY

Evaluating historical extracts

What is the value of Source 1 for a historian researching the attitudes of the English to their parish churches?

Religion's social role was evident in a number of other ways. Going on **pilgrimage** was another way in which the individual could gain relief from purgatory. A pilgrimage could involve visiting the tomb of a saint, such as Thomas Becket at Canterbury, or a shrine built where there had been a reported visitation of the Virgin Mary, such as at Walsingham in Norfolk. There is evidence to suggest that England's primary pilgrimage site, the tomb of Thomas Becket at Canterbury, was losing some of its popularity, and some late-medieval religious writers such as Thomas a Kempis were critical of pilgrimage as a practice. However, the vast number of pilgrimage sites made access relatively easy, and the practice of pilgrimage was, in Eamon Duffy's description, exuberant. A simpler form of pilgrimage happened on Rogation Sunday (Rogationtide) when the whole community would 'beat the bounds' of the parish (walking around the parish boundaries to pray for its protection), carrying banners and the parish cross to ward off evil spirits and reinforce the parish property. This event emphasised the importance of the parish as the key focus of local community in the lives of ordinary people at the time.

Although religion was emphasised as a social activity, the importance of individual religious experience should not be underestimated; indeed it became more important as the fifteenth century progressed. Individual religious experience was emphasised in the writing of mystics, who believed in the personal communication of the individual with God. The most obvious example of this approach in practice was that of Henry VII's mother, Lady Margaret Beaufort, whose piety was reflected in her widespread donations, especially to Cambridge University.

KEY TERM

pilgrimage: a journey to a place of religious devotion

CROSS-REFERENCE

For more information on the Reformation of religion and how England changed from a Roman Catholic state to a Protestant one, go to Chapter 12.

CROSS-REFERENCE

To read more on Lady Margaret Beaufort return to Chapter 2, page 10.

Fig. 2 *Lady Margaret Beaufort*

Religious orders

Monastic orders

It has been estimated that around one per cent of adult males in England by c1500 were monks, living in religious housing known as monasteries. The monks lived under the rule of the monasteries. Most of these lived in the 900 religious communities which were found all over the country.

The oldest and most common religious order was the Benedictines, named in honour of their founder St Benedict, who first devised the monastic rule. Many Benedictine houses were large. Some of the larger Benedictine houses, like Durham, also operated as the cathedral churches of their diocese, so fulfilling an important role in the community. Other religious orders included the Cistercians and Carthusians. Their foundation in the late eleventh century was prompted by the lack of zeal shown by Benedictines. Their monasteries were frequently situated in more remote rural areas – examples include the Yorkshire houses of Fountains and Mount Grace. Though monastic recruits came from a wide range of social backgrounds, it is evident that a large proportion of monks in the larger houses was drawn from the wealthier parts of society. It is also evident that many monasteries recruited predominantly from their own localities.

Friars

Orders of friars, who worked among lay people and who were largely supported by charitable donations, arose in the thirteenth century. The three main orders of friars were: the Dominicans (or black friars), a preaching order; the Franciscans (grey friars); and the Augustinians. Orders of friars seem to have recruited from lower down the social scale than the larger monasteries. By the late fifteenth century, as Christopher Harper-Bill has argued, the great days of the friars were over, though the various orders of friars continued to receive substantial bequests in the wills of the faithful.

Nunneries

Nunneries enjoyed much less prestige, given that they were mostly populated by women who were deemed unsuitable for marriage. A notable exception was the Bridgettine foundation at Syon near Isleworth in Middlesex. Most nunneries were relatively poor, though Syon again was an exception, and the quality of many novices was inadequate as they entered convents as a last resort.

The Lollards, heresy and anticlericalism

A small minority was critical of the beliefs and practices of the Church. Lollardy, for example, founded by John Wycliffe, emerged in England in the second half of the fourteenth century and was still to be found during the time of Henry VII. Lollards placed stress on the understanding of the Bible and therefore favoured its translation into English. They were sceptical about transubstantiation and the principles of the Eucharist, and considered the Catholic Church to be corrupt. They also denied the idea of the special status of the priesthood.

Lollard views were considered **heresy** but still persisted in parts of southern England, particularly in south Buckinghamshire and around Newbury in Berkshire. Though the movement seems to have been quite widespread at the end of the fourteenth and beginning of the fifteenth centuries, its popularity declined after the failed Lollard uprising of 1414. Lollards became fewer in number, the movement lost intellectual coherence and became geographically restricted. Other forms of heresy seem to have been rare. The burning of heretics had been introduced into English law in 1401, though relatively few had suffered this terrible fate.

Criticism of the Church did exist, and it has often been assumed that **anticlericalism** was widespread in late-medieval England, though this assumption has been challenged by historians such as Christopher Haigh who have argued that specific outbursts of anticlericalism were rare, that they were often politically motivated and that the continued healthy numbers of candidates for the priesthood showed that priests retained the support of most members of the **laity**.

KEY TERM

heresy: the denial of the validity of the key doctrines of the Church

anticlericalism: opposition to the Church's role in political and other non-religious matters

laity: refers collectively to those who were neither priests nor members of a religious order

STUDY TIP

The two extracts offer the opportunity to consider both what religious experience meant for ordinary people and the way in which the monarch could exploit the Church for his own purposes. Identify and evaluate the interpretation in each and provide a judgement on the more convincing.

AS LEVEL PRACTICE QUESTION

Evaluating historical extracts

With reference to Extracts 1 and 2, and to your understanding of the historical context, which of these extracts provides the more convincing interpretation of the role of religion in England during the reign of Henry VII?

Humanism, arts and learning

Humanism and humanists

A CLOSER LOOK

'**Humanism**' was derived from 'humanist' ('*umanista*' in Italian). It was a development of the **Renaissance** of the fourteenth century and was founded on the rediscovery of original Latin and Greek texts. Originating in Renaissance Florence, humanists were particularly concerned with establishing the reliability of Latin and Greek translations in order to purify the ideas of religious texts. As such, it was a broadly intellectual trend with specific learning objectives. Humanists were believers in the Catholic faith, particularly the notion of free will. Their work affected not only religion but also politics and economics. Christian humanism was the movement which arose when this approach was applied to biblical texts.

The earliest humanist scholars of significance in England were William Grocyn (c1449–1519) and Thomas Linacre (c1460–1524). Each of them had experienced humanist approaches to the classics in Florence in the late 1480s. Grocyn began to lecture at Oxford on the ideas of Plato and Aristotle. Linacre was particularly influenced by the scientific thinking which he acquired in Italy, and took a medical degree at the University of Padua. Even more influential as an educator was **John Colet** (1467–1519). He saw humanist scholarly approaches as a means of reforming the Church from within. His most important ally in this process was the renowned Dutch scholar **Desiderius Erasmus**, who paid his first visit to England in 1499. Erasmus, more than anyone else at least in his own estimation, epitomised the spirit of the new learning. His friendship with **Thomas More** would give a huge boost to humanist ideas in the early years of the reign of Henry VIII.

KEY PROFILE

Desiderius Erasmus (1466–1536) was a Dutch scholar whose influential book *The Handbook of a Christian Soldier*, published in 1504, sought to regenerate Christianity through emphasis on education and rejection of some of the Church's traditional ceremonies. His satirical works were highly critical of the abuses of the Church.

A CLOSER LOOK

Printing in England began with William Caxton in 1477, but it was more significant in Germany, the Netherlands and Italy. There was little connection in this period between printing, humanism and the new learning.

SOURCE 2

On 5 December 1499 Erasmus wrote a letter to Robert Fisher, an English agent in Rome:

I find the climate both pleasant and wholesome, and I have met with so much kindness and so much learning, not hackneyed and trivial, but deep, accurate, ancient Latin and Greek, that but for the curiosity of seeing it, I do not now care so much for Italy. When I hear my Colet, I seem to be listening to Plato himself, In Grocyn, who does not marvel at such a perfect round of learning? What can be more acute, profound and delicate than the judgement of Linacre? What has nature ever created more gentle, more sweet, more happy than the genius of Thomas More? I need not go through the list. It is marvellous how general and abundant is the harvest of ancient learning in this country, to which you ought all the sooner to return.

KEY PROFILE

John Colet (1467–1519), like Grocyn and Linacre, travelled to Italy and was introduced to humanist influences there. After following a largely academic career, he became Dean of St Paul's, and refounded St Paul's School in 1512. His one surviving sermon was highly critical of the standards of the clergy, and this has led many historians to assume that his views foreshadow those who favoured the growth of Protestantism.

KEY PROFILE

Sir Thomas More (1478–1535) was a distinguished lawyer and humanist scholar, most famous, perhaps, as the author of ***Utopia***. A valued councillor to Henry VIII, he was appointed Lord Chancellor on the fall of Wolsey in 1529, but resigned in 1532 in despair at Henry's religious changes. He was executed for treason, having denied the royal supremacy.

Fig. 3 *Sir Thomas More painted by Hans Holbein in 1527*

CROSS-REFERENCE

The full implications of the development of humanist influence are discussed in chapters 12, 14 and 16.

ACTIVITY

Evaluating primary sources

How convincing do you find Erasmus's portrayal of English humanism in 1499? Consider the source's provenance, including the fact that Erasmus knew his letter would likely be read widely in England.

KEY TERM

Renaissance: a cultural and intellectual movement which, beginning in Italy, emphasised a revival of interest in classical learning and the arts

KEY TERM

scholasticism: a system of philosophical analysis in the medieval period

ACTIVITY

Extension

Research more about the activities of Erasmus, especially his work as a satirist, for example *In Praise of Folly*. This would greatly enhance your appreciation of this period.

At the time of Henry VII's reign, **humanism** and the **Renaissance** had made little impression on England. English intellectual life continued to be dominated by traditional medieval **scholastic** philosophy, which humanists considered to be too formal and old fashioned.

Developments in education

This was also a period of widening educational opportunities. 'Song schools' and 'reading schools' provided elementary education for the very young. Much of what we would now consider 'secondary' education took place in grammar schools. Some of these had been in existence for centuries, but there was an increase in new foundations during this period; 53 new grammar schools were founded between 1460 and 1509. Nevertheless, while there was ample provision for the wealthy, for the majority access to education depended on where they happened to live.

Central to the grammar school curriculum was the study of Latin. Most schools probably continued to teach the subject in the traditional way, but the 1480s saw the beginnings of a humanistic approach, particularly at Magdalen College School in Oxford. The teaching of English remained a by-product of the teaching of Latin.

University education rested with the ancient universities of Oxford and Cambridge. Oxford had experienced substantial expansion with the foundation of new colleges in the first half of the fifteenth century, but this had ground to a halt. Cambridge, however, had several new colleges during this period, benefiting, in particular, from the generosity of Lady Margaret Beaufort who was responsible for the foundation of Christ's College and St John's College.

Drama

The most important popular art form of the time was drama. Plays were sometimes presented in association with church-ale festivals, for example at Bishop's Stortford in Hertfordshire in 1490. Troupes of players, sometimes sponsored by members of the nobility, toured the country. However, the most famous dramas were the mystery plays performed at the feasts of Corpus Christi by the guilds of towns and cities such as York, Lincoln, Wakefield and Coventry. The performances were important festive occasions in which churches, corporations and guilds combined in public celebrations which set out straightforward moral and religious messages for the moral improvement of their audiences.

Music

Music was also enjoyed at various levels in the fifteenth century from the local bagpipe and wind groups that entertained the crowds on saints' days – sometimes accompanying bawdy drinking songs – through to the great choral pieces sung in the country's cathedrals. This music underwent the beginnings of a 'renaissance' as single-line chants gave way to polyphonic choral music, where different parts of the choir sang independent melodic lines, which would be heard in cathedrals and other major churches.

Fig. 4 *The Eton Choirbook*

The most important surviving source for such music is the Eton Choirbook, compiled around 1505, a collection of 93 separate musical compositions. The two most important composers represented in the Choirbook each had very close links with the political establishment of Henry VII's reign: Thomas Browne was employed in the household of the Earl of Oxford and Robert Fayrfax benefited regularly from the patronage of Lady Margaret Beaufort as well as that of the king.

Music performed at court or in the homes of the wealthy (sometimes for a special occasion or, more regularly, given from the **minstrels' gallery** to accompany a meal) used instruments such as trumpets, **shawms** and **sackbuts** or, in softer music, stringed instruments, recorders and lutes. Browne and Fayrfax also composed **secular** songs used for entertainment. Carols, not then exclusively associated with Christmas, were also popular.

Art and architecture

There was a massive amount of building and rebuilding of parish churches that occurred at this time. The vast number of churches built in the **Gothic perpendicular style** is an indication of the scale of investment which took place; these include such important places of worship as Saint Mary Redcliffe in Bristol and the major wool churches of East Anglia, such as Lavenham and Long Melford. In 1502 Henry VII approved this architectural style for the Lady Chapel at Westminster Abbey.

English culture still followed the Gothic traditions of northwestern Europe, with an allegedly primitive visual style. The new industry of printing was still only concerned with traditional medieval culture. William Caxton, who established his printing press in 1478, printed works such as Chaucer's *Canterbury Tales* and other traditional medieval works, including **chivalric** romances and adaptations of the saints' lives. However, tastes began to change and by the time of Henry VII's death in 1509 humanist influences had reached England, particularly from Italy. Humanist scholars, foreigners like Erasmus

KEY TERM

minstrels' gallery: a minstrel was a medieval singer or musician who performed for the nobility, often from a form of balcony inside the great hall of a castle or manor house

shawm: a medieval and Renaissance wind instrument, forerunner of the oboe, with a double reed enclosed in a wooden mouthpiece, and having a penetrating tone

sackbut: a medieval wind instrument, forerunner of the trombone

secular: something not connected with religious or spiritual matters

KEY TERM

Gothic: the style of architecture prevalent in Western Europe in the twelfth to sixteenth centuries, characterised by pointed arches and large windows; English Gothic architecture is divided into Early English, Decorated, and Perpendicular categories

perpendicular style: the dominant form of church architecture in England from the later fourteenth, to the early sixteenth, century, so-called because of its emphasis on vertical lines; the most famous perpendicular building is probably the chapel of King's College, Cambridge

chivalric: refers to the code of conduct for medieval knights of the realm; the code of chivalry emphasised bravery, military skill, generosity in victory, piety, and courtesy to women

Fig. 5 *The Lady Chapel of Westminster Abbey, built in the perpendicular style by Henry VII but showing also the king's Renaissance-influenced tomb*

and Englishmen like Thomas More and John Colet, became more fashionable. The works printed by Caxton also became unfashionable, with the emergence of what historian Jack Lander called the 'humanist contempt for chivalric literature'.

Fig. 6 *The parish church of Lavenham, Suffolk, built in the perpendicular style*

ACTIVITY

Extension

Find and visit a church in your area which has perpendicular architecture. Identify its distinctive features and consider how its style differs from other churches you have visited.

Summary

ACTIVITY

Identify the strengths and weaknesses of the Church in Henry VII's reign for each of the following:

	Strengths	Weaknesses
King		
Nobility		
Leading churchmen		
Local community		
Ordinary people		

During the reign of Henry VII the English Church was in a generally healthy state. The relationships between both Church and State and between king and Pope were generally positive. The Church fulfilled its major functions tolerably well and there was remarkably little dissent, although patches of Lollard activity did undoubtedly exist. On the whole, however, the Church was remarkably effective at fulfilling what people perceived as their spiritual needs. Certainly, in the judgement of Christopher Harper-Bill, 'the institutions of the English church in the early sixteenth century do not appear to have been in urgent need of radical reform'. The relationships between the Church and education and culture remained strong. The speed of cultural change remained quite slow. Humanism had made inroads in education, but its major influence would not be felt until the reign of Henry VIII. Visual culture remained predominantly Gothic.

ACTIVITY

Evaluating historical extracts

Look back at Eamon Duffy's interpretation given at the beginning of the chapter (page 51). Can you find evidence in this chapter that can support or oppose his views?

AS LEVEL PRACTICE QUESTION

'The Church in England in the reign of Henry VII was riddled with abuses.' Explain why you agree or disagree with this view.

STUDY TIP

The importance of abuses should be set against the strengths of the Church in terms of its popular appeal at the time.

A LEVEL PRACTICE QUESTION

To what extent, by 1509, was the Church in England in need of reform?

STUDY TIP

Evaluation of the need for reform also implies a need to examine those aspects of the Church which were working well and which met the needs of worshippers effectively.

2 Henry VIII, 1509–47

7 The character and aims of Henry VIII

The character of Henry VIII

EXTRACT 1

Self-interest ruled at the accession of Henry VIII. The reaction against Henry VII's government was emotional and unsupported by hard evidence. After Henry VII's death Empson and Dudley were convicted of treason in show trials. They were imprisoned for a year, then beheaded; the executions were a calculated ploy to enable the new regime under Henry VIII to profit from the stability created by his father without incurring any of the stigma attached to it. Henry VIII showed his mind by these proceedings; something of his ruthlessness was revealed even though he was barely eighteen years of age by his accession.

Adapted from John Guy, *Tudor England*, 1988

Fig. 1 *Henry VIII in 1509, aged 18*

LEARNING OBJECTIVES

In this chapter you will learn about:

- the character of Henry VIII
- the legacy of Henry VII
- Henry VIII's aims.

KEY QUESTION

As you read this chapter, consider the following Key Questions:

- How important was the role of key individuals and groups and how were they affected by developments?
- How effectively did the Tudors restore and develop the powers of the monarchy?
- In what ways, and how effectively, was England governed during this period?

ACTIVITY

1. How does John Guy portray Henry VIII's character in Extract 1?
2. As you study this chapter, consider the view of John Guy presented in Extract 1. At the end of the chapter you will be asked to provide your own critique of Guy's judgement about Henry VIII's character.

KEY CHRONOLOGY

1509	21 Apr	Death of Henry VII
	23 Apr	Henry VIII proclaimed king
	11 Jun	Henry VIII marries Catherine of Aragon
	24 Jun	Coronation of Henry and Catherine
1514		Emergence of Wolsey as first minister

Henry VIII came to the throne two months before his eighteenth birthday. Seven years had passed since the death of his elder brother, Arthur, and in this time he had prepared for his new role as the future king of England. He had been well educated for the task, including some acquaintance with the new learning of humanism. He was well read, although, according to John Guy, his mind was able but second rate. The early impression he created was very positive. The modern historian, Eric Ives, describes Henry at this time as 'extrovert, affable and charming.'

EXTRACT 2

Henry VIII was educated and cultivated; he had courage, charm, even humour. He was pious and well versed in theology. Qualities of mind and character, his splendid physical presence and his chivalry would have impressed even if he had not been king. But he was a king of commanding will. **Sir Thomas More** warned, even as the reign began, that unlimited power tended to weaken good minds.

Henry's reign began, as it would end, with a comprehensive deception practised for high political purposes, as a courtier concealed the news of the old king's death. Courtiers colluded with some of Henry VII's councillors to secure the succession and organise a coup. Two days after his father died the new king was being served as though he were still Prince of Wales and Henry VII still alive. On the first day of the new reign, Henry VII's hated councillors Edmund Dudley and Sir Richard Empson were sent to the Tower, to the delight of the people, who saw them as agents of Henry VII's oppression rather than as victims of his son's. Already the ruthlessness of the young king seemed apparent.

Adapted from Susan Brigden, *New Worlds, Lost Worlds: the Rule of the Tudors, 1485–1603*, 2000

CROSS-REFERENCE

A Key Profile of Sir Thomas More is in Chapter 6, page 57.

Henry VIII's accession was welcomed as a breath of fresh air after the stultifying and rather sinister atmosphere associated with the influence of Empson and Dudley in the last years of his father's reign. For Sir Thomas More, it represented 'the end of our slavery, the fount of our liberty, the end of sadness, the beginning of joy'. However, Henry had had no experience of government or public affairs.

SOURCE 1

Thomas More stated in his 'Coronation Ode to King Henry VIII' in 1509:

For this day consecrates a young man who is the everlasting glory of our time and makes him your king – a king who is not merely to govern a single people but singly to rule the whole world – such a king as will wipe the tears from every eye and put joy in the place of our long distress.

The nobility, long since at the mercy of the dregs of the population, the nobility, whose title has too long been without meaning, now lifts its head, now rejoices in such a king, and has proper reason for rejoicing.

The merchant, heretofore deterred by numerous taxes, now once again ploughs seas grown unfamiliar.

Laws, heretofore powerless – yes, even laws put to unjust ends – now happily have regained their proper authority.

All are equally happy. All weigh their earlier losses against the advantages to come.

ACTIVITY

Evaluating primary sources

1. What do you understand by the phrase 'long distress' in Source 1?
2. How valid is the claim that the nobility had 'proper reason' for rejoicing?
3. What do you understand by the claim that 'laws … now happily have regained their proper authority'?
4. How valuable would this source be to a historian studying reactions to Henry VIII's accession? Consider the provenance of the source, including the tone, the occasion and intended audience. You may wish to look back at what you have learnt about Thomas More in Chapter 6 before attempting this question.

Henry VIII's version of kingship differed markedly from that of his father. He had a profound dislike for the business of government and found the writing and reading of State papers both tedious and painful. Yet he could intervene suddenly in the business of government, in the process contradicting decisions or actions which had already been taken. Such an impetuous approach had considerable implications for the quality of decision-making within Henry's administration, which was especially important given the nature of personal monarchy. Moreover, he certainly lacked the work ethic which many historians attributed to his father, instead preferring to pass the time with good company. This was evident in the courtly activities which followed his accession. There was much emphasis on pageants, revelry, sports, hunting and tournaments.

Fig. 2 *Henry VIII spent much of his youth at tilt yards where he learned to joust magnificently. This is an early sixteenth-century Flemish image of a jousting tournament*

Because Henry VIII was rarely engaged directly with the business of government, the structure of government evolved differently compared with the reign of Henry VII.

- In the short term there was a renewed emphasis on governing through council, which then made two comebacks at later stages of the reign (1529–32, 1540–47).
- Furthermore, for two periods during his reign Henry relied upon the work of a chief minister who shaped the structures of government to meet his own needs. The first of these was **Thomas Wolsey** who was particularly adept at using Star Chamber. The second was Thomas Cromwell, who developed his role as principal secretary.

A CLOSER LOOK

Wolsey was certainly richly rewarded for his efforts. He quickly acquired an impressive range of Church offices which ensured a lucrative living. Moreover, he also achieved recognition from the

KEY PROFILE

Fig. 3 *Henry VIII talking to Wolsey. The king was actively interested in foreign policy but content to leave the domestic economy and affairs to his chief minister*

Thomas Wolsey (c1471–1530) became the royal almoner (distributing money as charity to the needy on behalf of the king) upon Henry VIII's accession. He came to Henry's attention as a result of his organisational abilities and became, according to his servant and biographer George Cavendish, 'the most earnest and readiest among all the Council to advance the king's only will and pleasure.' This apparently minor member of the Council became more like a chief minister, interposing himself between the king and the experienced councillors who were increasingly frozen out from serious influence. Wolsey was not, however, simply the king's mouthpiece, because his intelligence and articulacy meant that he was exceptionally skilful at presenting the king's case.

papacy, being appointed cardinal by Pope Leo X in 1515. This was more important for its symbolism than for any political influence which it might have conferred. More important, however, was his appointment as papal legate in 1518, a post in which he was confirmed for life in 1524. This was significant in that it meant that Wolsey now outranked the ageing William Warham, Archbishop of Canterbury, and also gave him control over the religious orders in England. This acquisition of Church offices was complemented by an accumulation of secular posts within the king's government, culminating in his appointment as Lord Chancellor in 1515.

However, no politician who has attained the stature that Wolsey obtained can ever be free of enemies. It was Wolsey's enemies who brought him down in 1529 by exploiting the weakness in his relationship with the king, brought about by his failure to secure the annulment of Henry VIII's marriage to Catherine of Aragon.

CROSS-REFERENCE

Wolsey's work in government is discussed on pages 72–77 and Cromwell's work in government is discussed on pages 77–81.

Henry VII's financial and economic policies, and his use of councils in government, are discussed in Chapter 2.

CROSS-REFERENCE

Wolsey's management of the Church is covered in Chapter 7, page 66.

The annulment of Henry VIII's marriage to Catherine of Aragon was virtually an impossible task. This became known as 'the King's Great Matter'. It is covered in Chapter 8, pages 75–79.

The legacy of Henry VII

KEY QUESTION

- In what ways and how effectively was England governed during this period?
- How did relations with foreign powers change and how was the succession secured?

Henry VIII had essentially a fourfold legacy from his father:

- money – it is believed that Henry VII left around £300,000 upon his death
- unpopular mechanisms for extracting money
- a peaceful foreign policy
- a conciliar form of government – decisions were made through a council.

Each of these, however, would disappear during the first few years of Henry VIII's reign. The money Henry inherited from his father's reign would vanish as a result of paying for the revival of a traditionally aggressive foreign policy towards France. The conciliar form of government would disappear in the short term as a result of the emergence of Fox's former protégé, Thomas Wolsey, as the focus of government.

The start of Henry VIII's reign was marked by changes during which some members of the Council were able to dispose of others and establish themselves in power. The key person in this process was Richard Fox, who, assisted by Sir Thomas Lovell and Richard Weston, secured the arrest of Richard Empson and Edmond Dudley. Henry VIII was not himself responsible for this action, though he was undoubtedly responsible for their subsequent executions, which did not take place until the king had been on the throne for over a year. The Council Learned in the Law was abolished by Act of Parliament in January 1510. With the abolition of the Council Learned, the cancellation of many of the bonds and recognizances which the Council Learned had imposed, and the executions of Empson and Dudley, Henry not only distanced himself from his father's regime; he also ensured his own popularity amongst the nobility and propertied classes who considered themselves the victims of his father's approach to taxation.

CROSS-REFERENCE

Henry VII's foreign policy towards France is covered in Chapter 3, pages 23–24.

You can find Key Profiles of Henry VII's infamous advisors Empson and Dudley in Chapter 2, page 11.

The Council Learned in Law is described in Chapter 2, pages 10–11.

Bonds and recognizances are explained in Chapter 2, pages 14–15.

ACTIVITY

Pair discussion

Consider Henry VIII's motives in distancing himself so much from his father's regime. Was he justified in doing so?

ACTIVITY

Produce a piece of writing in the style of a newspaper article – or a poem – proclaiming the new king and welcoming the start of the reign.

The aims of Henry VIII's government

Henry's early aims

KEY QUESTION

- How effectively did the Tudors restore and develop the powers of the monarchy?
- In what ways and how effectively was England governed during this period?
- How did relations with foreign powers change and how was the succession secured?

In addition to dismantling the less popular aspects of his father's legacy Henry VIII had a number of other key aims in the first years of his reign:

- to establish his status amongst European monarchs through marriage
- to re-establish the role of the nobility
- to establish himself as a warrior king through success in battle.

Henry's marriage to Catherine of Aragon

A marriage between Henry and his brother Arthur's widow, Catherine of Aragon, had been discussed since Arthur's death, but had not been finally agreed while Henry VII was king.

Henry VIII, perhaps believing that Catherine had been unfairly treated, was anxious to conclude the marriage as quickly as possible. This suited Henry's councillors, who took the view that marriage for Henry would deflect him from political matters and enable them to conduct conciliar business as usual, and Henry and Catherine married on 11 June 1509. Not only was the marriage initially successful on a personal level, Catherine also exercised some influence over policy making in the first few years. However, by the mid-1520s Henry would repent of the rapidity of his marriage to a woman who was over five years older than he was, especially once it was clear that she could never present him with a healthy male heir.

Re-establishing the nobility

The nobility had been largely frozen out of direct political influence by Henry VII. Few of them had spent much time at court. Moreover, Henry's largely peaceable foreign policy had denied them their traditional outlet of the pursuit of military glory. This changed with the accession of Henry VIII, who shared the tastes and dominant military culture of the aristocracy. It was largely the sons of the nobility, generally young men who were slightly older than the king himself, who partnered Henry in the sports and revels which took up so much of his time and energy at the start of the reign. It was they who accompanied Henry to war in northern France, or the Marquis of Dorset to south-west France or the **Earl of Surrey** to Scotland. However, the nobles did not in the end achieve the political domination they had hoped for because Henry chose to promote the interests of Thomas Wolsey, the churchman who had organised the war in France on his behalf.

A CLOSER LOOK

The execution of Buckingham, 1521

Henry's treatment of the Duke of Buckingham is indicative of his ruthlessness towards the nobility early in his reign. Buckingham, like Henry VIII, was a descendant of King Edward III, and the only English duke at the start of the reign. He was regarded with suspicion by Henry, who wrote an undated letter to Wolsey setting out his concerns about Buckingham and four other nobles. Buckingham was certainly prone to muttering about issues such as the succession. Wolsey had even warned

Fig. 4 *Catherine of Aragon*

A CLOSER LOOK

Catherine's marriage to Henry's brother, Prince Arthur, had been brief. Following Arthur's death in 1502, Henry VII had insisted that Catherine stay in England. After the death of Catherine's mother, Isabella of Castile in 1504, Catherine was kept in a restricted environment at court, complaining to her father about her poor treatment.

ACTIVITY

Produce a document for Bishop Fox and other key members of the Council setting out the advantages and disadvantages of a marriage between Henry VIII and Catherine of Aragon.

him to be more cautious. Technically, any discussion of what might happen after the king's death could have been regarded as treasonable and it was on this basis that he was tried by a court of his peers, headed by Thomas Howard, Duke of Norfolk. This duly found him guilty and he was quickly executed. The reason for the proceedings against him remains obscure, and many historians, including Geoffrey Elton, have presumed that Wolsey had a hand in his downfall, though Wolsey's biographer Peter Gwyn has argued that there is no hard evidence to support this claim.

KEY PROFILE

Thomas Howard, Earl of Surrey and second Duke of Norfolk (1443–1524) came from a distinguished Yorkist family and fought for Richard III at the Battle of Bosworth after which he was imprisoned and attainted for treason. He was restored to his title in 1489 when he suppressed the Yorkshire Rebellion and led the victorious English army at the Battle of Flodden with Scotland, after which he was promoted to the Duchy of Norfolk. He served both Henry VII and Henry VIII as a soldier and administrator.

Foreign policy

Henry sought quickly to overthrow his father's foreign policy legacy. The pursuit of military glory, which fitted in closely with his rehabilitation of the traditional nobility, led directly to war in France, a theme which would recur regularly throughout the reign, usually with the same results: vast amounts of money were spent to achieve painfully small gains which had little or no strategic significance. To make matters even more confusing, these bouts of aggression were mixed with occasional alliances with the French against Spain and the Holy Roman Empire, though Henry was never quite foolish enough to go to war with the powerful Charles V.

CROSS-REFERENCE

Henry's foreign policy is covered in detail in Chapter 9.

Henry's later aims

The first five years of Henry VIII's reign had witnessed some celebrated events: his marriage, his coronation and a momentous victory over the Scots. For better or worse, he comprehensively destroyed his father's legacy through warfare and extravagance.

It would be a mistake to assume that Henry VIII had a consistent approach to his aims in government. Some themes recur, especially the pursuit of glory and the need to secure the succession to the throne, but for the most part he was remarkably little interested in the business of government except on an occasional and impulsive basis. He almost always gave priority to the pursuit of pleasure. Yet his reign would leave an enduring mark on English history: the broadening of the use of statute law (Acts of Parliament) to achieve his political ends, the resulting growing importance of Parliament, the destruction of much traditional religion and the plundering of much of the Church's wealth. The effects on the Church, however, were almost completely a consequence of the break with Rome, a policy decision which would have seemed inconceivable in the first 20 years of the reign.

CROSS-REFERENCE

The break with Rome, in which Henry transformed the Church in England in order to procure his divorce from Catherine of Aragon, is the subject of Chapter 12.

Henry certainly exhibited ruthlessness and cynicism, as demonstrated through his treatment of Empson and Dudley. This was a trait which was present throughout his reign. His resort to execution for treason, often on the flimsiest of charges, combined tyranny and insecurity in a way which completely overshadowed those positive qualities which witnesses such as More discerned in the young king.

He had also demonstrated his impulsiveness in the speed of his marriage to Catherine of Aragon, another characteristic which would come to the fore on crucial occasions later in the reign, for example with the marriages to Anne of Cleves and Catherine Howard. This impulsiveness was not restricted to his marital relationships. Thus, for example, he came to regret his impulsive decision to execute Thomas Cromwell. When combined with the sort of naivety demonstrated in his approach to foreign policy, the consequences would be potentially devastating for the governing of the country.

CROSS-REFERENCE

For Henry's later marriages, look ahead to Chapter 8, pages 80–82.

ACTIVITY

Summary chart

How much continuity was there between 1485 and 1521? Copy and complete the table, giving evidence to support all of your ideas.

	Change/continuity	Evidence
Government/council/ relationship with ministers		
Finance		
Parliament		
Foreign policy		
Relationship with nobility		

EXTRACT 3

The young Henry had remarkable attributes. For many years he could play the part expected of an ideal king. He was rich, splendid, vital, hearty, handsome, dashing, affable, ingratiating, athletic, musical, an accomplished linguist, a patron of the arts, orthodox, self-confident. He had charm and he had force of character. His extravagance could easily be taken for generosity after the miserly days of Henry VII. His throwing of Empson and Dudley to the wolves seemed to promise a more lawful mode of governing. The young king had brilliance, but his talents were ill-disciplined and ill-directed. He attended to the business of government only by fits and starts when the mood took him and when the pursuit of pleasure allowed.

Adapted from Christopher Morris, *The Tudors*, 1955

AS LEVEL PRACTICE QUESTION

Evaluating historical extracts

With reference to Extracts 2 and 3 and your understanding of the historical context, which of these two extracts provides the more convincing interpretation of the young Henry VIII as king?

STUDY TIP

One way of approaching this question would be to divide the individual comments made by the two historians into negative and positive judgements on the king. You will then need to establish some criteria by which you can evaluate and synthesise the specific judgements which you have come up with.

ACTIVITY

Look back at John Guy's interpretation at the beginning of the chapter (page 63). In small groups, consider whether you find his interpretation convincing. You will need to find specific evidence to support or refute his views.

A LEVEL PRACTICE QUESTION

'Henry VIII's actions as king destroyed Henry VII's legacy.' Assess the validity of this view of the years 1485 to 1514.

STUDY TIP

When faced with a complex quotation, it is important to break it down into its constituent parts and plan a response based on these parts. Here it is important to identify what might have been the positive aspects of Henry VII's legacy (stability, financial security, peace) as well as the negative aspects (greed, undermining of the nobility).

8 Henry VIII, government and Parliament

Government in Henry VIII's early and middle years (1509–40)

Fig. 1 *Henry VIII in procession prior to the state opening of Parliament, 1512*

EXTRACT 1

> Monarchy was personal. Everything, therefore, depended on the king's willingness to devote himself to business. Most State papers were read to or summarised to him and he did almost all his work by word of mouth. Only on issues which engaged him personally was he willing to become fully committed. On the other hand, Henry was not willing to delegate consistently. He also reserved the freedom to intervene as and when he wanted. The need to accommodate Henry VIII's particular version of personal monarchy explains much. In essence there were two options. The first was that the Royal Council should attempt to provide some continuity in government and the second that a chief minister should take over, leaving the king as overall director. Neither met the difficulties fully and the story of the reign is of fluctuation as the options were tried in turn and successively broke down.

Adapted from Eric W. Ives, 'Henry VIII' in *Oxford Dictionary of National Biography*, 2004

As Eric Ives has emphasised in Extract 1, Henry VIII liked to have an overview of his government, but he was happy to let others do the mundane work for him – be it his Royal Council or his chosen ministers. The style of government therefore varied across his reign. A further complicating factor was the existence of Parliament and the use to which this was put. Indeed, thanks to a very personal matter relating to Henry's concern for a son to succeed him, a major overhaul of relations between Crown and Parliament took place during Henry VIII's reign.

Before the 1530s, there was little to suggest that Henry VIII's view of the role of Parliament differed from that held by his father. Its two main functions remained, to grant extraordinary revenue to the Crown and to pass laws. Parliaments could also advise the monarch, though neither Henry VII, nor Henry VIII in his earlier years, saw the need to seek Parliament's advice. Indeed, before 1529 Henry VIII only summoned parliaments in 1510, 1512, 1515 and 1523. His first minister, Wolsey, in particular, seems to have regarded Parliament with some distaste and only one parliament (that of 1523) was called during his period of dominance (c1514–29).

LEARNING OBJECTIVES

In this chapter you will learn about:

- the relationship between Crown and Parliament during Henry VIII's reign
- the role and importance of key ministers such as Wolsey and Cromwell
- domestic policies under Henry VIII, including the establishment of the royal supremacy.

KEY QUESTION

As you read this chapter, consider the following Key Questions:

- In what ways and how effectively was England governed during this period?
- How important was the role of key individuals and groups and how were they affected by developments?

ACTIVITY

1. In pairs, using your knowledge from Chapter 7 and Extract 1, identify any key problems that you think might arise in government from Henry VIII's approach to monarchy and government.
2. As you study this chapter, consider the interpretation put forward by Eric Ives in Extract 1. At the end of the chapter, you will be asked to give your own views on whether or not his views are convincing.

CROSS-REFERENCE

The role of Parliament under Henry VII, including the granting of extraordinary revenue to enable him to wage wars and the passing of laws, is discussed in Chapter 2, pages 13–14.

Table 1 *Parliament under Henry VIII*

Parliament	Dates	Significance
1	Jan–Feb 1510	Abolished the Council Learned in the Law.
2	Feb 1512 – Mar 1514	Provided extraordinary revenue for invasions of France and Scotland; Anticlerical Act restricting benefit of clergy.
3	Feb 1515 – Dec 1515	Act restricting benefit of clergy not renewed despite the apparently anticlerical atmosphere of the House of Commons.
4	Apr 1523 – Aug 1523	Provided extraordinary revenue for invasion of France; Speaker of the House of Commons, Sir Thomas More, made the first known plea for freedom of speech for MPs. Despite Parliament's ill-temper, the level of anticlericalism seemed much reduced.
5	Nov 1529 – Apr 1536	'Reformation' Parliament.
6	Jun 1536 – Jul 1536	Called to enact a new Succession Act following the fall of Anne Boleyn.
7	Apr 1539 – Jul 1540	Called to provide extraordinary revenue with invasion threatened; produced divergent religious legislation, for example the dissolution of the greater monasteries and the Six Articles Act.
8	Jan 1542 – Mar 1544	Provided extraordinary revenue for invasions of Scotland and France; dealt once more with the issue of succession.
9	Nov 1545 – Jan 1547	Provided extraordinary revenue.

CROSS-REFERENCE

To find out more about the events in Table 1 read:

- Chapters 12 and 14 (on anticlericalism and dissolution)
- Chapters 9 (on the invasions)
- Chapter 9 (on the new Succession Act and the Six Articles Act).

In the first part of the reign it is evident that the use of Parliament by Henry VIII followed the pattern associated with his father. The primary reason for calling Parliament was to secure revenue. Wolsey seems to have been reluctant to use Parliament. On the other hand, Cromwell exploited its legislative possibilities much more thoroughly. Consequently, Parliament met much more frequently in the second half of Henry VIII's reign.

During Henry VIII's reign, governance via councils broke down for the first time because of conflict between the king's own impulsive personality and that of his more conservative councillors. It was Thomas Wolsey who came to Henry's rescue and provided the effective management of government which was required.

CROSS-REFERENCE

A conciliar government is one in which decisions are made by a council. Such a government, which Henry VIII inherited from his father, and initially continued, is discussed in Chapter 7, page 66.

To appreciate how significant Wolsey was to Henry VIII's reign in the early years, return to Chapter 7, page 65, for Wolsey's Key Profile.

Wolsey and the end of government by councils

The **conciliar** approach to government was adopted at the start of the reign, and lasted from 1509 to 1514. However, several factors combined to bring it to an end.

- Henry became disenchanted with the reluctance of some of his father's senior councillors to support a war with France.
- As he became more attuned to governing, he became increasingly his own man by asserting his undoubted right to control decision-making.
- Henry surrounded himself with like-minded young courtiers who reinforced his suspicions of the 'old guard'.
- He became particularly impressed by the organisational skills of Thomas Wolsey, whose contribution to the effective management of the French campaign earned him royal gratitude.

In the end, Wolsey, with his energy and organisational skills, emerged as the dominant political figure. He had the uncanny ability – at least in his early years – to give the king precisely what he wanted, or to convince the king of what he assumed he wanted.

Wolsey's influence was derived more from the closeness of his relationship with the king than from the formal positions he held. He complemented the king's customary 'hands-off' approach to the details of policy-making. In addition to the management of the Church and the conduct of foreign relations, Wolsey's main concerns were the legal system, the formulation of domestic policy and political decision-making.

Privy Chamber

The Privy Chamber was the one area of government which, before 1519, lay outside Wolsey's immediate control. The Privy Chamber had been established during the reign of Henry VII, but its role was extended in the early years of Henry VIII's reign when the king's 'minions' (a group of young courtiers who enjoyed Henry's personal favour) became Gentlemen of the Privy Chamber. This process transformed both their status and that of the Privy Chamber.

It was clear that, collectively, the minions distrusted Wolsey, who set himself the task of neutralising their influence. In 1519 he secured the removal of the minions and replaced them with his own supporters. However, most of the minions managed to recover their positions. The Privy Chamber thus retained some of its prestige and influence and was the one part of government which was outside Wolsey's immediate control.

CROSS-REFERENCE

To recap on the Privy Chamber and the king's household, look back to Chapter 2, pages 11–13.

For Wolsey's further attempt to curb the Privy Chamber through the Eltham Ordinances of 1526, see page 75.

Domestic policies under Wolsey (1514–29)

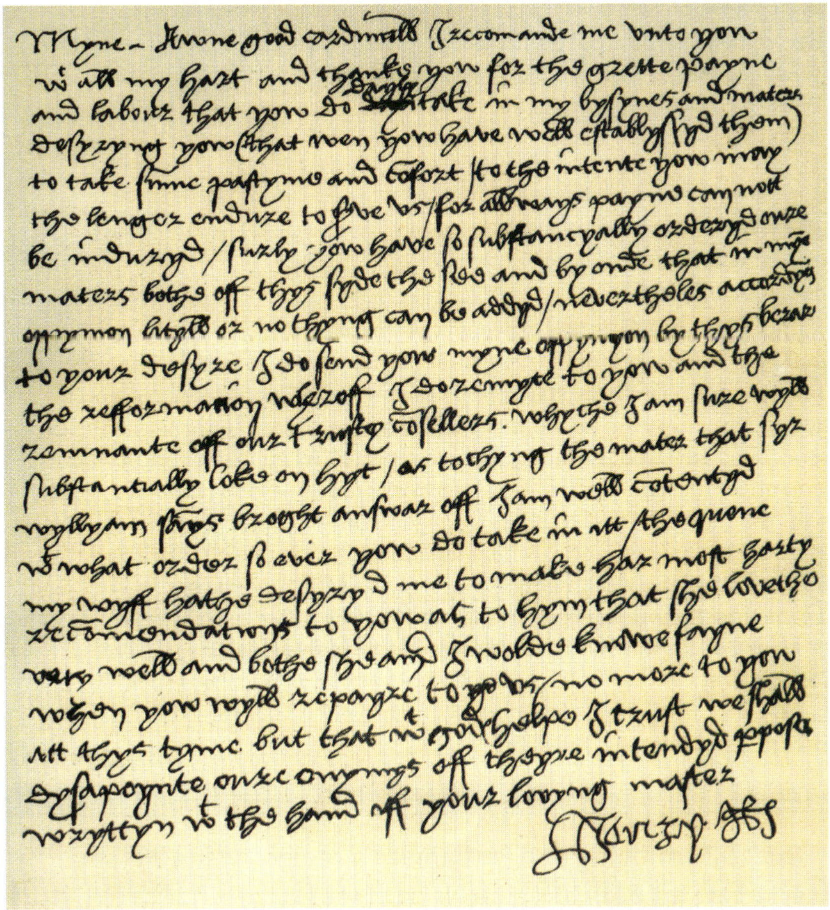

Fig. 2 *In this letter, Henry VIII thanks Wolsey for the trouble he had taken with domestic and foreign affairs, and urges him to take some 'pastime and comfort'. The letter concludes with a friendly greeting from the queen. It is evidence that the two men enjoyed a close relationship, sometimes referred to as a partnership*

Court of chancery

Wolsey was not a trained lawyer but, as Lord Chancellor he was responsible for overseeing the legal system. He had the right to preside over the court of **chancery** and he tried to use the court to uphold 'fair' justice. For example, he used the courts to deal with problems relating to enclosure, contracts and land left to others in wills. The main problem with the chancery court was that it became too popular and justice was slow since it became clogged up with too many cases.

KEY TERM

chancery: the main court of equity in the kingdom; in such courts justice was based on applying the principle of equity, i.e. fairness, rather than through a strict reading of the common law

CROSS-REFERENCE

The importance of enclosure (the system of fencing land and deeding it to specific owners) and of Wolsey's attempts to curb it are discussed more fully on page 112.

Court of Star Chamber

Wolsey's most distinctive legal contribution came through the operation of the Court of Star Chamber. This had been established by Act of Parliament in 1487, as an offshoot of the king's Council, and became the centre of both government and justice under Wolsey. Wolsey's motive in extending the use of the Star Chamber from 1516 was to increase cheap and fair justice. Wolsey heard cases of alleged misconduct by people who were dominant in their localities.

Wolsey also encouraged the use of the Star Chamber for private lawsuits. In this regard Wolsey proved too successful and he was forced to set up a series of 'overflow tribunals' to deal with the pressure of business. A permanent committee which he set up in 1519 became the ancestor of the later court of requests, whose job was to deal with cases involving the poor.

CROSS-REFERENCE

The Court of Star Chamber is introduced in Chapter 2.

ACTIVITY

Government can be divided into three parts: legislative (law-making); executive (ensuring the laws and actions are carried out) and judiciary (judging the laws). Create a chart-diagram to illustrate government in the early years of Henry VIII's reign (1509–c1530). Name the various sections and indicate their functions.

Finance

The 'Tudor subsidy'

As under Henry VII, it was expected that taxpayers, including the nobility, would provide extraordinary revenue (parliamentary taxation) when required. This was most effectively achieved by raising subsidies. Wolsey did not 'invent' the subsidy. However, he did make a substantial change in the way **subsidies** were collected – and his methods were repeated when later subsidies were demanded. Instead of using local commissioners to assess taxpayers' wealth (with the risk that they would be over-generous to the local nobility), Wolsey set up a national committee which he himself headed. With direct and realistic assessments of the wealth of taxpayers, the nation's revenue base consequently became much more realistic. In this way Wolsey raised extraordinary revenue for Henry VIII's war in France. However, the amount was insufficient. Consequently Wolsey attempted to raise unparliamentary taxation, through the so-called **'Amicable Grant'** of 1525. This led to widespread resistance, amounting almost to a rebellion.

CROSS-REFERENCE

To revise the financial position under Henry VII, look back to Chapter 2.

KEY TERM

subsidy: historically, this refers to a grant issued by Parliament to the sovereign for State needs; the 1523 subsidy imposed a tax of one shilling in the pound for land worth £50, and one shilling in the pound on personal savings and goods

Amicable Grant: in 1525 Wolsey ordered the implementation of 'Amicable Grant' to raise more money for war; in theory it was to be a freely given gift from his subjects to the king, but in reality it was a heavy tax, levied without Parliament's approval; the implications of this imposition are discussed later in this chapter

A CLOSER LOOK

The 1523 subsidy and Parliament's resistance to Wolsey

Most historians believe that Wolsey did not manage Parliament well. John Guy, for example, has described him as 'arrogant and insensitive'. This insensitivity was clear in his relationship with the 1523 Parliament, which had been called to grant the subsidy needed to finance the renewal of war against France. Instead of the broadly supportive parliaments of

Henry VII's reign, this parliament seems to have spent its time grumbling about Wolsey's financial demands, so much so that he proved unable to secure all he wanted. The atmosphere was so charged that the Speaker of the House of Commons, Sir Thomas More, felt obliged to ask the king's forgiveness for the boisterousness of some of the members, while at the same time More defended their right to express critical opinions.

CROSS-REFERENCE

Henry VIII's conflicts with France are discussed in Chapter 9.

The Eltham Ordinances

In 1526, Wolsey introduced the Eltham Ordinances in order to reform the finances of the Privy Council. In the guise of pushing forward proposals for a reduction of royal household expenditure, Wolsey secured a reduction in the number of the Gentlemen of the Privy Chamber, the one area of government over which he did not have control. Most importantly, he secured the removal of Henry's **Groom of the Stool,** Sir William Compton, replacing him with the more compliant Henry Norris.

KEY TERM

Groom of the Stool: the most intimate of an English monarch's courtiers, who became a man in whom much confidence was placed and royal secrets were shared as a matter of course

A CLOSER LOOK

The historiography of the Eltham Ordinances

The historian Peter Gwyn has argued that the purpose of the Ordinances was primarily financial; not only did several Gentlemen of the Privy Chamber lose their posts, but many more humble household servants suffered the same fate. However, according to David Starkey, the issuing of the Eltham Ordinances reflected Wolsey's fear that the Amicable Grant might make him so unpopular that he would be in danger of losing his political influence over Henry VIII.

The establishment of royal supremacy

The problems over resolving **'the King's Great Matter'** led in the short term to the downfall of Wolsey and in the longer term to the establishment of the royal supremacy. This was brought about under the direction of Wolsey's successor as chief minister, Thomas Cromwell, from 1532 by Parliament. Cromwell himself would later be destroyed on account of ensuing religious tensions and Henry's continued marital problems.

KEY TERM

the King's Great Matter: concerned the annulment of Henry VIII's marriage to Catherine of Aragon and his desire to marry Anne Boleyn; this was a complex situation which would ultimately lead to England's break from the Catholic Church.

CROSS-REFERENCE

The term 'papal dispensation' is defined on page 26, in Chapter 3.

The 'King's Great Matter'

By the mid-1520s Henry was becoming dissatisfied at the state of his marriage. Catherine, six years older than the king, was past childbearing age. Only one child, Princess Mary, had survived infancy. Henry was fearful for the kingdom should he die without a male heir. Henry even considered legitimating his son Henry Fitzroy (his son from his mistress Bessie Blount); a plan born of desperation which would have been unlikely to succeed.

To complicate matters, Henry had fallen madly in love with Anne Boleyn, the niece of Thomas Howard, the Duke of Norfolk. Anne, for her part, was unwilling to become the king's mistress (as her own sister had). Henry therefore required Wolsey to secure a papal dispensation for the **annulment** of his marriage to Catherine. This became known as 'the King's Great Matter'. It posed a major problem for Wolsey, who was faced with the task of securing the annulment.

It was in all probability Henry himself who found the biblical justification which could form the basis of an annulment; the book of Leviticus contained a prohibition on a man marrying his brother's widow. As Catherine had been very briefly married to Henry's brother Arthur, Henry argued that the papal

KEY TERM

annulment: refers to declaring something, in this case a marriage, legally invalid; it was generally accepted that only the Pope could authorise such a measure

CROSS-REFERENCE

The Duke of Norfolk served Henry VIII over a long period. He was also the uncle of two of Henry's wives: Anne Boleyn and Catherine Howard. More details are in Chapter 7, page 68.

Fig. 3 *Anne Boleyn*

CROSS-REFERENCE

The emperor was the elected head of the Holy Roman Empire. Return to Chapter 3, page 25, where this is covered in more detail.

dispensation issued by Julius II to permit his own marriage to Catherine was invalid. He claimed that in God's eyes his marriage was still illegal and that he was therefore free to marry Anne.

There was a fundamental problem with this argument. Catherine claimed that her marriage to Prince Arthur had never been consummated and that therefore the biblical ban did not apply. However, Henry insisted that Wolsey seek a dispensation for annulment based on the Levitican argument anyway.

A CLOSER LOOK

The papacy and the emperor in 1527

In normal circumstances the Pope might have been prepared to issue a dispensation for annulment – for the right fee. However, Pope Clement VII was not in a position to do so, for on 6 May 1527 Rome had been sacked by the troops of the Emperor Charles V and the Pope was in effect the emperor's prisoner. The emperor, Catherine's nephew, was not prepared to see his family insulted.

In May 1527 Wolsey used his power as the personal representative of the Pope to bring Henry before a fake court to 'accuse' him of living in sin with his supposed wife, a fault which Henry readily admitted. Catherine refused to accept the court's verdict and, in accordance with **canon law** (church law), appealed to the Pope.

Fig. 4 *This painting by Marcus Stone (1840–1921) depicts the rivalry between Catherine of Aragon and Anne Boleyn. Catherine, standing in a doorway, watches the king and Anne flirt. The little dog is an ironic touch because it represents fidelity*

The fall of Wolsey

Wolsey was only too aware that his own fate depended on securing an annulment. The Pope was aware of Wolsey's situation but all he could do was play for time, which simply increased Henry's frustration. After two years of fruitless diplomacy (1527–29) the Pope sent an envoy, Cardinal Campeggio, to hear the case along with Wolsey. This hearing opened in London on 15 June 1529, but Campeggio adjourned it on 30 July, thereby sealing Wolsey's fate: he had failed to give Henry his annulment.

Wolsey's fall, though sudden, was not entirely unexpected. He was already unpopular for forcing the 1523 subsidy through Parliament and imposing the Amicable Grant. Former associates had been distancing themselves from him. In October 1529 he was charged with **praemunire** and surrendered himself, with all of his possessions, including the sumptuous Hampton Court, to the king. On 4 November 1530 he was arrested. It was clear that the intention was that Wolsey should be tried and executed, but he cheated the executioner's axe and died at Leicester Abbey on 29 November.

KEY TERM

***praemunire*:** a parliamentary statute enacted in 1393 to prevent papal interference in the rights of the Crown to make appointments to Church office

ACTIVITY

Re-enact Catherine's tribunal, with members of the class taking the parts of Catherine, Henry, Wolsey and Campeggio. Shakespeare's version of the event can be found in *Henry VIII*, Act 2, Scene 4.

A CLOSER LOOK

The historiography of Thomas Wolsey

Wolsey's career has been the subject of much debate. Contemporary judgements were hostile. Polydore Vergil, writing after his fall, claimed that he 'aroused against himself the hatred of the whole country'. The poet John Skelton claimed that 'Hampton Court hath the pre-eminence'; in other words, it was more important than the king's court and was therefore a monument to Wolsey's arrogance. For many years his standing among historians was poor, though much of the evidence against Wolsey came from his enemies. More recently, historians have become more willing to acknowledge Wolsey's qualities. John Guy considers him England's most gifted administrator for over 300 years, although he tempers that judgement with criticisms.

KEY PROFILE

Fig. 5 *Thomas Cromwell, painted by Hans Holbein in around 1532–34*

Thomas Cromwell (c1485–1540) rose from a humble background to become a lawyer and secretary to Wolsey and then principal secretary to Henry VIII. It was Cromwell who suggested Henry place himself as head of an English Church; he masterminded the dissolution of the monasteries but later fell from favour and was executed at the Tower of London on 28 July 1540.

Domestic policies under Cromwell (1532–40)

Conciliar government continued for nearly three years following the fall of Wolsey, though with no sign that the 'King's Great Matter' might be resolved. It was the emergence of **Thomas Cromwell** which brought this phase of conciliar government to an end. Cromwell had advanced his career under Wolsey and, following the cardinal's death, he rose swiftly, not least because of his proposal to enable Henry to secure his marriage annulment. He suggested that Henry make a break with Rome and place himself as head of an English Church. By 1532, he was the king's chief minister.

Although Cromwell never had the range of influence enjoyed by Wolsey, he came to dominate royal government for the rest of the 1530s, much to the annoyance of the Duke of Norfolk, who was hostile to Cromwell's religious reforms.

Parliament's role in government developed during the years 1529 to 1536 when the so-called 'Reformation Parliament' was in session. The initial reason for calling another parliament – dealing with Wolsey – died along with the minister in 1530. After this, its attention was turned towards Henry's divorce and the Church.

The divorce from Catherine of Aragon and its impact on the Church

Ultimately, both the divorce and the break with Rome were accomplished through the use of statute law (Acts of Parliament), whose supremacy over canon law (the law of the Church) was firmly established.

Exploiting weaknesses in the Church

The fact that the Church had become weaker in a number of aspects made Cromwell's task easier:

- The Catholic Church as an institution had been weakened by the **humanist** criticisms of Colet and Erasmus and the anticlerical satire of Simon Fish.
- The Church's claims to *legal* supremacy had been challenged in 1528 by the lawyer Christopher St German, who asserted the superiority of English law over the canon law of the Church. This helped to prepare the way for the parliamentary attack on the Church's power, which was masterminded by Cromwell.
- Henry had been supplied with more intellectual justifications by means of the ***Collectanea Satis Copiosa***. This was a collection of historical documents compiled by two Cambridge theologians, **Thomas Cranmer** and Edward Foxe, which looked to justify the king's divorce on the basis of legal and historical principles.
- To add to the pressure on the papacy, Henry had sought and received expert opinions on his marital situation from a number of continental universities, some of which were favourable to his position. The king himself humiliated the Lord Chancellor Sir Thomas More by requiring him to present these favourable opinions to both houses of Parliament.

CROSS-REFERENCE

Humanism, including the ideas of Colet and Erasmus, is discussed in chapters 6 and 12, and the anticlerical satire of Simon Fish is covered in Chapter 12.

Thomas Cranmer, who later became Archbishop of Canterbury, is profiled on page 79.

A CLOSER LOOK

In compiling the ***Collectanea Satis Copiosa***, Cranmer and Foxe had, according to the historian John Guy, 'redefined the boundaries between royal and ecclesiastical power' by asserting that kings of England had always enjoyed both a secular and spiritual authority over the Church.

Pressurising the Pope

Henry and Cromwell had tried to pressurise the Pope in a number of ways.

	Measure	Significance
1531	Clergy collectively accused of *praemunire* and fined	This began a sustained attack on the clergy and forced from the clergy an acknowledgement that the king was 'Protector and Supreme head of the English Church' so far as 'the law of Christ allowed'.
1532	Act in Conditional Restraint of **Annates**	This was designed to increase pressure on the papacy by withholding conditionally the first year's income from the office of bishop which the papacy had traditionally enjoyed.
1532	House of Commons **Supplication against the Ordinaries**	This was designed to increase anticlerical pressure within the House of Commons.
1532	Formal **submission of the clergy** to Henry VIII	This provoked the resignation of Sir Thomas More as Lord Chancellor

KEY TERM

annates: revenue paid to the Pope by a bishop or other cleric on his appointment; they were effectively church taxes collected in England and sent to Rome and were also known as the 'First Fruits' (*primitiae* in Latin), a concept which dates back to earlier Greek, Roman, and Hebrew religions

Supplication against the Ordinaries: a supplication was a form of petition; in this case it was addressed to the king by the House of Commons and directed against alleged abuses of *ordinary* jurisdiction, i.e. the jurisdiction exercised in church law by archbishops and bishops

submission of the clergy: this was the formal surrender of the Church's independent law-making function

Henry's marriage to Anne Boleyn

It was Anne Boleyn who forced the annulment issue. She took matters into her own hands by finally consenting to have sexual relations with Henry. In doing so she was gambling that by becoming pregnant she would force him to take decisive action. This would require open defiance of the Pope by both Henry and the authorities of the English Church. Henry's path was eased by the death of the Archbishop of Canterbury, **William Warham**. He was replaced by **Thomas Cranmer**, who received his authority from Rome but would also become a leader of the Reformation. This was just as well for Henry as it was known by December 1532 that Anne was pregnant. The couple married in a secret ceremony on 25 January 1533. According to the Catholic Church the marriage was invalid.

The former marriage of Henry and Catherine was annulled in May 1533 by Archbishop Cranmer, and Anne was crowned shortly afterwards. Her child was born – legitimate in English law – on 7 September, but to Henry's grief it was a girl, the Princess Elizabeth. The problem of the succession had not been solved.

Acts of Parliament (1533–34)

From 1533 onwards Cromwell passed a series of measures to achieve the break from Rome and establish royal supremacy.

- **The Act in Restraint of Appeals** was drafted expertly by Cromwell in April 1533 and founded on the evidence in the *Collectanea*. The preamble to the Act declared that the monarch possessed an **imperial jurisdiction** which was not subject to any foreign power (i.e. the papacy). The act declared that appeals could not be made to Rome regarding Church court decisions 'in causes matrimonial' and other areas. The Act meant that Catherine could not appeal to Rome against her marriage annulment.
- **The Act of Supremacy** (November 1534) gave legislative force to the royal supremacy. It stated that 'the king's majesty justly and rightfully is and oweth to be the Supreme Head of the Church of England'. This act effectively accomplished the break from Rome.
- The legal basis for the enforcement of the break with Rome was also strengthened.
- The **Act of Succession** (April 1534) declared that:
  - Henry's marriage to Catherine was void
  - the succession should be vested in the children of his marriage to Anne
  - to deny the validity of Henry's marriage to Anne was treasonable
  - an oath should be taken to affirm an individual's acceptance of the new marriage.
- The **Treason Act** (November 1534) was tightened so that treason could be committed by the spoken word as well as by deed or writing and so that it was treasonable to describe the king as 'heretic, schismatic, tyrant, infidel or usurper of the Crown'.

A CLOSER LOOK

The **Treason Act** has been seen as savage by some historians, though Geoffrey Elton and Steven Gunn have both defended its application, the latter suggesting that its use was fairly selective and that the authorities had no real interest in prosecuting ordinary people who had made incautious remarks about the royal supremacy. On the other hand, the Treason Act was used to ensnare some high-profile victims, the most eminent of whom was **Sir Thomas More**, who was convicted and executed in July 1535 for denying the royal supremacy.

KEY PROFILE

William Warham (c1450–1532) was Archbishop of Canterbury from 1503 and a councillor under Henry VII. He lost political influence under Henry VIII.

Thomas Cranmer (1489–1556) was a Cambridge academic, who came to Henry VIII's attention through the *Collectanea Satis Copiosa*. He later became Archbishop of Canterbury, and always enjoyed Henry VIII's personal confidence, though his relationship with the Duke of Northumberland in Edward VI's reign was uneasy (see Chapter 14). He was burnt for heresy under the Catholic Queen Mary I.

KEY TERM

imperial jurisdiction: official powers to make legal decisions and judgements belonged to the king and could not be challenged by the Church or any other power

CROSS-REFERENCE

Sir Thomas More had once been a valued councillor to Henry VIII, as discussed in Chapter 7, page 64.

- **The Act Annexing First Fruits and Tenths to the Crown** (November 1534) was a typically cynical move by Henry and Cromwell. The Annates paid by a bishop, which had been 'intolerable' when paid to the Pope, now became perfectly acceptable when paid to the king. This Act increased the financial burden on the clergy, and strengthened the royal supremacy.

By 1534, the relationship between England and Rome which had endured for almost a millennium had been smashed to pieces. Royal supremacy over the Church had been created. Despite the assertion made in the Act of Supremacy that the king's role was recognised by the clergy, the supremacy had come about largely by means of parliamentary statute. In the process, Parliament's role as a law-making body had been strengthened. Henry now had control over the Church in England, and religious policies would essentially be based on royal whim.

The most important such policy was the dissolution of the monasteries. Begun in 1536 and completed by 1542, the dissolution ensured that a vast amount of the Church's land was confiscated by the Crown. This significantly increased the wealth and therefore the power of the Crown. However, the benefit to Henry was short-lived as much of the property was granted away or sold, often below the market price, so that the Crown could raise money to finance its foreign policy.

CROSS-REFERENCE

The dissolution of the monasteries is covered in detail in Chapter 12.

Henry's expensive foreign policy is discussed in Chapter 9.

The fall of Anne Boleyn

At first Queen Anne was a considerable advocate of Church reform. Indeed, as Eric Ives has pointed out, she had been responsible for helping to push the king in a more Protestant direction. But relations between Anne and Cromwell publicly broke down. Cromwell was insecure enough to feel that his relationship with the king, as well as his life, was threatened. He therefore allied with the conservatives and together they persuaded Henry that Anne's flirtatious manner had led to adultery. Anne's downfall was sudden and spectacular. Always a target for the conservatives, she was rendered more vulnerable when Catherine of Aragon died in January 1536. Accused of adultery (and also incest), which for the wife of the monarch constituted treason, she was executed in 19 May 1536. In Catholic eyes Henry was now a widower and free to remarry, and he already had his eye on one of Anne's ladies-in-waiting, **Jane Seymour**.

KEY PROFILE

Jane Seymour (c1509–37)

A lady-in-waiting to both Catherine of Aragon and Anne Boleyn, Jane's demure personality appealed to Henry, who had wearied of Anne's feisty sophistication. She and Henry married on 30 May 1536, and she gave birth to Prince Edward on 12 September 1537 but died on 24 October from complications after childbirth.

EXTRACT 2

That the reign of Henry VIII was enormously significant is beyond question. His rejection of western Christendom in favour of a national Church, the innovative use of statute law and the resulting change on the qualitative role and importance of Parliament, all these left a deeper mark on English history than any monarch since the Norman conquest and any who followed him. Even more profound has been the consequence of Henry's decision to require, for the first time ever, that subjects should accept belief as defined by the State. From that point on it ceased to be sufficient any longer to offer the Crown loyalty and ability; the monarch needed to search hearts. Ideological conformity and nonconformity became substantial and permanent features of English life.

Adapted from Eric W. Ives, 'Henry VIII' in *Oxford Dictionary of National Biography*, 2004

The fall of Thomas Cromwell

By 1540 Cromwell's influence was declining. However, the catalyst for his downfall, as with Wolsey, was his failure to manage the king's marital affairs satisfactorily. In 1537 Henry's third wife, Jane Seymour, had died, after giving birth to the long-awaited male heir, Prince Edward. In 1540 Cromwell had tried to reconcile Henry with the League of Schmalkalden, an organisation of German princes and free cities within the Holy Roman Empire who supported the reformer Martin Luther and his rejection of the Catholic Church, by arranging a marriage with a German

Protestant princess, Anne of Cleves. This was an unhappy partnership on multiple levels: Anne proved unsuitable to Henry personally, and the match had become unwelcome politically. The marriage was quickly annulled, destroying what remained of Cromwell's credibility with the king.

This gave his enemies, led by the Duke of Norfolk, the chance to bring about his downfall. Norfolk was once again aided by having a niece, the Catholic Catherine Howard, at court and conveniently free to wed the king. Cromwell was accused of treason and heresy at a Council meeting and was executed on 28 July 1540. Henry and Catherine married on the same day.

Two days later, the message that the Protestant Reformation cause was in tatters was reinforced by the burning for heresy of three Protestant theologians. Henry, however, demonstrated his even-handedness by ensuring the execution on the same day of three Catholic priests, who had been imprisoned for six years, for treason in denying the royal supremacy.

CROSS-REFERENCE

The German religious reformer and theologian Martin Luther, and his influence on the development of the Protestant Church, is discussed in more detail in Chapter 12, page 119.

Fig. 6 *Henry VIII saw a painting of Anne of Cleves and liked what he saw. However, he did not like what he saw when they later met in person*

A CLOSER LOOK

The historiography of Thomas Cromwell

To many historians Cromwell was a grubby and unprincipled operator who was happy to do the king's dirty work. Geoffrey Elton attempted in 1953 to rehabilitate him, seeing him as the architect of the Tudor revolution in government, in which English government was transformed from the amateurish and medieval to the professional and modern. Few current historians now accept Elton's argument and a more subtle view of Cromwell has emerged as an effective, though occasionally unscrupulous, administrator and skilful lawyer who was a convinced religious reformer. His most important achievement was bringing about the break with Rome and securing for Henry VIII the royal supremacy over the English Church.

Government in Henry VIII's last years (1540–47)

The major political implication of the conservative revival of 1539 to 1540 was that a form of conciliar government was restored. It was, however, a different form of government, as the fall of Cromwell saw the emergence of a Privy Council with fixed membership, supported by a secretary who kept a formal record of proceedings. There is some debate as to the actual amount of power wielded by the king. On the one hand, he is seen as being firmly in control; on the other hand, he is seen by some historians as essentially weak and prey to the factions which existed at court. In 1540, however, power, at least temporarily, lay with the conservatives in the Council such as Norfolk, **Stephen Gardiner** and **Thomas Wriothesley**. Once again, however, it was the problems created by Henry's marital issues which helped shift the balance of power.

ACTIVITY

Thinking point

How successful was Thomas Cromwell as a minister? In groups or pairs discuss your judgements of Cromwell and back up your response with evidence.

KEY PROFILE

Stephen Gardiner (c1495–1555), having progressed initially in the service of Wolsey, became principal secretary to Henry VIII and then bishop of Winchester. He supported the break with Rome, but retained conservative Catholic views. This led to his imprisonment under Edward VI, but he returned to favour under Mary I.

Thomas Wriothesley (1505–50) owed his advancement to Cromwell's patronage. He was appointed joint principal secretary in 1540, survived Cromwell's downfall and attached himself to the conservative Gardiner. He was appointed Lord Chancellor in 1544. A slippery figure, he again switched sides when involved in the downfall of Norfolk in 1546.

The execution of Catherine Howard and Henry's marriage to Katherine Parr

In his eagerness to benefit politically from a marriage between his family and the king, Norfolk had overlooked the unfortunate fact that his niece Catherine Howard, despite her youthfulness, was already sexually experienced. To make matters worse there were allegations of an affair between Catherine and her distant cousin, Thomas Culpepper. The whole business devastated Henry. Catherine and her lady of the bedchamber were executed for treason on 13 February 1542. Several of Catherine's relatives were also implicated and disgraced.

Although Norfolk managed to extricate himself from the whole affair, he was wounded politically. His problems were reinforced when Henry chose as his sixth wife the Protestant Katherine Parr. Norfolk was fully aware of the danger which Katherine, as a Protestant, posed to his ambitions and tried unsuccessfully to embroil her in accusations of heresy.

KEY PROFILE

Edward Seymour (c1500–52), Marquis of Hertford and later Duke of Somerset, was the brother of Henry VIII's third wife, Jane Seymour, and therefore the uncle of Edward VI. A soldier, he became politically very influential towards the end of Henry's reign and was Lord Protector to Edward before his own downfall in 1549.

Political rivalries and the death of Henry VIII

As the king's health began to deteriorate, political rivalries intensified: whoever was most influential in the king's last months was likely to be in a position to dominate under his successor. In this battle, Norfolk's rival **Edward Seymour** could play his trump card as the uncle of Jane Seymour's son, the male heir to the throne. Norfolk was also compromised by the overambitious arrogance of his son Henry Howard, Earl of Surrey, who threatened the king's throne and was executed for treason. The dying king consented to Norfolk's death, but Norfolk was spared the axe by the king's death on 28 January 1547; the new Council did not want to inaugurate the reign with bloodshed. Norfolk remained a prisoner in the Tower for the whole of young Edward VI's reign.

Henry VIII's government: a summary

Henry VIII had reigned for almost 38 tumultuous years. Some aspects of the reign, particularly the marital politics, read almost like a sixteenth-century soap opera. Nevertheless, the reign changed England permanently, though how much for better or for worse might be debated. Historians' judgements on the reign have varied enormously. The king can be seen negatively as a bloated and unpredictable tyrant who destroyed much of what was positive about English life, or positively as the embodiment of an English national identity and the person responsible for transformational and necessary change.

EXTRACT 3

Throughout his reign Henry kept an eye on some details and dealt with some business, but he never did enough of either to save himself from having to follow the lead given by his ministers. He delegated power in the confidence that he could rely on his advisers and agents; he knew he could always discard the policy with the minister. His attitude to business shows that he was wise enough to realise that there are other things in life. But the evidence is strong that while a minister held power it was he and not the king who controlled and devised policy. In the hands of Henry VIII personal monarchy did not mean personal attention to the business of government. It meant the putting of the king's personal force behind policies not of his devising. It is doubtful if he was the architect of anything, least of all the English Reformation.

Adapted from Geoffrey R. Elton, *Henry VIII*, 1962

A LEVEL **PRACTICE QUESTION**

Evaluating historical extracts

Using your understanding of the historical context, assess how convincing the arguments in Extracts 1, 2 and 3 are, in relation to Henry VIII's rule in England.

STUDY TIP

All these extracts consider to what extent Henry VIII was successful as a ruler. In order to assess whether or not you find their interpretations convincing, it would be helpful to clarify the contexts in which you might evaluate success and split the reign into manageable sub-periods about which to make interim judgements.

ACTIVITY

Summary chart

Divide into small groups to decide whether or not Henry VIII was well served by his ministers.

	Quality of service	Supporting evidence
1509–14 Conciliar government (see also Chapter 7)		
1514–29 Wolsey		
1529–32 Conciliar government		
1532–40 Cromwell		
1540–47 Conciliar government		

AS LEVEL **PRACTICE QUESTION**

'Henry VIII was content to allow ministers to "rule" for him.' Explain why you agree or disagree with this view with reference to the years 1526 to 1547.

STUDY TIP

Henry was content to let Wolsey and Cromwell rule for him. However, the former was losing influence in 1539 to 1540. It is important, therefore, to consider why Henry ceased to be 'content' with Wolsey and Cromwell and why he avoided having a chief minister from 1529 to 1532 and again from 1540 to 1547.

9 Foreign relations and securing the succession

Foreign relations

EXTRACT 1

In foreign affairs, where Henry was most continuously and most personally active, he followed the devices and desires of his own heart. Before 1527 his object was to establish his credentials as a monarch of European standing. From 1527 policy became dominated by the 'King's Great Matter' and the need to protect the action he had taken. In the 1540s, the revival of Henry's personal obsession with winning territory in France led him to mishandle opportunities.

Adapted from Eric W. Ives, 'Henry VIII' in *Oxford Dictionary of National Biography*, 2004

ACTIVITY

With reference to Extract 1 list the stages by which Henry's foreign policy evolved. As you read this chapter find examples of actions to accompany each stage.

LEARNING OBJECTIVES

In this chapter you will learn about:

- England's relations with Scotland and other foreign powers
- Henry VIII's securing of the succession.

KEY QUESTION

As you read this chapter, consider the following Key Questions:

- How did relations with foreign powers change and how was the succession secured?
- How important was the role of key individuals and groups and how were they affected by developments?

Foreign policy 1509–14

Henry VIII's reign began with a conflict of interests between the king and some of the councillors whom he had inherited from his father. His councillors sought a continuation of peace and, indeed, negotiated the renewal of the **Treaty of Etaples** in 1510. At the same time it was evident that Henry was thinking along different lines. He signalled his intentions early by commissioning a translation of the life of his warlike predecessor Henry V. He sent Christopher Bainbridge, Archbishop of York, to Rome to persuade the Pope, Julius II, to enter an alliance against the French. This bore fruit with the creation of the Holy League, which joined England, Spain, the Holy Roman Empire, Venice and the Papacy in an anti-French alliance.

What Henry did not realise was the extent to which he was being used by his shrewd father-in-law, Ferdinand of Aragon, and the Holy Roman Emperor, Maximilian I. In 1512 Henry sent a substantial army of 10,000 men to southwest France under the command of the Marquis of Dorset. However, this achieved nothing, and was used by Ferdinand as a diversionary tactic while he successfully conquered Navarre.

In 1513 Henry himself led a force to northeastern France. This was successful not only in winning the 'Battle of the Spurs' (in reality little more than a skirmish but claimed in propaganda to be a stunning victory) but also in capturing the towns of Thérouanne and Tournai. How much all of this mattered can be debated. To Geoffrey Elton it was nothing more than a futile sideshow.

Perhaps to Henry VIII's private dismay, much more important was the Anglo-Scottish conflict at the Battle of Flodden in September 1513. King James IV had crossed the border with a substantial force, but was defeated by a smaller English army hurriedly put together and capably led by the veteran soldier, the Earl of Surrey. James himself was killed, along with much of the Scottish nobility. This left the throne of Scotland in the hands of the infant James V, but Henry VIII did little to build on the advantage which Flodden had given him. Nothing was gained from Henry's military adventures of 1513:

- The war was very costly and Henry was forced to liquidate assets inherited from his father to pay for it.
- In a rerun of the problems of 1489, there were rumblings about the taxation in **Yorkshire**, which only narrowly failed to turn into a full-scale revolt.
- The renegotiated French pension was lost.

CROSS-REFERENCE

To recap on Henry VII's relations with France and Scotland, look back to Chapter 3.

KEY CHRONOLOGY

Foreign policy 1509–14

1510	Renewal of Treaty of Etaples
1512	First invasion of France
1513	Second invasion of France and war against Scotland
1513 September	Battle of Flodden

CROSS-REFERENCE

The Treaty of Etaples, signed in 1492, is outlined in Chapter 3, page 24.

CROSS-REFERENCE

The Yorkshire Rebellion of 1489 is outlined in Chapter 4, pages 39–40.

- Tournai was eventually sold back to the French for rather less than the English had paid to repair its defences after the siege.

A further campaign was contemplated in 1514, but it was quickly abandoned once Ferdinand and Maximilian each made a separate peace with France. It was left to Wolsey to pick up the pieces, which he did with considerable skill, recovering the Etaples pension and securing a marriage alliance between Henry's younger sister, Mary, and the much older king of France, Louis XII.

KEY CHRONOLOGY

English foreign policy, 1514–26

1514	Marriage of Louis XII of France and Princess Mary, sister of Henry VIII
1515	Death of Louis XII; succeeded by Francis I
1516	Death of Ferdinand of Aragon Treaty of Noyon establishing peace between Spain and France
1517	Treaty of Cambrai establishing peace between the Holy Roman Empire and France Duke of Albany, heir presumptive to Scottish throne, sent by Francis to Scotland to stir up trouble between Scotland and England
1518	Treaty of London establishing general European peace
1519	King Charles of Spain elected Holy Roman Emperor
1520	Field of the Cloth of Gold
1521	Treaty of Bruges between England and the emperor, Charles V
1522	England at war with France
1525	Charles V victorious over the French at the Battle of Pavia Peace with France
1526	England linked with anti-Imperial League of Cognac

Foreign policy, 1514–26

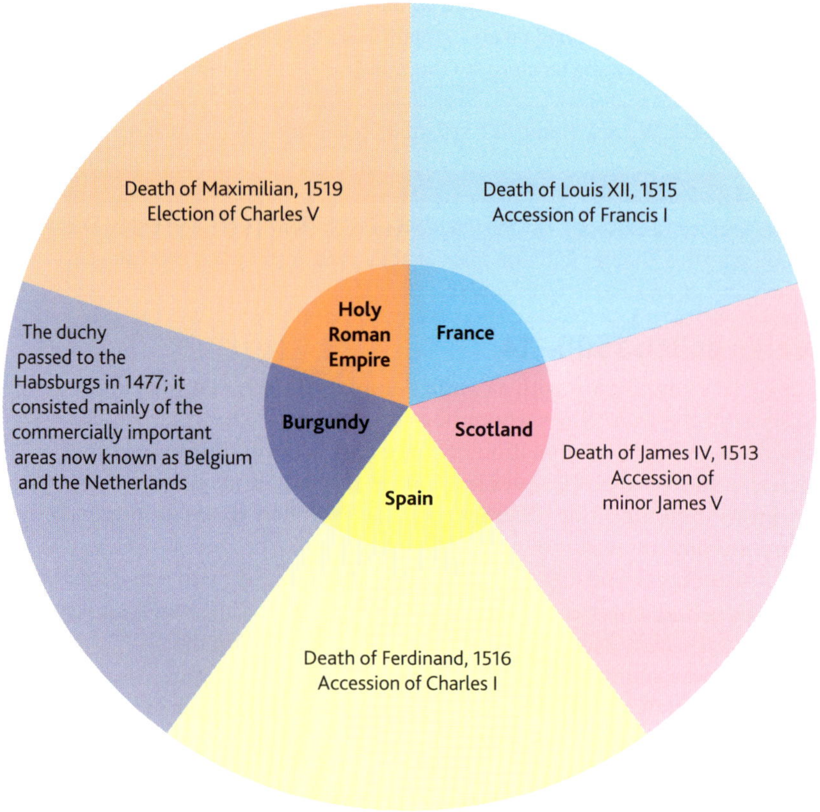

Fig. 1 *The main players in foreign relations, 1514–26*

There is no really clear theme to the foreign policy pursued by Henry and Wolsey from late 1514 to 1526. Alliances were made – and just as quickly broken. However, three points can be made about the basis of policy making at this time.

1. England remained a relatively minor power and could not really compete on level terms with the major powers of France and Spain.
2. Henry significantly overestimated English power. Wolsey then had to frame the details of foreign policy based on that false assumption.
3. The 'auld alliance' between France and Scotland remained strong. Consequently, when England and France were on amicable terms there tended to be few issues with Anglo-Scottish relations. On the other hand, clashes between England and France almost always led to increased tension between England and Scotland.

By the end of 1514 Henry VIII had run out of money to continue a warlike foreign policy. This had two major consequences.

1. He was unable to exploit the weakness of Scotland following the death of James IV at Flodden.
2. He sought peace with France, the settlement being reinforced by the marriage of his younger sister Mary to the French king, Louis XII. The marriage, however, was short-lived.

A CLOSER LOOK

The marriage of Louis XII and Princess Mary

The marriage ceremony took place on 9 October 1514. However, there was a considerable disparity between the ages of the young princess and her husband. Louis XII died on 1 January 1515, amid much gossip and innuendo about the cause of his death. Within weeks Mary had remarried; the fact that her second husband was the Duke of Suffolk denied her brother the opportunity to use her a second time for diplomatic purposes. The king considered himself dishonoured by the secrecy of the whole business and it was some time before he was reconciled with his favourite sister and the man who had hitherto been his closest friend.

The death of Louis XII left the French throne in the hands of **Francis I**, a charismatic young king whom Henry immediately saw as a personal, as well as a political, rival. His immediate response was to seek an alliance with Ferdinand of Aragon. However, Ferdinand died in 1516 and his grandson and successor, **Charles V**, sought an alliance with the French. In the following year Charles and his other grandfather, the Emperor Maximilian, agreed the Treaty of Cambrai with the French, leaving England dangerously isolated.

One consequence of that isolation was that it offered Francis I the opportunity to undermine Anglo-Scottish relations. He was able to do this because the Duke of Albany, **heir presumptive** to the Scottish throne, was, in fact, a member of the French nobility. Albany was able to consolidate his position by being appointed as regent to the Scottish throne. This alarmed Henry and Wolsey who saw Albany simply as a French agent. However, any threat from Albany was minimised because of poisonous divisions among the Scottish nobility. On the other hand, Henry showed himself incapable of exploiting divisions and weaknesses within Scotland.

Wolsey was successful in ending England's isolation very quickly and with the Treaty of London in 1518 he emerged as the leading diplomat in western Europe. Prompted by Pope Leo X, who desired a united Christian front against what he saw as the threat of the Ottoman Turks, this treaty had its origins in the peace negotiations between England and France. However, its scope widened and eventually it became a 'treaty of perpetual peace', a non-aggression pact agreed to by England, France, Spain, the Holy Roman Empire and numerous smaller states. Future conflicts would suggest that the treaty was essentially meaningless. That is not how it appeared, however, in the immediate aftermath of its signing. Firstly it was a diplomatic coup for Wolsey; secondly, the Pope's need for a united Christian front meant that he appointed Wolsey as **papal legate** over England. In 1518 Wolsey was undoubtedly at the height of his power and prestige as Henry VIII's chief minister.

ACTIVITY

Produce a piece of writing, in the form of a newspaper article, commenting on the Treaty of London and on Wolsey's role in its formulation.

The newfound friendship between England and France continued. England agreed to return Tournai to France, but the French once again agreed to pay the English a pension to compensate for its loss. In addition, the French agreed to keep Albany out of Scotland, which ensured more peaceable relations on the Anglo-Scottish border. The French, in particular, were concerned about the increased power which Spain could exert with the election of

KEY PROFILE

Fig. 2 *Francis I of France*

Francis I (1494–1547) reigned from 1515 to 1547. He and Henry were intense personal rivals. However, at times they were willing to ally, because of their shared suspicion of Emperor Charles V.

Charles V (1500–58) was successively Duke of Burgundy, King of Spain from 1516 to 1556 and Holy Roman Emperor from 1519 to 1556. This made him the dominant ruler in western Europe. He was the nephew of Henry VIII's first wife, Catherine of Aragon.

KEY TERM

heir presumptive: the person who is first in line of succession but whose position could be displaced by a new heir with a better claim; in this case, Albany would cease to be first in line for the throne once the infant James V of Scotland had a legitimate child as an heir

papal legate: the personal representative of the Pope; being appointed papal legate gave Wolsey control over the English Church and meant that he had superior status to the Archbishop of Canterbury

the Spanish king to the post of Holy Roman Emperor and this, rather than Wolsey's diplomatic brilliance, encouraged the French change of attitude. The improbably good relations between France and England were reinforced by the most extravagant and expensive diplomatic encounter of the period, the **Field of the Cloth of Gold** in June 1520.

Fig. 3 *The Field of the Cloth of Gold, 1520*

CROSS-REFERENCE

For Parliament's resistance to granting extraordinary revenue in 1523, look back to Chapter 8, pages 74–75.

CROSS-REFERENCE

The Amicable Grant is outlined in Chapter 8, page 74; the controversy surrounding it is covered in detail in Chapter 10.

CROSS-REFERENCE

The 'King's Great Matter' is discussed in Chapter 8.

ACTIVITY

Prepare a group presentation on Wolsey's conduct of foreign policy from either a broadly supportive perspective or from a hostile perspective.

A CLOSER LOOK

The **Field of the Cloth of Gold** is the name given to a meeting which took place over more than two weeks in June 1520 between Henry VIII and Francis I. The location was in France, but quite close to the town of Calais which was held by the English. Each king, accompanied by a large retinue, set up a base in a lavishly decorated pavilion which was used for dining and entertainment. The hospitality was sumptuous, but the event lost some of its attraction in Henry's eyes because he was defeated by Francis in a wrestling match. It has been estimated that the event cost Henry's royal treasury about £15,000.

In diplomatic terms nothing was really achieved by the Field of the Cloth of Gold. Conflict arose between Francis I and Charles V and in August 1521 Wolsey negotiated the Treaty of Bruges with Charles. Henry had compelling motives to side with Charles:

- He could improve his relations with the Pope, who was anxious to reduce French control over northern Italy.
- He believed that he might gain more territory within France.
- Part of the deal entailed a marriage alliance between the emperor and Henry's young daughter, the Princess Mary.

Consequently, English armies invaded northern France in both 1522 and 1523. The campaigns gained little but proved costly, with Parliament proving reluctant to grant the extraordinary revenue necessary to cover the costs.

Henry showed his lack of strategic awareness by the crass way in which he attempted to benefit from the emperor's crushing defeat of the French at the **Battle of Pavia** in 1525, suggesting to Charles that they launch a joint invasion of northern France in order to achieve territorial gains. Historian Peter Gwyn considers that England's contribution to the Imperial triumph was paltry. In such a context it was no surprise that Charles would not agree to this. Moreover, the controversy over the Amicable Grant showed that there was a lack of public support for the adventure. This episode had three major consequences:

- Henry, his ego bruised, was obliged to back down.
- His resentment towards the emperor was reinforced when Charles repudiated his marriage contract with Princess Mary.
- Wolsey's domestic prestige never really recovered from the episode.

A CLOSER LOOK

The **Battle of Pavia** was a crucial moment in the recurring conflict of the Italian Wars which lasted from 1494 to 1559 and which regularly involved conflict between France on the one hand, and Spain and the Holy Roman Empire on the other. Both sides saw Italy as their main strategic focus. In this context, therefore, England was merely a sideshow. The battle was particularly important because Francis I was captured and held captive for a time by Charles V.

The fracturing of the Anglo-Imperial alliance led Henry and Wolsey once more in the direction of a pro-French foreign policy. This became most evident when Henry lent support to the League of Cognac, which had been put together by the Pope in order to counterbalance what he considered to be the excessive power of the emperor in northern Italy following his victory at Pavia. This proved not to be the best time to be on poor terms with the emperor, and the emergence of the problems created by the 'King's Great Matter' created a new complication in foreign policy which not even a politician as skilful as Wolsey could resolve. In the process it would not only bring down Wolsey; it would also make Henry an object of suspicion to the whole of Catholic Europe.

Foreign policy, 1527–40

The failure of Henry VIII to resolve his 'Great Matter' by diplomatic means emphasises the extent to which England remained a relatively minor power in Europe. Henry and Wolsey were forced by their weak position to make an anti-Imperial alliance with the French at the Treaty of Amiens in 1527. Wolsey sought to pressurise the emperor by imposing a trade embargo with the Burgundian lands, but Charles's retaliation created widespread unemployment and social problems in England, forcing Wolsey to back down. Moreover, Charles V's strength, as exemplified by his victory over the French at the Battle of Landriano in 1529, and his dominance over the Pope, as demonstrated by the Peace of Cambrai in the same year, ensured that Henry's attempts to solve his marital issues by diplomatic means were doomed to failure. Characteristically, Henry had to blame someone else for this failure, and this resulted in Wolsey's fall from power in 1529.

A CLOSER LOOK

The Peace of Cambrai in 1529 required the French to give up their ambitions in Italy. It also reinforced the papacy's political dependence on the emperor. It made clear an international political context in which the dominant individual was Catherine of Aragon's nephew, the emperor, who made his commitment to family honour very clear.

KEY CHRONOLOGY

English foreign policy, 1527–40

1527	Sack of Rome, leaving Pope Clement VII a virtual prisoner of the emperor England offers support to France against the Holy Roman Empire/Spain at the Treaty of Amiens
1529	French defeated at Landriano Peace of Cambrai between France and the Holy Roman Empire Fall of Wolsey
1532	Defensive alliance between England and France
1533	Henry begins break with Rome
1536	Renewal of fighting between France and the Holy Roman Empire/Spain
1538	Peace between France and the Holy Roman Empire
1539	Fear of invasion in England as Pope attempts to unite Catholic powers in an anti-English crusade
1540	Henry marries Anne of Cleves; marriage quickly dissolved

Fig. 4 *The illuminated title page for the Treaty of Peace signed between Henry VIII and Francis I of France at Amiens in 1527*

STUDY TIP

Answering questions such as this requires you to bring balance to your judgement. Your analysis of Henry's responsibility needs to be set alongside the responsibilities of other individuals as well as other reasons which go beyond individual responsibility.

AS LEVEL PRACTICE QUESTION

'Henry VIII was responsible for the failures of English foreign policy in the years 1514 to 1529.' Explain why you agree or disagree with this view.

In 1532, Henry tried to shore up his position by making a fragile alliance with France, though France was also in a weak position so that together they could put little pressure on the emperor. In any case, the limited usefulness to Henry of a French alliance began to unravel as Francis sought to establish a marriage alliance between his son Henry and the Pope's niece, Catherine de Medici.

In the circumstances Henry had little alternative but to resolve his 'Great Matter' by breaking with Rome. Though this horrified the Catholic powers, there were no repercussions in the short term because Charles was primarily concerned with the threat posed by the Ottoman Turks to Christian Europe. Henry tried to reinforce his position by making an alliance with the League of Schmalkalden, which foundered amid mutual mistrust.

CROSS-REFERENCE

The League of Schmalkalden, an organisation of German princes and free cities which supported the reformer Martin Luther and his rejection of the Catholic Church, is introduced in Chapter 8, page 80.

Henry was fortunate that the pressure upon his position was reduced in 1536. There were two main reasons for this:

1. The death of Catherine of Aragon and the execution of Anne Boleyn opened up the possibility of a renewed alliance with the emperor.
2. The renewal of fighting between the emperor and Francis I reduced the potential danger of England's isolated position.

This relief was short-lived, and in 1538 Henry's position had once again weakened.

1. Charles and Francis once again buried their differences in the Treaty of Nice and they each agreed to sever connections with England.
2. Pope Paul III published a **bull** deposing Henry and thereby absolving English Catholics from the need to obey their ruler.
3. The Pope sent envoys to both France and Scotland to rouse support for a Catholic crusade against Henry.

KEY TERM

bull: a letter or formal declaration issued by the Pope; it is named after the seal (*bulla*) that was added to the end to authenticate it

In reality Henry's position was more secure than it appeared. Neither Francis nor Charles trusted each other and each had more important immediate priorities. However, the situation did appear to Henry to be dangerous, and this helps to explain his enthusiasm for the Six Articles Act of 1539, which was intended to reassure Catholic opinion in England. It also helps to explain his decision to marry Anne of Cleves. His first encounter with Anne coincided with a meeting between Charles and Francis. Henry's natural fear was that they were conspiring to invade England and he believed that therefore the marriage with Anne, accompanied by another attempt at an alliance with the League of Schmalkalden, would be a useful insurance policy. The marriage soon became as politically redundant as it was personally unsuitable once the short-lived friendship between Charles and Francis broke down, leaving Henry in a much more secure position.

Fig. 5 *The Emperor Charles V*

CROSS-REFERENCE

The passing of the Six Articles Act is discussed in Chapter 12, page 122.

Ireland

For the first part of Henry VIII's reign the king had had few concerns regarding Ireland. The English authorities remained in control of the Pale, the area of land surrounding Dublin. At the same time Gerald Fitzgerald, ninth Earl of Kildare, was the dominant Irish nobleman. He managed for a time successfully to play a complex double game in which he was both an English courtier and servant of the Crown and the most powerful of the Gaelic chiefs. It did, however, prove difficult to sustain this ambiguous role, especially after the revival of the Geraldine–Butler feud, and the relationship between Kildare and the king broke down. Henry VIII's problem was that he found it difficult to govern Ireland with Kildare; without him he found it impossible.

Kildare's dismissal led in 1534 to a major rebellion, led by his son Thomas Fitzgerald, Earl of Ossory, which was only suppressed with difficulty and at considerable expense. The attempt to refashion Irish government in 1534 by bringing it more directly under English control failed utterly. It required royal government through an English-born deputy, supported by a substantial military presence. Ireland therefore became an increasing drain on the Crown's resources.

This was made worse by the scale of resentment amongst the Gaelic lords. Two of these nobles, Con O'Neill and Manus O'Donnell, invaded the Pale in 1539. The government eventually regained control and tried to pacify Ireland by establishing it as a separate kingdom in 1541, imposing English law and creating counties out of the Gaelic lordships. In return some of the Gaelic lords received peerage titles and the Irish were to be entitled to the same legal protections as their English counterparts. However, the government lacked the resources to follow through the reforms, there was no residual Irish loyalty to the English Crown, and in any case after 1534 the relationship between England and Ireland had become even more complex because of the religious differences which began to emerge between the two.

CROSS-REFERENCE

To recap on the Geraldine–Butler feud, look back to Chapter 3, page 27.

Foreign policy, 1540–47

The final years of Henry VIII's reign mark a distinct contrast with the experience of the previous decade. In the 1530s the focus of foreign policy had been to minimise the response of foreign powers to the break from Rome. In the 1540s Henry returned to the aggressive foreign policy which had characterised the early years of his reign, launching attacks on both Scotland and France.

Scotland

England's invasion of Scotland in 1542 met with immediate military success. The Scots were forced into military action by being faced with demands which they could not possibly have met. As a result the Scots were heavily defeated at the Battle of Solway Moss. To make matters worse for the Scots, James V died shortly after hearing news of the defeat, leaving as his heir his one-week-old daughter Mary. The Scottish position therefore seemed hopeless.

Henry might at this point have launched a full-scale invasion which would have been virtually impossible for the Scots to repel. It seems clear, however, that Henry's main interest was an invasion of France; he therefore looked primarily to diplomatic pressure as a means of securing his Scottish objectives, while he himself sought military glory in France.

KEY CHRONOLOGY

English foreign policy up to 1547

1542	Invasion of Scotland
1543	Treaty of Greenwich between England and Scotland
	Anglo-Imperial alliance
1544	Invasions of Scotland and France
1545	French counter-invasion of the Isle of Wight
1546	Peace with France

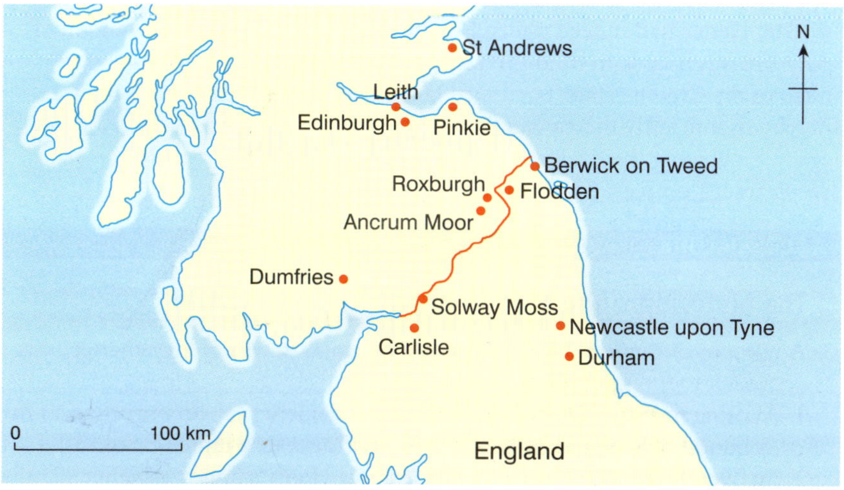

Fig. 6 *The Anglo-Scottish border*

The Scottish policy became known as the 'rough wooing'. Henry sought to marry the young Prince Edward to the even younger Mary, Queen of Scots. For a time this policy objective seemed to enjoy the support of the Scottish regent, the Earl of Arran, though the English ambassador in Edinburgh, Sir Ralph Sadler, reported that there was widespread suspicion of English intentions, and the Scots refused to allow Henry's request that Queen Mary be brought up in England. The children were formally betrothed according to the terms of the Treaty of Greenwich of 1543. However, Arran deserted the English cause and the Scottish parliament refused to ratify the treaty. This prompted an enraged Henry to order the Earl of Hertford to carry out a punitive raid on Edinburgh, Leith and St Andrews.

Henry can be criticised for the failure of his Scottish policy on several counts.

1. He neglected the opportunity to secure his policy by military force when he had the opportunity in 1542.
2. He failed to heed Sadler's warnings about Scottish hostility to his intentions.
3. His ordering of Hertford into Scotland was simply a matter of retaliation. This gave no thought to possible strategic objectives and simply served to antagonise the Scots still further.

France

To facilitate the French invasion, Henry had agreed an alliance with the emperor. That Henry's main concern was France can be seen from the size of the army which was assembled in 1544. Henry himself, desperate for military glory, set off at the head of his army, despite his health problems and the efforts of councillors to persuade him not to. Typically, Henry gave little thought to strategic objectives, though he did realise that an attempt to march on Paris, to which he had committed himself in the Imperial alliance, was likely to prove unsuccessful. Consequently, the English army confined itself to the vicinity of Calais, besieging Montreuil unsuccessfully but capturing Boulogne. By this time, however, the emperor had had enough of the conflict and had made a separate peace with Francis I.

Matters got even worse for Henry in 1545 when:

- Francis I sent troops to Scotland to reinforce a possible invasion of England from across the Scottish border
- the English were defeated at the Battle of Ancrum Moor
- a separate French force landed in the Isle of Wight
- Henry's flagship, the *Mary Rose*, sank in the Solent.

However, the French failed to recapture Boulogne and the invasion of northern England never materialised. In the end both sides were happy to sue for peace as neither could afford to continue the conflict. Peace was agreed in 1546. Henry had indeed paid a high price for his final and vain pursuit of glory. He was unable to fund the war from extraordinary revenue, he sold much of the Crown estate, borrowed large sums and debased the coinage, thereby significantly increasing the rate of inflation. This was indeed a toxic legacy. 'Following the devices and desires of his own heart', as Eric Ives put it (see Extract 1 on page 85), proved to be a complete disaster.

CROSS-REFERENCE

The strategy of debasing the coinage to raise money is discussed in Chapter 11, page 111, and in Chapter 13, page 126.

A CLOSER LOOK

The historiography of foreign policy in the 1540s

A number of theories have been put forward as to why Henry changed his approach to foreign policy in the 1540s:

1. Writing in 1902, Albert Pollard argued that Henry's main purpose was the conquest of Scotland, as part of a project to create a united British Isles.
2. In 1966 R. B. Wernham, like Pollard, saw Henry's policy as being primarily about Scotland. However, he believed that his approach was

fundamentally defensive, given the threat to English security which Scotland represented in the event of full-scale war against France, and the fear that King James V might threaten the English throne were Henry to die whilst Prince Edward was still young.

3. Two years later John Scarisbrick, in his biography of Henry VIII, argued that Henry was primarily motivated once again by the lure of glory and territorial gains in France; in that context, therefore, the invasion of Scotland was essential to ensure that the Anglo-Scottish border remained secure once an invasion of France was launched.
4. Michael Bush has attempted to disentangle Scotland from France by arguing that Henry was motivated mainly by his desire to punish his nephew James V for a number of presumed offences: harbouring English rebels, twice marrying French princesses, ignoring pressure from Henry to break with Rome and failing to turn up for a meeting arranged with Henry at York.

ACTIVITY

Group work

Divide into four groups. Each group should address one of the historiographical approaches put forward here. What evidence can be found in the material on foreign policy from 1540 to 1547 to support your chosen historiographical approach?

Securing the succession

KEY CHRONOLOGY

Succession issues

1516	Birth of Princess Mary, heir presumptive
1532	Pregnancy of Anne Boleyn
1533	Annulment of marriage of Henry and Catherine of Aragon
	Birth of Princess Elizabeth
1534	Succession Act confirms Elizabeth as heir presumptive and declares Mary illegitimate
1536	Death of Catherine of Aragon and execution of Anne Boleyn
	Marriage of Henry and Jane Seymour
	Succession Act repeals the 1534 Act, declares Elizabeth illegitimate and lays down that Henry can determine the succession by will in the absence of an heir apparent
1537	Birth of Prince Edward as heir apparent
1544	Succession Act receives the royal assent, repeals the 1536 Act, reinstates Mary and Elizabeth in the succession and reaffirms that Henry could determine the succession by will
1546	Henry VIII's will confirms the terms of the 1544 Succession Act and lays down that in default of heirs to Edward, Mary and Elizabeth the succession should pass to the heirs of his sister Mary

Securing the succession, ideally with an adult male heir, proved to be an obsession with Henry for the whole of his reign. It was the problem of succession which would ultimately bring about the break with Rome. It also helped cause rebellion (the Pilgrimage of Grace), and contributed to many of the wider political problems which Henry faced. In the end, his attempt to rule from the grave was cast aside as the terms of his will were altered by Lord Protector Somerset.

Henry's problems in this regard came from the failure of his first wife, Catherine of Aragon, to produce a healthy male heir. Catherine and Henry

CROSS-REFERENCE

The political aspects of the break with Rome are discussed in Chapter 8, and the religious implications in chapters 10 and 12.

Reaction against this reform, including the Pilgrimage of Grace, is covered in Chapter 10.

The overturning of Henry's will by Somerset is covered in Chapter 13.

had two baby sons; one was stillborn and the other died at the age of seven weeks. There were several miscarriages, and the only surviving child, Princess Mary, was born in 1516. As Catherine reached the end of her childbearing years, Henry came increasingly to believe that the lack of a son was God's punishment for marrying Catherine contrary to canon law. It was essential therefore that Henry should remarry. Eventually he was able to marry Anne Boleyn in January 1533. On 7 September 1533 she gave birth to the Princess Elizabeth. Elizabeth's position as the heir presumptive was confirmed by the Succession Act of 1534, which declared Mary illegitimate.

Henry still had no male heir, but despite what many historians have assumed, there was no immediate breach in his relationship with Anne. However, the fact that she had two subsequent miscarriages left him wondering whether he was again being afflicted with divine punishment. Anne's execution for treason led to the 1536 Succession Act, which declared Elizabeth illegitimate. Henry now had no legitimate heir, but he did have three illegitimate children. It was in this context that Henry turned to the possibility of legitimating the succession of his son, the Duke of Richmond. The 1536 Succession Act broke new ground by laying down that, in the absence of a legitimate heir, the king could determine the succession by will or by **letters patent**. This could theoretically have led to Richmond's succession, but the latter's death ended this possibility.

Henry did acquire a legitimate male heir in Prince Edward, born in 1537. Moreover, the fact that Henry had not married Edward's mother, Jane Seymour, until after the deaths of both Catherine and Anne meant that Edward's legitimacy could not be denied by any interpretation of canon law. However, by 1543 problems with Henry's health made it increasingly likely that Edward would still be a minor when he succeeded to the throne. Thus, there was potential uncertainty and anxiety, especially on Henry's part, about what the succession might entail. Consequently, the Succession Act which passed through the Commons and the Lords in 1543 and received the royal assent in 1544, re-legitimated Mary and Elizabeth. It also reaffirmed Henry's right to determine the succession by will or by letters patent.

Henry confirmed the succession arrangements in his will which was dated 30 December 1546. The will further laid down the right of succession to the heirs of Henry's sister, Mary Duchess of Suffolk, if Edward, Mary and Elizabeth died without issue. It also set up a regency council to act on Edward's behalf. Very little was to be seen of the regency council in Edward's reign.

KEY TERM

letters patent: legal instruments issued by the monarch in the exercise of his or her prerogative powers

EXTRACT 2

Left to himself, King Henry VIII turned his hand to the search for personal glory and national aggrandisement, playing a part he had always fancied and never been fit for either in his personal capacities or the resources of his realms. His achievement must strike the reflective mind as remarkable: a grave threat of invasion from France, an continuous threat of war from Scotland, the wasting away of the Crown's recently enlarged resources, a country drained by the heaviest taxation for centuries (some of it dubiously legal), and a major crisis in what had been the least crisis-prone of the economies of western Europe. That his achievements did not destroy the monarchy which his father, Wolsey and Cromwell had fashioned, nor produce a real collapse and a class war in England, was none of his doing.

Adapted from Geoffrey R. Elton, *Reform and Reformation: England, 1509–1558*, 1977

EXTRACT 3

To contemporaries, Henry was everything a king should be. For them, whether they might like or loathe his policies, Henry was everything a king should be; he had all the monarchical virtues in full measure. The first was magnificence, immediately obvious in his personal appearance. The reputation of the Field of the Cloth of Gold spread throughout Europe, not simply as a costly expensive exercise in image building, but as regal glory in action. A second contemporary royal virtue was military power and success. Henry's fascination with military technology, most notably heavy guns on board ship and the consequent need to encourage cannon-founding, was entirely in the kingly tradition. So was war. No one was allowed to forget Henry's triumph at the Battle of the Spurs, even though it was a skirmish fought in his absence. His armies not only won massive victories which culled two generations of Scottish nobles; in 1544 they savaged the lives of ordinary Scots and ruined the lowland economy. Supremely, with the capture of Boulogne, Henry became the only king to win territory in France for more than a century.

Adapted from Eric W. Ives, 'Henry VIII', in *Oxford Dictionary of National Biography*, 2004

AS LEVEL PRACTICE QUESTION

Evaluating historical extracts

With reference to Extracts 2 and 3, and your understanding of the historical context, which of these two extracts provides the more convincing interpretation of Henry VIII's foreign policy?

STUDY TIP

In answering a question such as this it is important to draw upon evidence and support from the whole of the reign. It is also perfectly reasonable to conclude that each of the interpretations might be more convincing at different points of the reign, depending on the specific context.

ACTIVITY

Summary

Evaluate whether or not English foreign policy was successful.

	Scotland	France	Spain	Holy Roman Empire
1509–14				
1514–27				
1527–40				
1540–47				
Conclusion				
Overall summary				

ACTIVITY

Evaluating historical extracts

Look back at Eric Ives's interpretation, given at the beginning of this chapter (page 85). In small groups, consider whether you find this interpretation convincing. You will need to find specific evidence to support or refute his views.

A LEVEL PRACTICE QUESTION

To what extent was Henry VIII himself responsible for the failures of English foreign policy during his reign?

STUDY TIP

The question requires you to balance Henry's personal responsibility against other factors. These other factors can include the responsibility of other individuals, for example ministers such as Wolsey and rivals such as Francis I. They can also include other factors such as underlying national weaknesses.

10 English society in the reign of Henry VIII

EXTRACT 1

There was a long tradition of popular revolt in England. Tudor chronicles told of the revolt of 1381, when peasants and townspeople had denounced their oppressors and wrought havoc. The fear was always that the common people would rise again. Yet the people rarely showed their power. The poor would be cast weeping from their homes when land was enclosed, yet offer little resistance. Yet, when really provoked, they might take action. Rebellion of a greater or lesser kind – whether against the Crown or revolt against landlords – was, perhaps, the natural consequence of a political system which allowed the great majority no channel for grievances, in which any appeal for redress was taken as rebellion.

Adapted from Susan Brigden, *New Worlds, Lost Worlds: the Rule of the Tudors, 1485–1603*, 2000

LEARNING OBJECTIVES

In this chapter you will learn about:

- the social status of members of the elites and commoners
- regional issues and their importance
- the social impact of religious upheaval
- the significance of rebellions.

KEY QUESTION

As you read this chapter, consider the following Key Question:
How did English society and economy change and with what effects?

Elites and commoners

Elites

The reign of Henry VIII witnessed a dynamic period in English society in which remnants of the feudal system still existed, but, in contrast, there was the growth of a professional and commercial bourgeoisie. However, the traditional nobles (or peers) and the greater gentry still represented a social elite which wielded considerable political and economic influence.

ACTIVITY

What views of the ordinary people of England are expressed in Extract 1? When you have studied this chapter, reflect on whether you feel these views are justified.

The nobility

The size of the peerage increased during the reign of Henry VIII, though by the end of the reign there were only nine more peers than there had been at the beginning. The creation of new peers had been to a large extent offset both by 'natural wastage' and by the number of attainders during the reign. Most of the new peers had achieved their rank as a result of successful royal service as courtiers or soldiers. In some cases this was enhanced by a close family relationship; for example the king's brother-in-law Edward Seymour was elevated to the earldom of Hertford.

England had only one duke when Henry VIII came to the throne, Edward Stafford, Duke of Buckingham, who never enjoyed royal favour. Henry VIII only promoted two non-royal ducal titles, Norfolk and Suffolk. Their holders served the king as soldiers and courtiers. There was a distinction to be made between the two. Norfolk was restored to the title which had been enjoyed by his father. In contrast, Suffolk seems to have been promoted on account of the closeness of his personal relationship with the king in a move which prompted criticism in some quarters, for example by Erasmus.

Henry did sometimes bestow property on nobles to enable them to exert royal authority in particular areas. Thus, Suffolk was endowed with property in Lincolnshire after the rebellion there in 1536 and the king ordered him to move there to ensure that he could exert that authority in person. Similarly, **John, Baron Russell**, was raised to the peerage and endowed with lands in Devon to bolster royal authority in the south-west following the execution of the **Marquess of Exeter**.

CROSS-REFERENCE

The structure of society under Henry VII is described in Chapter 4.

CROSS-REFERENCE

The ranks of the peerage are outlined in Chapter 4, pages 33–35.

Attainders, by which a nobleman lost his title and lands, are described in Chapter 1, page 3.

KEY PROFILE

John, Baron Russell and Earl of Bedford (c1485–1555)

Russell had a long career as a courtier. He served Henry VIII as a diplomat and soldier, and became a councillor in 1536. Following Exeter's fall, Russell was granted a huge amount of monastic land in Devon to bolster royal support in the southwest.

KEY PROFILE

Henry Courtenay, Marquess of Exeter (c1498–1538)

A grandson of Edward IV, Exeter was dominant in the southwest. He had had a close relationship with Henry, but his identification with the Aragonese faction and his enmity towards Cromwell strained the relationship.

ACTIVITY

Why was Henry VIII willing to bestow large amounts of property on nobles? Here are some suggested reasons. Discuss with a partner which would be the most important and place them in order of priority.

- Create a different atmosphere among the aristocracy from that in his father's reign.
- Reward loyalty.
- Ensure control in provincial areas.
- Show his generosity as a king.
- Ensure he had nobles willing to follow him to war.
- Ensure he had homes if he travelled around the country.

KEY TERM

affinity: described all those who had relationships with a person of higher status based on landholding and/or holding a position within the household

Nobles were expected to have great households and offer hospitality to their **affinity** and neighbours. To do so too openly could make a noble an object of royal suspicion, as was the case with Buckingham. On the other hand, noble households remained critical to the maintenance of local influence and to the recruitment of royal armies. (The Earl of Shrewsbury raised over 4000 men for the invasion of France in 1513.) Bastard feudalism had not died away completely. Gradually, however, the nobility was being brought more under the control of the monarch. This helps to explain the fate of Thomas Fiennes, Baron Dacre of the South. In 1541 not only was he tried for the murder of a neighbour's servant but he was convicted and hanged like a common criminal. It would have been very difficult to envisage either of these events happening two generations earlier at the start of the Tudor period.

Fig. 1 *The arrest and execution of Sir Thomas More, one of the leading nobles executed; painted in 1591 by Antoine Caron*

Many other nobles fell victim to Henry VIII in more orthodox fashion. The Duke of Buckingham was executed for treason on the vaguest of charges in 1521. The king's relatives, Henry Pole Baron Montague and Henry Courtenay Marquess of Exeter, were accused of treasonable conspiracy and executed in 1538. Montague's mother, Margaret Pole Countess of Salisbury, having been attainted of treason, was held in the Tower for over two years before eventually being executed, arguably the most vindictive of all of Henry's punitive actions. Lords Darcy and Hussey were executed for their roles in the rebellion of 1536, Henry's actions being perfectly justified according to the legal standards of the day.

The gentry

John Guy has suggested that there were about 5000 gentry families in England in 1540. Some aspects of gentry status were specific. Knighthoods were conferred as a sign of royal favour, and it was assumed that a knight would possess an income which reflected his status. Susan Brigden has suggested that there were about 200 knightly families in 1524. A gentleman who was entitled to bear a coat of arms was deemed an esquire. Such status was certified by the royal heralds. By 1530 heralds were unwilling to grant or confirm the title to anyone with lands worth less than £10 per annum or goods worth under £300. The term 'gentleman' itself lacked legal precision, and 'gentility' was often acquired as a result of the proceeds of office, profession or business.

Though it is difficult to be precise, the number of gentry increased during the reign of Henry VIII. Moreover, the increase in the number of justices of the peace (JPs) increased the numbers of those who participated in local administration. In addition to the JPs, many other members of the gentry were drawn into unpaid administration on behalf of the Crown. Members of the gentry were increasingly keen on their sons acquiring the legal training which would make them better able to take on such roles as could offer the basis for local advancement. Moreover, whereas the Crown's local administrators had formerly been likely to be clergymen, increasingly they were laymen, whose office holding often generated the income which would bring about landownership and gentry status.

Commoners

There was little dramatic change in the standard of living of commoners during the first half of the reign of Henry VIII. However, the rise in the rate of inflation did lead to a drop in real incomes which contributed to the ill feeling felt by many towards the imposition of the Amicable Grant. The social structure remained substantially unchanged, with the vast majority of people having very few possessions and little chance of regular and secure employment. Governments were always fearful of such people, with some justification because, while full-scale rebellion was relatively rare, outbreaks of disorder were much more common – and these were held to upset the good ordering of society.

Regional issues

Tudor society was not only divided by class and title, it was also regionally divided, with local loyalties often being stronger than national ones. In order to bind the country as one nation, measures were taken to create a single unified state.

CROSS-REFERENCE

The rebellion of 1536 is outlined later in this chapter, on pages 104–107.

ACTIVITY

Discuss in pairs or in small groups why the nobility continued to be attracted to Henry VIII's court.

Fig. 2 *This shows the coat of arms of John Dudley, Earl of Warwick*

CROSS-REFERENCE

The imposition of the Amicable Grant is discussed below on page 103.

Creating a unitary state

Fig. 3 *Wales after the 1535 Act*

Wales

Before 1536 Wales was a separate territory from England, though in practice it was under English control, even though the ruling dynasty was Welsh in origin. Wales comprised **marcher** (i.e. border) lordships and the Principality of Wales. It had neither a single unified administration nor a formal political link with England. That was changed by the Laws in Wales Act of 1536 which:

- divided Wales into shire counties which operated on the same basis as their English counterparts
- gave the Welsh shires direct representation in the House of Commons at Westminster for the first time
- brought Wales into the same legal framework as England.

In practice this meant that Wales became incorporated into England with little of a separate identity except for the survival of the Welsh language in some parts of the country. Control over Wales continued to be exercised on the Crown's behalf. However, increasingly this became the responsibility of members of the aristocracy, such as the earls of Pembroke, and by members of an anglicised Welsh gentry who controlled county politics, were elected to Parliament and became increasingly prominent within the legal profession.

The English palatinates

Three English counties, Lancashire, Cheshire and Durham, were technically 'palatinates'. In other words, they were separate jurisdictions from the rest of the kingdom. This mattered little in Lancashire and Cheshire, where the exercise of palatinate jurisdiction had long since fallen back into royal hands. Durham was still technically separate, with palatinate jurisdiction being exercised by the bishop. The Act Resuming Liberties to the Crown of 1536 reduced the level of independence enjoyed by the bishop, but did not destroy it completely. For example, the palatinate court of chancery continued to operate. The change therefore seems to have been as much evolutionary as revolutionary.

Border administration

The Anglo-Welsh border

The lands which were governed as part of the Principality of Wales, along with the four bordering English counties – Shropshire, Herefordshire, Worcestershire, Gloucestershire – came under the jurisdiction of the Council of Wales and the Marches, which was based at Ludlow in Shropshire. This offered relatively cheap and local access to the law and could therefore be seen as a benefit to the area under its jurisdiction.

The Anglo-Scottish border

This remained a problematical area for Henry VIII. The border with Scotland was difficult to police; much of it was remote and often inhospitable in the winter months. Both sides of the border had a reputation for lawlessness. Cattle and sheep rustling were rife and violence was common.

In order to deal with such problems the border with Scotland was split into three marches, each under the jurisdiction of a warden. The filling of these posts could be difficult for the king. Appointing from a local noble family ran the risk that the noble would exploit his office to enhance his own power at the king's expense. In any case Henry had little time for such border magnate families as the Percies and the Dacres. The other option was to appoint local officers who came from the gentry class (e.g. Thomas Lord Wharton, only recently raised to the peerage and a man of relatively humble origins, was appointed in 1542) or those who were complete outsiders: these two groups were more likely to owe complete loyalty to the king, but they had limited ability to influence the conduct of local people who often saw themselves as owing a primary loyalty to a local magnate.

The Council in the North

The north of England posed problems of governance to a regime based far away in London. This was demonstrated particularly strongly with the huge number of supporters of the **Pilgrimage of Grace** in 1536. This led Henry and Cromwell to re-establish the Council as a permanent body based in York with a professional staff. It had both administrative and legal functions. It showed its worth by helping to keep the north quiet during the summer of rebellions in 1549.

CROSS-REFERENCE

The Pilgrimage of Grace is described later in this chapter, on pages 104–105, and the rebellions of 1549 in Chapter 14, pages 139–141.

Fig. 4 *The King's Manor in York, formerly the residence of the abbot of St Mary's, became the headquarters of the Council in the North after coming into the Crown's hands in 1539*

STUDY TIP

It is possible for questions to extend across more than one reign. Revisit Chapter 4 before writing this essay.

A LEVEL PRACTICE QUESTION

'The people of northern England, Cornwall and Wales had little reason to be grateful for the rule of Henry VII and Henry VIII.' Assess the validity of this view.

CROSS-REFERENCE

To recap on the structure, organisation and beliefs of the Church in the late fifteenth and early sixteenth centuries, reread Chapter 6.

The reform of the Church under Henry VIII, including the dissolution of the monasteries which had played an important social role, is described in detail in Chapter 12.

Sir Thomas More is profiled in Chapter 6, page 57, and his fall from favour and execution are outlined in Chapter 8, page 79.

Cromwell's attacks on the monasteries in 1536 and 1539, and the royal injunctions of 1536 and 1538, are discussed in Chapter 12.

The social impact of religious upheaval

At the start of Henry VIII's reign there was little sign that there would be fundamental changes to the English Church. Although complaints were made occasionally about, for example, the worldliness of the clergy, on the whole the Church appears to have fulfilled the requirements of the bulk of the people to whom it ministered. There had even been some improvement in the early sixteenth century in the quality of the clergy and Cardinal Wolsey had dissolved some redundant monasteries, using their endowments for educational purposes. No one would credibly have predicted the destruction of Catholic England.

However, in the 1530s a major change took place in the English Church when Henry VIII broke with Rome and became head of a new English Church. Though a small minority of people undoubtedly welcomed the religious change this brought, there was no groundswell of popular support for the changes. There were executions of some who denied the royal supremacy, most notably Sir Thomas More.

Monasteries were an important feature of the appeal of the pre-Reformation Church. Cromwell's dissolution of the monasteries, begun in 1536, and his royal injunctions of 1536, attacked many of the traditional practices of Catholicism, such as holy days, pilgrimages and the veneration of relics. This provoked fears that these reforms might be accompanied by an attack on parish churches. The most important consequence of this was a major rebellion which broke out in the autumn of 1536 in Lincolnshire and parts of the north of England; this became known as the Pilgrimage of Grace.

The religious upheaval had long-lasting social consequences:

1. A huge amount of land was removed from the Church and taken by the Crown. This theoretically should have made the king more powerful.

However, the expense of the warlike foreign policy of Henry's final years led to the widespread sale of Church and monastic property, often at knock-down prices, thereby increasing both the size and the wealth of the landholding gentry. By 1547 almost two thirds of the monastic land acquired by the Crown had been sold off or granted away.

2. Many monasteries had been noted for their educational provision. With their demise, most monastic schools were lost also.
3. Many monks and nuns were rendered unemployed at a stroke. Some monks were able to secure employment as secular priests and many others received pensions. The position of nuns was very precarious.
4. Some monasteries played a very considerable role in the communities in which they were situated. As well as providing education, they also offered employment and business opportunities. Some major monastic churches, such as Durham, were the cathedrals of their dioceses; many others doubled up as the local parish church. Dissolution was seen as a potential disaster and some communities went to considerable lengths to try to protect their monasteries. At Hexham in Northumberland, for example, royal commissioners were prevented from beginning the process of dissolution by a gathering of armed men.

CROSS-REFERENCE

Henry's costly foreign policy in his later years is discussed in Chapter 9.

Rebellions

Henry VIII's reign saw various instances of disorder and disobedience which the authorities managed, with difficulty, to keep under control. It also contained one major rebellion, the Pilgrimage of Grace.

KEY QUESTION

- How was England governed?
- How important was the role of key individuals and groups?

Resistance to taxation: the Amicable Grant

Just as in Henry VII's reign, the imposition of taxes to pay for foreign wars brought instability and disorder. There were complaints in Yorkshire, particularly in upland areas, about the subsidy to raise money for Henry's campaigns in 1513. The taxation demands for some of the areas affected were eventually written off.

Similarly, many refused to pay the Amicable Grant in 1525. Opposition was geographically widespread, but the strongest resistance occurred in north Essex and south Suffolk. The Earl of Essex reported that 1000 people had gathered at the Essex–Suffolk border and were determined to resist payment. The dukes of Norfolk and Suffolk also faced about 4000 taxation resisters, in particular, unemployed cloth workers who found it impossible to pay the levy. The dukes handled the matter sensitively and the king backed down. Wolsey publicly begged the king to offer pardon to those whom he saw as his Suffolk countrymen and the leaders of the resistance were treated leniently. The whole business demonstrated very clearly that Henry could not operate in defiance of the taxpaying classes. When next he opted to invade France he supplemented his extraordinary revenue with cash from the sale of monastic lands.

CROSS-REFERENCE

The introduction of the Amicable Grant, which was neither amicable nor a grant, but a forced loan (in other words a tax imposed without the approval of Parliament) is outlined, in its political context, in Chapter 8, page 74.

SOURCE 1

Adapted from a report by the Duke of Norfolk to Cardinal Wolsey, 11 May 1525:

And unto us came the inhabitants of the town of Lavenham and Brent Eleigh who were offenders to a great number. They came all in their shirts and, kneeling before us with piteous crying for mercy, showed that they were the king's majesty's most humble and faithful subjects and would continue during their lives, saying that this offence by them committed was only for lack of work so they knew not how to get their living. And for their offence most humbly

ACTIVITY

Group work

Working in pairs or small groups assess Norfolk's performance in dealing with the Amicable Grant rebels.

A CLOSER LOOK

Key events in the Lincolnshire Rising and Pilgrimage of Grace

1536	
2 Oct	Lincolnshire Rising begins at Louth
4 Oct	Lincolnshire Rising spreads to Horncastle; murder of Dr Rayne, chancellor of the diocese of Lincoln
7 Oct	Lincolnshire rebels converge on Lincoln Cathedral
8 Oct	Pilgrimage of Grace proper begins in the East Riding of Yorkshire under the leadership of Robert Aske
10 Oct	Pilgrimage of Grace spreads to the West Riding of Yorkshire
18 Oct	Lincolnshire Rising ends
20 Oct	Pontefract Castle surrendered to the rebels
25 Oct	Rebellion spreads to high Pennines and Lake District
26 Oct	Rebels meet Duke of Norfolk near Doncaster
Nov	East and West Riding rebels gradually disperse
3 Dec	Royal proclamation offering pardon to rebels
16 Jan	Renewed rebellion in the East Riding of Yorkshire led by Sir Francis Bigod

besought us to be means to the king's highness for pardon and remission, unto whom we made a long rehearsal the best we could to aggravate their heinous offence declaring the same to be high treason. Finally we tried out four of the principal of the offenders. We gave all the rest leave to depart.

The Lincolnshire Rising and the Pilgrimage of Grace

Fig. 5 *The Lincolnshire Rising and the Pilgrimage of Grace, showing the routes taken by the various groups of rebels*

Together, the Lincolnshire Rising and the Pilgrimage of Grace comprised the largest single rebellion in the history of Tudor England. It began as a rising which started in Lincolnshire in early October 1536, spread over the Humber into the East Riding of Yorkshire and continued from there into parts of the West Riding around Wakefield and Pontefract.

A second and more militant rising started in the dales between Ripon and Richmond, spread west into Cumberland, Westmorland and north Lancashire, north into Durham and southwest into the Craven area of the West Riding of

Yorkshire. The rebels here were more radicalised and more hostile towards the gentry because of the strength of their grievances against their landlords. Class antagonism was clear from letters sent out in the name of 'Captain Poverty', in a way which contrasted markedly with the Lincolnshire and the East Risings. The recreation of the 'Captain Poverty' movement helps to explain the revival of rebellion in Cumberland early in 1537.

Causes of the rebellion

The causes of the rebellion were complex, and various secular motives played a part. However, it is undoubtedly the case that opposition to the impact of Henry VIII's religious changes figured among the rebels' grievances. What sparked off rebellion was the huge resentment felt about a government which was pushing too quickly for fundamental religious change that most ordinary people could neither sympathise with nor even understand.

Religious motives

1. Dissolution of the monasteries
   By the early autumn of 1536 the work of dissolving the smaller monasteries was well under way. It was clear that the dissolution would have a number of effects which many people found undesirable:
   - the loss of the charitable and educational functions which some monasteries provided
   - the possible loss of parish churches which were monastic properties
   - the fear that the north would be impoverished by monastic land falling into the hands of southerners
   - the usefulness of the facilities and services which the monasteries offered.

   The importance of monasteries to the rebels can be seen in their attempts to restore some of the houses which had been suppressed. The rebel leader, **Robert Aske**, was a convinced supporter of the monasteries.
2. Fear for parish churches and traditional religious practices
   The 1536 Injunctions drawn up by Cromwell were seen as attacking traditional religious practices.
   - The celebration of locally important saints such as St Wilfrid in parts of Yorkshire had been discouraged.
   - This was linked to the discouragement of pilgrimage.
   - There were rumours that church plate and jewels, which had been bequeathed by parishioners, would be confiscated and that parishes might be amalgamated.

Secular motives

Several secular motives have also been attributed to the rebellion.

1. The ordinary rebels were generally more motivated by economic grievances, including resentment of taxation, than their leaders.
2. The Crown's attempts to impose the Duke of Suffolk upon Lincolnshire as a great magnate may initially have sparked the rebellion in Lincolnshire.
3. It has been argued, most strongly by Geoffrey Elton, that the rebellions of 1536 were brought about primarily by a courtly conspiracy prompted by councillors who had been supporters of Catherine of Aragon, who had died in January 1536. Their main motive was the restoration of Princess Mary as heir. These courtiers were able to exploit the religious and financial concerns of northerners to put pressure on the king as part of the factional politics of the reign.
4. The extension of the rebellion west of the Pennines into Cumberland and Westmorland has been linked in particular to tenants' grievances.

It is, of course, difficult to disentangle completely the motives of the rebels, especially given the huge geographical area covered by the rebellion and the varied identities of those most prominently involved.

A CLOSER LOOK

The Pontefract Articles

These give the most comprehensive set of rebel demands and incorporate a range of grievances: some of which were widespread while others were specific to particular areas, and some were highly contentious, while others were very minor. There is no sense of organisation and prioritisation about the Articles. They do express a range of religious grievances, some of which can be linked to the religious experiences of ordinary folk while others reflected the concerns of the clergy. Anger was directed against Cromwell and members of his circle. The desire for Parliament to meet at York suggested strongly held regional resentment.

KEY PROFILE

Robert Aske (c1500–37) led the Pilgrimage of Grace and devised its name which gave it its distinctive religious flavour. A capable leader, he turned the varied movements of the rebels into a cohesive whole. He tried to negotiate a settlement with the king but was executed after the outbreak of renewed rebellion in January 1537.

Fig. 6 *The banner of the Five Wounds of Christ was used in both the Pilgrimage of Grace in 1536 and the Northern Rebellion of 1569 to symbolise the religious motives of the rebels*

A CLOSER LOOK

The historiography of the rebellion

The difficulty in analysing the rebels' motives is reflected in the work of historians, who have asserted a multiplicity of motives. John Scarisbrick, in his biography of Henry VIII published in 1968, sees the rebellion as a comprehensive attack on the whole range of Henry VIII's policies, though he does accept the primacy of religion. One school of thought suggests the rebellion was led by aristocrats and gentry – particularly Lord Darcy (in Yorkshire) and Lord Hussey (in Lincolnshire) – and was 'planned and organised from above'. Another emphasises the view that the rebellions were risings of the commons.

EXTRACT 2

The whole course of the rebellion – its start, its spread, its open and secret purposes, its end – becomes clearer when it is recognised that it was at heart the work of a political faction which utilised the social, economic and religious grievances to be found in the disaffected north, grievances linked not to feudal or popular uproar but to the increasing distrust felt by the regional gentry towards a thrusting and revolutionary court policy. A common interest joined the defeated court faction with the anti-court 'country' and offered an opportunity for forcing Henry to change course. In Lincolnshire the conspiracy proved rather incompetent, perhaps because Hussey, old and dithery, was not up to it: he never controlled the rising which evidently started before everything was ready, and his intended allies among the gentry lost the taste for politics when they began to fear they had let loose the elements of social rebellion.

Adapted from Geoffrey R. Elton, 'Politics and the Pilgrimage of Grace' in *After the Reformation: Essays in Honor of J. H. Hexter,* 1980

EXTRACT 3

The Pilgrimage was threatening because nobles, gentry, clergy and people combined forces, and because they shared an ideology. Indeed this revolt was neither a clash between different social groups nor a split within the governing class, but a popular rising by northerners in general. They wore badges of the Five Wounds of Christ; they swore an oath that contradicted the Crown's oath of supremacy; and they circulated ballads connecting the theme of the Church in danger to the socio-economic distress they believed would result from the loss of monastic charity. Their oath bound them to take up Christ's cross, to defend the Catholic Church, to strive for suppression of heretics and to expel evil councillors from the king's council. The Pilgrimage followed medieval patterns of dissent – that is, protest combined with protestations of loyalty to the king and the established order.

Adapted from John Guy, *Tudor England*, 1988

EXTRACT 4

The revolts of 1536 to 1537, the Lincolnshire Revolt, the Pilgrimage of Grace and the Captain Poverty risings in October, and the renewed risings in January and early February 1537 must be understood as risings of the commons which the gentry, ultimately successfully, worked to tame through the re-establishment of their authority. In their attempts to harness the commons, the gentry were hindered, first by one of their number – Aske – who saw political and personal advantage in furthering the revolts and led the commons into a stand-off with a royal force at Doncaster; and second, by the refusal of Henry VIII to make concessions. The first revolt took place in Lincolnshire and east Yorkshire and was stimulated by fears for religion in the parish churches. The second revolt in the uplands was concerned with agrarian discontents.

Adapted from Richard Hoyle, *The Pilgrimage of Grace and the Politics of the 1530s*, 2001

A LEVEL PRACTICE QUESTION

Evaluating historical extracts

Using your understanding of the historical context, assess how convincing the arguments in these three extracts are in relation to the reasons for the outbreak of the Pilgrimage of Grace.

STUDY TIP

In answering questions such as this which deal with causation it is advisable to integrate your contextual knowledge as far as possible with the causes identified in the extracts. Use your contextual knowledge to expand upon and develop the points which you identify in the extracts.

The suppression of the rebellions

Estimates of the numbers involved vary. However, it is evident that not only were these the most geographically widespread set of rebellions in Tudor England, they were also the most popular in terms of participation. Though the Lincolnshire Rebellion quickly collapsed when faced with the forces of the Duke of Suffolk, the northern rebels occupied York and Hull and captured Pontefract Castle. The rebellions therefore caused great alarm to both the king and many of his ministers.

The king sent an army north under the command of the Duke of Norfolk. When Norfolk encountered the rebels near Doncaster he was hugely outnumbered. Norfolk therefore sought to defuse the rebellion through the issue of a pardon and the promise that the dissolved monasteries would be restored and a free parliament established. The king almost certainly had not the slightest intention of honouring these promises. They did, however, secure their strategic objectives and most of the rebel forces dispersed.

Henry had the excuse he needed to go back on his word when rebellion was renewed in Cumberland and the East Riding in February 1537. The Duke of Norfolk quickly suppressed the renewed rebellion, declared martial law and hanged 74 rebels, though after that initial harshness he behaved relatively mercifully and with a concern for proper legal process. A number of rebel leaders including Darcy and Hussey, several members of the gentry and heads of monastic houses were brought to London, tried and executed.

The Pilgrimage of Grace shook Henry VIII. His own record in dealing with the rebellion was poor; he ignored warnings about the increase in resentment which he did not wish to hear. He was fortunate that the Duke of Norfolk showed common sense and flexibility. The Pilgrimage did not, however, slow the pace of religious change.

ACTIVITY

Evaluating historical extracts

Look back at Susan Brigden's interpretation at the beginning of this chapter. In the light of this chapter, consider whether her views are convincing.

ACTIVITY

Summary chart

Complete the chart below, to summarise the evidence for each of the reasons for disorder and rebellion under Henry VIII.

The reasons for disorder and rebellion

Reasons	Specific supporting evidence
Religious reasons	
Economic reasons	
Opposition to government policies	
Influence of gentry/nobles	
Regional/local factors	

STUDY TIP

In answering a question such try to draw on evidence from across the whole reign. Levels of disorder might vary across the reign and between regions.

A LEVEL PRACTICE QUESTION

'English society in the reign of Henry VIII was characterised more by disorder than by order.' Assess the validity of this view.

STUDY TIP

Look back to Chapter 4 and remind yourself of the rebellions faced by Henry VII. Use this information and your summary chart to assess the reasons for rebellion and evaluate the importance of economic factors.

AS LEVEL PRACTICE QUESTION

'Tudor rebellions before 1540 were primarily driven by economic factors.' Explain why you agree or disagree with this view.

11 Economic development in the reign of Henry VIII

EXTRACT 1

England and Wales were predominantly agrarian societies, subject after 1520 to sustained population pressure. Obvious opportunities sprang from the enhanced level of demand that stimulated the development of capitalistic agriculture and a more commercialised industrial economy, but inflation, speculation in land and foodstuffs, unemployment, poverty, vagrancy and urban squalor were the inevitable consequences of the sudden rise in population. The power of the State was negligible when faced by demographic, economic and social changes, but we can take a relatively optimistic view of the period for one overriding reason: some regional crises apart, Tudor England managed to feed itself.

John Guy, *Tudor England*, 1988

LEARNING OBJECTIVES

In this chapter you will learn about:

- the importance of trade to the English economy
- the economic contribution of exploration
- the extent of prosperity and depression during the reign.

KEY QUESTION

As you read this chapter, consider the following Key Question:
How did English society change and with what effects?

ACTIVITY

What is John Guy's view in Extract 1? List the positive and negative points made about Tudor England.

CROSS-REFERENCE

To recap on trade, exploration, prosperity and depression during the reign of Henry VII, reread Chapter 6.

Trade

Though there were occasional downturns, the volume of English trade increased during the first half of the sixteenth century. There was a continued rise in cloth exports, though the market for raw wool declined. Woollen cloth exports almost doubled during Henry VIII's reign. This was accompanied by significant increases in the export of hides and tin. These exports were counterbalanced by an increase in the import of wine, which suggests that the spending power of the more prosperous classes increased.

The leading route for exports, particularly of cloth, was from London to Antwerp, from where it was frequently sent to customers in Central Europe and the Baltic. An increasing proportion of exported cloth was routed through London. This had a negative impact on some other ports, especially Bristol, and also east-coast ports such as Hull and Boston. Provincial traders seem to have found it difficult to compete against their London rivals. Southampton enjoyed a boom, especially in trade with Venice, but it was short-lived and was over by the middle of the century. Though broadcloths continued to be exported, the biggest change in the cloth industry was the increase in cheaper fabrics such as **kersey**.

KEY TERM

kersey: a coarse woollen cloth which was lighter than the traditional English broadcloth and which took its name from the village of Kersey in Suffolk, a centre of the cloth trade; its lightness broadened its popular appeal

The profits of the cloth trade did not always find their way into English pockets. Although 70 per cent of cloth exports were transported by English merchants from the 1550s, much of the trade was in foreign hands before this. Nevertheless there were certainly profits to be made in cloth, and the woollen industry grew in the first half of the sixteenth century in order to keep pace with increasing demand.

The ability of the cloth trade to supply its markets depended on the effectiveness of the woollen industry. The industry certainly grew in the first half of the sixteenth century, though by precisely how much is difficult to determine. The industry operated largely on a domestic basis with children carding the wool, women spinning and men weaving it. The wool was then passed from the domestic sphere for more specialist treatment such as fulling

Fig. 1 *Major trade routes from England to the Continent*

A CLOSER LOOK

It is significant in this context that the Crown seems not to have contested the tales of hardship recounted by textile workers who could not afford to pay the Amicable Grant (see Chapter 10, page 103).

and dyeing which existed as small-scale industries throughout much of the country. The three areas which undoubtedly saw the greatest growth in the cloth industry were the West Riding of Yorkshire, East Anglia (especially south Suffolk) and parts of the West Country (especially Gloucestershire, Wiltshire and Devon). The work was not always secure and this could lead to poverty.

On the other hand, there were serious profits to be made, especially by rich and entrepreneurial clothiers who were able not only to acquire wealth but also to enhance their social status. The best such example is William Stumpe of Malmesbury in Wiltshire who became MP for Malmesbury, high sheriff of the county, wealthy landowner and beneficiary from the dissolution of the monasteries.

There was some growth in the mining industries. Cornish tin remained a prize export. Lead mining in the high Pennines and coal mining in the northeast of England were growing in importance, with Newcastle supplying an increasingly important London market by sea. Blast furnaces produced an increasing amount of iron ore in the Weald of Sussex and Kent. By the middle of the century their number totalled 26. However, the upsurge in iron ore smelting would come in the second half of the century.

ACTIVITY

Indicate on a blank map of England the areas most involved in the woollen industry and cloth trade and the major ports from which wool and cloth were exported.

Fig. 2 *Abbey House, built by William Stumpe in the grounds of the dissolved Malmesbury Abbey in Wiltshire*

Exploration

Henry VIII was uninterested in exploration and made no attempt to build on the early achievements of Cabot and the Bristol merchants at the end of the fifteenth century. Although Robert Thorne, a Bristol trader, continued his involvement in an Iceland and Newfoundland fishery, other merchants that showed an interest in further exploration found themselves unable to win royal support for any venture.

Sebastian Cabot remained in Spain for most of Henry VIII's reign apart from two short visits to England, and it was only after Edward VI took the throne that he returned. Interestingly, however, he was assisted in his map-making activities by Robert Thorne's son who bore the same name as his father.

Prosperity and depression

John Guy has argued that 'England was economically healthier, more expansive and more optimistic under the Tudors than at any time since the Roman occupation'. There are a number of points which can be put forward to support this view.

- The population began to grow significantly from about 1525 with, allowing for fluctuations, a decline in the rate of mortality.
- From the 1520s, agricultural prices rose significantly, therefore there was an increase in farming incomes, enhanced in some cases by the practice of **engrossing**.
- **Debasement** of the coinage created a short-term artificial boom in 1544 to 1546, but at a long-term cost to living standards.

On the other hand:

- Bad harvests (for example 1520–21 and 1527–29) led to temporary but significant increases in food prices. Food prices almost doubled across Henry VIII's reign. John Guy has suggested that this caused problems in particular for urban workers.
- Real wages, after a period of stability, began to decline for many. This process was at its worst at the end of Henry VIII's reign when the effects of debasement were particularly evident.
- Assessment for subsidies indicated considerable urban poverty. For example, over half the population of Coventry were recorded as having no personal wealth. The same was true for a third of the population of Yarmouth.

CROSS-REFERENCE

John and Sebastian Cabot and their voyages in the time of Henry VII are covered in Chapter 5, pages 48–49.

Fig. 3 *Sebastian Cabot*

KEY TERM

engrossing: the joining together of two or more farms to make a single agricultural unit; it could be seen as improving efficiency and output at the cost of rendering families homeless

debasement: the reduction in the silver content of coins and its replacement by base metal; debased coins were regarded with suspicion and, as a result, merchants and shopkeepers put up their prices which resulted in an increase in the rate of inflation whose impact was greatest on low wage earners

CROSS-REFERENCE

See the table in Chapter 5, page 49, regarding the wage rates of building craftsmen and agricultural labourers.

- There is evidence of growing unemployment amongst rural labourers, some of whom found work in rural industries such as weaving and mining or moved to towns and cities. There were over 5000 migrants a year adding to the population of London.
- Some people seem to have been made homeless on account of engrossing, though its extent and effects are difficult to determine and legislation regarding the problem was ineffective.

CROSS-REFERENCE

The nature of open-field husbandry in lowland areas is discussed in Chapter 5, page 44.

Impact of enclosure

Enclosure of common fields had existed in the fifteenth century, but had had relatively little impact. It was, however, perceived as creating a moral problem in that it led to the poor being forced to leave their homes. Rather muddled legislation had been passed against enclosure in 1489 and 1515, but there was no real grasp of its extent or the scale of the problem. Its harmful social effects had been highlighted in Thomas More's *Utopia*, published in 1516. In response, Wolsey launched an enclosure commission in the following year to ascertain the scale of the problem, and proceedings were launched successfully against no fewer than 188 defendants who were found to have enclosed illegally. Enclosure at this time was, however, a largely regional practice, most commonly found in east Midlands villages. In any case, the bulk of the damage caused by enclosure and conversion of land from tillage to pasture had taken place before 1485. That did not prevent further legislation in 1534 which attempted to limit sheep ownership and engrossing – with predictably limited results.

Population

The main underlying cause of economic distress was the increase in population. This put a considerable strain on the supply of food which made it difficult at times to meet the rising demand. This problem was made worse by the fact that wages were at best stagnating, with a plentiful supply of cheap labour. The beneficiaries of population increase were wealthier farmers and landowners. Agricultural prices, and therefore income from farming, rose. There was a growing class of substantial farmers who were able or fortunate enough to respond effectively to changing market conditions and who enjoyed much better material conditions as a result. Thus, as John Guy has argued, 'agricultural improvement promoted economic growth at the cost of peasant distress; increased production generated prosperity for landlords and impoverishment for wage-earners'. Society became more polarised, which undermined traditional ideals of good lordship and social responsibility. Consequently, 'the upper strata of society became richer, but the poor became poorer.' Increasingly, the former assumed that the latter were poor on account of their own idleness, which would lead in the long run to much sterner measures taken against vagrancy and begging.

ACTIVITY

Summary

Working in pairs or small groups, choose one of the following features of the economy during the reign of Henry VIII: low wages; enclosing and engrossing; urban poverty; harvest fluctuation. Produce an argument that your chosen feature was the most important factor in ensuring low standards of living.

EXTRACT 2

England was a country of subsistence farming. Here and there, among the great landed proprietors of Norfolk, there were sheep flocks running into thousands, and there may have been cattle farmers in the Midlands and the northern hills who farmed in a big way for a specialised market. Over the country as a whole, however, nine farmers out of ten worked with their families to get enough to eat and make a small annual surplus with which to buy household goods and clothes at the nearest fair. Henrician England was a country of very slow economic growth, if any.

Adapted from W.G. Hoskins, *The Age of Plunder: the England of Henry VIII, 1500–1547*, 1976

EXTRACT 3

By the time of Henry VIII, the economic crises of the Middle Ages were no more. Agricultural improvement promoted economic growth, although at the cost of peasant distress. Increased production generated prosperity for landlords but impoverishment for wage-earners. The effect of economic change was to divide society. The diet of the poor deteriorated, and they were forced to live in bare cottages or rural hovels.

Adapted from John Guy, *Tudor England*, 1988

AS LEVEL PRACTICE QUESTION

Evaluating historical extracts

With reference to these extracts and your understanding of the historical context, which of these two extracts provides the more convincing interpretation of the development of the English economy during the reign of Henry VIII?

STUDY TIP

It is important that you draw on contextual knowledge when considering how convincing each of the extracts is. You must provide an overall judgement as well.

A LEVEL PRACTICE QUESTION

'The performance of the English economy remained weak throughout the reigns of the first two Tudors.' Assess the validity of this claim.

STUDY TIP

To answer this question effectively you will need to cover the whole period from 1485 to 1547. It will help to draw on information from chapters 5 and 11. It is important that you ask yourself what the characteristics of weak economic performance might have been during this period.

12 Religion, ideas and reform

EXTRACT 1

Erasmianism – a blend of humanism and reform and the joint manufacture of More and Erasmus, swayed undoubtedly by the fervent genius of John Colet – was characteristic of the whole English humanist community in the years before the crisis of the royal divorce, and its influence extended far beyond the **Oxford reformers**. This group developed their basic ideas within the framework of their religious beliefs to take an active role in shaping the English religious settlement.

Adapted from James K. McConica, *English Humanists and Reformation Politics under Henry VIII and Edward VI*, 1965

LEARNING OBJECTIVES

In this chapter you will learn about:

- the influence of Renaissance ideas on England
- the reforms of the English Church
- religious continuity and change by 1547.

KEY QUESTION

As you read this chapter, consider the following Key Question.
How far did intellectual and religious ideas change and develop and with what effects?

ACTIVITY

Evaluating historical extracts

As you study this chapter, you should reflect on how convincing is James McConica's treatment of both the intellectual influence of humanism and the link between humanism and the shaping of religious reform.

Renaissance ideas

Renaissance ideas in intellectual life and culture had made a tentative appearance in England during the reign of Henry VII. However, it was during the reign of Henry VIII that Renaissance ideas began to flourish at least among some of the elite groups within English society. To some extent this can be attributed to the king himself. He certainly encouraged thinkers such as More and Erasmus and some of his cultural patronage, particularly the commissioning of the effigies on his parents' tomb, showed the influence of fashionable artistic trends which had arrived in England from Italy.

Humanism and education

The most significant humanist voice in English education was John Colet. In his refoundation of St Paul's School, London, Colet showed his initiative in two respects. Firstly, he appointed as the school's governors members drawn from a city guild rather than choosing clergymen. Secondly, the school's statutes laid down a curriculum, including some works by Erasmus, and teaching methods derived from humanist principles. Colet reinforced the type of school he envisaged by appointing as head, William Lily, a humanist.

Schools like St Paul's and Magdalen College School in Oxford were at the forefront of educational reform, and firmly adopted **Platonist** educational principles, teaching many boys who would later become prominent in the religion and politics of Tudor England. Their influence steadily grew. Similar concepts influenced the foundation of Corpus Christi and Cardinal colleges in Oxford and St John's College in Cambridge. No less a figure than Cardinal Wolsey, much praised by Erasmus, gave his personal commitment to educational improvement by founding his college and also a school in his home town of Ipswich, as well as endowing a professorship in Greek at Oxford. By the end of Henry VIII's reign, humanist influences had gained a lasting hold on university curricula.

CROSS-REFERENCE

Humanism, including the humanist scholars Erasmus, More and Colet, is introduced in Chapter 3. Sir Thomas More is profiled in Chapter 7, page 57.

KEY TERM

Erasmianism: the body of ideas associated with Erasmus and his followers

Oxford reformers: men such as Grocyn, Linacre and Colet who were amongst the first English scholars to adopt humanist ideas and approaches

CROSS-REFERENCE

To recap on humanism, arts and learning under Henry VII, look back to Chapter 6.

John Colet is profiled in Chapter 6, page 57.

A CLOSER LOOK

Desiderius Erasmus and his influence

Erasmus visited England four times; his most important visit was that from 1509 to 1514 when he was appointed to a professorship at Cambridge University and was also a well-known figure in and around Henry VIII's court. In 1516 he published a Greek New Testament complete with a new Latin translation.

A CLOSER LOOK

Platonism refers to the ideas of the Greek philosopher Plato. Interest in Plato's ideas had been revived in fifteenth-century Florence and had then spread round much of Europe. Plato held that the main function of education was to produce 'philosopher kings': what this meant in practice was that pupils should have the ideal of public service instilled into them.

Erasmus was received with enthusiasm in English intellectual circles. He was a friend of Fisher and More and he had some influence on a younger generation of English humanists. More demonstrated his support for Erasmus in 1518 when controversy over the Greek New Testament at Oxford University had led some dons to condemn the study of Greek.

It is important, however, not to exaggerate the importance of Erasmian humanism. Its scope was quite limited and much of the change that took place stemmed from the influence of new religious thinking rather than simply scholarly Renaissance humanism.

Renaissance ideas and English culture

Before Henry VIII came to the throne there were few signs of the influence of Renaissance ideas on English culture. That situation changed during the course of his reign as:

- knowledge of classical learning increased amongst the elite groups in society
- a growing number of schools became influenced by humanist approaches to education
- Henry VIII saw himself as a promoter of new ideas and of humanism
- the Crown needed well-educated diplomats who could communicate with their counterparts in other countries in a fashionably elegant style.

The most important English humanist writer was Thomas More, who combined his intellectual interests with his work as a lawyer and statesman. A number of other writers also demonstrated humanist influences, for example, Thomas Lupset and Thomas Starkey.

Renaissance ideas also had an increasing influence on visual culture. Henry VIII commissioned the Italian sculptor Pietro Torrigiano to produce the tombs of his parents and of his grandmother, Lady Margaret Beaufort. Both tombs were produced in the Renaissance style and are situated in the Lady Chapel of Westminster which Henry VII had

Fig. 1 *The tomb of Henry VII and Elizabeth of York, commissioned by Henry VIII from the Florentine sculptor, Pietro Torrigiano*

commissioned. The contrast in styles is clear. The Lady Chapel is one of the finest examples of late fifteenth-century perpendicular Gothic architecture; the tombs are influenced by the classical concerns of the Renaissance. Another example of Renaissance style within a famous perpendicular setting is the rood screen erected in the early 1530s in the chapel of King's College, Cambridge. It celebrates the marriage of Henry VIII and Anne Boleyn. However, it should not be assumed that Renaissance influences predominated during the reign. Richard Marks has argued that Gothic remained the predominant cultural form.

The same is true of painting. The dominant painters at Henry VIII's court were from the 'northern Renaissance', which owed far more to Gothic influences than it did to the Italian Renaissance. The best-known painter at the court was the German Hans Holbein, though the best paid was the Fleming Lucas Horenbout. Much more esteemed at the time than paintings were tapestries, most of which were Flemish in origin and often displayed chivalric themes from medieval culture. It is also evident that Henry was more conservative in his building tastes than was Cardinal Wolsey. Little remains of the massive building programme, for example Nonsuch Palace, which Henry instituted, but surviving evidence does show a continuing taste for the Gothic, whereas Wolsey's palace at Hampton Court clearly exhibited more classical influence. Henry was also a generous patron of music and musicians and was himself an amateur composer of some skill. Cardinal Wolsey too was noted as a musical patron. Again, however, the most distinctive influence, certainly on the church music heard in the Chapel Royal and in cathedrals, was Flemish. What is evident across the cultural range was that while Italian Renaissance influences were becoming more fashionable, England's main cultural links reflected the close commercial ties which existed between England and the Low Countries.

CROSS-REFERENCE

Architecture in the reign of Henry VII is discussed in Chapter 6, pages 59–60.

ACTIVITY

Prepare class presentations on humanists and artists working in England in this period. Find out something about their lives, their work and their influence.

Reform of the Church

Between 1532 and 1540 Henry VIII, assisted by Thomas Cromwell and Archbishop Cranmer, withdrew the English Church from the jurisdiction of the papacy, established the king as supreme head of the Church, dissolved the monasteries and began to alter the Church's doctrine and practices. This was a hugely significant process which could not have been foreseen in the earlier years of Henry's reign, when the Church appeared broadly popular and effective, albeit with weaknesses.

Fig. 2 *Henry VIII painted by Lucas Horenbout in about 1527*

Weaknesses of the Church

Corruption

A range of offences involving corruption was associated with the Church. These included pluralism (receiving the profits of more than one post), simony (the purchase of Church office) and non-residence (receiving the profits of a post but not being present to perform the duties associated with it). The best example of a corrupt clergyman was Cardinal Wolsey, but many other clergymen were guilty, especially as the Crown used Church offices as a way of rewarding those of its officials who were clergymen.

Anticlericalism

Anticlericalism, or opposition to the political and social importance of the clergy, has often been cited as a weakness of the Church. Some common lawyers objected to the influence of canon law, the law of the Church, and there were objections to the legal privileges of the clergy. There were certainly some instances of clerical misconduct which did cause considerable criticism. The worst example concerned the death of **Richard Hunne**.

A CLOSER LOOK

The murder of Richard Hunne, 1514

Hunne, a London merchant, was found dead in his cell in the Bishop of London's prison. He had apparently hanged himself, but it was evident to the coroner's jury that Hunne could not have killed himself, that he had therefore been murdered and that there had been a clumsy attempt to cover up the murder by dressing it up as a suicide. (Almost certainly what had happened was that an attempt at torture had gone dreadfully wrong and the torturers panicked.) The case was disastrous in the short term for the reputation of the Church, but the time which had elapsed between the case and the start of the break with Rome suggests that by then it was much less likely to have been at the forefront of the minds of critics of the Church.

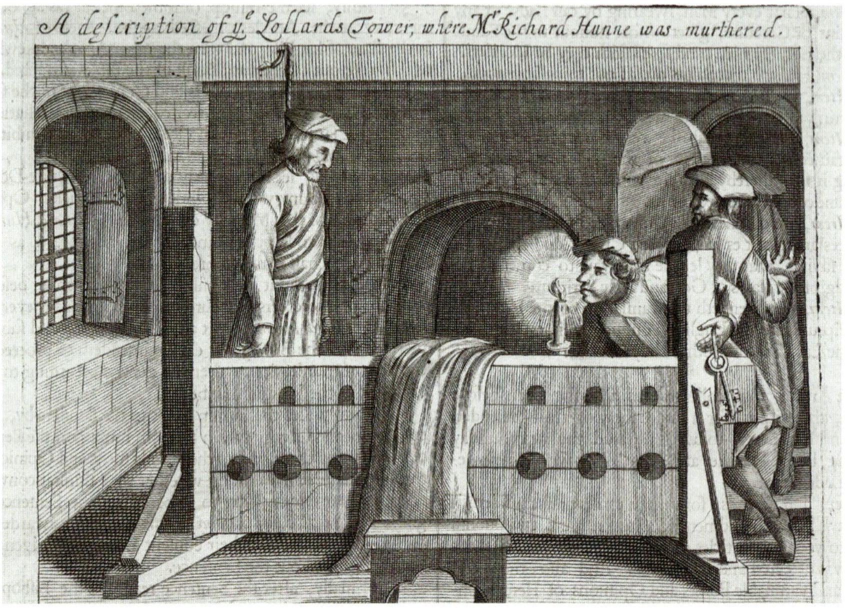

Fig. 3 *The murder of Richard Hunne, as depicted in Foxe's 'Book of Martyrs'*

A CLOSER LOOK

The *Supplication of the Beggars*, written by Simon Fish who was an early English Protestant convert, was dedicated to Henry VIII. It was a vicious and powerful attack on many aspects of the Catholic Church, which was portrayed in exaggerated terms as being greedy, corrupt and treacherous.

The Crown itself was perfectly capable of stirring up anticlerical passions. It is in this context that the much-quoted 1529 attack on the clergy, Simon Fish's *Supplication of the Beggars*, should be seen. There were occasional disputes over tithes and other causes of concern. However, these were relatively rare, and this has led Christopher Haigh to conclude that anticlericalism was less a cause but rather more a consequence of the Reformation.

Decline of monasticism

It has been argued that the operation of the religious houses was open to criticism. Precedents for dissolving the monasteries already existed by the 1530s. Wolsey secured the dissolution of around twenty houses in the 1520s to fund the establishment of Cardinal College, Oxford. Some historians have suggested that monasticism was a relic of a bygone age and had lost its sense of direction; and that the larger monasteries had become, in effect, substantial businesses with huge resources in terms of land and buildings. The ease and speed with which the monasteries were dissolved is held to lend support to this argument. On the other hand, some orders, such as the Observant Franciscans and Bridgettines, were clearly flourishing right up to the final days of the dissolution.

Evidence of early English Protestantism

There is little evidence of a substantial movement towards Protestantism in the years following **Martin Luther**'s attack on the Catholic Church which started in 1517. Certainly some Lollard beliefs survived, and there is evidence of the influence of the German reformers in London and the east-coast ports in the 1520s. At an intellectual level there was a nucleus of future reformers based in Cambridge in the 1520s who met for religious discussions at the White Horse. The leading figure in this group was Robert Barnes, who had been converted to Protestantism by Thomas Bilney. (Both would be burned as heretics later in Henry VIII's reign.) The most influential member of this group proved to be the future Archbishop Cranmer. Otherwise, evidence for committed evangelism is fairly thin.

Erasmianism and the Reformation

James McConica argued that the years from 1529 showed a group of humanists with shared ideals based on the ideas of Erasmus helping to shape royal policy. The evidence for this argument seems rather slender, given that the two most influential humanists in royal circles, Sir Thomas More and Bishop Fisher, paid with their lives for their opposition to the religious changes. Some of the reformers certainly did have humanist connections. These included Archbishop Cranmer. However, not all reformers were humanists – and many humanists either were not reformers at all, or, like Bishops Gardiner and Tunstall, went along with reforms in which they did not believe in order to maintain their lives and positions.

There is, however, some evidence that a humanist approach to reform persisted during the final years of Henry VIII's reign. Cranmer continued to enjoy the king's favour, even when he was being subject to attack by enemies such as the Duke of Norfolk. The king turned to the humanists John Cheke to be the tutor to his son and heir, Edward, and Roger Ascham to be the tutor to Princess Elizabeth. There was a humanist circle around the king's last wife, Katherine Parr. She herself had had a humanist education, unusual enough for a woman of her generation, and was a generous patron of the arts and literature.

EXTRACT 2

The sponsorship for this devout humanism came from the highest quarters and was never far from the royal family itself. The association of the London humanists with the mercantile community was amply evident from the careers of Colet and More and from the involvement of the Mercers' Company with St Paul's School. Most obvious was the concentration of important patronage in a very few hands and the close industry of this sponsoring group, including courtiers, administrators, ecclesiastics and reforming abbots. Finally, at the centre of this whole group of patrons was the king himself. Equally important was the opposition to Erasmus. Only one man of stature in learned circles opposed him, Edward Lee, later Archbishop of York.

Adapted from James K. McConica, *English Humanists and Reformation Politics under Henry VIII and Edward VI*, 1965

EXTRACT 3

The humanism of Erasmus and More was fragile. Even without Luther's challenge the humanists would have split because of differences in religious stance. More believed in the supremacy of faith; Catholic beliefs must be defended because God commanded them. Erasmus believed in human reason, and could not accept that God tested people's faith by making them believe things that humanist scholarship had thrown into question. So these splits weakened humanism. Instead, new exponents of reform caught public attention.

Adapted from John Guy, *Tudor England*, 1988

KEY PROFILE

Martin Luther (1483–1546) was a German monk who challenged the Catholic Church's teaching on salvation in 1517. His challenge broadened into an attack on papal supremacy. He gained the support of many secular rulers in Germany, who withdrew their territories from allegiance to Catholicism.

CROSS-REFERENCE

Thomas Cranmer, who became Archbishop of Canterbury in 1532, is profiled in Chapter 8, page 79.

Bishop Stephen Gardiner is profiled in Chapter 8, page 81.

A CLOSER LOOK

Erasmian reformers

What was important about this group of humanist reformers was not the influence it had on religious policy during the reign of Henry VIII, but that it was in a position to influence policy-making during the reign of his successor. However, by the time the young Edward VI came to the throne, the moderation of many of the humanist reformers would be supplanted by more radical strands of reform.

STUDY TIP

You should consider the ways in which each extract is both convincing and unconvincing by applying your own knowledge to support or challenge the points made by each author. Try to provide an overall conclusion in which you justify your decision as to which is the most convincing.

AS LEVEL PRACTICE QUESTION

Evaluating historical extracts

With reference to Extracts 2 and 3 and your understanding of the historical context, which of these two extracts provides the more convincing interpretation of the importance of humanism in Henry VIII's reign?

Changes to the Church's structure

Change	Significance
King becomes supreme head of the Church	This was *confirmed* by the Act of Supremacy in 1534. The Act did not confer the supremacy on the king.
King appoints Cromwell *Vicegerent in Spirituals*, 1534	Cromwell was second only to the king and therefore outranked the archbishops and bishops. This gave Cromwell considerable power over the Church. The post, however, died with him.
Six new **dioceses** (areas under the jurisdiction of a bishop) were created, though one was soon abolished	This was an attempt to improve the Church's administration.

No other changes were made to the structure of the Church. Spiritual jurisdiction continued in the hands of archbishops and bishops. In this way the Church of England differed from reformed churches in continental Europe.

KEY CHRONOLOGY

1535 Compilation of *Valor Ecclesiasticus*

Start of 'visitations' to monasteries

1536 Act to dissolve the smaller monasteries

1539 Act to dissolve the remaining monasteries

1540 All religious houses dissolved

Dissolution of the monasteries

The process of dissolution can be traced back to the compilation of the *Valor Ecclesiasticus*, a survey set up by Cromwell in 1535 to discover exactly how wealthy the Church was. This gave Cromwell a broadly accurate indication of the resources which were available for the Crown to plunder.

The next stage was amassing the evidence which could be used to justify dissolving the monasteries. Accordingly, four 'visitors' were sent round the country to inspect all monastic institutions. They found much to criticise, though they had clearly been instructed to find evidence of weakness and corruption, and the most fair-minded of the visitors, Tregonwell, often mixed his criticism with praise for the holiness and conscientiousness of those whom he was inspecting.

The visitors provided Cromwell with enough evidence to justify bringing in an Act of Parliament in 1536 to dissolve the smaller monasteries, defined as those with an income of under £200 per annum or less. This was presented as a mechanism for preserving and improving the quality of monasticism, the argument being that it was the smaller religious houses which had allowed standards to slip.

However, the scope of dissolution widened after the Pilgrimage of Grace, as the heads of religious houses that had been implicated in the rebellion voluntarily surrendered to the Crown. It was probably Cromwell's intention all along to get rid of the monasteries once the softening-up process had taken effect and in 1539 an Act dissolving the remaining monasteries was passed. By March 1540 all of the remaining religious houses had been dissolved.

CROSS-REFERENCE

The social implications of the dissolutions are discussed in Chapter 10, page 105.

Fig. 4 *Fountains Abbey in Yorkshire*

The attack on traditional religious practices

This began with the issue in 1536 of the first set of royal injunctions and was taken much further with the issue of the second set two years later. As well as encouraging more moral conduct, the 1536 injunctions placed a restriction on the number of holy days to be observed and discouraged pilgrimages. In 1538 pilgrimages and **veneration** of relics and images were condemned as 'works devised by men's fantasies'. Clergy who had upheld the virtues of pilgrimages, relics and images were required publicly to recant. The implications of the 1538 injunctions for traditional worship were undoubtedly radical.

The English Bible

The injunctions of 1538 required each parish church to acquire an English Bible and encourage 'every person to read the same, as that which is the lively word of God, that, every Christian man is bound to embrace'. (In practice, few would actually be able to read this Bible. For the majority, religious messages still came primarily from visual images.) The first edition of the Great Bible appeared in 1539, complete with a title page showing Henry VIII graciously 'offering' the word of God on the one hand to Cranmer and his bishops and on the other to Cromwell and other politicians.

Within four years, Henry had tired of this role and had become fearful of allowing the wrong sorts of people to read the wrong parts of the Bible. The Act for the Advancement of True Religion of 1543 therefore restricted the public reading of the Bible to upper-class males. Women and men of other classes had 'increased in divers naughty and erroneous opinions and by occasion thereof (have) fallen into great division and dissension among themselves'. The word of God was all very well, but not if it loosened the bonds of social control on which good order depended.

Changes to doctrine

At this stage of the Reformation changes in doctrine were less important than the challenge to traditional religious practices. In any case, there was no consistent pattern of doctrinal change, which reflected the king's inability to make up his mind definitively about such matters.

KEY CHRONOLOGY

1536	First set of royal injunctions
1538	Second set of royal injunctions
1539	First edition of the Great Bible
1543	Act for the Advancement of True Religion

KEY TERM

veneration: the honouring with awe and reverence of a religious object

Fig. 5 *The front cover of the Great Bible*

ACTIVITY

In pairs or small groups, discuss why the image of Henry VIII as portrayed in the Great Bible was important as royal propaganda.

Measure	Proposal	Significance
1536 Ten Articles	Only three sacraments, baptism, penance and Eucharist, were seen as necessary to salvation (Lutheran) but the definition of Eucharist was ambiguous. Confession (Catholic) was praised. Praying to saints for remission of sins was rejected (Lutheran) but praying to saints for other purposes was still deemed 'laudable'.	This was an ambiguous document which showed both Lutheran and Catholic influences on the development of doctrine.
1537 Bishops' Book	Restored the four sacraments omitted from the Ten Articles, but the four restored sacraments were given a lower status.	This was therefore a more conservative document than the Ten Articles.
1539 Six Articles Act	This reasserted Catholic doctrine. Denial of transubstantiation was deemed heretical.	This was a triumph for the conservatives. It was founded on the assumption that there had been too much religious controversy and that this undermined the good ordering of society. Two reforming bishops resigned their posts.
1543 King's Book	This revised the Bishops' Book.	The emphasis was largely conservative, but with some Lutheran hints.

CROSS-REFERENCE

To recap on the fall and execution of Cromwell, look back to Chapter 8, pages 80–81.

ACTIVITY

Look back at James McConica's interpretation at the beginning of this chapter (page 115). How convincing do you find his claim about the role of humanism in religious reform in England?

Continuity and change in religion and culture by 1547

Some aspects of the English Church in 1547 would have been familiar to someone who had been alive at the start of Henry VIII's reign in 1509. The hierarchy of the Church remained largely intact; there had been little attempt as yet to alter the interior of churches; and services remained largely traditional in form. Moreover, the passing of the Six Articles Act in 1539 and the fall of Cromwell in 1540 had seriously weakened the cause of religious reform. Services continued to be held in Latin and music continued to play an important role in services in cathedrals and collegiate churches.

Much, however, had changed. The jurisdiction of the Pope had been destroyed; the king was a much more visible authority figure than the Pope, whose grip on the English Church had been remarkably loose much of the time; the monasteries had been dissolved, many monastic buildings were falling into ruin and there had been a massive transfer of resources from the Church to the Crown through the dissolution; parish churches were required to possess Bibles in English (though many of them did not). Religious culture had been influenced by humanism. This had certainly contributed to the undermining of the traditional Church and by the end of Henry VIII's reign humanism looked poised to achieve even greater influence. On the other hand, however, the undoubted humanism of Catholic martyrs like More and Fisher shows how diverse humanist influence had become. Wider Renaissance culture had become firmly entrenched at court and in the circles of the wealthy and well educated and would retain its cultural prominence for the rest of the century.

ACTIVITY

Summary

Evaluate the importance of the key changes which took place in the English Church during the reign of Henry VIII.

	Importance
Supremacy	
Church organisation	
Doctrine	
Religious practice	
Monasteries	

A LEVEL PRACTICE QUESTION

'Henry VIII might have made himself supreme head of the Church of England, but he did little else to change the Church.' Assess the validity of this claim.

STUDY TIP

The greater the number of areas in which you can evaluate change and continuity, the easier the question becomes. It is possible, of course, to decide that some areas showed considerable change whereas others were more noted for their continuity. Make sure that you produce a conclusion to the essay which fully reflects such differing outcomes.

3 Instability and consolidation: 'the mid-Tudor crisis', 1547–63

13 Edward VI, Somerset and Northumberland

EXTRACT 1

Edward's life, after he ascended the throne, was played out mainly in the Privy Chamber, the focus of the court's political life, to which access was closely guarded by the four principal gentlemen of the Chamber, of whom the most important was **Sir Michael Stanhope**, Somerset's brother-in-law. Until the **Protector**'s fall in October 1549, Edward was a cypher in politics, exercising little influence of his own. He was like the king on a chessboard, having little room for manoeuvre, but crucial to the development of the game. Control of the person determined the possession of power.

Adapted from Penry Williams, *The Later Tudors: England, 1547–1603*, 1995

LEARNING OBJECTIVES

In this chapter you will learn about:

- the roles and importance of Edward VI, Somerset and Northumberland
- royal authority during the reign of Edward VI
- the problems of succession
- relations with foreign powers.

KEY PROFILE

Sir Michael Stanhope (d. 1552)

Stanhope, a Nottinghamshire gentleman, owed his position to the marriage of his sister to the Duke of Somerset (then Sir Edward Seymour). The two remained closely linked and Stanhope was a key household officer under Edward VI as Groom of the Stool and Chief Gentleman of the Privy Chamber. In other words, he was the king's keeper. He was imprisoned when Somerset fell from power and executed following his involvement in Somerset's attempted coup against Northumberland.

KEY QUESTION

As you read this chapter, consider the following Key Questions:

- How effectively did the Tudors restore and develop the powers of the monarchy?
- In what ways and how effectively was England governed during this period?
- How important was the role of key individuals and groups and how were they affected by developments?

Royal authority under Edward VI

Fig. 1 *Edward VI, pictured as Prince of Wales a year before he came to the throne*

KEY TERM

Protector: the term used to describe Edward Seymour, the Duke of Somerset, who was in charge of the kingdom as Edward was too young to rule in his own right; Somerset's rule is described as a 'protectorate' or 'protectorship'

ACTIVITY

Evaluating historical extracts

As you study this chapter, consider how convincing you find the interpretation in Extract 1 of Edward VI's role in government.

CROSS-REFERENCE

Edward Seymour, Earl of Hertford, who became Duke of Somerset in 1547, is profiled in Chapter 8, page 82.

For the religious upheaval that had taken place under Henry VIII, look back to Chapters 10 and 12.

The wars against France and Scotland and the poor state of England's finances that resulted from them are discussed in Chapter 9.

The accession of a nine-year-old king created many problems. It was by no means clear that the new king, on whose behalf the reins of government had been seized by an uncle – **Edward Seymour**, Earl of Hertford and subsequently Duke of Somerset – would have a trouble-free accession. Furthermore, he had a difficult inheritance:

- the country was divided on religious grounds
- Crown finances had been ruined by expensive wars against France and Scotland
- to pay for the wars the coinage had been debased, leading to a considerable rise in the rate of inflation and a substantial decline in real incomes for many
- the Crown had compromised its own long-term security by selling off monastic lands, often at a considerable discount, in order to raise money quickly.

Henry VIII, in his will, had set up a Regency Council to govern England during Edward's minority. This comprised sixteen members, supported by a further twelve who were required to assist as required. Decisions of the Council were to be by majority. The Regency Council was balanced between Protestants such as Hertford, Cranmer and Sir Anthony Denny and religious conservatives such as Thomas Wriothesley, now the Earl of Southampton, and Lord St John (later Marquis of Winchester). There were several administrators and lawyers who might have been expected to ensure the interests of good government. On the other hand, the great noble families were under-represented. The Regency Council did not last long; it promptly delegated its power to Hertford who was appointed Protector.

The government was fearful for good order and security. The tone of Archbishop Cranmer's **homily** *on Obedience*, published in 1547, to be read in parish churches, made this very clear. The clergy in their pulpits were required to reinforce to their congregations that obedience to the authority of the king was in accordance with the will of God; disobedience was, therefore, a **mortal sin**.

KEY TERM

mortal sin: a sin, which if unforgiven, could lead a person's soul to be subject to eternal damnation

homily: a published reading which could be substituted for a sermon produced by a clergyman

The Duke of Somerset

Hertford counted on the support of Archbishop Cranmer, **Viscount Lisle** (later **Earl of Warwick** and **Duke of Northumberland**), and **Sir William Paget**. He rewarded his supporters and himself with promotions within the peerage (he became Duke of Somerset) and substantial grants of Crown lands.

Fig. 2 *The Duke of Somerset*

KEY PROFILE

John Dudley, Viscount Lisle, Earl of Warwick, Duke of Northumberland (1504–53) was son of Henry VII's tax gatherer, Edmund Dudley, and he was a soldier whose political career progressed during the 1540s. He initially enjoyed a good working relationship with Somerset, but this deteriorated. He overthrew Somerset in October 1549 and became Lord President of the Council and in 1551 Duke of Northumberland. He was executed for treason after the failure of the plot to place Lady Jane Grey on the throne.

Sir William Paget (c1505–63) prospered as a diplomat and administrator under Henry VIII. He was appointed clerk to the Privy Council in 1540 and in 1543 became one of Henry's two principal secretaries. He was close to Somerset, but also served Northumberland and Mary. He was excluded from the Privy Council by Elizabeth.

Within weeks Somerset had awarded himself control, governing largely with members of his own household, only one of whom, Sir Thomas Smith, was appointed a member of the Privy Council. He reinforced this power by controlling the Privy Chamber through the appointment of his supporter, Sir Michael Stanhope, as Chief Gentleman. Increasingly, members of the Privy Council felt resentment at the protectorate; within a few weeks one of them, the Earl of Southampton, had been arrested. Moreover, there could be no guarantee of wider public acceptance of Somerset's protectorate. Consequently, there were widespread fears about the breakdown of law and order.

The atmosphere within Somerset's regime was quickly soured by factional rivalries. The first victim was Somerset's brother, **Thomas Seymour**. Seymour not only sought to turn Edward VI against his brother, the Protector, but also tried to plot with the Earl of Southampton against Somerset. This gave Somerset little choice but to bring treason charges against Seymour. He was assisted by Southampton who denounced Seymour and thereby achieved his readmission to the Council.

Such problems were reinforced by policy failings under Somerset. At the heart of these failings lay Somerset's approach to foreign policy, especially with regard to Scotland. Moreover he badly mishandled the rebellions that broke out in 1549. Even before 1549, however, misgivings about Somerset had been growing. His arrogant and dictatorial manner created enemies, especially Southampton who resented his earlier imprisonment. His style of government and his policy failures combined to weaken him in the minds of many of those who had originally supported him. The most important such enemy was the Earl of Warwick, and the apparent feebleness of Somerset's response to the rebellions of 1549 gave Warwick the opportunity to strike.

At some stage in August 1549 Warwick and Southampton, along with two other conservative noblemen, the Earl of Arundel and Lord St John, decided that Somerset's control should be brought to an end. Initially they tried to secure the support of Princess Mary, but she decided to steer well clear of any conspiracy. By October the conspirators were ready to strike. There was a stand-off between the conspirators, based in London, and Somerset who was at Hampton Court but who crucially still had control over the king. Somerset and Edward retreated to Windsor but, in the end, Somerset, having been promised that no treason charges would be pressed against him, surrendered.

The Duke of Northumberland

As a result of the coup against Somerset and the protectorate, Warwick, as the leader of the plot, found himself first among equals. He was anxious to avoid the excessive concentration of power that had itself done so much to bring Somerset down, and so there was no attempt to re-establish a protectorate. Warwick presided as Lord President of the Council, but at first it was unclear exactly what type of regime he was going to preside over. Many of his key supporters in the coup had been conservatives; some of these hoped for a regency led by Princess Mary. The nature of the regime was made clearer by Warwick's second coup, this time directed at the conservatives. It was later assumed that Warwick always intended this second coup so that he could exercise unlimited power. However, it seems more likely that Warwick acted because he feared that he himself might be ejected by the conservatives.

The purging of the conservatives Southampton and Arundel, Cranmer's support and the king's own increasingly assertive Protestantism determined the religious character of the regime. Warwick himself was promoted to Duke of Northumberland. Already Lord Chamberlain, he appointed his own hardman, Sir John Gates, as Vice-Chamberlain of the household to ensure his control over the court.

A CLOSER LOOK

Thomas Seymour, who had been left out of the Regency Council, had married Henry VIII's widow, Katherine Parr. This brought him into close proximity to Katherine's stepdaughter, Princess Elizabeth, and led to rumours of an affair.

CROSS-REFERENCE

Somerset's handling of policy towards Scotland is discussed on pages 129–130.

The rebellions of 1549 are outlined in Chapter 14, pages 139–141.

Fig. 3 *John Dudley, Duke of Northumberland; three of his signatures are included below the picture*

ACTIVITY

In pairs or small groups, produce a paper written from the perspective of an adviser to the Earl of Warwick (the Duke of Northumberland from 1551). In the paper you should explain the following:

- the key problems facing the government
- what measures might be taken to deal with these problems
- what Warwick needs to do to consolidate his political position.

KEY PROFILE

Sir John Gates (1504–53) owed his initial advancement to the support of his brother-in-law, Sir Anthony Denny, and became Vice-Chamberlain of the household and one of the Chief Gentlemen of the Privy Chamber. He incurred the animosity of Princess Mary by preventing her from attending Mass and this helped to seal his fate; he was executed along with Northumberland.

ACTIVITY

Class debate

Set up a class debate on the Duke of Northumberland. Use the material in this chapter to argue whether or not he deserves Dale Hoak's description of being 'remarkably able'.

CROSS-REFERENCE

William Cecil was to fall from favour during Mary's reign, but became very close to the Princess Elizabeth, whom he was to serve as chief minister for almost 40 years. He is profiled in Chapter 17, page 166.

A CLOSER LOOK

The historiography of Northumberland

For several centuries Northumberland enjoyed a bad press from historians. He was seen as particularly ruthless and unscrupulous on account of his coups against Somerset and then the conservatives, his securing of Somerset's execution and his failed attempt to alter the succession. There was a simple contrast between Somerset 'the good duke' and Northumberland 'the bad duke'. Moreover, Northumberland's unscrupulousness was apparently combined with incompetence. In more recent years Northumberland's reputation has been favourably reassessed. This process was begun by the American historian Dale Hoak who argued that Northumberland was no more unscrupulous than any other leading Tudor politician. Moreover, Hoak went much further in claiming that Northumberland was 'one of the most remarkably able governors of any European state during the sixteenth century', solving many of the problems which he had inherited from Somerset. More recently, David Loades has offered a more measured evaluation in the *Oxford Dictionary of National Biography* (2004). On the one hand, he views him as 'a major figure in English government for a crucial decade'; on the other hand, though a 'hardened professional', he 'destroyed himself by a major miscalculation which left his reputation as discredited as his career'.

Northumberland did for a time operate an effective government through the Privy Council, although his task in this respect was undoubtedly made easier by the expulsion of the Earl of Southampton. Paget had drawn up a set of guidelines for the more effective operation of the Privy Council, some of which Northumberland instituted, although Paget was to find himself increasingly excluded from decision-making processes. Instead, William Cecil, who had originally prospered as one of Somerset's men, was able to transform himself, after a brief period of imprisonment, into Northumberland's key administrator.

EXTRACT 2

The secret of Northumberland's power was that he took Edward seriously. He knew that he must accommodate the boy's keen intelligence and also his sovereign will. This first showed itself in 1550 when at the confirmation of Bishop Hooper, Edward with his own pen angrily deleted from the oath of supremacy all reference to saints. By October 1551 the king clearly possessed a powerful sense that he and not his council embodied royal authority. Edward stood on the threshold of power but Northumberland was skilfully guiding the king for his own purposes by exploiting the boy's precocious capacity for understanding the business of government. He did this with the help of his clients and confidants in the Privy Chamber.

Adapted from Dale Hoak, 'Edward VI', *Oxford Dictionary of National Biography*, 2004

However, this broadly collective approach to government did not survive Somerset's attempt at a counter coup. Having been readmitted to the Council, Somerset plotted to recover his old position, but was outwitted by Northumberland. Somerset was executed, an action which, according to Dale Hoak, saved England from a revival of the chaos that had characterised the protectorate. Northumberland reacted to the coup attempt by becoming less conciliar in his approach to government. In other words, he started to behave in precisely the way that Somerset had before he was removed. Presumed enemies such as Paget were removed from the Council and

Paget himself was sent to the Tower. Power lay increasingly in the hands of Northumberland and his henchman Gates, who had possession of the dry stamp with which he could affix the king's signature to documents.

Problems of succession

While Northumberland restored stability, his reputation has been tarnished by his attempt to alter the succession.

In his will Henry VIII had laid down that he should be succeeded by his son Edward, but that if Edward should die without children, then he should be succeeded by Princess Mary. For much of Northumberland's time in power this was not an issue. Although Edward's health was never particularly robust, he was nevertheless expected to reach adulthood. However, in February 1553 he was taken ill and by the end of March the Venetian ambassador reported that he was dying.

The rapid decline in Edward's health created an immediate problem for Northumberland. It was obvious that if Mary were to come to the throne, Catholicism would be restored. Northumberland, who had enthusiastically supported a more radical form of Protestantism, would thus be ruined and his life would be in danger.

A plan, known as the *Devyse*, was consequently produced to alter the succession and the original idea may well have come from Edward rather than Northumberland. Edward was anxious to ensure the continuation of Protestantism in the event of his death and was prepared to exclude both his half-sisters (Mary and Elizabeth, who was second in line) from the succession. To Edward, both were illegitimate. Northumberland's preferred choice as the next monarch was **Lady Jane Grey**. Jane was married to Northumberland's son, Guildford Dudley. In June 1553, Mary and Elizabeth were both declared illegitimate and preparations were made to call a parliament to ratify the new succession. However, Edward died on 6 July 1553 before that parliament could meet. Without parliamentary sanction the *Devyse* was patently illegal.

Surprisingly, for someone who was such an effective political operator, Northumberland seemed to have no plans in place for what to do when the king actually died. It took him three days to carry out his plan and not until 9 July 1553 did he proclaim Lady Jane Grey as queen.

Relations with foreign powers

In 1547 Somerset inherited a potentially ruinous foreign policy from Henry VIII. Somerset's aggressive approach to Scotland was determined by the strategic objective of reasserting the ancient claim of Edward I to the Scottish throne. His aim was to enforce the marriage between Edward VI and the infant Mary, Queen of Scots and thereby unite the crowns of England and Scotland. The difference between the approaches of Henry and Somerset was that for Henry an aggressive policy towards the Scots was a sideshow with the main action being in France, whereas for Somerset Scotland was his main priority.

Somerset's chosen strategy was to defeat the Scots in battle, build and garrison a number of forts in the borders and south of Scotland and force the Scots into submission. Matters began well for Somerset, who defeated the Scots at the Battle of Pinkie in September 1547. However, the strategy soon began to unravel. The forts proved difficult and expensive to garrison, the English could not capture the strategically significant castles at Dunbar and Edinburgh, Somerset underestimated the amount of cooperation between Scotland and France and failed to block the Firth of Forth properly, thereby enabling the French to relieve Edinburgh. In the process the French were able to gain control of the young Queen Mary, who was duly taken to France in August 1548 to marry the Dauphin, the heir to the French throne.

KEY QUESTION

How did relations with foreign powers change and how was the succession secured?

CROSS-REFERENCE

To recap on the terms of Henry VIII's will, look back to Chapter 9, page 93.

KEY PROFILE

Lady Jane Grey (1537–54) was a great-granddaughter of Henry VII. A Protestant, she had married Guildford Dudley, son of the Duke of Northumberland and became the object of the *Devyse*. Having been declared queen by the Privy Council after Edward VI died, she was deserted by most of her councillors once they realised the extent of Mary's popular support. Though initially spared by Mary, she was executed for treason in 1554.

CROSS-REFERENCE

To see how Northumberland's plans collapsed, read about Mary's response to the crisis at the beginning of Chapter 15.

Fig. 4 *The ruins of Roxburgh Castle, showing its strategically important position above the River Tweed*

This had disastrous consequences for Somerset. He had engaged in a military strategy that proved unaffordable at a time of financial pressure. Moreover, he had failed in his political objective: to secure the marriage of Queen Mary and King Edward. To make matters worse for Somerset, the deteriorating relationship with France led in 1549 to the threat of war and the prospect of a French invasion of southern England – at precisely the moment when he was at his most vulnerable as a result of the rebellions which in turn heightened resentment among members of the Privy Council about his autocratic style of government.

Northumberland, on the other hand, was able to reduce foreign policy expenditure in order to help stabilise the Crown's finances. He ended the wars against Scotland and France. To end the French war Northumberland was forced to return Boulogne to the French. Though this might have been perceived as a humiliating defeat, it did serve to bring about an immediate improvement in the Crown's financial position. The occupation of Boulogne had proved a constant drain on resources. Moreover, the French were willing to pay the substantial sum of £133,333 to recover the port. This financial gain was reinforced by the abandonment of the remaining English garrisons in Scotland; the financial benefit from this clearly outweighed any fears about continuing French influence over affairs in Scotland.

CROSS-REFERENCE

Henry VIII's foreign policy, including the proposed marriage between Edward VI and Mary, Queen of Scots, is the subject of Chapter 9.

The negative impact on the economy caused by Somerset's spending on the war, and the resulting increase in social distress that culminated in the rebellions of 1549, are covered in Chapter 14, pages 138–141.

ACTIVITY

Summary chart

Compare the effectiveness of Somerset and Northumberland as rulers of England:

	Somerset	Northumberland
Relationship with king		
Relationship with Council		
Foreign policy		
Maintenance of order		

ACTIVITY

Revision

Look back at the interpretation by Penry Williams set out at the beginning of this chapter (Extract 1). To what extent is his view that Edward was essentially an easily manipulated puppet borne out by what you have read?

EXTRACT 3

Dependent upon personal influences and relationships, Tudor government varied in style from one reign to another. Henry VII relied very much upon a corps of household servants and other officers operating under special commissions outside the formal institutions of government. Henry VIII put his trust in two great ministers, both of whom built up institutions which they could dominate: Wolsey developing chancery and Star Chamber; Cromwell working through the secretaryship and the new financial courts. In their relations with the nobility Henry was mean with new creations and grants of land. Henry VIII and Edward VI by contrast raised many to the peerage and endowed them generously.

Adapted from Penry Williams, *The Tudor Regime*, 1979

EXTRACT 4

Edward's character remains in many ways unclear, no wonder since he lived so short a time. On the other hand, more writings survive from his hand than from that of any other Tudor, and these have led to much speculation, especially in the notion of a highly intelligent young ruler who in his mid-teens was composing profound State papers. In such memorials Edward demonstrably was copying other people's drafts, though no doubt he contributed this or that point himself; more purely personal is the diary he kept from early in the reign to the days of his last illness. The king's 'majesty' comes through strongly in his frequent assertion of personal authority. Edward was a boy tyrant. Whoever, therefore, really devised policy, no one could afford to ignore the king's religion.

Adapted from Geoffrey R. Elton, *Reform and Reformation: England, 1509–1558*, 1977

A LEVEL **PRACTICE QUESTION**

Evaluating historical extracts

Read Extracts 1, 3 and 4. Using your understanding of the historical context, assess how convincing the arguments in these three extracts are in relation to the quality of government in the years 1485 to 1553.

STUDY TIP

This question takes a broad theme across three reigns. Answers do not require detail, but they do require you to try to synthesise your ideas and judgements across reigns.

A LEVEL **PRACTICE QUESTION**

To what extent did English government respond effectively to the domestic problems which it faced in the years 1529 to 1553?

STUDY TIP

The question invites you to consider a wide range of domestic problems. These can include the implementation of religious change, dealing with popular responses to such changes and problems with the economy and royal finance, as well as issues of government. It is important, therefore, that you develop your skill to synthesise material from a range of contexts in order to respond to this and similar questions effectively.

14 The social impact of religious and economic change under Edward VI

The social impact of religious and economic change

LEARNING OBJECTIVES

In this chapter you will learn about:

- the social impact of religious and economic change under Edward VI
- the rebellions arising from religious and economic change
- intellectual developments including humanism and religious thought.

EXTRACT 1

The **evangelical** establishment were determined to join the religious revolution in the rest of Europe: to destroy the old conservative and Catholic world of devotion in the English Church, which was now severed from its link with European Catholicism. Edward's leading political advisers were ready to implement an alternative programme for making religion more radical. They could not have failed to notice that a programme of religious change also gave the possibility of diverting some of the Church's huge wealth to their own pockets.

Adapted from Diarmaid MacCulloch, *Tudor Church Militant: Edward VI and the Protestant Reformation*, 1999

KEY QUESTION

As you read this chapter, consider the following Key Questions:

- How did English society and economy change and with what effects?
- How far did intellectual and religious ideas change and develop and with what effects?

ACTIVITY

Evaluating historical extracts

Extract 1 is written by a modern historian who is an expert on both the English and the continental Reformations. What impression does he convey of the attitudes of 'Edward's leading political advisers'? As you read the chapter, reflect on Diarmaid MacCulloch's view and look for evidence which both supports, and disagrees with, what he has written.

Fig. 1 *Edward VI and the Pope. The unclear words are as follows: on the Bible – 'The Word of the Lord endureth for ever'; by the Pope's shoulder – 'idolatry'; under the Pope's right hand 'feyned' (pretended) holiness*

KEY TERM

evangelical: term used by historians in this context to describe anyone who favoured further religious reform; those who were opposed to further religious reform are usually described as conservatives

ACTIVITY

1. What message is being conveyed by the dying Henry VIII?
2. What is happening to the Pope and the monks?
3. What is the overall message of the painting?

KEY CHRONOLOGY

Major religious changes in the reign of Edward VI

Jul 1547	Issue of royal injunctions which are radical in nature
Dec 1547	Dissolution of the chantries
Jan	Act of Uniformity, which laid down the publication of the Book of Common Prayer
May 1549	Book of Common Prayer introduced
Mar 1552	Second Act of Uniformity, which laid down the publication of the second Book of Common Prayer
Dec 1552	Revised Book of Common Prayer introduced
Jun 1553	Forty-Two Articles of Religion published

Religious change

Religious changes under Somerset

Religious policy under Edward VI saw a considerable move in the direction of **Protestantism**. Somerset himself seems to have been a genuine, albeit somewhat late, convert to Protestantism, and he welcomed religious radicals such as John Hooper and Thomas Becon into his household.

CROSS-REFERENCE

Bishop Stephen Gardiner is profiled in Chapter 8, page 81.

For the most part, religious policy under Somerset proved cautious. This is exemplified by the moderate Book of Common Prayer written in 1549 by Archbishop Cranmer, who was himself cautious by temperament and anxious to avoid an increase in religious tension. It had two key objectives: it established a single form for services within the Church of England and it translated the services into English to enhance understanding of the key texts. It therefore simply translated into English many of the traditional Latin services. Indeed, it included an ambiguous Eucharistic declaration which the **Catholic Bishop Gardiner**, a prisoner in the Tower, thought could still imply the acceptance of transubstantiation.

However, a much more radical approach was adopted in some areas, despite the reluctance of public opinion to embrace religious reform. In fact, Somerset's period of power experienced a sustained attack on popular religious practice, particularly in London.

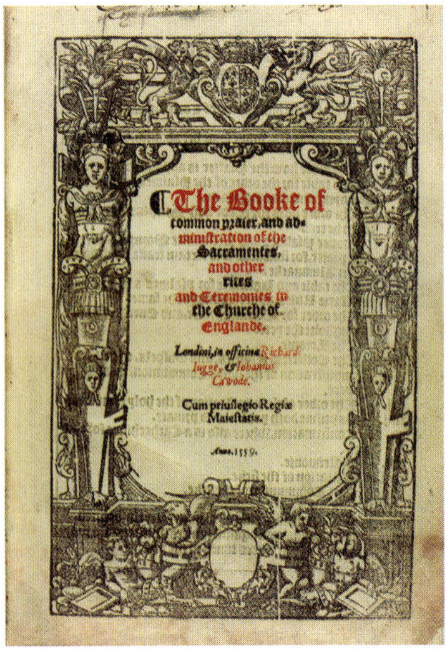

Fig. 2 *A page from the Book of Common Prayer of 1549*

A CLOSER LOOK

Protestantism

Convinced Protestants were in a small minority at the start of Edward's reign. Susan Brigden has suggested in *The Reformation in London* (1991) that roughly 20 per cent of Londoners were Protestant by 1547, which does mean, of course, that 80 per cent were not. The leaders of London Protestantism, especially Nicholas Ridley, were a vocal lobby who were well placed among Somerset's supporters. Kent, East Sussex, Essex, Bristol and the East Anglian ports were other places with entrenched Protestant minorities. Elsewhere, it was almost non-existent. Meanwhile, Catholic survivalism remained strong in the north, especially Lancashire, in Midland counties such as Staffordshire and Worcestershire, and in the far south-west (look ahead to Chapter 16, page 157, for a map of the distribution of Catholic and Protestant areas in the UK at this time).

Table 1 *Religious changes under Somerset*

Date	Policy change	Reason for change	Significance of change
Feb 1547	Denunciation of images in London	Reflected radical attitudes among churchmen, especially **Nicholas Ridley**	Ridley was supported both within government and by Protestant activists within London who engaged in widespread **iconoclasm.**
Jul 1547	Injunctions issued	Reflected radical attitudes in government	Attacked many features of popular Catholicism, such as lights, images, stained glass, processions and practices associated with Candlemas, Ash Wednesday and Palm Sunday.
Dec 1547	Dissolution of chantries and religious guilds	Crown needed money to pay for expensive foreign policy	Chantries, guilds and lay brotherhoods abolished and their property seized by Crown. This represented a further attack on popular Catholicism.
May 1549	Introduction of Book of Common Prayer	Need for uniform approach to religious services	Imposed a more moderate approach to religious reform than that which had been followed in 1547.

A CLOSER LOOK

To encourage acceptance of the religious changes, Archbishop Cranmer published a book of homilies. Homilies were 'off-the-shelf' substitutes for sermons whose purpose was to encourage obedience to both Church and State.

The social impact of these religious changes was highly significant, given that they amounted to a sustained attack on the religious experience of ordinary people, and enabled a renewed plundering of the Church's resources. The injunctions of 1547 attacked many traditional Catholic practices. The subsequent attack on chantries and the plundering of their assets by the Crown destroyed one means of connecting the dead to the communities of which they had once been part, whilst the attack on guilds and confraternities meant that the Crown confiscated money and property which had previously underpinned charitable activities, feasts and celebrations. There was widespread fear that this would only be the start of systematic asset stripping of the Church.

Religious change under Northumberland

Northumberland had a twofold strategy in relation to the Church:

1. He wished to continue the Protestant reforms initiated by Somerset.
2. He sought to plunder more of its wealth.

Moreover, the wider political context helped to shape a more radical approach to Protestantism than might have been expected of a political figure like Northumberland, who had seemed hitherto to be fairly cautious in religious matters. There were a number of reasons for this.

1. The tactically cautious Cranmer was beginning to move in a more radical direction. This was reflected in the much more radical Book of Common Prayer which he introduced in 1552.

KEY PROFILE

Nicholas Ridley (c1500–55) was a Cambridge-educated reformer. He was a chaplain to Henry VIII and quickly emerged as a prominent reformer in Edward VI's reign. He was successively bishop of Rochester and London, and was burnt as a heretic in Mary's reign.

KEY TERM

iconoclasm: the breaking of images; more radical Protestants assumed that images were prohibited because of the wording of the third of the Ten Commandments in the Book of Exodus in the Old Testament

Table 2 *Changes introduced by the revised Book of Common Prayer, 1552*

Key change	Reason for change	Significance of change
Removal of remaining 'conservative' ceremonies	No longer fitted in with the regime's religious radicalism	Conservatives could no longer find anything in the prayer book which they could accept
Rewriting of baptism, confirmation and burial services	To make services more easily understood by congregations	Showed Cranmer's desire to see greater simplicity in church services
Radical reform of communion service, including replacement of wafer by ordinary bread	Need for decisive change from ambiguity of 1549 prayer book	Showed influence of **Zwinglianism** in the Eucharistic declaration, 'Do this in remembrance that Christ's blood was shed for thee'
Ban on use of 'popish' vestments	Seen as objects of 'superstition'	Simpler clerical vestments were seen as more in keeping with the simpler approach to services
Restriction on use of church music	Moderate Protestants thought that church music hindered religious understanding; radical opinion considered it idolatrous	Simpler approach to music reflected the emphasis on greater simplicity in church services

KEY PROFILE

John Hooper (c1495–1555) was Edward VI's most radical bishop. He had travelled extensively in Protestant areas of Europe and returned to England in 1549 when he was appointed a chaplain to Somerset. Northumberland appointed him bishop of Gloucester, and he showed much inflexible radicalism in that post. He was burnt as a heretic in Queen Mary's reign.

A CLOSER LOOK

Protestant reformers were very keen to return to what they saw as biblical purity and often drew parallels between their reforms and similar events in biblical times. In the Old Testament Josiah succeeded to the throne of the kingdom of Judah at a similar age to Edward VI and drove idolatry out of the kingdom. Edward was therefore the 'new Josiah' who would drive out Catholicism.

A CLOSER LOOK

The term **Zwinglian** refers to the religious ideas of Ulrich Zwingli (1484–1531), a Protestant reformer from Zurich in Switzerland; his ideas, which were more radical than those of Martin Luther, were the most important continental influence on the English Church during Edward VI's reign; in Zwingli's view the Eucharist was simply a commemoration of Christ's sacrifice, and no transformation in the 'elements' (the bread and the wine) took place.

2. More radical senior clergy such as Nicholas Ridley, Bishop of London, and the even more radical **John Hooper**, Bishop of Gloucester, were becoming more influential.
3. Eminent continental reformers such as Martin Bucer and Peter Martyr had moved to England and were becoming influential in decisions on religious matters. Moreover, there were very close links between many English reformers and the Swiss reformer, Heinrich Bullinger of Zurich, who had carried on the Zwinglian Reformation in that city.
4. Most importantly, it reflected the increasing influence, as the reign progressed, of Edward VI on the policy-making process. The king took his role as head of the Church very seriously and believed it was his mission to destroy idolatry.

The firmly Protestant nature of official doctrine was confirmed in Cranmer's **Forty-Two Articles of Religion**, although these left some ambiguity between competing varieties of Protestantism.

In addition to the adoption of a more strongly **Protestant** approach, the Crown, still in financial difficulties after the ruinous expenditure of the protectorate, pursued a systematic policy of asset stripping, extracting wealth from the Church through the plundering of the property of bishoprics. For example, the dioceses of Gloucester and Worcester were combined, with two thirds of the Worcester estate going to the Crown; the bishops of Exeter and Winchester made substantial 'grants' from their property to the Crown; and there was a plan, never implemented, to divide the bishopric of Durham and to appropriate much of its wealth to the Crown.

Impact on society of the religious changes

Evidence from churchwardens' accounts suggest that the Crown's orders regarding the destruction of old Catholic habits seem gradually to have been put into effect, although responses to the restoration of Catholicism in 1553 were often rapid. Expenditure on church goods declined after 1540. This seems to have been a reaction to the destructive attitudes of the Crown. In other words, people increasingly felt that there was little point in leaving money to the Church if there was a chance that their bequests might be confiscated by the Crown.

The **evidence from wills** has been much debated. Many wills have not survived and in any case most people did not leave them. It is sometimes possible to make deductions about religious beliefs both from declarations of faith, found at the beginning of wills and from individual bequests, although such evidence needs to be treated with some caution. What is evident is that by the reign of Edward VI people were much less likely to leave money to their parish church.

To historian Christopher Haigh, this represents nothing less than a crisis in religion at the parish level. 'As services became plainer, plays and ales were suppressed, guilds and special funds were abolished, so churches attracted less affection – and much less money – from their people.' There is evidence of a decline in church attendance in the diocese of Exeter and it has also been claimed that there was a decline in the number of candidates for ordination as priests, which could potentially have left the Church with a severe manpower shortage.

In 1550 the radical Hooper admitted that the pace of reform was hampered by uncooperative public opinion. The crisis at parish level was made worse by fear of a Crown attack on church plate. Many parishes tried to avoid this by selling their treasures. Such actions proved justified because in January 1553 the Crown started to confiscate church plate, although some resourceful parishes were able to hide their treasures. Not only was this an attack on the assets of parishes, it was also, as Eamon Duffy has argued, an attack on the history and collective memory of each parish, which encouraged a 'climate of discontent and disobedience'. In such a climate it was, perhaps, unsurprising that the accession of Queen Mary should have witnessed a spontaneous return to the old ways in many parishes.

Fig. 4 *An example of a former chantry chapel; this one is in Buckingham and was used as a school until 1907*

A CLOSER LOOK

The Forty-Two Articles of Religion

The Forty-Two Articles were issued by Archbishop Cranmer in June 1553 and defined the essentials of the faith of the Church of England. As such, they reflected the influence on Cranmer of the Swiss reformers Zwingli and Bullinger. They confirmed the firmly reformed path along which the Church had headed in Edward VI's reign. However, the king's death within a few weeks of their issue meant that they were never implemented. A revised and more moderate version, the Thirty-Nine Articles, was adopted in Elizabeth's reign.

Fig. 3 *Thomas Cranmer, by Gerlach Flicke*

A CLOSER LOOK

Evidence from wills

According to Christopher Haigh's figures, 70 per cent of northern wills between 1540 and 1546 left money to their parish but only 32 per cent did so during Edward VI's reign. In Lincolnshire and Huntingdonshire the decline was even more steep: from 66 per cent in 1545 to just 10 per cent in 1552.

EXTRACT 2

Henry VIII carried the great conservative bulk of the nation with him in his dual action – the severance of England from Roman jurisdiction and the curtailment of the wealth and privileges enjoyed by the English Church. The quiet advances of Protestantism during Henry's last years account for the ease with which Somerset established it as the new official religion from the beginning of the new reign. The Edwardian years display a rough poetic justice. The seizure of chantries and church goods marred the public image of the Reformation in the eyes of many people. The fund of social idealism amongst the reformers, deeply impressive on paper and in the pulpit, availed little at this stage to check the profiteering which it so loudly denounced.

Adapted from A. G. Dickens, *The English Reformation*, 1964

EXTRACT 3

By the end of Edward VI's reign in most churches the altars and statues were gone. Whatever the Crown commanded, the people, for the most part, did. When resistance erupted it was often because of specific local provocations or social and economic crisis. For historians convinced of the bankruptcy of late medieval Catholicism there is nothing here to surprise. Thus, for A.G. Dickens the chantries could be dissolved and the altars demolished because people no longer believed in intercession and the Mass as sacrifice. However, the vigour, richness and creativity of late medieval religion was undiminished and continued to hold the imagination and loyalty of the majority of the population. In the majority of English villages people breathed easier for the accession of a Catholic queen.

Adapted from Eamon Duffy, *The Stripping of the Altars: Traditional Religion in England, c1400–1580*, 1992

STUDY TIP

The phrase 'religious changes' can be applied to a variety of contexts: the motives of monarchs and ministers who imposed the changes, the degree of cooperation of those who had the responsibility for implementing the changes and the attitudes of ordinary people who experienced the changes.

A LEVEL PRACTICE QUESTION

Evaluating historical extracts

Read Extracts 1, 2 and 3. Using your understanding of the historical context, assess how convincing the arguments in these three extracts are in relation to religious changes in England in the years 1532 to 1553.

KEY QUESTION

How did English society and economy change and with what effects?

CROSS-REFERENCE

Henry VIII's expensive wars against Scotland and France are covered in Chapter 13, page 126.

Economic changes

Economic changes under Somerset

There were a number of interconnected economic factors which helped bring about discontent during Somerset's period of rule. These included:

- inflationary pressures
- agrarian issues, particularly enclosure and harvest failure
- taxation.

The rate of inflation had been increasing rapidly during the later stages of Henry VIII's reign, bringing about a marked reduction in real wages for many people, particularly those at the lower end of the income scale. These problems grew worse under Somerset. He continued Henry's disastrous policy of debasing the coinage in order to finance the war against Scotland. Although this raised £537,000, it heightened the inflationary pressures and added to the social distress that many were feeling at the time. A poor harvest in 1548 reinforced inflationary pressures even more.

CROSS-REFERENCE

For previous problems with enclosure, including Wolsey's policies in this area, look back to Chapters 8 and 11.

Enclosure became a serious political issue during Somerset's protectorate. Somerset was much influenced by the writer John Hales who argued that enclosure was the root cause of many of the country's social and economic problems. Somerset therefore, like Wolsey before him, agreed to set up a commission to investigate the problem and issued a proclamation against enclosure. Enclosure commissioners were duly appointed, but little was achieved apart from raising the expectations of the poor, and annoying landowners. In fact, despite the scale of controversy, the rate of enclosure seems to have been slowing down and Somerset's proclamation might well have been wrong-headed.

Taxation caused great discontent. Money had to be raised to pay for the Scottish war; this was mostly financed by land sales and borrowing, which simply added to the long-term problems of Crown finance. What caused even more short-term problems was a failed social experiment. The main driver of increasing amounts of enclosure was perceived to be the profits that could be gained by converting land from arable to pasture in order to graze large flocks of sheep; these would provide wool and cloth for the export market. In order to deter this process Somerset introduced a tax on sheep. It was intended to deter enclosure. Its main effect, however, was to create huge financial pressure on small farmers in upland areas who had little choice but to rely on sheep for subsistence.

Economic changes under Northumberland

After the disastrous final years of Henry VIII's reign and the protectorate, Northumberland achieved a measure of stability in the national finances. He brought an end to the wars against Scotland and France, and this not only ensured a considerable reduction in Crown expenditure but also brought in £133,333 as a French payment for the return of Boulogne. He succumbed to the temptation of one final debasement, but then abandoned the practice. Crown income improved, although some of this improvement was achieved by increasing revenue form the Church by unscrupulous methods, including the melting down of church plate for bullion. Under the influence of Walter Mildmay, a commission produced a detailed analysis of the shortcomings in royal financial administration and plans were made for the streamlining of financial administration, although most of these did not come to fruition until the reign of Queen Mary.

Rebellion

The year 1549 was perhaps the worst year of the whole of the Tudor period. There were major rebellions in East Anglia and the south-west, as well as considerable levels of disorder throughout much of the rest of the country. It was, according to John Guy, 'the closest thing Tudor England came to a class war'. To make matters worse, Somerset's government found it difficult to cope with the rebellions, not least because the thin resources of the Tudor State were overstretched with substantial numbers of troops engaged in the garrisoning of the south of Scotland, while others were stationed in the south-east of England to ward off a potential French invasion.

There were a number of reasons for rebellion and disorder:

- In some parts of the country religious reasons predominated.
- In the Midlands and East Anglia agrarian and social grievances were most important, with the Council receiving numerous reports of riots and of uprooting of enclosures.
- Resentment of taxation appears to have been a consistent factor.

Most of the risings died out fairly quickly, either because of insufficient support or through prompt action from the local nobility and gentry, such as the Earl of Arundel who managed to calm matters down in strategically sensitive Sussex. Arundel heard grievances and punished a few oppressive landlords and disorderly peasants even-handedly, restoring what he considered to be a 'quavering quiet'. Similar methods seemed to work in Cambridgeshire, Yorkshire and the Midlands. However, the south-west lacked a resident aristocrat of Arundel's stature who could bring matters under control, and both the Western Rebellion and Kett's Rebellion in East Anglia required significant military action to suppress them and restore order.

The Western Rebellion, 1549

The Western Rebellion in Devon and Cornwall was prompted particularly by religious grievances. This rebellion has been described as the 'prayer book rebellion' on account of the description by the rebels of the new Book of **Common Prayer** as a 'Christmas game'. However, the rebels had had little chance to experience the new prayer book and the actual religious grievances ran much deeper. The rebels wanted to reverse the religious reforms which were destroying the way in which people had experienced religion. Both the traditional rituals of the church services and much of the Church's wider role in the community had gone.

CROSS-REFERENCE

The introduction of the new Book of Common Prayer in 1549 is discussed on page 136.

A CLOSER LOOK

The extent of resentment in Cornwall was evident in the murder at Helston in April 1548 of William Body. This archdeacon's insensitive approach to the removal of traditional objects of veneration had preceded the introduction of the Book of Common Prayer by over a year, and demonstrated the level of tension which already existed in the county.

SOURCE 1

Extract from the demands of the western rebels, 1549:

Item. We will have the mass in Latin, as was before.
Item. We will have the Sacrament hung over the high altar, and there to be worshipped as it used to be, and they which will not thereto consent, we will have them die like heretics against the holy Catholic faith.
Item. We will have the holy bread and holy water made every Sunday ... images to be set up again in every church, and all other ancient old ceremonies used as heretofore by our mother, the holy Church.

However, the rebellion was also provoked by distrust between the rural labourers, on the one hand, and the landowners on the other, and grievances over taxation. The peasant labourers resented the **sheep tax**, which they regarded as an imposition by an uncaring and ignorant government in London. Their resentment had been made worse by its implementation by insensitive local officials.

A CLOSER LOOK

Sheep tax was introduced in March 1549. It was intended to deter the conversion of arable land to pasture, which was often accompanied by enclosure and driving out of the poor; while its application might have made some social sense in, for example, the east Midlands, it proved a significant burden on hill farmers who struggled to make a living from sheep farming on marginal highlands such as Exmoor and Dartmoor.

A CLOSER LOOK

The Western Rebellion, 1549

6 Jun	Formation of Cornish rebel camp near Bodmin
11 Jun	Start of Devon rebellion at Sampford Courtenay
20 Jun	The two rebellious groups converged on Crediton
21 Jun	Dispute between the rebels and Sir Peter Carew, a Devon JP and courtier
23 Jun	Rebels camp at Clyst St Mary, near Exeter
2 Jul	Rebels besiege Exeter
28 Jul	Lord Russell began his advance on the rebels
4 Aug	Rebels defeated at Clyst Heath
17 Aug	Final defeat of rebels at Sampford Courtenay

CROSS-REFERENCE

For more detail on the sheep tax, look back to page 139 of this chapter.

Kett's Rebellion in East Anglia

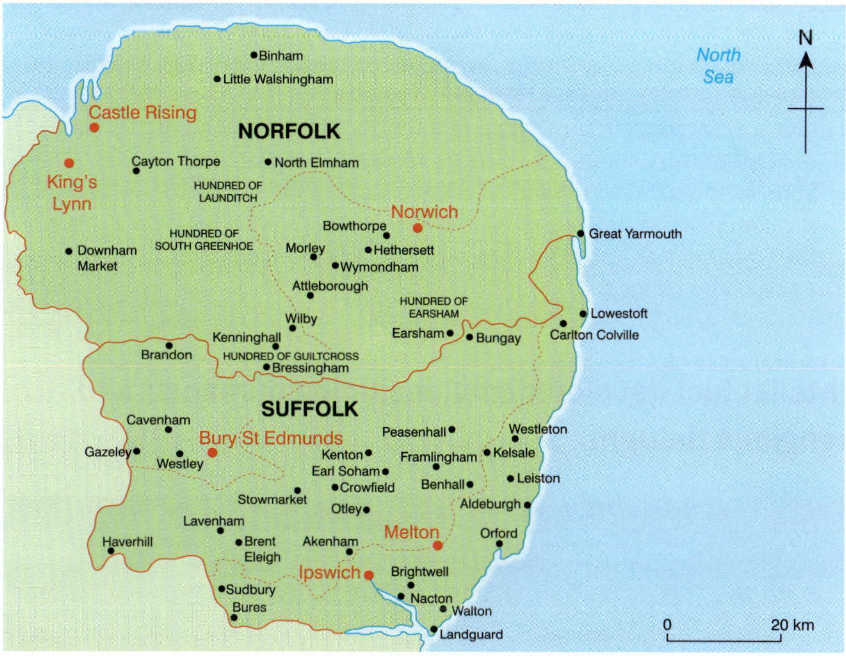

Fig. 5 *East Anglia, showing the main areas of rebel activity in 1549*

There was little evidence in East Anglia of conservative religious tendencies among the leadership, and the rebels at Norwich had services conducted according to the Book of Common Prayer. What the Norwich rebels shared with the Western Rebellion, however, was a sense of class antagonism which was less evident in those counties where the 'commotions' were more easily resolved. Diarmaid MacCulloch has emphasised a number of specific grievances:

- hatred of local government officials
- resentment of the abuse by landowners of the **Norfolk foldcourse** system
- the release of pent-up frustrations about the maladministration locally of the Howards.

A CLOSER LOOK

Kett's Rebellion

8 Jul	Tearing down of hedges near Wymondham
9 Jul	Protestors begin heading towards Norwich
12 Jul	Rebels begin camping on Mousehold Heath, overlooking Norwich; other camps are set up elsewhere in East Anglia
21 Jul	Rebels begin firing on the city
22 Jul	Norwich in hands of the rebels
1 Aug	Failure of Earl of Northampton to recapture Norwich
27 Aug	Rebels finally defeated by forces led by the Earl of Northumberland

A CLOSER LOOK

Norfolk foldcourse

A foldcourse was the right to graze sheep on an enclosed piece of common land. In some villages in Norfolk and Suffolk many of these rights were held by peasant farmers, but problems were caused in some villages by landowners denying access to the foldcourse. (In practice, therefore, peasant holders of foldcourse rights were anxious to defend their own enclosures.) The denial of access to foldcourse was one of the factors that increased levels of peasant discontent and contributed to the outbreak of the rebellion.

However, what the rebels wanted the government to do was to act on the promises of reform which had been made (or which they thought had been made) by Somerset in his proclamation against enclosures in April. This contrasts with the western rebels who wished to reverse government policy. In the process they camped at Mousehold Heath just outside Norwich, where their leader, the tanner and property owner Robert Kett, not only achieved the remarkable feat of maintaining order and discipline but was also able to negotiate with the civic authorities In Norwich.

KEY TERM

mercenary: professional soldier who offers his services to the highest bidder

The suppression of the rebellions

- Somerset had appointed Lord Russell, a rising nobleman with estates in the West Country, to deal with the Western Rebellion. Eventually Russell had enough forces, including foreign **mercenaries**, to be able to defeat the rebels at Clyst Heath near Exeter on 4 August.
- The government's original attempt to crush the East Anglian rebellion by the Earl of Northampton had ended in humiliating failure.
- Somerset was forced to send an army including foreign mercenaries under the command of the Earl of Warwick to deal with the rebels. On 27 August the rebellion was brutally suppressed and Kett was convicted of high treason and hanged.

Intellectual developments, including humanist and religious thought

Fig. 6 *This woodcut from the first edition of Foxe's 'Book of Martyrs' (published in 1563) shows the Protestant preacher **Hugh Latimer**, preaching a sermon*

CROSS-REFERENCE

To find out what happend to Hugh Latimer, the Protestant preacher, during the reign of Mary I, read Chapter 16, page 156.

ACTIVITY

Divide into groups. Acting as advisers to Protector Somerset, write a plan of how he should allocate his scarce military resources in dealing with rebellions, the Scots and the French in the summer of 1549.

The reign of Edward VI witnessed a contest between two reforming traditions:

- the tradition of evangelical humanism associated with those who identified with the teachings of Erasmus
- more radical forms of Protestantism.

Moderate humanism, though it had been weakened by the divisions of the 1530s, still exerted some influence.

- Archbishop Cranmer had been influenced by humanism.
- The 1547 injunctions required each parish church to acquire a copy of the *Paraphrases* of Erasmus.
- The humanist Sir John Cheke had been Edward's tutor.
- The humanist writer Nicholas Udall received government encouragement.
- William Cecil, then junior secretary of state in Northumberland's administration, encouraged humanist scholars at Cambridge.
- Significantly, the humanist-influenced reformers Peter Martyr and Martin Bucer were invited to work in England during Edward's reign. Cranmer secured for Bucer a Crown appointment as Professor of Divinity at Cambridge.

- Even more significantly, the great Lutheran and humanist scholar Philip Melanchthon, the leading continental moderate reformer, was invited to be Bucer's replacement. (Melanchthon, in the middle of a bruising battle with more militant Lutheran opinion in Germany, seems to have taken the invitation very seriously, though Edward VI's death in July 1553 brought this prospect to an end.)

On the other hand, a more militant and less comprehensive approach to reform gained pace under Northumberland. This was partly brought about by the strained relationship which existed between Northumberland and Cranmer. Northumberland seems to have come more under the influence of the radical figure John Hooper, whom Cranmer found divisive. With the move towards more radical reform in 1552 and 1553 it looked as if this movement was gaining ground. However, the death of Edward VI destroyed both contending groups.

The impact of religious change during Edward VI's short reign was profound. Never before, throughout the whole of English history, had the population been subjected to so much religious change so quickly. For many people the experience was disorientating. Perhaps one should conclude that rather than criticising the government for dealing rather ineptly with the two major rebellions of 1549, they should be praised for implementing the policy with so little disruption.

CROSS-REFERENCE

Although Somerset managed to suppress the rebellions, his political credibility was badly damaged. Look back to Chapter 13 to see how this played a significant part in his downfall.

A CLOSER LOOK

Erasmian and radical reformers

Both groups reformed at the beginning of Elizabeth's reign, with the queen herself showing a preference for moderate evangelical humanism.

ACTIVITY

Summary chart

For each of the religious changes, identify its social and/or economic impact.

Change	Social impact	Economic impact
Denunciation of images		
1547 injunctions		
Dissolution of the chantries		
Introduction of Book of Common Prayer		

ACTIVITY

Revision

Look back at the interpretation by Diarmaid MacCulloch given at the beginning of this chapter (Extract 1). In small groups, consider whether you find his interpretation convincing. You will need to find specific evidence to support or refute his views.

A LEVEL PRACTICE QUESTION

To what extent was the English Church in 1553 different from what it had been in 1532?

STUDY TIP

Such questions target the concepts of difference and similarity. Try to identify a range of similarities and a range of differences at the planning stage. Establish the relative importance of these before you start writing, so that you have a clear line of argument in mind before you start writing your answer.

15 Mary I and her ministers

EXTRACT 1

When the moment for action came Mary was courageous, decisive and determined. But she had little experience of government or of politics, and not much inherent sense of manoeuvre. Her presence lacked the majesty of her father and her sister. She worked hard at the business of government, was brave and resolute in the face of opposition, but lacked the quality of 'magnificence' which was an essential quality of Renaissance monarchy. The men who had administered Mary's household when she was princess – Robert Rochester, Edward Waldegrave, Henry Jerningham – were loyal, honest and devoutly Catholic, but also lacked the political experience or social weight to rule the country.

Adapted from Penry Williams, *The Later Tudors: England, 1547–1603*, 1995

LEARNING OBJECTIVES

In this chapter you will learn about:

- royal authority under Mary I
- problems of succession
- England's relations with foreign powers.

KEY QUESTION

As you read this chapter, consider the following Key Questions:

- In what ways and how effectively was England governed during this period?
- How did relations with foreign powers change and how was the succession secured?

ACTIVITY

Evaluating historical extracts

Read Extract 1. As you read through this chapter, look for evidence that Mary 'worked hard at the business of government' but also look for evidence of her limitations as a monarch.

Royal authority under Mary I

Fig. 1 *Mary I portrayed by Antonis Mor, 1554*

Lady Jane Grey might have been proclaimed queen in 1553. However, popular support for Mary was quick to appear. Thus, according to Christopher Haigh, 'to the surprise and embarrassment of those politicians and local leaders who had supposed that there was no choice but to obey Northumberland, Mary was swept to power by a revolution'.

CROSS-REFERENCE

To recap on the attempt by Edward VI and Northumberland to manipulate the succession by means of the *Devyse* to install Lady Jane Grey on the throne, look back to Chapter 13, page 129.

Northumberland's role in suppressing Kett's Rebellion in East Anglia is outlined in Chapter 14, pages 141–142.

A CLOSER LOOK

The historiography of Mary's accession

Until recently it was widely assumed by historians that the people of England were well disposed towards religious reform. It was therefore argued that the popularity of Mary's accession was a reflection of the regard that the English people had for the legitimate succession. However, Christopher Haigh has asserted that the scale of Mary's popularity reflected the considerable devotion to the Catholic faith held by most English people. Indeed, he suggests that confiscations of church goods ensured that 'religion may now be recognised as one of the elements of Mary's appeal'.

CROSS-REFERENCE

England's religious experience under Mary I is discussed in Chapter 16, pages 154–158.

ACTIVITY

Produce a newspaper article commenting on the problems which were facing the new government in July 1553.

A CLOSER LOOK

The failure of Northumberland's *Devyse*

On learning of Northumberland's intentions to proclaim Lady Jane Grey queen, Mary had gathered together Catholic supporters, including members of the nobility, in Norfolk. Northumberland immediately summoned troops and sent a naval squadron to wait off the coast by Great Yarmouth to intercept Mary should she try to set sail. However, there was little love for Northumberland in Norfolk because of the cruelty with which he had put down Kett's Rebellion and the ships he sent proved disloyal to him and declared allegiance to Mary. At this, other members of the Council decided to proclaim Mary as queen on 19 July 1553. Northumberland realised his plan had failed and proclaimed Mary as queen in the marketplace at Cambridge on 20 July.

The failure of the *Devyse*

Northumberland's plans failed for a number of reasons. He had attempted to interfere with the legitimate succession and had compounded this by promoting the claims of his son's wife, thus leading many people to draw the conclusion that the whole business was simply a sordid attempt to hold on to power. His behaviour was, moreover, illegal and upset even some of his more committed supporters on the Council. Although Northumberland had generated less enmity than Somerset among his colleagues, he had little positive support. Mary, on the other hand, had acted bravely, decisively and quickly, gathering support from nobility, gentry and ordinary folk.

Royal government under Mary

It is undeniably the case that Queen Mary's accession was, on the whole, greeted favourably by the English people, though it has been debated whether this was primarily because the English people supported the legitimate succession or because they welcomed England's probable return to the Catholic faith. Certainly, from Mary's point of view, the restoration of the Catholic faith took priority over all other issues of government.

The popular acclaim for Mary obscured some considerable problems.

- She inherited a kingdom that had fundamental religious divisions.
- She was Catholic in a kingdom which had a substantial Protestant minority.
- She had not been brought up to rule, and had little in the way of political instinct to help her cope with the challenges with which she was confronted.
- Her loyal and trusted supporters, such as Robert Rochester, Edward Waldegrave, Sir Henry Jerningham and Sir Henry Bedingfield, had no serious experience in government.
- Mary would have to rely on those who had served her half-brother and were therefore implicated in the introduction of religious reforms that were distasteful to her.

Her new councillors included:

- Bishop **Stephen Gardiner**, who had been her father's secretary and had been a steadfast upholder of religious conservatism during Edward's reign in which he had suffered imprisonment
- other churchmen, who had been excluded from influence during Edward's reign
- some of the more conservative councillors who had at various times served Edward, most importantly Lord Paget.

A CLOSER LOOK

Mary's councillors

Mary appointed 50 councillors during her brief reign. This has led some historians to assert that such a large number of councillors inevitably led to inefficient and faction-ridden government, and to back this claim with the fact that Mary's most important decision – to marry Philip of Spain – was never discussed formally in Council. However, this is misleading. Mary seems to have regarded 'councillor' as an honorary title; the working council board was much smaller and was dominated by such experienced figures as Gardiner, Marquis of **Winchester** and **Paget**. In any case, her trusted group of advisers included Cardinal Pole, who was never a member of the Privy Council.

A CLOSER LOOK

Stephen Gardiner (profiled in Chapter 8, page 81), had lost his post as bishop of Winchester and been imprisoned in the Tower under Edward VI because of his conservative Catholic views. He returned to favour under Mary, was restored to Winchester and appointed Lord Chancellor.

CROSS-REFERENCE

For more on Winchester and a profile of Paget, see Chapter 13, page 126. Pole is profiled below.

Mary was never quite at ease with her key councillors. She lost confidence in Paget on account of his opposition to her religious programme, and she never fully trusted Gardiner, who had failed to support her mother, Catherine, at the time of the break with Rome. She did, however, regard him as indispensable, and his death in 1555 left a gap in government that was never satisfactorily filled, particularly as **Cardinal Pole** distanced himself from secular issues. As a consequence Mary was thrown back on to the advice of the two foreigners whose judgement she trusted implicitly: her husband from 1554, Philip of Spain, and Simon Renard, the ambassador of her cousin and father-in-law, Charles V.

The relationship between Mary and Parliament was usually one of cautious cooperation. A substantial minority of MPs (about 80) opposed the reversal of the Edwardian religious legislation, and there were other examples of opposition to Crown policies. Concern for property rights, doubtless motivated by self-interest in many cases, ensured that ex-monastic property would not be restored to the Church, and Mary did not press the point. Moreover, a bill in 1555 to allow the seizure of property of Protestant exiles was defeated. Mary also quarrelled with Parliament over the issue of the succession.

Fig. 2 *Lord Paget*

ACTIVITY

Make a wall chart to illustrate some of Mary's key councillors, with a little detail on each.

Problems of succession

KEY QUESTION

How important was the role of key indivisuals and groups and how were they affected by developments?

The Spanish marriage, 1554

Once queen, Mary was anxious to get married. She regarded it as essential that she produce an heir so that a Catholic succession might be guaranteed and her relatively advanced age (37) required that the marriage take place as soon as possible. This immediately raised the issue of whom she could marry. There was one English candidate for marriage, Edward Courtenay, Earl of Devon, who was Gardiner's choice – possibly to prevent a foreign marriage. However, this caused problems. Marriage to an Englishman brought with it the threat of factional rivalry, as the husband's family would inevitably become more

KEY PROFILE

Cardinal Reginald Pole (1500–58), a grandson of Edward IV's brother the Duke of Clarence, went into exile in Italy rather than accede to Henry VIII's religious reforms. He was made a cardinal in 1536 and was an influential figure under Popes Paul III and Julius III. He returned to England as Archbishop of Canterbury in 1554 under Mary, but his wider influence diminished under Pope Paul IV, who disliked him and regarded him as a heretic.

KEY PROFILE

Philip of Spain (1527–98) was the son of Mary's cousin, Emperor Charles V. In 1554 Philip was ruling the Netherlands on behalf of his father, whom he succeeded as king of Spain in 1556. He shared Mary's devout Catholicism.

Fig. 3 *Mary I with her husband, the future Philip II of Spain*

influential. Moreover, Courtenay lacked courtly skills and was therefore seen as an unsuitable candidate by many, including Mary herself, who never took him seriously as a potential husband.

Mary's personal preference for **Philip of Spain** was clear, and her view was easily reinforced as her main adviser on this issue was the ambassador Simon Renard, who was himself a Spanish subject, Catholic and politically experienced. Philip's father, Charles V, had offered advice, guidance and moral support throughout Mary's years of unhappiness and was more keen on the match than was his son, although Philip was prepared to 'do his duty'.

However, the matter was not concluded without difficulty. English public opinion was hostile, as Gardiner had predicted, and a parliamentary delegation had attempted unsuccessfully to dissuade Mary from her intentions. In an attempt to allay fears a detailed marriage treaty was drawn up:

- Philip was to be given the title of king but was to exercise none of the power that went with the title
- no foreigners were to be permitted to hold English offices
- if Mary predeceased Philip then the latter could have no claim on the English Crown.

The marriage duly took place in 1554, but Philip was not impressed by his new wife. He resolved to spend as little time as possible in England.

A CLOSER LOOK

The marriage of Mary and Philip

The couple met for the first time on 23 July 1554 and the marriage ceremony took place in Winchester Cathedral two days later. Philip's initial experience reinforced his prejudices. The weather was foul, the English court and people were unwelcoming, there was instant hostility from English courtiers, and Philip found himself marrying a woman who was 11 years older than he was, who seemed prematurely middle-aged in many respects but whose attitude towards love and marriage seemed remarkably childlike. Philip resolved to spend the minimum time possible in his new kingdom.

Parliament was not happy either. In 1554 Parliament rejected a bill that would specifically have included Philip along with Mary in a proposed new law on treason and in 1555, it prevented Philip's coronation as king.

CROSS-REFERENCE

Wyatt's Rebellion, which took place in January 1554 partly in protest at Mary's proposed marriage to Philip of Spain, is discussed in Chapter 16, pages 159–161.

ACTIVITY

Make a chart to show the (a) advantages and (b) disadvantages to Mary of her marriage to Philip of Spain.

Plans for the succession

Mary's overthrow of Northumberland and Edward's *Devyse* had restored Henry VIII's will, as established under the Succession Act of 1544, as the legal mechanism for determining the succession. Under its terms, Mary would be succeeded by her half-sister, Elizabeth, should she die childless. This created an immediate issue for Mary, as Elizabeth was known to be a Protestant and was therefore likely to move religious policy back in a Protestant direction.

Mary had no love for her half-sister, who personified the reason for the breakdown of her mother's marriage to Henry VIII. Indeed, she could never believe that Elizabeth was other than illegitimate and had therefore no moral right to succeed to the throne. However, to deny her the right of succession would require either parliamentary legislation to overturn the 1544 Act or Elizabeth's disqualification through treason.

Following **Wyatt's Rebellion** of January 1554, Elizabeth had been confined in the Tower of London. However, although Mary suspected that Elizabeth was implicated in the rebellion, she had no proof, and was more reluctant than her father to pursue treason charges where there was no compelling evidence. Elizabeth was therefore released from the Tower after two months, though she was in effect kept under house arrest in a succession of country residences. Meanwhile, attempts to change the succession through Act of Parliament came to nothing.

The childless Mary was thus forced reluctantly to accept that Elizabeth would be her successor. Philip had also decided that, from a Spanish perspective, Elizabeth was the least unacceptable option. As Mary's health worsened, Elizabeth came to realise that all she required was the patience to wait for her inheritance. By the later stages of Mary's reign, Elizabeth's confinement at Brocket Hall in Hertfordshire had become fairly comfortable. Few restrictions appear to have been placed on visitors and therefore she was well acquainted with the details of Mary's final illness. Mary formally named Elizabeth as her successor on 6 November 1558. She died 11 days later, knowing that her kingdom would fall into the hands of the sister whose religion she despised.

A CLOSER LOOK

Although Philip was a committed Catholic, the potential succession of the Catholic Mary, Queen of Scots, in reality as much French as she was Scottish, was something he was not prepared to accept.

ACTIVITY

Produce a document on behalf of Philip II outlining from a Spanish perspective the advantages and disadvantages of Elizabeth succeeding Mary.

Relations with foreign powers

KEY CHRONOLOGY

Foreign relations under Mary I

Jan 1554	Marriage treaty between Mary and Philip drawn up Wyatt's Rebellion against the Spanish marriage
Jul 1554	Marriage between Mary and Philip takes place
May 1555	Election as Pope of the fiercely anti-Spanish Paul IV
Apr 1557	Scarborough raid followed by England declaring war against France
Jan 1558	England loses Calais

When she came to the throne Mary had two main aims in terms of her relationship with **foreign powers:**

- to restore England to **papal supremacy**
- to marry Philip, the heir to the Spanish throne.

Both of these was achieved, though in each case it took longer than Mary had anticipated. What she could not have anticipated, however, was the extent to which very soon the two foundations of her foreign policy would come into conflict.

It was evident that it would be very difficult for England to remain neutral in any Franco-Spanish conflict. To make matters even more complicated for Mary, one of the main instigators of renewed Franco-Spanish conflict was the virulently anti-Spanish Pope, Paul IV. England was dragged into the war against France and Mary found herself effectively at war with the papacy, a terrible blow for such a loyal daughter of the Catholic Church.

England finally declared war on France in 1557 following a bizarre landing at Scarborough of French troops led by Thomas Stafford, grandson of the Duke of Buckingham who had been executed in 1521. (Stafford might have been set up by Paget who was the English minister most anxious for war.) Many members of the nobility were enthusiastic about the prospect of war, which also offered a way for those who had been in disfavour because of their links with Edward's regime to regain some credit with the Crown.

CROSS-REFERENCE

The restoration of papal supremacy is discussed on page 161.

CROSS-REFERENCE

For more on the difficulties posed by the relationship between Mary and Pope Paul IV, look ahead to Chapter 16, page 155.

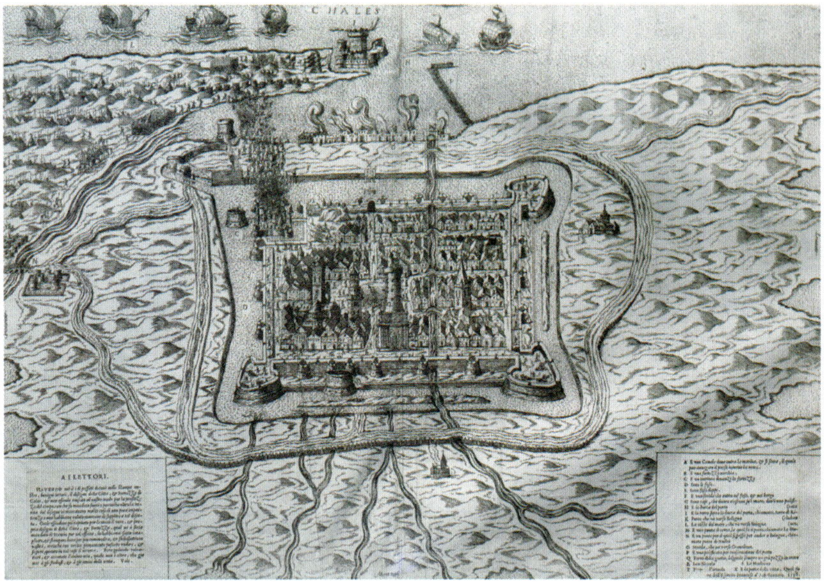

Fig. 4 *The Capture of Calais from the English in 1558, by Francis de Lorraine, Duke of Guise*

Militarily, the campaign had a promising start, assisting the Spanish at the successful siege of St Quentin and dealing easily with a minor incursion into England by the Scots. However, it soon turned into a disaster, with the humiliating loss in January 1558 of Calais, which had been in English hands for centuries. No attempt was made to recapture the town, and a full-scale attack on the port of Brest in the summer of 1558 failed dismally. The story that Mary declared that when she died Calais would be found inscribed on her heart might not be true, but it symbolises the disasters which had befallen the country in the latter stages of the reign.

CROSS-REFERENCE

The Battle of the Spanish Armada of 1588 is covered in Chapter 20, page 202.

A CLOSER LOOK

Naval and militia reforms

Mary's reign also witnessed significant naval and militia reforms. There was a complete reorganisation of the administration and finance of the navy. Six new ships were built, many other ships were repaired and the Crown finances budgeted for a peacetime allocation of £14,000 to the navy, a sum that Elizabeth subsequently reduced. The system worked effectively with the highly efficient treasurer to the navy, Benjamin Gonson, now answerable directly to Lord Treasurer Winchester. In the long term, these reforms laid the basis for the organisation of the navy which, crucially for Elizabeth, was to defeat the Spanish Armada. Also reformed at the end of Mary's reign were the methods for the raising of troops, always important in a country that lacked a standing army. This was effected through two complementary Acts of Parliament, which provided in John Guy's words 'a landmark in English military organisation'.

Summary

Mary had a mixed record as queen. In foreign policy she must be accounted a failure, as both she and the country felt the humiliation of the loss of Calais. Her marriage failed in its most basic requirement – the production of a Catholic heir to the throne. This left Mary unable to prevent the succession of her despised half-sister Elizabeth, whom she knew would overturn the religious changes which she had been so anxious to introduce. Mary was not, however, without her strengths: she showed her character and determination admirably when seizing the throne and later when facing down rebellion. Her main failing, ultimately, was something she could not control, dying after just over five years on the throne.

ACTIVITY

Summary chart

Complete the following chart, to summarise success and failure in Marian government.

	Success/evidence	Failure/evidence
Securing the throne		
Marriage		
Foreign policy		

When you have studied subsequent chapters, you will be able to insert additional rows in this grid relating to Wyatt's Rebellion, the implementation of religious change and the introduction of naval and militia reforms.

EXTRACT 2

Mary was arrogant, assertive, bigoted, stubborn, suspicious and rather stupid. Her portraits show a bitter and narrow-minded woman, curiously unlike her father, brother and sister. Certainly, she had led a truly unhappy life. For twenty years before her accession she had lived in the shadows. Her experience would very probably have soured a sweeter and more tolerant temper. The fact remains she was ill-prepared to be England's first woman sovereign. She had ever been her mother's daughter, devoid of political skill, unable to compromise; set only on the wholesale reversal of a generation's history, she was a manifest portent of strife. If it is not clear whether she leant towards the new rigour of the rising Counter-Reformation, or a pre-Lutheran conventional piety, this is mainly because she never gave any sign of a genuinely intelligent interest in the issues that confronted her. She seized a power rightfully hers for the exercise of which she was utterly unsuited.

Adapted from Geoffrey R. Elton, *Reform and Reformation: England*, 1509–1558, 1977

EXTRACT 3

Mary was swept to power by a revolution. In part, it was her own doing. She had escaped to Suffolk, and immediately summoned some reliable supporters to join her and others to prepare to tackle any opposition. In response major figures supported her. But it was popular support for Mary's bid which determined the outcome. On 19 July Mary was proclaimed queen. 'Great was the triumph here at London, for my time I never saw the like', wrote one chronicler. There were 'bonfires in every street in London, with good cheer at every bonfire, the bells ringing in every parish church, and for the most part all night till the next day at noon'. It was the same everywhere. There had been a mass rejection of Northumberland and approbation of Mary.

Adapted from Christopher Haigh, *English Reformations: Religion, Politics and Society under the Tudors*, 1993

EXTRACT 4

From a childhood in which she was adored and feted and then violently rejected, a fighter was born. Mary maintained her faith and her self-belief. Despite repeated attempts to deprive her of her life and her right to the throne, the warrior princess turned victor, and became the warrior queen. The boldness and scale of her achievements is often overlooked. The campaign that Mary led in the summer of 1553 would prove to be the only successful revolt against central government in sixteenth-century England. In the moment of crisis she proved decisive and courageous, and won the support of the English people as the legitimate Tudor heir. Mary proved to be a conscientious and hard-working queen who was determined to be closely involved in government business and policy-making. She was also a woman who lived by her conscience and was prepared to die for her faith.

Adapted from Anna Whitelock, *Mary Tudor: England's First Queen*, 2009

STUDY TIP

This question deals with both the acquisition of power and the exercise of that power once it had been acquired. It might be perfectly reasonable for you to conclude that Mary's performance in one context was significantly better or worse than her performance in another. When looking at Mary as queen, remind yourself once again of those responsibilities which were exercised by other English monarchs in the sixteenth century.

A LEVEL PRACTICE QUESTION

Evaluating historical extracts

Read Extracts 2, 3 and 4. Using your understanding of the historical context, assess how convincing the arguments in these three extracts are in relation to Mary I as queen.

STUDY TIP

Try to link what you have learnt about Mary's foreign policy to the material which you studied on the reigns of Henry VIII and Edward VI. When discussing the success of foreign policy, ask yourself what that foreign policy was trying to achieve. Remember that foreign policy objectives can change over time.

A LEVEL PRACTICE QUESTION

How successful was English foreign policy in the years 1529 to 1558?

16 The social impact of religious and economic changes under Mary I

EXTRACT 1

Marian Catholicism was incomplete. Although the liturgical rites returned and religious art and drama enjoyed a partial renaissance, the cults of saints, pilgrimages, and belief in purgatory were permanent casualties of Henry VIII's and Edward VI's reigns. Few shrines and relics reappeared, while miracles aroused scepticism. The oral tradition that Catholics held to be equivalent to scripture had largely disappeared, and the dissolution of the chantries made Catholic re-education difficult at a popular level. A minority of guilds and fraternities were re-established but with more limited functions. Lastly, the size of church attendance is doubtful. Congregations declined when the Edwardian prayer books were introduced, but it is unclear that they recovered under Mary.

Adapted from John Guy, *Tudor England*, 1988

Fig. 1 *St John's was one of two Oxford colleges founded during Mary's reign to further the Catholic faith; its banner included Catholic images such as the assumption of the Virgin Mary and the emblem of the Five Wounds of Christ*

LEARNING OBJECTIVES

In this chapter you will learn about:

- the social impact of religious and economic change under Mary I
- rebellion under Mary I
- intellectual developments including humanist and religious thought.

KEY QUESTION

As you read this chapter, consider the following Key Question:
How did English society and economy change and with what effects?

ACTIVITY

Evaluating historical extracts

What impression is given by John Guy in Extract 1 about the state of Marian Catholicism? As you read through the chapter, note both the evidence which appears to support Guy's arguments and the evidence which appears to contradict them.

KEY QUESTION

How far did intellectual and religious ideas change and develop, and with what effects?

Religious change under Mary and its social impact

Many parts of the country anticipated that Mary would restore Catholicism, even while the Edwardian religious legislation still technically remained in force. Although the restoration of Catholicism caused trouble in some areas, for the most part local enthusiasm produced large sums of money, raised at great speed, to devote to popular conservative religious projects. It is certainly evident that the first religious changes of Mary's reign were generated not by government action but by the willing anticipation of a largely enthusiastic populace.

Mary's key religious reforms

There was never any doubt that Mary would restore the English Church to papal jurisdiction and initial enthusiasm suggested this might be relatively straightforward. However, the whole process proved to be much more fraught than Mary had originally anticipated.

Mary faced several problems.

- Protestantism, although a minority faith, had attracted adherents in London and in other parts of the south.
- The reformed Protestant Church of England was protected in statute law.
- Many members of the political elites, on whose support Mary depended, had benefited financially from the acquisition of monastic land and had no desire to surrender what Mary saw as their ill-gotten gains.

Mary began cautiously, although some of the most prominent Protestant clergy, including seven bishops, were deprived of their livings and, in some cases, imprisoned. Foreign Protestants were ordered to leave the country, but most of them had already left voluntarily. The legislative attack on Protestantism began with the meeting of Mary's first parliament in October 1553.

- The **religious laws** that had been passed during Edward VI's reign were repealed.
- The order of service as at the time of the death of Henry VIII was restored.
- All clergy who had married when permitted to do so could be deprived of their livings.
- The legal status of the Church of England was upheld.

However, Mary faced a dilemma. To rely on parliamentary legislation to reverse the royal supremacy would mean acknowledging that the original laws passed during Henry VIII's reign were legally valid. In other words, Mary would have to accept the superiority of statute law over divine law, precisely the opposite of her own fundamental belief.

The status of the Church was not finally resolved until the meeting of Mary's third parliament, which lasted from November 1554 to January 1555. What delayed the process was the issue of what should happen to the lands from dissolved monasteries which had fallen into private hands. It was made clear to Pope Julius III and his legate **Reginald Pole** that there was no question that such land could be restored to the Church. The **Imperial ambassador Renard** had told Charles V that more ex-monastic land was in the hands of Catholics than Protestants.

However, the Pope and Pole wanted the English Church to submit to Rome first before dispensations might be awarded to landowners on an individual basis. The Council, along with the emperor, Charles V and Philip, was aware that this would be politically impossible. In the end Julius reluctantly accepted Charles's advice. Once this had been agreed, Cardinal Pole arrived in England in November 1554 to take up a position as legate and Archbishop of Canterbury.

Mary's third parliament reversed the Henrician Act of Attainder that had been passed against Pole. Royal assent was given the day before Pole's

A CLOSER LOOK

About 80 MPs went so far as to vote against the repeal of the Edwardian **religious laws**. Moreover, about 800 persons, mostly drawn from the political elites, their families and servants, went into exile at centres of European Protestantism such as Strasbourg, Geneva, Frankfurt and the port of Emden in north Germany.

ACTIVITY

Refer back to Chapter 8 and use the information there to help explain why Mary was so reluctant to use statute law to re-establish papal supremacy.

CROSS-REFERENCE

Reginald Pole and the Imperial ambassador Renard are introduced in Chapter 15, page 147.

arrival. However, until the issue of the former Church lands was resolved there could be no final religious settlement. There were furious debates between Pole and councillors who asserted the view that no foreigner could have jurisdiction over English property. Mary sympathised with Pole and even threatened to abdicate, although doubtless she was bluffing since abdication would necessarily have been followed by the rapid restoration of Protestantism.

In January 1555, the Act of Repeal revoking the royal supremacy was passed. However, Pole's grudging attitude on the subject of Church property had made him an object of suspicion among landowners and his reputation never really recovered. Furthermore, Mary had been forced to acknowledge, however reluctantly, the jurisdiction of statute law in matters involving religion.

Pope Julius III died in 1555 and was succeeded by the anti-Spanish Paul IV. Not only was Paul IV hostile towards Mary's husband Philip, he was also suspicious of Pole whom he regarded as a **heretic**. Paul IV's hostility towards Philip was demonstrated in his open hostility towards the Spanish side in a war which broke out in 1555 and into which Mary's England was later dragged. To all intents and purposes, Mary found herself at war with the papacy.

Paul IV's attitude towards Pole was made clear when he dismissed him as papal legate in April 1557. Not only was this a considerable blow to Pole's prestige, it also meant that he could no longer act directly on behalf of the Pope in his supervision of the English Church. The Pope went on to accuse Pole of heresy but Mary refused to let him go to Rome to face the charge.

The Pope named a new legate, William Peto, but Mary trusted Pole, and in effect refused to acknowledge superior papal authority that placed Peto in a higher position in the English Church than the Archbishop of Canterbury. This placed Mary in a difficult legal relationship with the Pope, so that her reward for restoring England to what she regarded as the true Catholic faith was meagre.

The burning of heretics

Mary's historical reputation has come to rest on the burning of Protestant heretics. This policy earned her the nickname of 'Bloody Mary'. The fate of Mary's victims was recorded at length in John Foxe's *Acts and Monuments* (more familiarly known as **Foxe's 'Book of Martyrs'**).

A CLOSER LOOK

Foxe's 'Book of Martyrs'

This was first published in 1563 and went through five editions in Elizabeth's reign. It became probably the most widely read book in England apart from the Bible and established the notion of the English as God's elect (and Protestant) nation. Mary was therefore condemned for her cruelty and ungodliness, and such views have long tended to influence historians' interpretations of her reign and of her conduct. In possibly the most famous extract from the book, Foxe made it easy for his readers to draw the appropriate moral. He quoted Hugh Latimer's alleged comment to Nicholas Ridley as they were about to suffer together. 'Be of good comfort, Master Ridley, and play the man. We shall this day light such a candle, by God's grace, in England, as I trust shall never be put out.'

KEY CHRONOLOGY

Religion under Mary

1553	First statute of repeal, which repealed the religious legislation of Edward VI's reign
Nov 1554	Mary's third parliament assembled Heresy laws restored Return of Cardinal Pole to England
1555	Second statute of repeal, which repealed anti-papal legislation from Henry VIII's reign
Feb 1555	First burnings for heresy
21 Mar 1556	Burning of Archbishop Cranmer

CROSS-REFERENCE

Heresy is explained in Chapter 6, page 56.

The war between France and Spain and the difficulty that this caused for Mary are discussed in Chapter 15, page 149.

ACTIVITY

Write a letter which Mary might have sent to the Pope at this time, explaining her concerns and seeking his support.

A CLOSER LOOK

The geography of martyrdom is also significant. There were 60 burnings in London, which reflects the extent of Protestant penetration there. The other main locations of burnings were all in the south-east of England: Canterbury (Kent), Lewes (Sussex) and Colchester (Essex). More than three quarters of the martyrs were to be found in the south-east and East Anglia, the regions where Protestantism was most highly developed, as indicated by the map in Fig. 3. On the other hand, there were no burnings, for example, in the diocese of Durham.

ACTIVITY

Work in small groups. Each member of the group should use the Internet to identify from Foxe's 'Book of Martyrs' an execution for heresy which took place during the reign of Queen Mary. Put these accounts together and identify:

a. The specific offences of which victims were accused.

b. The ways in which Foxe demonstrates his sympathy for his victims and his hostility towards their persecutors.

KEY TERM

Catholic Reformation: the attempts of the Catholic Church across Europe to reform itself

legatine synod: a joint assembly summoned by a papal legate; in this context, Pole as papal legate had the right to summon clergy from both provinces of the English Church – Canterbury and York – to a legatine synod; other Archbishops of Canterbury did not have this right

Fig. 2 *The burnings of bishops Latimer and Ridley*

Altogether, 289 Protestants (237 men, 52 women) were burnt at the stake for heresy. Some of the victims were famous. These included three bishops at the time of Mary's accession – Archbishop Cranmer and bishops Hooper and Ridley – as well as Hugh Latimer, a noted preacher and former bishop of Worcester. Twenty-one other clergymen suffered; eight victims were from the gentry. However, the bulk of the sufferers were men and women of fairly humble status, in contrast to the more exalted background of those who had gone into exile once Mary became queen. This suggests that Protestantism was important to some people who did not simply benefit financially from religious change.

It is difficult to be certain about the effects of the burnings. At one level the Crown's strategy appears to have misfired. The first two victims, John Rogers and Rowland Taylor, who suffered at Smithfield in London and Hadleigh in Suffolk respectively, seem to have been chosen on account of their popularity as preachers. Their deaths appear to have elicited widespread public sympathy. Moreover, extending the range of victims to include humble persons seems to have strengthened the sympathy for their martyrdom.

That the Council started worrying about the effects of the burnings is evident in the measures which it took in attempting to ban servants, apprentices and the young in general from attending burnings. It ultimately failed to extinguish heresy. In some continental countries such strictness succeeded, and the failure of the policy in England may have been a consequence of lack of time rather more than the extent of popular feeling. What is certain, however, is that the policy did nothing for Mary's reputation.

Mary's other religious reforms

Mary's religious policy was not purely repressive. Pole, in particular, saw his role in largely pastoral terms. The resources of the Church, which had been eroded for 20 years, needed to be restored, and both the quality and the quantity of priests needed to be improved.

Pole tried to ensure the quality of pastoral provision. Most of the new bishops whom Mary and he appointed took their pastoral responsibilities seriously and in a manner that was perfectly in accord with the spirit of the **Catholic Reformation**. Pole's **legatine synod** of 1555 to 1556 made his expectations clear. Bishops were to reside in their dioceses, they were to preach and they were to oversee carefully the religious life of their parishes. Also within the spirit of the Catholic Reformation there was a proposal, never put into effect, that each cathedral should have a seminary attached for the training of new recruits to the priesthood.

With greater time at his disposal, Pole's reforms might have worked. However, the chances of success largely depended on commitment at parish level. Although this could be guaranteed in Catholic Lancashire or Durham, which proved fertile territory for recruiting new priests, matters were much less straightforward further south; for example, there were very few candidates for ordination in Kent. There was wide variation in practice in the City of London, where some parishes re-embraced Catholicism enthusiastically whereas other churches were virtually in ruins.

Fig. 3 *English counties, showing the areas which were strongly Catholic and strongly Protestant*

The extent to which Mary had transformed the religious situation by 1558

The bulk of the country remained Catholic in sentiment, a point that Protestants returning from exile after Elizabeth's accession were only too keen to emphasise. Clearly, given time and resources, Pole and Mary might well have succeeded in their mission to re-Catholicise England. Nevertheless, more could have been achieved in religious terms during Mary's reign. The delay in properly restoring the Church's institutional structure and the divisions between Crown and papacy did not help but Mary certainly never completed what she set out to do.

KEY QUESTION

How did English society and economy change and with what effects?

Economic change and its social impact

Mary's brief reign had a mixed economic record. On the one hand, various converging trends continued to produce inflation (driving up prices) during this period.

- The continued pressure on demand brought about by the rapid increase in the population. This was the key long-term factor in increasing inflation.
- The inflationary impact of debasement of the coinage. This was the key medium-term factor.
- Harvest failures in 1555 and 1556. These brought severe food shortages and severe strain on real wages for the poor.
- The devastating impact of the 'sweating sickness', a virulent form of influenza which swept through the country in 1557 and 1558. (The death toll was probably the worst of the century, possibly the worst since the Black Death.)

On the other hand, the Crown made several improvements in financial administration; in the long term the country largely benefited from these.

Fig. 4 *An English sixpence from 1557, showing the heads of Philip and Mary*

Financial reforms

One area in which progress was made was revenue administration. The Duke of Northumberland had sought to improve the administration of Crown finances by setting up a commission to investigate the shortcomings of the system and to recommend reforms. Edward's premature death prevented any of the recommendations from being implemented in his reign. However, some of the changes were implemented in 1554 even though the person largely responsible for making the recommendations, Walter Mildmay, was regarded with suspicion on religious grounds: the **Court of Exchequer** took over both the **Court of First Fruits and Tenths** and the **Court of Augmentations**, but in the process adopted some of the more recent courts' superior methods. Financial administration, under Lord Treasurer Winchester, was competent.

A CLOSER LOOK

The **Court of First Fruits and Tenths** and the **Court of Augmentations** were both set up in the 1530s to deal with new 'revenue streams' which the Crown had acquired. The former dealt with funds which had previously gone to the papacy; the latter dealt with the income from monastic lands. As new institutions, they had operated more efficiently than the old-fashioned **Court of Exchequer.**

Mary made one big mistake, remitting the final part of Edward's last subsidy. This bought her some cheap popularity but at some financial cost. Although the level of royal indebtedness rose during the reign, it did not do so dramatically given that England was at war with France during the later stages of the reign. For a government at war, its financial record was satisfactory. The long-term security of Crown finances was boosted by the plans for recoinage drawn up from 1556 to 1558 but implemented under Elizabeth. Inflationary pressures had been caused by the proliferation of debased coins in circulation. It was the thoroughness of preparation under Mary that enabled efficient implementation under Elizabeth. Elizabeth also reaped the benefit from the introduction of a new Book of Rates in 1558, which raised customs revenue dramatically.

CROSS-REFERENCE

Mary's war against France is outlined on pages 149–50.

The debasement of the coinage during Edward VI's reign is discussed in Chapter 14, page 138.

Poor relief

Marian government did itself become more active in areas relating to poor relief. At one level this was a response to the extent of the problems the country faced from 1556 to 1558. These were dreadful years. There was a huge mortality rate from the influenza epidemic of those years, there were a series of harvest failures and taxation was high in order to pay for the war against France. Particular emphasis was placed on the enforcement of laws against grain hoarders and there was strong encouragement to convert pasture land to tillage. However, it is very difficult to assess the effect of these measures.

Wyatt's Rebellion

As some of Mary's ministers feared, the prospect of a Spanish marriage was enough to provoke rebellion. This was despite the fact that the **marriage treaty** of January 1554 had attempted to allay fear by minimising Spanish influence.

A rebellion had, in fact, been planned in November 1553. There were to be four simultaneous risings: in Devon (which would be led by **Edward Courtenay**, Earl of Devon), Hertfordshire, Leicestershire and Kent. The plans leaked out in January 1554, forcing the rebels into action. However, only Kent experienced a serious rising. Sir Thomas Wyatt raised a force of about 3,000 men.

The rebels had a mixture of motives:

- Although the government tried to play this down, some of them were motivated by religion, with many of Wyatt's urban supporters coming from Maidstone, a Protestant stronghold.
- Xenophobia (fear or dislike of foreigners) certainly motivated many of the rebels.
- The decline in the local cloth industry might well have prompted some poorer rebels to use the revolt as a means of expressing their social and economic grievances.
- The rebellion seems also to have attracted some gentry who had lost office within the county.

However, resentment of the proposed royal marriage was clearly the main grievance, especially amongst the rebellion's leaders. There was an implicit objective of getting rid of Mary, though this was never stated openly. (To cause further confusion for the rebels, the involvement of Jane Grey's father in the rebellion implied a desire to restore Jane to the throne; other rebels would undoubtedly have preferred Elizabeth.)

KEY QUESTION

- How effectively was England governed during this period?
- How important was the role of key individuals and groups and how were they affected by developments?

CROSS-REFERENCE

The marriage treaty between Mary I and Philip II of Spain is discussed in Chapter 15, page 148.

Edward Courtenay, who had been a marriage candidate for Mary, is introduced in Chapter 15, page 147.

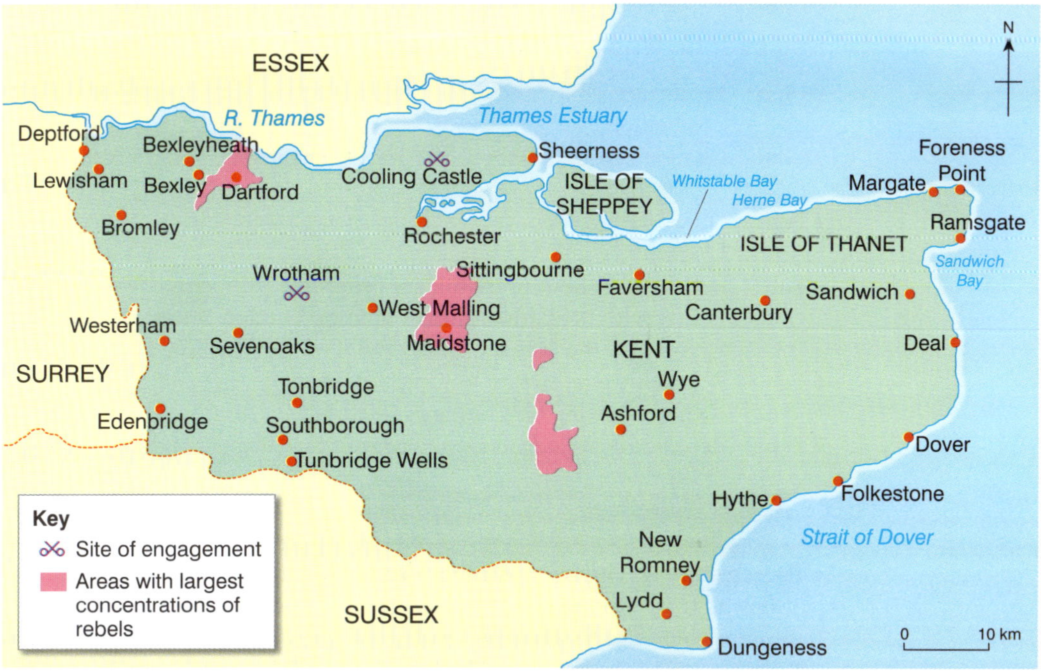

Fig. 5 *Wyatt's Rebellion, 1554*

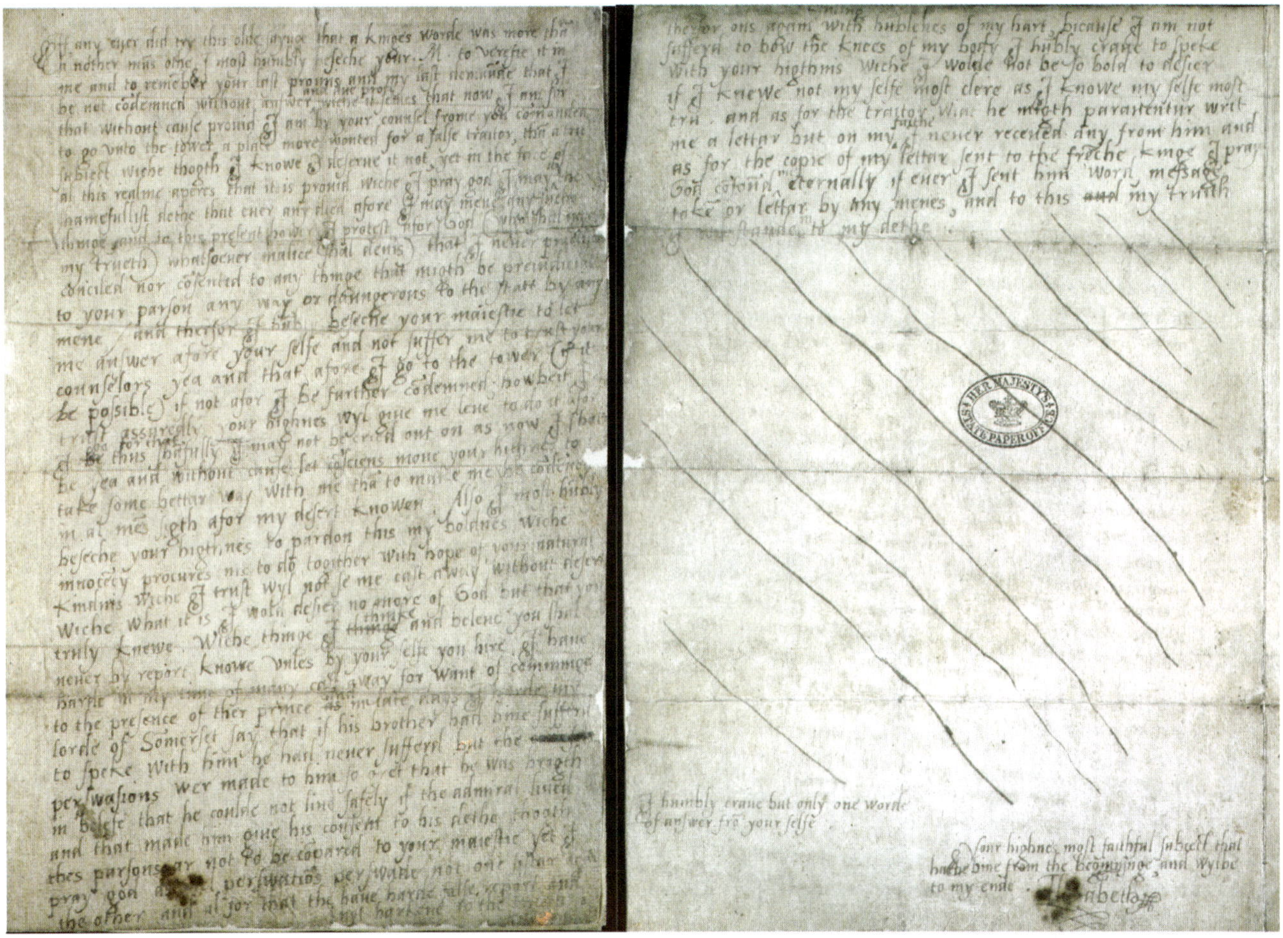

Fig. 6 *Elizabeth protests her innocence. The diagonal strokes have been inserted to prevent the forgery of additional material*

A CLOSER LOOK

Key events: Wyatt's Rebellion, 1554

25 Jan Wyatt raises his standard in Maidstone to signify the start of the rebellion

28 Jan Duke of Norfolk's force unable to engage the rebels; Norfolk forced to retreat

1 Feb Queen rallies support with a speech at Guildhall in the City of London

3 Feb Rebels reach Southwark but are prevented from crossing to the City with the Crown's forces holding London Bridge. This is probably the critical turning point of the rebellion

6 Feb Rebels move upstream to Kingston upon Thames and cross river there, moving back towards London

7 Feb Rebels stop at Ludgate on the edge of the City of London. Wyatt surrenders

The rebellion was highly significant in a number of respects:

- It showed that, although Protestants were in a minority, their religious opinions could not be ignored.
- It demonstrated the extent to which there was popular suspicion of the proposed Spanish marriage.

- It resulted in the execution of Lady Jane Grey, an innocent victim of her father 's support for the rebellion.

Elizabeth herself was arrested and confined to the Tower. Mary was convinced that Elizabeth was aware of the rebels' intentions. However, Wyatt did not implicate her. Moreover, each of her interrogators, Gardiner and Paget, had a vested interest in not finding out the full truth: Gardiner because of his links with Courtenay, and Paget because he recognised that Elizabeth was likely one day to be queen and therefore he was eager not to alienate her. In the end, the allegations against Elizabeth could not be substantiated and she was eventually released.

Wyatt came close to success. He had raised – and kept – a large following, outmanoeuvred the Duke of Norfolk and come close to securing the City of London. Had he succeeded in taking the City, Mary's reign might well have come to a premature end. However, for the second time in a crisis she behaved bravely and resolutely, and her councillors kept their heads with no important defections to the rebel cause.

A CLOSER LOOK

Though most early Tudor rebellions had at least some socio-economic causes, this was not really the case with Wyatt's Rebellion. It is possible that there was a link between the decline in the local cloth industry in and around Maidstone and popular support for the rebellion, though there is little that can be proved. There is an intriguing hint of popular discontent which concerns a carpenter from Norwich who claimed that as a result of the Spanish marriage 'we should lie in swine sties in caves and the Spaniards should have our houses and we should live like slaves'. However, there was no rebellion in Norfolk, perhaps because the area was still feeling the punitive effects of the suppression of the 1549 rebellion, and this comment might well have been isolated.

Intellectual developments, including humanist and religious thought

KEY QUESTION

How far did intellectual and religious ideas change and develop, and with what effects?

The reign of Queen Mary showed little influence of humanism. There was no scope under Marian Catholicism for the expression of the **evangelical humanism** which had been linked to religious reform. There was very little sign also of the Catholic humanism which had been so closely associated with the Catholic martyrs.

Reginald Pole's governance of the Church seemed to have been little influenced by the humanism which he had experienced in his younger days. In any case the Catholic Church seemed consciously to wish to dissociate itself from humanism. Pope Paul IV regarded the greatest of all Catholic humanist scholars, Erasmus, as a heretic. His works were placed on the Catholic *Index Librorum Prohibitorum* (Index of Prohibited Books), a list of titles the papacy forbade Catholics from reading.

CROSS-REFERENCE

Evangelical humanism is covered in Chapter 14, page 142.

Official religious thought in Marian England, while it might have lacked the intellectual thrust of humanism, was designed at a more practical level to assist the process of Catholic reform at a parish level. Edmund Bonner, bishop of London and chief villain in Foxe's 'Book of Martyrs', published *A Profitable and Necessary Doctrine*, which explained the faith at a straightforward level, and a **book of homilies** to replace that which had been published by the Edwardian Church. Pole was keen to stress the importance of papal supremacy, which had not been an especially strong feature of pre-Reformation Catholicism. This was somewhat ironic given Paul IV's hostility towards him. Had Pole and Mary survived and outlived Paul IV, the nature of English Catholicism would have developed into a very different form compared with its pre-Reformation character.

CROSS-REFERENCE

For the book of homilies published by Archbishop Cranmer at the beginning of Edward VI's reign, turn back to Chapter 14, page 135.

On the Protestant side, the exiles sent back to England numerous publications. They were not, however, a united group, being divided between those who were happy to use the 1552 prayer book as the basis for church services and those who wished to move in a more radical direction. This did not merely reflect religious discipline; it also reflected a split between those who wished to operate politically within existing structures and those, led by John Knox and Christopher Goodman, who wished to adopt a more radical approach involving active resistance to the regime. Foxe, exiled in Frankfurt and then in Basle, spent much of his exile collecting material which would be used eventually in his 'Book of Martyrs'. This would enjoy official approval during Elizabeth's reign. On the other hand, the translation of the Bible begun in Geneva by William Whittingham would be regarded with suspicion by many of the Church's authorities after 1558.

It became conventional for historians to regard the reign of Mary and the ecclesiastical administration of Pole with disdain. It was assumed that their failure was somehow inevitable. However, it is clear that the five years of Mary's reign were pivotal to the way in which English religion and society might have developed in the longer term. Although Mary suffered a poor reputation at the hands of subsequent generations of Protestants, there were some positive advances made during her reign and had she not died prematurely of cancer in 1558, the future of Catholicism in England might have been very different.

ACTIVITY

Summary chart

How well did Mary and Pole handle the religious changes which they introduced?

Religious change	Successfully handled	Unsuccessfully handled
Reversing of Edwardian changes		
Monasteries		
Restoration of papal supremacy		
Treatment of heretics		
Pastoral improvement		

EXTRACT 2

The persecution set the seal on Mary's failure to restore the Church of Rome in England, but that failure was pretty much guaranteed also by Pole's policies and by the fact that the earlier Reformation had taken a much firmer hold than has often been supposed. The signs are everywhere. The steadfastness of those executed proved so effective because they were setting their example to men and women more than half persuaded. The new owners' determination to retain the secularised lands not only demonstrated an understandable attachment to property, but also testified to the continued absence of any scruple about sacrilege. Despite herself, Mary throughout acted as the ruler of a Church which yet she believed was ruled solely by the Pope, a point underlined when Philip and Pope Paul IV had a serious argument and Pole lost the special papal authority which had lent some credibility to the notion that everything was done by and for Rome.

Adapted from Geoffrey R. Elton, *Reform and Reformation: England, 1509–58*, 1977

EXTRACT 3

At the parish level English Catholicism recovered under Mary – not everywhere and in all respects, since the past could not be entirely undone, but on the whole. The Church showed signs of health which had not been seen since the 1520s, and promise for the future. In clerical recruitment, for example, twenty-five years of decline were reversed, though career prospects had not improved very much. Under Edward VI ordinations had almost ceased; in Mary's reign they boomed. Again, after two decades in which the printing press had been used to undermine traditional religion, there were numerous books of Catholic teaching and devotion. The Marian Church was the Church of the 1520s writ later: a vigorous pastoral episcopate; high levels of clerical recruitment; best-selling works of personal edification and piety; active investment in parish religion – and a troublesome cardinal, distrust of clerical authority and a heresy problem.

Adapted from Christopher Haigh, *English Reformation: Religion, Politics and Society under the Tudors*, 1993

EXTRACT 4

The constructive aspects of Marian Catholicism were less dramatic than the persecutions, but even so were not negligible. Mary and Pole were able as a result of deprivation and death to appoint – or in some cases to restore – bishops of unquestioned loyalty to the Catholic faith. The leaders of the Marian Church were as well qualified to provide pastoral guidance and discipline as any bench of bishops in the century. Yet able and devoted as they were, they lacked the calibre or the spirit to inspire a true rebuilding. Pole himself had been defeated at the Council of Trent and now put his trust in ceremony and obedience. He was, besides, an old, sick man, whose last eighteen months were marred by his quarrel with Pope Paul IV.

Adapted from Penry Williams, *The Later Tudors: England, 1547–1603*, 1995

A LEVEL PRACTICE QUESTION

Evaluating historical extracts

Using your understanding of the historical context, assess how convincing the arguments in Extracts 2, 3 and 4 are in relation to the Church in Marian England.

STUDY TIP

Examination questions in this specification cover at least 20 years. It is important therefore when you are revising Mary and religion that you place it in a wider chronological context of religious developments.

A LEVEL PRACTICE QUESTION

'Religious changes in the years 1532 to 1558 enjoyed little popular support.' Assess the validity of this view.

STUDY TIP

This question embraces a range of religious changes across three reigns. Try to concentrate on the key phrase 'popular support'. You could identify a range of important religious changes and divide them into two sections: those which were largely popular and those which were largely unpopular. Make sure that you have identified an effective line of argument before you start writing.

17 Elizabeth I: character and aims

EXTRACT 1

Elizabeth the politician and Elizabeth the person can never be disentangled, but some things can be concluded about her preferences. In the matter of religion she was a Protestant. Although it is difficult to tell exactly what theology she preferred, it is obvious that she would not tolerate a Church independent from the State. The royal supremacy was at the very centre of both her political and religious ideals. Elizabeth gained a reputation for being a conservative in matters of church ceremony and decoration, if not dogma, but this only became obvious after the parliament of 1559. She was Protestant but tolerant towards Catholic behaviour. To say that she preferred a bit of colour in her religion and had a good opinion of Mary, the mother of Christ does not mean, however, that Elizabeth rejected the second Book of Common Prayer, or the theology espoused by the Swiss Protestant reformers.

Adapted from Norman Jones, *Faith by Statute: Parliament and the Settlement of Religion, 1559*, 1982

ACTIVITY

Evaluating historical extracts

What opinion of Elizabeth's religious views does Norman Jones put forward in Extract 1? As you read this chapter, what evidence can you find which supports or challenges his suggestions?

The character and aims of Elizabeth I

Elizabeth acceded to the throne at the age of 25, significantly younger than Mary had been at her accession. There were, however, considerable differences in character and experience between the two. Elizabeth was considerably better educated, had a much shrewder grasp of political processes in their widest sense and was, for the most part, a shrewder judge of character than her half-sister. She had also learned much from her personal and political experiences, including a brief and tempestuous relationship with **Thomas Seymour**, and what may have been her treasonable implication in **Wyatt's Rebellion**.

A CLOSER LOOK

Elizabeth showed the development of her political skills as a result of each of these developments. Her succinct dismissal of the executed Thomas Seymour as a man of much wit but little judgement showed that she had learnt from the temporary disgrace of their relationship. Her clear-headedness under interrogation and marking a letter to her half-sister Queen Mary with diagonal lines so that it couldn't be doctored were remarkable for someone who was aged only 20.

Elizabeth clearly believed that she was entitled to rule the kingdom directly, and from the start of her reign it was clear who was in charge. In December 1558 the Spanish ambassador, the Count of Feria, noted that Elizabeth was more feared than her sister had been and gave orders 'as absolutely as her father did'. Moreover, she readily invoked her father 's memory, telling Parliament in 1559 that 'we hope to rule, govern and keep this our realm in good justice, peace and rest, in like wise [sic.] as the king my father held you in'.

LEARNING OBJECTIVES

In this chapter you will learn about:

- the character and aims of Elizabeth I
- Elizabeth I's consolidation of power
- the Elizabethan religious settlement
- Elizabeth's relations with foreign powers up to 1563.

KEY QUESTION

As you read this chapter, consider the following Key Questions:

- How effectively did the Tudors restore and develop the powers of the monarchy?
- How did relations with foreign powers change and how was the succession secured?
- In what ways and how effectively was England governed during this period?
- How important was the role of key individuals and groups and how were they affected by developments?

CROSS-REFERENCE

Elizabeth's relationship with Thomas Seymour is outlined in Chapter 13, page 127.

Her implication in Wyatt's Rebellion is discussed in Chapter 16, page 161.

CROSS-REFERENCE

The religious settlement is covered later in this chapter, pages 167–170.

The pursuit of peace with France is discussed in Chapter 17, pages 171–172.

Elizabeth had no desire to involve herself in the details of government in the manner of her grandfather, Henry VII. However, she took an informed interest in decision-making processes. Most importantly, she was determined to preserve the prerogative powers of the Crown, which meant that she insisted on taking the most important decisions.

On coming to the throne she had a number of key short-term aims:

- to consolidate her position
- to settle religious issues
- to pursue a peaceful settlement with the French.

KEY PROFILE

Fig. 1 *Sir William Cecil*

Sir William Cecil, first Baron Burghley (1521–98) first enjoyed prominence under Somerset but managed to transfer allegiance to Northumberland. He enjoyed the trust of the Princess Elizabeth, managed her succession smoothly and served her when she became queen for almost 40 years, first as principal secretary and then from 1572 as Lord Treasurer.

Elizabeth I's consolidation of power

Queen Mary died in the early hours of 17 November 1558. Within a few hours, **Sir William Cecil** had ridden the 16 miles north to Hatfield to tell the Princess Elizabeth that the long-awaited accession had arrived. Mary 's councillors were only too well aware that Elizabeth did not share their religious views; many of them guessed that their political careers were over. However, they made no attempt to interfere with the lawful succession as defined by Henry VIII. In any case, Mary had recognised Elizabeth as her successor and her husband Philip of Spain had signified his recognition of Elizabeth's right of succession when he sent his envoy, the Count of Feria, to see Elizabeth a month before Mary's death.

In other respects, however, it was a difficult succession. England had suffered a series of bad harvests, hence food was scarce and expensive. Moreover, the country had suffered grievously from the ravages of a flu epidemic which had brought about the highest rate of mortality since the Black Death over two centuries previously. The political and religious situations were delicate. England had fought a disastrous war against France which had resulted in the loss of Calais. The question of the queen's marriage had become the subject of endless speculation. Finally, it was evident that there would be changes to the Catholic faith, as re-established by Queen Mary.

There were several key features to Elizabeth's consolidation of power.

- Her path to power was eased by the acceptance of her succession by Mary's key councillors. On the morning of 17 November Nicholas Heath, Mary's Lord Chancellor and Archbishop of York, announced Mary's death to Parliament and proclaimed Elizabeth's succession. Legally he had no right to do so; Mary's death should, in law, have brought about the immediate dissolution of Parliament. Politically, however, it was a significant move because it showed that the political elite of the nation collectively assented to Elizabeth's accession. Within a couple of days, nine of Mary's councillors rode to Hatfield to assure Elizabeth of their loyalty. There would therefore be no attempt to deny Elizabeth's succession by devout Catholics who had never accepted the validity of her father's marriage to Anne Boleyn.
- William Cecil was appointed principal secretary. Their political partnership would last for almost 40 years. Elizabeth also made some household appointments. At this stage, however, she did not announce any further appointments. It certainly made political sense for her to keep Mary's councillors guessing about her intentions and speculating about their chances of retaining some measure of royal favour.
- Elizabeth showed herself familiar with the customs associated with monarchs who had newly acceded to the throne by taking herself to the Tower, from which she emerged on several occasions to show herself to her new subjects and to benefit from pageants which were organised on her behalf by the City of London.
- Elizabeth also proceeded quickly (within two months) to her coronation. On the basis of astrological advice, the chosen date was 15 January.

CROSS-REFERENCE

The impact of poor harvests and the influenza epidemic is outlined in Chapter 16, pages 158–159.

The French war and the loss of Calais are covered in Chapter 15, pages 149–150.

- Elizabeth gained some measure of international confirmation. The Spanish ambassador, the Count of Feria, had already visited Elizabeth several days before Mary's death and after her accession tried to broker a marriage alliance between Elizabeth and Philip II. Nothing came of that, but it did demonstrate that Philip was unwilling to do anything to disrupt the smoothness of Elizabeth's succession.

Fig. 2 *Elizabeth, having been crowned, carries the orb and sceptre – symbols of her authority. The coronation robes were in essence the same as those worn by Mary I; perhaps designed to suggest continuity of authority*

The Elizabethan religious settlement

One of the major priorities of the new Elizabethan regime was to decide on the form of religion the country would experience. There were two key aspects to this: the legal status of the Church and the liturgical books to be used in church services.

The legal status of the Church had not been altered with the death of Queen Mary. Until the law could be changed, the English Church remained part of the Catholic Church of Rome. There was never any doubt that this relationship would be severed and that the Church of England would be reinstated as an established (or State) Church with the monarch at its head. What *was* in doubt was the nature of that established Church. Would it be:

- essentially an 'Anglo-Catholic' Church, in other words a Church whose doctrines and practices remained essentially Catholic even though it had rejected papal supremacy?

ACTIVITY

Produce a tabloid-style newspaper account of one of Elizabeth's public appearances in London prior to her coronation. You may wish to conduct further research to find out more about how the public reacted to the queen.

- an apparently moderate Protestant Church similar to that implied by the **Act of Uniformity of 1549**?
- a more radically evangelical Church as implied by the Act of Uniformity of 1552?

The Elizabethan settlement essentially embraced two Acts of Parliament (the Act of Supremacy and the Act of Uniformity), the issue of a set of royal injunctions to enforce the Acts and, to meet liturgical needs, the publication of a new Book of Common Prayer. In addition, although not part of the original settlement of 1559, the **Thirty-Nine Articles** of Religion were introduced in 1563.

The Act of Supremacy, 1559

This Act restored in law the royal supremacy in the Church, which had been established under Henry VIII and then removed under Queen Mary.

- The papal supremacy, which had been restored by statute law under Queen Mary, was rejected.
- The Reformation legislation of Henry VIII's reign was restored.
- The heresy law revived under Mary was repealed.
- The powers of royal visitation of the Church, as enjoyed by Henry VIII, were revived. This allowed the Crown to appoint commissioners to 'visit, reform, order, correct and amend all such errors, heresies, and abuses'. (This gave huge amounts of potential power to the commissioners, not least because it did not define the 'heresies' against which they might take action.)
- The Act described the queen as 'supreme governor' rather than as 'supreme head' of the Church of England as her father had been. (This has been interpreted in a number of ways: as a concession to Catholic opinion, as a reflection of contemporary misogynistic attitudes towards women derived from the teachings of St Paul and as a reflection of the assumption that only God could be head of the Church.)
- An oath of supremacy was to be taken by clergymen and church officials; there were penalties for refusing to do so. (Most of the Marian bishops felt unable to take the oath of supremacy and were deprived of their posts.)

A CLOSER LOOK

Because of the disappearance of most of the relevant records, it is impossible to estimate how many parish clergymen were deprived of their offices. One estimate puts the number at 2000 – about a quarter of the total. This is almost certainly an overestimate. The visitors empowered to administer the oath under the terms of the Act may well have been reluctant to deprive too many clergy because of the difficulty of replacing them. Furthermore, the most important surviving piece of direct evidence, the Act Book of the Visitors in the Province of York, seems to indicate that the visitors were only really interested in the more important members of the clergy – bishops, deans, cathedral canons – and appeared not to be too bothered about ordinary parish clergy.

The Act therefore restored the legal position of the Crown in relation to the Church which had been first established in the reign of Henry VIII. It gave legislative authority for the Crown to act in matters relating to the Church.

The Act of Uniformity

This Act specified the use of a single Book of Common Prayer, which was a modified version of the second and strongly Protestant book that Cranmer had introduced in **1552**. The two modifications were that:

- variations in Eucharistic belief were possible in that both the **1549** wording ('The body of our Lord Jesus Christ, which was given for thee …'), which even the conservative Bishop Gardiner felt able to accept at the time, and

CROSS-REFERENCE

To recap on the Acts of Uniformity of 1549 and 1552, look back to Chapter 14, page 134.

ACTIVITY

Group work

Assume that you are advisers to Sir William Cecil. You are anxious once again to bring about a break with Rome and, like your boss Sir William, want to return religion roughly to the state it was in in 1552. You suspect that there might be opposition to this suggestion and particularly fear that the queen, to whom you are fanatically loyal, might not share your religious perspective. Working in pairs or small groups, produce a list of the factors (a) promoting and (b) hindering the religious reforms you want to see brought about.

CROSS-REFERENCE

For the Thirty-Nine Articles of 1563, look ahead to Chapter 18, pages 178–179.

the 1552 wording derived from the beliefs of the Swiss reformer Zwingli ('Take and eat this in remembrance ...') were permitted

- the 'Black Rubric', which had been included in the 1552 prayer book to explain away the practice of kneeling at the administration of the Eucharist, was omitted.

The Act also specified that 'such ornaments of the church and of the ministers thereof' should be those that were in place during the second year of the reign of Edward VI, in other words *before* the passing of the Act of Uniformity of 1549, which was passed during the third year of the reign. This would subsequently become an issue of contention. Many returning Protestant exiles, including some of the new bishops appointed by Elizabeth, simply assumed that this dating was an error and did not expect the clause to be enforced, particularly in relation to the dress of clergymen. This would cause problems because many **Calvinist** clergy saw the 'ornaments' as 'Popish' and therefore objected strongly to them.

CROSS-REFERENCE

The prayer books of 1549 and 1552 are discussed in Chapter 14, pages 168–169.

KEY TERM

Calvinism: refers to the ideas on Church doctrine and organisation put forward in Geneva by the French reformer John Calvin

The royal injunctions, 1559

These were a set of instructions about the conduct of church services and government of the Church issued in the queen's name as supreme governor. On three previous occasions (1536, 1538 and 1547), royal injunctions had been used by the Crown as a mechanism for imposing its will in relation to church practices.

The first injunction made clear their Protestant character. It emphasised 'the suppression of superstition' (i.e. Catholic practices) and the need 'to plant true religion to the extirpation of all hypocrisy, enormities, and abuses'. These injunctions emphasised that the Eucharist be administered at a simple communion table rather than at the altar, which was a clear signal that religious practice should move in the direction of reform. They called for the removal from the churches of 'things superstitious'. Such traditional Catholic practices as pilgrimages and the use of candles were described as 'works devised by man's fantasies'. In other words, the injunctions, like those of 1547, were drafted in a way which intended that they were to be an attack on traditional Catholic practices.

In addition, parish churches were required to purchase an English Bible, reasserting the 1538 injunctions, and a copy of Erasmus's *Paraphrases*, as previously required in 1547. Moreover, the visitors nominated by Cecil to enforce the injunctions were strongly Protestant. On the other hand, the injunctions reflected some of Elizabeth's personal idiosyncrasies. For example, her disapproval of clerical marriage was signalled by the fact that prospective wives of clergy had to produce a certificate signed by two justices of the peace signifying their fitness for such a role. Also typical of the queen herself was the desire to persuade people to 'forbear all vain and contentious disputations in matters of religion'.

CROSS-REFERENCE

The royal injunctions of 1536 and 1538 are outlined in Chapter 12, and those of 1547 are discussed in Chapter 14.

Fig. 3 *Brooke Church, in Rutland, has an interior which was refurbished in Elizabeth's reign in line with the Act of Uniformity and the 1559 injunctions*

The significance of the settlement

There has been much debate among historians about the settlement. For many years the dominant interpretation was that put forward in 1950 by John Neale. He argued that the queen faced pressure from radical clergymen, as well as from their allies in the House of Commons, the so-called 'Puritan Choir'. The queen had to back down and accept a much more Protestant prayer book and settlement than she had really wanted.

The challenge to Neale's interpretation came from three American historians.

- William Haugaard argued in *Elizabeth and the English Reformation* (1968) that Elizabeth saw the settlement as final, rather than, as Neale had suggested, a precursor to further reform. Many of the subsequent religious controversies of Elizabeth's reign therefore become easily explicable in this light.
- Winthrop Hudson in *The Cambridge Connection and the Religious Settlement of 1559* (1980) argued that Elizabeth and her ministers always intended that the settlement should be firmly Protestant and that there was never any serious intention to restore the first Edwardian prayer book, but that appearances to the contrary had to be maintained, mainly to keep support in the conservative House of Lords.
- Norman Jones in *Faith by Statute* (1982) argued that Elizabeth and her ministers wanted a complete religious settlement from the start. The political opposition they faced came not from the Puritan Choir but the Catholic bishops and conservative peers in the House of Lords. Though the bishops and conservative peers grudgingly accepted the restoration of the royal supremacy, they provided much more opposition to the uniformity bill, which was only passed in the Lords by three votes.

KEY CHRONOLOGY

Apr 1559	Treaty of Câteau-Cambrésis
Jun 1559	Death of Henry II of France; succeeded by Francis II, husband of Mary, Queen of Scots
Feb 1560	Treaty of Berwick
Mar 1560	English army sent to Scotland to assist the Lords of the Congregation
Jul 1560	Treaty of Edinburgh upholds power of (Protestant) Lords of the Congregation
Dec 1560	Death of Francis II
Oct 1562	English intervention in France on the side of the Huguenots
Apr 1564	Treaty of Troyes

CROSS-REFERENCE

Mary I's war with France, including the loss of Calais, is outlined in Chapter 15, pages 149–150.

KEY QUESTION

How important was the role of key individuals and groups and how were they affected by developments?

England's relations with foreign powers, 1558–64

The Treaty of Câteau-Cambrésis, 1559

When Elizabeth came to the throne, England was in conflict with France. Not only had this war gone very badly for England with the loss of Calais, it had also seriously weakened the Crown's finances. Elizabeth wanted to extricate England from this war and, fortunately, the financial state of both France and Spain meant that neither Philip II nor Henry II of France had the stomach to continue the fight.

A peace treaty was concluded at Câteau-Cambrésis in April 1559, in which England and France also reached an agreement over the vexed issue of Calais. France would retain Calais for eight years, after which time Calais would be restored to English control provided England had kept the peace in the meantime. If France failed to return Calais, they agreed to pay 500,000 crowns (£125,000) to England.

Intervention in Scotland

Further problems emerged after the death in June 1559 of Henry II of France following an accident in a jousting match. Henry II was succeeded by his eldest son Francis II, whose wife was Mary, Queen of Scots, Elizabeth's cousin and the main Catholic claimant to the English throne. Francis's accession also brought the strongly Catholic Guise faction to power in France. The Guises sought once again to use Scotland as an instrument of French policy. French troops were sent to garrison major Scottish fortresses, much to the alarm of John Knox, the radical Calvinist who was the leader of the Scottish Reformation, and his political allies, the Lords of the Congregation, who were seeking power in Edinburgh. This led to conflict, with the Lords of the Congregation requesting assistance from their fellow Protestants south of the border.

A CLOSER LOOK

John Knox published *The First Blast of the Trumpet against the Monstrous Regiment of Women* in 1558. It was an attack on the female and Catholic rule of Mary Tudor and Mary of Guise, mother of Mary, Queen of Scots. In this, Knox asserted that there was no biblical justification for female rulership. Female rule was therefore, he argued, repugnant to nature.

Elizabeth was cautious about interfering in the domestic affairs of another nation in which subjects were rebelling against sovereign authority and was reluctant to intervene in Scotland. She loathed Knox, who had written against 'the monstrous regiment of women'. Cecil, on the other hand, strongly supported intervention. He sympathised with the religious predicament of Scottish Protestants and knew that England would be more secure without a French force north of the border. However, he also sought the removal of Mary, Queen of Scots, which would weaken her influence as a potential Catholic claimant to the English throne, and wanted to incorporate Scotland within a wider 'imperial' British State, which he considered necessary for the survival of Protestant England. This was admittedly a minority position on the Council, in which he was even opposed by his normal ally and brother-in-law Sir Nicholas Bacon. Cecil persuaded Elizabeth to intervene by playing on her insecurity. He pointed to the action of Francis and Mary in using the English royal coat of arms on their own heraldic device. He even suggested his own resignation if Elizabeth failed to support him. The process of intervention in Scotland, therefore, is a clear illustration of the way in which decision-making in foreign policy could be influenced both by religious considerations and a key individual.

Initially, intervention was limited to money and armaments, but towards the end of December 1559 the navy was sent to the Firth of Forth to stop French reinforcements from landing. The Lords of the Congregation were offered conditional support at the Treaty of Berwick in February 1560, and in March 1560 an army was sent north. The army and navy blockaded Leith, just outside Edinburgh and where most of the French force was situated, from land and sea. The siege failed, but other circumstances forced a French withdrawal; the French fleet was severely damaged by storm, and the regent Mary of Guise died. Cecil was therefore able to secure favourable terms in the Treaty of Edinburgh in July.

The Lords of the Congregation were accepted as a provisional conciliar government and, with the death of Francis II in December, the Guises fell from power, Mary Stuart's influence on French policy came to an end and she had to return to Scotland. Here, she was forced to accept the political and religious power of her enemies. Cecil had triumphed – the interests of Scottish Protestants had been protected and the political influence of Mary had been significantly reduced. However, Elizabeth was conscious that success had been achieved through good fortune (the death of Francis II) and she would proceed more cautiously in the future.

Intervention in France

Conflict broke out between Catholics and Protestants in France in March 1562. **Robert Dudley**, later **Earl of Leicester**, encouraged Elizabeth to put military pressure on the French Crown when it was in a relatively weak state so as to ensure the return of Calais. Elizabeth promised the **Huguenot** leader, the Prince of Condé, 6000 men and a loan of £30,000, with control of the port of Le Havre as security.

Unfortunately for Elizabeth and Leicester, the luck that had assisted the English in Scotland now deserted them. The Huguenot army was defeated and Condé was captured; on the Catholic side the Duke of Guise was assassinated. With both sides leaderless, the French factions agreed to accept peace terms

Fig. 4 *An official portrait of Mary, Queen of Scots, commissioned when she was ruling in Scotland*

ACTIVITY

Prepare a document for Sir William Cecil's use, outlining the advantages and disadvantages of intervening in Scotland. How would Cecil have persuaded Elizabeth to intervene?

KEY PROFILE

Robert Dudley, first Earl of Leicester (1532–88), a younger son of the Duke of Northumberland, was a childhood friend of Elizabeth. He survived the downfall of his father to become Elizabeth's favourite over many years.

KEY TERM

Huguenot: term used in the sixteenth and seventeenth centuries to denote French Protestants

and united to drive the English out of Le Havre. The English were therefore forced to seek an unfavourable peace settlement at the subsequent Treaty of Troyes in 1564.

Elizabeth not only lost the indemnity she had secured at Câteau-Cambrésis, she lost Calais as well, this time permanently. Although in the long run that might have proved an advantage (Calais was expensive to maintain and it was too tempting to use it as a starting point for invasion), the blow to Elizabeth's prestige was significant. Thereafter, she became much more cautious about supporting Protestant causes on the European continent: possibly too cautious in the case of **her subsequent attitude to the Netherlands**.

CROSS-REFERENCE

Elizabeth's relationship with the Netherlands in the 1560s is discussed in Chapter 20, pages 198–201.

Summary

Elizabeth, despite the problems in foreign policy, had made a broadly impressive start as queen. With the assistance of Cecil she had managed her accession and coronation very skilfully, in the process impressing such experienced foreign observers as the Spanish ambassador with her style of rulership. She had achieved a settlement in religion which attempted, with some success, to be relatively comprehensive. There were still many unanswered questions, especially in regard to marriage and succession, but she had established herself as queen with remarkable success.

ACTIVITY

Summary chart

What were the main features of the religious settlement?

Church doctrine	
Church services	
Appearance of churches	
Role of the monarch	
Relationship between Church and State	

EXTRACT 2

It is clear from the Privy Council's own registers that nine privy councillors ran the country from 1541 to 1547. Although Henry intervened, he did so spasmodically and in matters that had always concerned him: diplomacy, military strategy, theology and his wives. The irony is that the Duke of Norfolk was not among the nine. After the fall of Catherine Howard the entire Howard connection was threatened with destruction, and the reformed cause revived at court when Henry married his sixth wife, Katherine Parr, in 1543. However, factionalism was encouraged by the hottest political issue of the king's last years – the succession, a battle won by the Earl of Hertford (later Duke of Somerset). As Protector to Edward VI, Somerset's arrogance aroused resentment. He mishandled the revolts of 1549 and his overthrow became inevitable.

Adapted from John Guy, *Tudor England*, 1988

EXTRACT 3

From a childhood in which she was adored and feted and then violently rejected, a fighter was born. Mary maintained her faith and her self-belief. Despite repeated attempts to deprive her of her life and her right to the throne, the warrior princess turned victor, and became the warrior queen. The boldness and scale of her achievements is often overlooked. The campaign that Mary led in the summer of 1553 would prove to be the only successful revolt against central government in sixteenth-century England. In the moment of crisis she proved decisive and courageous, and won the support of the English people as the legitimate Tudor heir. Mary proved to be a conscientious and hard-working queen who was determined to be closely involved in government business and policy making. She was also a woman who lived by her conscience and was prepared to die for her faith.

Adapted from Anna Whitelock, *Mary Tudor: England's First Queen,* 2009

EXTRACT 4

Elizabeth gained her kingdom without having to fight for it, but never forgot the danger which had lain in her way. In January 1559, leaving the Tower which once, as a prisoner in Mary's reign, she had thought never to leave except in her coffin, she thanked God for saving her as He had Daniel from the lion's den. By this Old Testament analogy she offered a deliberate promise to all those who waited for a Protestant princess to bring their own deliverance. As even her enemies admitted, Elizabeth had 'powers of enchantment', and as she passed through her capital to her coronation she displayed them. Mary had made no response to the pageants which had greeted her, but Elizabeth promised her new subjects a reign of mutual love and undying royal self-sacrifice. With a new monarch came a new court and Council. Even Paget was dispensable. Elizabeth's Privy Council was composed, at first, of laymen. A few great magnates, even those of suspect loyalty, stayed, but her Council was far from baronial. Most were trained to public life at the universities and Inns of Court.

Adapted from Susan Brigden, *New Worlds, Lost Worlds: the Rule of the Tudors, 1485–1603,* 2000

A LEVEL PRACTICE QUESTION

Evaluating historical extracts

Using your understanding of the historical context, assess how convincing the arguments in Extracts 2, 3 and 4 are in relation to the nature of Tudor rule in the years 1541 to 1563.

STUDY TIP

Try to look at arguments put forward about 'rule', rather than what is said about individual monarchs. You should assess the views and provide a summary conclusion.

18 The impact of economic, social and religious developments in the early years of Elizabeth's rule

EXTRACT 1

Wretched harvests, mortal epidemics of influenza in 1557 and 1558, and heavy expenditure on war had combined to present the government with social, military and financial problems at least as pressing as religious dissensions. There were many signs that the conjunction of dearth and epidemic had inflicted alarming wounds upon society. The population fell. Labourers were said to be 'out of obedience', deserting their masters and demanding excessive wages, apprentices were becoming undisciplined; vagabonds and thieves abounded. Several bills were introduced into the parliament of 1559 to deal with this but none passed into law. During the next four years both central government and local authorities tried to establish some order. The culmination of tentative and sometimes contradictory efforts by national and local rulers came with the celebrated Statute of Artificers in 1563.

Adapted from Penry Williams, *The Later Tudors: England, 1547–1603*, 1995

LEARNING OBJECTIVES

In this chapter you will learn about:

- the impact of economic and social developments, from 1558 to 1563
- the impact of religious developments, from 1558 to 1563.

ACTIVITY

According to Penry Williams, what economic and social problems dominated the early years of Elizabeth's rule? Look back at chapters 11 and 17, 20 and 22.

1. Prepare a chart to show the main economic issues faced by the Tudors. Add in detail of attempts to address these by the first four Tudor monarchs.
2. As you read this chapter add any further material from Elizabeth's early years. Complete the chart after reading Chapter 22.

KEY QUESTION

As you read this chapter, consider the following Key Question:
How did English society and economy change, and with what effects?

The impact of economic and social developments, 1558–63

Fig. 1 *'Marriage Feast at Bermondsey', painted in 1569 by Joris Hoefnagel*

Elizabeth came to the throne at a difficult time for the English economy. The combination of bad harvests, high mortality rates, high taxation and, for many people, a significant cut in real wages meant that there was considerable fear about social instability. The high level of mortality, which reduced the supply of labour, did, however, increase the bargaining power of survivors. It was in this context that various pieces of legislation were proposed during Elizabeth's first parliament to deal with the range of problems, but none was passed into law. This meant that central government was left with two rather ineffective mechanisms for dealing with the situation: instructions issued to JPs and other officials, and royal proclamations. Often, issuing royal proclamations was effectively an admission of government impotence. This was hardly surprising. The government was dealing with problems which it only dimly understood.

A CLOSER LOOK

Local initiatives

Various local authorities also tried to deal with economic and social issues. Although we now know that real wages were falling, most thought that wages were too high. The Council of the North tried to get the corporations of York and Hull to enforce a schedule of wage rates which had applied in 1514, and 113 labourers were charged with unlawfully high wages. Counties such as Northamptonshire, Buckinghamshire and Worcestershire tried to establish appropriate wage rates for various trades.

The Statute of Artificers (1563) was a national attempt to try to sort out this problem. It established a number of rules:

- compulsory labour, especially at harvest time
- a minimum period of one year for the hire of workmen during which they could not leave their masters or be dismissed without good cause
- a prohibition on anyone following a craft unless they had served a seven-year apprenticeship
- the setting of maximum wage rates by JPs in every county.

However, the government lacked powers of enforcement. There was no army of bureaucrats to traverse the country investigating wage rates in every district. It was difficult even for JPs to manage this within their own counties.

Poor relief

The problems of poverty and vagabondage (people who wander from place to place without a home or job) remained widespread in late Tudor England. There were a number of causes of poverty. Partly as a result of the increase in population, real wages for the labouring poor in Elizabethan England were lower than they had been a century earlier, with wage rates consistently falling behind rises in prices. Harvest failures created food shortages, especially in the mid-1550s and mid-1590s. The old and the infirm suffered particularly badly.

Despite the impact of religious changes, offerings of private benefactors (who, for example, traditionally left money for the establishment of almshouses for the poor) continued. However, this was no longer enough. Cecil was particularly concerned that large numbers of homeless and unemployed people could present a serious threat to law and order.

Contemporaries differentiated between the 'deserving' and the 'undeserving' poor, with the former being deemed entitled to receive some form of limited assistance to alleviate their condition whereas the latter were entitled to be punished. The deserving poor included the old, widows and those whose disabilities prevented them from securing employment. Before the Reformation, the main responsibility for providing poor relief had lain

ACTIVITY

Extension

Research the treatment of the poor in the sixteenth century. Create an illustrated timeline to show attitudes, continuity and change.

with the Church. The Reformation had destroyed most such institutions offering poor relief; this meant that alternative forms of relief were necessary.

Parliament had made various stumbling attempts to deal with the problem. Acts had been passed in 1552 and 1555. The Elizabethan regime continued this process. A further ineffective Act was passed in 1563, but its impact was haphazard. National legislation continued to lag behind local provision which had been set up in a number of boroughs, most notably Norwich and Ipswich. It was not until the 1570s that parliamentary legislation began seriously to get to grips with the problem.

CROSS-REFERENCE

Attempts to improve the condition of the poor under Mary I are outlined in Chapter 16, pages 158–159.

The legislation of the 1570s is discussed in Chapter 22, page 222.

Stabilising the currency

The government was more successful in restoring confidence in the currency. Both Northumberland and Mary had sought to re-stabilise the currency. However, it was Elizabeth who was able to do so. Early in the reign a scheme was announced for the withdrawal of debased coins and their replacement by soundly minted coins. While some individuals suffered as a result of the scheme, it did ensure that only sound coins were in circulation and the government wisely did not resort again to debasement during the rest of the century. Prices still continued to rise but at least the government could no longer be held responsible for the problem.

Fig. 2 *A ten shilling coin from the reign of Elizabeth I*

The impact of religious developments, 1558–63

The Elizabethan settlement was undoubtedly Protestant – but *how Protestant?* Many returning Protestant exiles initially saw the queen as the 'English Deborah', the Old Testament heroine who had protected the Israelites from their Canaanite enemies. By analogy, Elizabeth would protect the godly from what they regarded as the evils and superstitions of Catholicism. Elizabeth, for her part, was a somewhat reluctant 'Deborah', and many of the religious problems of the reign were to stem from Elizabeth's unwillingness to fulfil the role allotted to her by her more religiously enthusiastic councillors. This created the fundamental paradox of Elizabeth's reign: her most enthusiastic

KEY QUESTION

How far did intellectual and religious ideas change and with what effects?

supporters often demonstrated a Protestant zeal which ensured their loyalty to the queen but which was wholly at variance with Elizabeth's own sceptical and sometimes conservative approach to religious matters.

KEY PROFILE

Matthew Parker (1504–75) was Anne Boleyn's chaplain, after which he had a successful academic career in Cambridge. As a married clergyman, he was deprived of his livings during Mary's reign, but he did not go into exile. He was a reluctant appointee as Elizabeth's first Archbishop of Canterbury.

ACTIVITY

Extension

Look up on the Internet the 'Song of Deborah' in the Book of Judges in the Old Testament of the Bible. Why do you think that it was so popular in 1558 and 1559 to draw the parallel between Queen Elizabeth and Deborah?

The Protestant emphasis can be seen in the appointment of new bishops, but one of Mary's bishops refused to continue to hold office. Some of the early appointments to bishoprics were of moderates, particularly the appointment of **Matthew Parker** as Archbishop of Canterbury. Parker had not been in exile during Mary's reign, but was trusted by Elizabeth, having been chaplain to her mother, Anne Boleyn. However, most of the new bishops were returning exiles and their appointments were part of a conscious strategy to reshape the hierarchy of the Church of England along more evangelical lines. On the other hand, Elizabeth disapproved of clergy marrying, distrusted preaching and ensured the preservation of the musical culture of the cathedrals and university colleges. Whatever else may be debated about the settlement, however, it is clear that it emphasised the **Erastian** nature of the Church of England.

CROSS-REFERENCE

To recap on the concept of Erastianism, look back to Chapter 6, page 52.

CROSS-REFERENCE

Look back to Chapter 14, page 133, for a definition of 'evangelical'.

ACTIVITY

Using the material both in this chapter and in Chapter 17, identify those aspects of religion in the early years of Elizabeth's reign which might be described as 'evangelical' and those aspects which might be deemed 'conservative'. What conclusions can you draw about the nature of the early Elizabethan Church?

The queen's view essentially was that the settlement was merely an act of State which defined the relationship between Crown and Church, and it established the Church's doctrinal position conclusively. Others believed the settlement represented the starting point for a process of spiritual renewal which would bring about the establishment of a true Church in England and which saw the English as God's elect nation. This was the view held by many of the queen's key advisers, including Cecil and Robert Dudley, and it was from this view that Puritanism would emerge.

CROSS-REFERENCE

Puritanism was the belief amongst extreme Protestants that the Church of England needed to be 'purified' of any remaining 'superstitious' (i.e. Catholic) practices; it is discussed in more detail in Chapter 23.

The character of the settlement was defined by two developments over the next four years:

1. The 1562 publication of *An Apology of the Church of England* by John Jewel, bishop of Salisbury. Jewel, who had been in exile during Queen Mary's reign, argued that the Church of England was returning to the true position abandoned many centuries earlier by the Church of Rome. 'We are come, as near as we possibly could, to the church of the apostles and of the old Catholic bishops and fathers.' There was thus an essential continuity between the early Church, as described in the Acts of the Apostles, and the beliefs of the reformers.
2. The publication in 1563 of the Thirty-Nine Articles of Religion. The Articles sought to define the difference between the Church of England and the Catholic Church. They were broadly supportive of reformed doctrine, especially that which was emerging out of Switzerland, though they attempted to adopt a broad and comprehensive approach to essential

CROSS-REFERENCE

To see how the Thirty-Nine Articles of Religion fitted in to the Elizabethan religious settlement, look back to Chapter 17, page 168.

beliefs. However, the convocation proved to be unsuccessful in achieving the wider aims of its leading members concerning the remaining features of Catholic practice within the Church and its structures, disciplinary procedures, services and clerical dress. Their vision of reform was not shared by the queen. Thus, the Church of England, though it was rapidly becoming Calvinist in its official doctrine was 'but half reformed' in its structures.

EXTRACT 2

As the Catholics had done in 1553, the Protestants now took their revenge. At Exeter those citizens most noted as devotees of images were made to throw them into the fire before the cathedral. When there was opposition to the demolition of the rood-loft at Throwley in Kent, one man was forced to be present when it was taken down 'for that he was an accuser in Queen Mary's time'. At Bures in Suffolk some of the parishioners hacked down the rood-screen. But usually resistance by conservatives was more evident than exuberance by radicals. Many parishes were slow to take down their altars and images, and others hid them away. Only 23 per cent of the senior clergy in the province of York endorsed the new arrangements. Elizabeth seems to have been outraged by the results of the visitation, both by the provocative iconoclasm, of the Protestants and of the surly disobedience of the conservatives.

Adapted from Christopher Haigh, *English Reformation: Religion, Politics and Society under the Tudors*, 1993

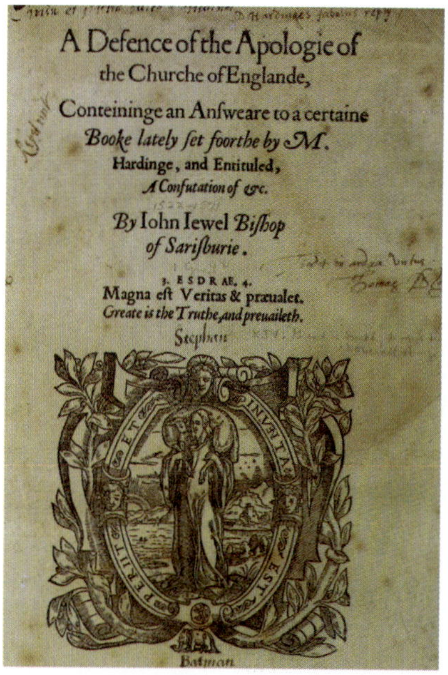
A Defence of the Apologie of the Churche of Englande,
Conteininge an Anſweare to a certaine *Booke lately ſet foorthe by M.* Hardinge, and Entituled, *A Confutation of &c.*
By Iohn Iewel *Biſhop of Sariſburie.*
3. ESDRAE. 4.
Magna eſt Veritas & præualet.
Greate is the Truthe, and preuaileth.

Fig. 3 *John Jewel's 'Apology or Answer in Defence of the Church of England' came out in 1562, shortly after Queen Mary died and the Anglican Church was able to return to England; it became the standard text for identifying Anglican views as they differed from the Catholic Church*

EXTRACT 3

Devout Protestants were delighted to see the removal of the Mass – but the strictest had scruples about the things retained by the new Church that reminded them of Catholicism. They expected the Church to be purged, and they believed that the queen would continue the reform. Certainly the bishops were of the opinion that she would take 'further orders' as the statute said. This meant that in the first few years of the reign the Godly, as they thought of themselves, were waiting expectantly and worshipping as they believed proper. The bishops, when they took office, often encouraged this behaviour, believing in the queen's commitment to a further reformation. In order to get a partially reformed Church most were willing to live within it for a short time, philosophically reminding themselves of the concept of *adiaphora*, that held that things unnecessary for salvation could be tolerated.

Adapted from Norman Jones, *The Birth of the Elizabethan Age: England in the 1560s*, 1993

EXTRACT 4

For nine months after the parliamentary statutes were carried out Elizabeth ruled the Church directly. Injunctions for its government were issued during the summer of 1559. For the most part these followed the Edwardian injunctions of 1547, commanding strict performance of duties by the clergy, the destruction of 'monuments of idolatry' and the avoidance of contention and strife. Reluctantly, Elizabeth permitted the clergy to marry, pointing out that many had previously been indiscreet in their choice of wives. At the same time she appointed royal visitors to secure the subscription of the clergy to the royal supremacy. Only the visitation records for the northern province have survived; they indicate a fairly low proportion of refusals but a higher number of absentees. Outright refusal was rare amongst parish priests, commoner in cathedral chapters and the universities. The large numbers who avoided committing themselves suggest that the Elizabethan Church was a long way from winning firm support. But by the beginning of 1560 the foundation of that Church had been laid and Elizabeth was able to delegate the task of administering it to her bishops.

Adapted from Penry Williams, *The Later Tudors: England, 1547–1603*, 1995

STUDY TIP

When evaluating the impact of the Settlement you should consider not only the impact of Acts of Supremacy and Uniformity but also that of the 1559 royal injunctions, which heavily influenced what went on at the level of the individual parish.

A LEVEL PRACTICE QUESTION

Evaluating historical extracts

Using your understanding of the historical context, assess how convincing the arguments in Extracts 2, 3, and 4 are in relation to the impact of the Elizabethan religious settlement.

A mid-Tudor crisis?

The concept of a mid-Tudor crisis has been employed to explain the significance of the reigns of Edward VI and Mary I as well as, in some accounts, the last years of Henry VIII and the first few years of the reign of Elizabeth. The concept rests, however implicitly, on the assumption that the reigns of Edward and Mary pale into insignificance when compared with the solid achievements of the reigns of Henry VIII and the later years of Elizabeth. In such readings the mid-Tudor years were unproductive, uncreative and strife-ridden. Such views were implicit in the interpretations of many Tudor historians through much of the nineteenth and twentieth centuries, most significantly Albert Pollard and Stanley Bindoff. The concept was made explicit in a book entitled *The Mid-Tudor Crisis*, published in 1973 by Whitney Jones, a student of Bindoff. Jones argued that the 11 years from 1547 to 1558 were marked by religious strife, inefficiency in government, economic and social distress and failures in foreign policy.

The apparent popularity of the concept as an aid to explaining the dynamics of the period is undoubtedly a reflection of the importance of Henry VIII and Elizabeth I, who are certainly the most distinctive and recognisable of all English monarchs. Both enjoyed long and dramatic reigns and, in contrast, the reigns of Edward and Mary seem limited in comparison.

However, a team of historians gathered together by Jennifer Loach and Robert Tittler in *The Mid-Tudor Polity*, published in 1980, challenged this idea and stressed both the positive features of the period from 1547 to 1558 and argued that the less desirable features of those years – for example, rebellions that explicitly challenged the Crown's religious policies and social dislocation – were as apparent in the mid-1530s as in 1549.

A CLOSER LOOK

The most important perspective was that offered by Dale Hoak who, in an influential essay, served to rehabilitate the Duke of Northumberland and thereby gave much force to his period of dominance. Similarly, Robert Tittler and David Loades have suggested that the reign of Queen Mary contained much that was worthy of credit. Historians such as Eamon Duffy and Christopher Haigh have gone much further in demonstrating the extent to which Mary was working with the grain of public opinion. Even the religious policies of the early part of the reign of Edward VI, castigated as chaotic by John Guy, have been rehabilitated by Diarmaid MacCulloch who has argued that they made perfect strategic sense given the Crown's religious priorities at the time.

ACTIVITY

Summary chart

1. Working in groups, for each of the main areas listed in the following table, give a mark from 1 (lowest) to 10 (highest) for the government's handling of the situation, providing evidence to justify your decision. In reaching your judgement you should, where possible, consider what the government was trying to achieve. Compare your findings with other groups and justify your decisions.

	1540–47	Somerset	Northumberland	Mary	1558–63
Crown finances					
Administration					
National security					
Religion					
Foreign policy					

2. Reflect on the chart you created at the beginning of this chapter. Can you explain why governments failed to deal effectively with economic issues in this period?

A LEVEL PRACTICE QUESTION

Is it fair to describe English government in the years 1540 to 1562 as 'consistently weak'?

STUDY TIP

You need to tease out the full implications of 'consistently'. This requires you to assess developments across these years to provide a supported conclusion which may subdivide the years to suggest government was sometimes weaker at one time than another.

4 The triumph of Elizabeth, 1563–1603

19 Elizabethan government, 1563–1603

EXTRACT 1

Elizabeth's reign was a period of order and good government, such as had not been seen in England since the 1520s. The Privy Council met twice a week, usually with up to ten of the courtiers and bureaucrats in attendance. The formal business was dispatched briskly and only foreign policy issues and the treatment of Mary, Queen of Scots required lengthy discussion. There were some disagreements amongst councillors, but no struggles for power. The key members were related, and shared the same ambitions and assumptions. The queen rarely saw her Council as a whole, and dealt privately with Burghley, Leicester, Walsingham, Sussex and, later, Hatton, so their leadership was assured. The wider royal court was dominated by the same individuals and families, and the **factionalism** of the 1560s had passed. The parliaments of 1571, 1572, 1576 and 1581 were carefully managed by the councillors and their agents. It was a narrow, but coherent and effective regime.

Adapted from Christopher Haigh, 'Politics in an Age of Peace and War, 1570–1630' in *The Oxford Illustrated History of Tudor and Stuart Britain*, 1996

KEY QUESTION

As you read this chapter, consider the following Key Questions:

- In what ways and how effectively was England governed during this period?
- How important was the role of key individuals and groups and how were they affected by developments?

LEARNING OBJECTIVES

In this chapter you will learn about:

- the place of the royal court in Elizabethan government
- the role of ministers
- factional rivalry
- Elizabethan parliaments.

KEY TERM

factionalism: in this context, factionalism refers to the fragmentation of the political system into separate groups competing against each other for patronage and advancement and, in the process, reducing the effectiveness of government

ACTIVITY

Evaluating historical extracts

1. What interpretation does Christopher Haigh advance in Extract 1?
2. Haigh has written extensively on the reign of Elizabeth. He is often described as a 'revisionist' historian. On reading through this chapter, identify those points on which he has 'revised' traditional views of Elizabethan government.

KEY TERM

patronage: the system by which the Crown distributed favours to those that were seen as loyal

The royal court

The royal court was important to the Elizabethan decision-making processes as here, Elizabeth could seek advice on an individual basis. The court was part theatre and partly a place for **patronage.** It existed wherever the queen happened to be at a particular time, whether she was resident at one of her palaces or visiting members of the nobility on one of her royal progresses. The court had two main areas: the Presence Chamber and the Privy Chamber.

The Presence Chamber was a relatively open area to which anyone with the right status or connections might expect to have access. The Privy Chamber was both more private and more important, though considerably less influential than it had been during the reigns of the Tudor kings because the Gentlemen of the Privy Chamber no longer had the rights of access to the monarch which they had formerly enjoyed. Admission to the Privy Chamber was carefully guarded.

The operation of the court came under the jurisdiction of the Lord Chamberlain. Elizabeth always appointed a member of the nobility to the post. (Three of her Lords Chamberlain were, in addition, close relatives, for example her cousin Lord Hunsdon, appointed in 1585.) Moreover, the ceremonial aspects of courtly life became much more important as the reign progressed. Increasingly, as Christopher Haigh has argued, Elizabeth turned her politicians (such as Cecil) into courtiers and her courtiers (such as the Earl of Leicester and Sir Christopher Hatton) into politicians.

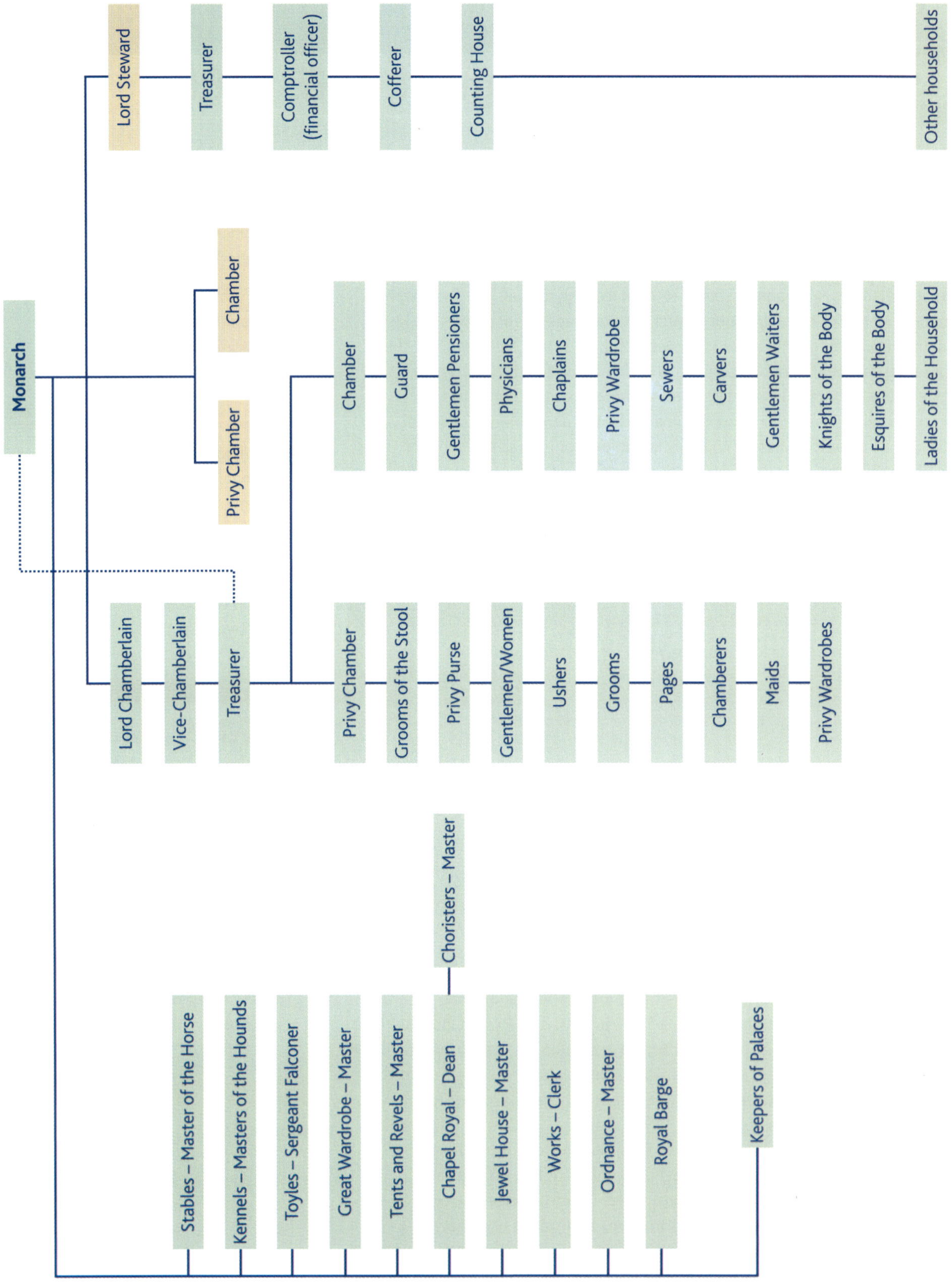

Fig. 1 *The royal court; the politically important posts are those towards the top and the centre of the diagram*

The role of ministers

EXTRACT 2

Elizabeth's Privy Council never had more than nineteen members and towards the end of the reign had only eleven. In her early years it met three days a week, but in the final decades was meeting on six or seven. According to John Herbert, who became second Secretary of State in 1600, it had three principal functions: the business of the queen, in which it 'doth handle principally question and consultations of State'; disputes between party and party, which might involve either criminal or civil suits or a mixture of the two; and disputes 'wherein the queen is a party'. Its business ranged widely from the apparently trivial to the significant. Its registers, however, omit one vital aspect of the Council's work. They record only action actually taken in the shape of orders and letters sent out; they tell us nothing about discussion about policy, of general decisions taken, of advice tendered to the queen. Yet such discussion certainly took place, normally without the queen.

Adapted from Penry Williams, *The Tudor Regime*, 1979

The main formal body in which the queen's principal ministers came together was the Privy Council, which was responsible for policy advice and administration. It met regularly, with most meetings attracting an attendance of about ten members. Its importance as a decision-making body should not be overestimated, however, as Elizabeth often consulted with ministers on an individual basis.

Fig. 2 *Key functions of the Privy Council*

In understanding the relationship between Elizabeth and her ministers, it is important to remember that Elizabeth fully intended to rule as well as to reign. An intelligent and sophisticated woman, she had, as a result of her traumatic adolescence, developed political skills that ensured her survival in difficult times. She was also conscious of the importance of her royal prerogative, which she was not prepared to restrict.

William Cecil was established as Elizabeth's key minister at the beginning of the reign, and he came to dominate the Council. He had already anticipated his rise to power even before Mary's death. Within a month of this event he was described by the Spanish ambassador as 'the man who does everything'. He was joined in the Council by a number of close associates including Sir Nicholas Bacon, Francis Russell Earl of Bedford and Sir Francis Knollys. The Council did contain some ministers of more conservative views. These were usually drawn from the traditional aristocracy and included the premier peer of the realm, the young and impetuous Thomas Howard, fourth Duke of Norfolk. Steadier conservatives included the Lord Treasurer the Marquis of Winchester and the earls of Sussex and Shrewsbury. However, the offices held by the latter pair usually kept them away from court and reduced their direct political influence. Elizabeth's favourite, **Robert Dudley**, Earl of Leicester, joined the Council in 1562.

CROSS-REFERENCE

William Cecil and Robert Dudley are profiled in Chapter 17, pages 166 and 171 respectively.

Some reshaping of the Privy Council took place in the 1570s. The influence of the traditional conservative aristocracy was reduced with the downfall and execution of Norfolk and the death of Lord Treasurer Winchester.

In the 1570s, a nucleus of firmly Protestant councillors was appointed: Sir Francis Walsingham, Sir Walter Mildmay, Sir Ralph Sadler, Sir Thomas Smith, Sir Henry Sidney and the Earl of Leicester's brother, the Earl of Warwick. Their advancement was balanced by the promotion of more conservative figures such as Sir James Croft and Sir Christopher Hatton. According to John Guy, these changes resulted in an 'inner ring' of eight councillors. Some of these were militant Protestants (Walsingham, Leicester, Mildmay, Knollys, the Earl of Bedford) along with Burghley (the title taken by Cecil when he was ennobled in 1571); the only relatively conservative figures were Sussex and Hatton.

Fig. 3 *Sir Christopher Hatton*

ACTIVITY

Group work

Working in small groups, prepare short presentations on the following Elizabethan ministers: Sir Nicholas Bacon, Sir Francis Knollys, Sir Walter Mildmay, the Earl of Sussex, Sir Christopher Hatton. You can access information on such figures in the *Oxford Dictionary of National Biography* at www.oxforddnb.com. You can view the website on any computer so long as you have a library card from one of the libraries that has right of access. Most public libraries in the UK offer this service.

CROSS-REFERENCE

The execution of Mary, Queen of Scots is covered in Chapter 20, page 198.

Despite the changes in personnel, the Council offered cohesive decision-making. There were disputes over foreign policy and a breakdown in relations between Elizabeth and her Privy Council brought about by the execution of **Mary, Queen of Scots**, in 1587, but Elizabethan ministers, on the whole, served their queen well.

ACTIVITY

The acts of the Privy Council for the reign of Elizabeth have been published online at www.british-history.ac.uk. Choose a date at random from the reign of Elizabeth, identify which councillors attended the Council meeting on that date, and note the range of business which was conducted. What conclusions can you draw about the nature and effectiveness of the Council and its business?

Several problems weakened Elizabeth's Council from the later 1580s:

- A number of ministers died in quick succession. The death of the Earl of Leicester in September 1588 was a blow Elizabeth took very personally. She also lost a number of other administratively able ministers. By 1597 the Council had only 11 members.
- The queen made matters worse by failing to make immediate replacements and when she did, she tended to rely on the middle-aged sons of former councillors who often lacked their fathers' skills.
- There was an absence of senior noblemen on the Council. As Paul Hammer has pointed out, this absence of great aristocrats mattered because it suggested that Elizabeth's Council no longer included the country's most important families.
- Elizabeth refused to allow Burghley to retire, although his effectiveness diminished during the 1590s. He appointed his son, Robert Cecil, to the Privy Council and the latter had to undertake an immense administrative burden on account of his father's ill health.
- The promotion of the younger Robert Cecil angered the Earl of Essex (stepson of the Earl of Leicester and a favourite of the queen); Essex was a temperamental man who made an enemy of Cecil.

A CLOSER LOOK

Sir Ralph Sadler died in 1587, the long-serving Chancellor of the Exchequer Sir Walter Mildmay in 1589, Sir Francis Walsingham, Sir James Croft, Leicester 's brother the Earl of Warwick and the Earl of Shrewsbury all in 1590 and Sir Christopher Hatton prematurely in 1591.

CROSS-REFERENCE

The problems of government in the later stages of Elizabeth's reign are discussed in detail on pages 192–193.

Factional rivalry

It has often been thought that conciliar government was affected by factional rivalries throughout Elizabeth's reign. However, the structure of Elizabethan government, at least in the early stages of the reign, helped to prevent factional rivalry from getting out of hand. No single minister, not even Cecil, had complete control over patronage. The various influential families at court and within the Council balanced one another. Thus, relatives of the Boleyns featured in the senior ranks of Crown service in substantial numbers, while Elizabeth's late stepmother's family, the Parrs, along with their close connections, also featured strongly, certainly early in the reign. Family connections could overcome religious differences. Although the Earl of Leicester and Cecil disagreed over the queen's potential marriage, they tended to cooperate over other issues, being able to work together most of the time because they needed each other.

KEY PROFILE

Sir Robert Cecil (1563–1612) was the only son of Lord Burghley's second marriage. He was groomed for high office by his father and became a member of the Privy Council in 1593 and was appointed secretary of state in 1596.

Robert Devereux, second Earl of Essex (1566–1601) was the stepson of the Earl of Leicester. He was active in the military service of the Crown, but his apparent charisma did not make up for his lack of political judgement. He lost favour following the failure of his mission in Ireland and responded to this situation with a so-called rebellion in 1601, which resulted in his execution for treason.

A CLOSER LOOK

Factional rivalry – differing interpretations

It has been asserted that there were clear divisions between Cecil and his allies, who favoured moderate and pragmatic policies, and Protestant ideologues led by Robert Dudley, Earl of Leicester. In recent years, however, historians such as Stephen Alford and John Guy have challenged this argument. This is partly because they see Cecil as a more radical figure in religious terms than has sometimes been acknowledged and partly because disputes between Cecil and Leicester tended to be occasional and focused on specific policy issues.

The coherence of government, which had been evident for much of Elizabeth's reign, began to decline during the 1590s when fierce clashes between Robert Cecil and the Earl of Essex made governance difficult. These problems came to a head in the Essex 'rebellion' of 1601.

CROSS-REFERENCE

The importance of the factional rivalries of the 1590s is discussed below.

Fig. 4 *The Earl of Essex*

CROSS-REFERENCE

For Essex's role in Ireland, look ahead to Chapter 21, pages 211–212.

A CLOSER LOOK

The declining influence of the Earl of Essex

Essex, once the bright young star of the Elizabethan court, lost his influence, his political judgement and eventually his head. His career suffered from a number of related problems: he had been largely frozen out of court by Sir Robert Cecil and his allies and had consequently lost his power as a faction leader. He was in deep financial trouble, which was made worse when Elizabeth refused to renew his monopoly on the import of sweet wines. He had also failed as a military leader in Ireland and had brought shame upon himself by his misbehaviour on his return from Ireland when he burst into the queen's bedchamber.

Essex's response to his declining influence was to plan an armed coup which would bring down Cecil and his other enemies. However, his plans were rumbled. Cecil was well prepared and Essex was finally forced to surrender. He was quickly tried and executed in 1601. Essex might have been an incompetent political figure who was hopelessly lacking in judgement. However, by this time the rule of Elizabeth and Cecil had become unpopular and the attitudes of Essex and his associates reflected a larger discontent, tied in with the queen's diminishing authority.

EXTRACT 3

Most accounts of the court have tended to emphasise factional strife and a vicious atmosphere of place-seeking, enmity and competition surrounding an alternately goddess-like or hag-like queen. Yet much of the evidence for factional strife has been drawn from the 1590s and by no means reflects the reality of the previous decades. The court was never completely free from conflict. But such conflict was less the product of faction among courtiers than of disputes between an able, charming, yet imperious and idiosyncratic queen, and councillors and intimates who in general shared a high degree of social, political and cultural homogeneity. It is not surprising to find some of the strongest criticisms of court life from men at the centre. Yet compared to that of Henry VIII Elizabeth's governance was mild and merciful. Elizabeth may have been imperious, vain and sharp of temper, but she was unwilling to go to extremes.

Adapted from Simon Adams, 'Eliza enthroned? The court and its politics', 1984

EXTRACT 4

Elizabeth I carefully managed her own policy. As Sir Robert Naunton later explained, 'Though very capable of counsel, she was absolute enough in her own resolution, which was apparent, even to her last'. She knew her mind; her instinct to power was infallible. When her privy councillors tried to manipulate her, they were rarely successful; she would lose her temper and the matter would rest in abeyance. Yet she repeatedly postponed important decisions; unless panicked, she could procrastinate for years. Her successive ditherings drove Sir William Cecil to distraction. Francis Bacon put his finger on the essence of Elizabethan politics: first, that to succeed at court politicians had to pretend to be in love with the queen; secondly, that the conduct of the 'game' of courtship was Elizabeth's most effective tool of policy.

Adapted from John Guy, 'Tudor monarchy and political culture', 1996

A LEVEL PRACTICE QUESTION

Evaluating historical extracts

Using your understanding of the historical context, assess how convincing the arguments in Extracts 1, 3, and 4 are in relation to Elizabethan government.

STUDY TIP

You should consider the ways in which each extract is both convincing and unconvincing by applying your own knowledge to support or challenge the points made by each author. Try to provide an overall conclusion in which you justify your decision as to which is the most convincing.

Parliament

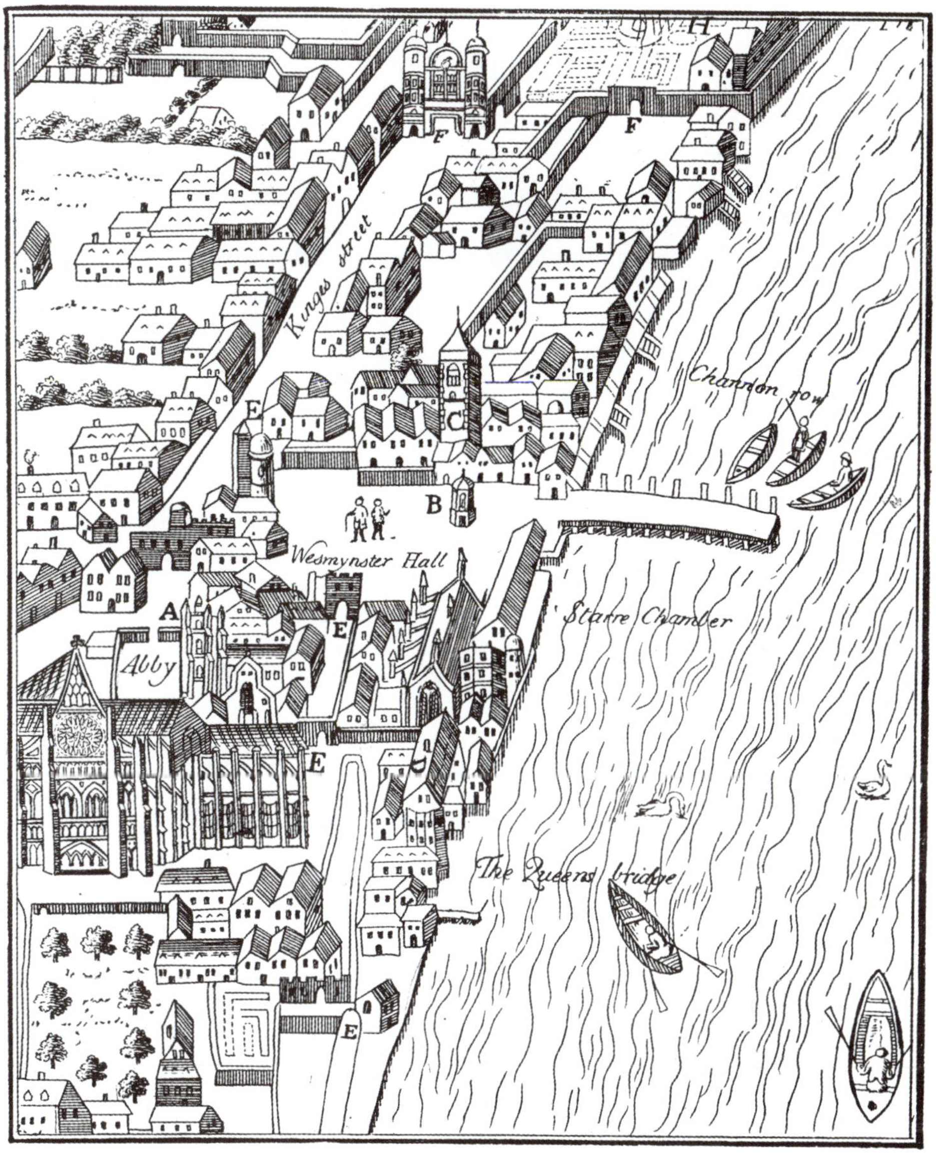

Fig. 5 *A contemporary image of Westminster, showing Parliament, Westminster Hall and Westminster Abbey*

Parliament was less important under Elizabeth than it would become in the seventeenth century. Possibly, it was also less important under Elizabeth than it had been under Henry VIII. Elizabeth tended to regard Parliament as a necessary but occasional evil; something she had to put up with for its tasks of law making, granting of taxation and (as the Members of Parliament believed), giving advice. So, while occasionally important for legislative and revenue-raising purposes, it was largely a secondary feature of the Elizabethan political system.

Table 1 *Elizabeth's Parliaments, 1559–1601*

Dates	Reason(s) called	What happened	Significance
Jan – May 1559	Settlement of religion.	Settlement pushed through because of the efforts of strongly Protestant councillors (Cecil, Knollys, Cooke, Bacon) in the face of conservative opposition in the House of Lords.	Legal status of the Church and forms of worship were established for the whole of the reign.
Jan – Apr 1563 (first session) Sep 1566 – Jan 1567 (second session)	Elizabeth wanted money.	A large number of MPs urged Elizabeth to marry, even though they were infringing the royal prerogative by doing so. In 1563 members of the Privy Council openly pressed the issue; in 1566 they were more subtle, prompting MPs to do their bidding. In 1566 Elizabeth prevented the passage of bills for further religious reform which were favoured by Cecil and many of the bishops.	This parliament saw the first difference of opinion between Members of Parliament and the queen on an issue which she considered to be part of the royal prerogative.
Apr – May 1571	Elizabeth wanted money to pay for the suppression of the 1569 rebellion and the Council also sought a tightening of the treason law and laws against Catholics.	Parliament granted Elizabeth a subsidy and was happy to support the tightening of laws against Catholics. William Strickland proposed a bill to reform the Book of Common Prayer, which upset the queen.	Strickland annoyed the Council, which was trying to secure further religious reform by more subtle means, and it was the Council which took the initiative in removing him from attendance at the Commons.
May –Jun 1572 (first session) Feb – Mar 1576 (second session) Jan – Mar 1581 (third session)	There was no request for money. Parliament considered issues of security following the exposure of the Ridolfi Plot. Parliament recalled. Parliament recalled.	Parliament called for the execution of the Duke of Norfolk and Mary, Queen of Scots. Parliament granted subsidy to the queen. The House of Commons itself imprisoned MP Peter Wentworth for infringement of the royal prerogative. Parliament granted a subsidy and once again tightened the anti-Catholic laws.	The calls for the execution of Norfolk were orchestrated by members of the Privy Council. Elizabeth refused to back calls for Mary's execution.
Nov 1584 – Mar 1585	Parliament was called at a difficult time in international relations following the assassination of William of Orange.	Parliament once again tightened the anti-Catholic laws.	Parliament's passing of the Act for the Surety of the Queen's Person, which gave a statutory basis to the Bond of Association, illustrates the level of uncertainty which was felt at the time.
Oct 1586 – Mar 1587	Parliament was called at a difficult time both in international relations and in the aftermath of the Babington Plot.	Parliament debated the issue of whether or not Mary, Queen of Scots should be executed.	Elizabeth disregarded the habits of her entire reign by seeking parliamentary advice concerning what to do with Mary, Queen of Scots. Parliament petitioned Elizabeth for Mary to be executed. A few Presbyterian MPs sought religious reform; their leaders were imprisoned for their infringement of the royal prerogative.

Dates	Reason(s) called	What happened	Significance
Feb – Mar 1589	Parliament was called so that revenue could be raised for the war against Spain.	Parliament voted a double subsidy.	The positive atmosphere of this parliament can be attributed to its having assembled in the aftermath of the Armada triumph.
Feb – Apr 1593	This session was largely concerned with legislation against those who refused to attend church.	Parliament voted a triple subsidy.	Peter Wentworth was imprisoned a second time, on this occasion for raising the issue of the succession, thereby infringing the royal prerogative.
Oct 1597 – Feb 1598	Elizabeth was desperately short of cash at a time of economic and social crisis.	The most important legislative achievement was the introduction of a comprehensive poor law. Parliament once again granted a triple subsidy.	The issue of monopolies generated considerable controversy.
Oct 1601 – Dec 1601	Elizabeth remained short of cash.	The 1598 poor law was revised. Elizabeth was able to demonstrate her political skill for one last time in her 'Golden Speech'. Parliament granted a quadruple subsidy, amidst much moaning about monopolies.	There was even more controversy over monopolies.

Law making

Altogether, 438 Acts were passed by Elizabeth's parliaments. Probably the most important related to religion (the Acts of Supremacy and Uniformity in 1559 and the penal laws against Catholics) and social policy (especially the Acts of 1598 and 1601 which addressed poor relief).

Granting taxation

To Elizabeth, as to the previous Tudor monarchs, the most important function of Parliament was to grant extraordinary revenue to the Crown. Of the 13 parliamentary sessions in Elizabeth's reign, all but 2 were asked to grant revenue. The distinction between 'ordinary' and 'extraordinary' revenue had been lost during the reign of Henry VIII and, despite her attempts to economise, Elizabeth was frequently forced to resort to levying 'extraordinary' revenue to pay for the Crown's 'normal' expenditure because the level of her ordinary revenue had fallen in real terms. However, persistent failure to reform the system of direct taxation meant that the yield of extraordinary revenue through the subsidy declined also in real terms.

Giving advice

Most of the time Elizabeth was not at all interested in listening to the advice of MPs. Indeed, she became particularly irritated when MPs ventured into areas that she considered fell within the royal prerogative. On the other hand, meetings of Parliament gave useful opportunities to members of the Privy Council and other senior figures to gauge opinion amongst members of the 'political nation'. As such, Parliament served as a useful means of communication and a clear point of contact between councillors and those who administered the localities on their behalf.

CROSS-REFERENCE

For more details about each of these parliamentary events turn to:
- Chapters 17–18, pages 167–169 and 190 (for religious settlement and anti-Catholic laws)
- Chapters 20–22 (for plots, war against Spain and economic issues)
- Chapter 19, page 193 (Elizabeth's marriage)
- Chapter 19, page 193 (Peter Wentworth's second imprisonment).

CROSS-REFERENCE

The Acts of Supremacy and Uniformity are outlined in Chapter 17, pages 168–169.

The Acts of 1598 and 1601 are covered in Chapter 21, page 208.

CROSS-REFERENCE

The distinction between 'ordinary' and 'extraordinary' revenue, defined in the fifteenth century by Sir John Fortescue, is explained in Chapter 2, page 13.

ACTIVITY

Research

You can find out more about the operation of Elizabeth's parliaments by reading *Elizabethan Parliaments, 1559-1601* by Michael Graves (1987). Another useful resource is the website of the History of Parliament Trust: go to www.historyofparliamentonline.org/research, and select the section on '1558-1603' under the heading 'Parliaments'.

A CLOSER LOOK

Parliament and the patronage system

It used to be thought that the Crown devoted much energy into ensuring that the House of Commons was packed with its own supporters. (To support the claim it was pointed out that Elizabeth's reign saw the creation of no fewer than 62 new borough seats – the assumption being that these were created to ensure the return of the Crown's own direct supporters.) This view has now been disputed – most of the impetus for the creation of such seats came from aristocrats, badgered by local gentry who wanted the prestige conferred by membership of the House of Commons. The creation of borough seats thereby enabled the Crown to oblige its aristocratic servants who were, in turn, able to reward their local supporters, a perfect example of the patronage system of Elizabethan England in operation.

A CLOSER LOOK

The historiography of Elizabeth and her parliaments

For many years the interpretation of Elizabeth and her parliaments which held sway was that of John Neale. Conscious of the importance of the parliamentary challenge to royal authority which culminated in civil war in the 1640s, Neale traced the roots of that challenge back to what he saw as the emergence of oppositionist elements in Elizabeth's reign, particularly the Puritan Choir of around 40 MPs who challenged Elizabethan religious legislation (see Chapter 18). His arguments were attacked by Geoffrey Elton and, later, Michael Graves.

Fig. 6 *The frontispiece of* Journals of All the Parliaments during the Reign of Queen Elizabeth, *published in 1682 by Sir Simonds D'Ewes*

Managing Parliament

Even if Parliament's functions were limited, it was important to Elizabeth's ministers that sessions were carefully managed. Sir William Cecil played an important role in preparing the Crown's legislative programme, 'framing and often shaping bills'. In such activities he was assisted by the Council's 'floor managers' in the House of Commons, at first Sir Francis Knollys and from 1576 Sir Christopher Hatton. He used his own men of business to help him manage the Commons. Typically, these MPs were lawyers and experts on parliamentary procedure who could promote measures which Cecil considered important.

Privy councillors often began parliamentary sessions by setting the tone and outlining the Crown's priorities. Moreover, privy councillors frequently introduced bills and sat on the committees that gave detailed consideration to the content of parliamentary bills. In short, as John Guy has put it, 'legislative business was properly directed'.

However, despite the attempts at control, there were times when her parliaments irritated the queen, particularly if they challenged what she considered to be her prerogatives. She gave vent to outbursts of irritation in 1563 and 1566 when the House of Commons, at the urging of members of the Privy Council, sought to debate the issues of marriage and succession. Moreover, she readily intervened to prevent the passage of bills of which she disapproved and refused the royal assent to some bills that had passed through both houses. Across the whole of her reign she refused the royal assent to over 60 bills, including no fewer than 15 in 1585 alone.

By 1593, many of the traditional methods of parliamentary management began to have less success. Elizabeth tried to use both charm and flattery but there were differences about how to deal with religion. The Crown, urged on by **Archbishop Whitgift**, sought the passing of a punitive act against **sectaries**, even though this was openly opposed by MPs such as Sir Walter Raleigh with close links to the Crown. One of Burghley 's associates made a Commons speech criticising Whitgift and the queen took this as personal criticism – barring the politician's advancement.

Another feature of the 1593 Parliament was the imprisonment of Peter Wentworth for arguing for a named successor to Elizabeth. Infuriated once again by such an attack on her royal prerogative, the queen had Wentworth and three colleagues imprisoned in the Tower. Her actions were not unconstitutional but showed how the queen's temper had worsened with age.

KEY PROFILE

John Whitgift (c1530–1604) made his name as Vice Chancellor of Cambridge University as an opponent of the Presbyterian Thomas Cartwright. He dismissed Cartwright from his professorship and in a subsequent pamphlet was a resolute defender of the royal supremacy. He was rewarded by being appointed bishop of Worcester in 1577 and promoted to Archbishop of Canterbury in 1583. He was the only churchman to be appointed by Elizabeth to membership of the Privy Council.

KEY TERM

sectaries: members of Protestant sects which had rejected the Church of England and the royal supremacy

A CLOSER LOOK

The Golden Speech of 1601

This was delivered by Elizabeth to a number of MPs as the final parliamentary session of her reign drew to a close. It is difficult to avoid the conclusion that Elizabeth was aware that this was likely to be the final parliament of her reign, so the speech did take the form of a valediction or farewell. Elizabeth's performance was masterly, as she drew a discreet veil over the poor relations which had blighted this parliamentary session. 'Though God hath raised me high, yet this I account the glory of my Crown, that I have reigned with your loves. This makes me that I do not so much rejoice that God hath made me to be a Queen, as to be a Queen over so thankful a people, and to be the means under God to conserve you in safety and to preserve you from danger. It is not my desire to live or reign longer than my life and reign shall be for your good. And though you have had, and may have, many mightier and wiser princes sitting in this seat, yet you never had, nor shall have, any that will love you better.' Many MPs reportedly left the chamber in tears.

The relationship between Elizabeth and her parliaments broke down entirely at the end of her reign over the issue of monopolies in 1601. The debate over monopolies was the one occasion when the Crown's officers lost control over the House of Commons and this was not helped by the problems faced by Robert Cecil who lacked skill as a parliamentary manager and had considerably fewer resources to undertake this task than had been available to his father. In the end a compromise was achieved and the session ended with the queen presenting her Golden Speech to a crowded gathering of around 140 MPs in the Council chamber at Whitehall.

A CLOSER LOOK

The case of Peter Wentworth

Wentworth gained notoriety as he was twice imprisoned for comments which he made in the House of Commons. The first occasion came in 1576, when he was actually imprisoned on the orders of the House of Commons itself for asserting the right of Parliament to discuss matters which Elizabeth regarded as part of her prerogative powers. In 1576 he was quickly released on the queen's own orders. Wentworth was less fortunate in 1593 on the second occasion when he offended the queen, this time because she took offence at his raising of the sensitive issue of the succession. He remained imprisoned until his death in 1597. It would be a mistake to see Wentworth as an opponent of the Crown. He himself saw his role as being that of a loyal and candid friend to the monarch.

Summary

In evaluating the quality of government over a period as lengthy as the reign of Elizabeth, a mixed picture of successes, partial successes and failures will emerge. On the whole, government was well conducted, especially over the first 30 years of the reign, and there was a broad consensus, religion excepted, amongst the governing classes concerning royal policies and their enforcement within the country. Elizabeth was fortunate that she had a number of talented individuals, such as Cecil, Walsingham, Mildmay and Hatton to work for her, but she herself demonstrated effectiveness and often wisdom in her choice of ministers. Her one serious blind spot in this regard was her reluctance to come to terms with the deficiencies in character and ability of the Earl of Essex, but this should perhaps be seen as part of wider issues in government in the final years of the reign.

CROSS-REFERENCE

The issue of monopolies is discussed in Chapter 19, page 193.

ACTIVITY

Summary chart

For each of the issues below, work in pairs to evaluate the success of central government in Elizabeth's reign. You should agree a mark out of 10 as to how well she handled the issue, from 1 (very poor) to 10 (outstanding), and provide evidence to support your judgement. Add up the marks and devise an overall conclusion concerning her success. You will need to refer to the material in this chapter and also in chapters 17, 18 and 24.

Context	Mark	Evidence to support judgement
Consolidation of power		
Implementation of religious settlement		
Directing policy through ministers		
Relationship between Crown and Parliament		

STUDY TIP

Your first task in planning an answer to this type of question is to identify what you consider to be the relevant aspects of Elizabethan government. Organise your material into those areas which you consider in broad terms to have been weak and those which you consider in broad terms to have been strong. You should also consider the importance of change across time during the reign. In particular, you need to judge which aspects of government might have declined during the later years of the reign.

A LEVEL PRACTICE QUESTION

'Elizabethan government had more weaknesses than strengths in the years 1558 to 1588.' Assess the validity of this view.

20 Foreign affairs

EXTRACT 1

The problem of Elizabeth's successor was perhaps the most long-running issue of the reign. After the death of Mary Stuart (Queen of Scots) in 1587, the field of possible candidates was large. The legal situation was complicated. Under the Succession Act of 1544, Henry VIII had been empowered to nominate heirs should his own children fail to produce offspring – as they did. In his will, he laid down that the Crown should pass, after Edward, Mary and Elizabeth, first to Lady Frances Grey and her heirs, second to Lady Eleanor Clifford , younger sister to Lady Frances, and her heirs and third to the 'next rightful heirs' – a vague phrase indeed. This gave low priority to the Stuart line. However, the protagonists of the Scottish, Stuart succession, who were many and influential after the execution of Mary, held that Henry's will was invalid, having been signed with a stamp, not with his own hand. If this were accepted then the best hereditary claim lay with James VI of Scotland. But there were two obstacles to his succession: his mother had been condemned for treason and he himself was a foreigner. Both could be held legally to debar him.

Adapted from Penry Williams, *The Later Tudors: England, 1547–1603*, 1995

KEY QUESTION

As you read this chapter, consider the following Key Question:
How did relations with foreign powers change and how was the succession secured?

LEARNING OBJECTIVES

In this chapter you will learn about:

- the importance of the succession as a political issue
- the relationship between Elizabeth and Mary, Queen of Scots
- relations between England and Spain.

ACTIVITY

1. Look back at the family tree on page xv. Explain the line of succession as established by Henry VIII's will.
2. Explain the claim of the 'protagonists of the Scottish, Stuart succession'.
3. Explain fully the problems faced by the Scottish succession.

As you read through the first part of this chapter, examine the range of choices open to Elizabeth and her councillors with regard to the succession and consider how much control Elizabeth had over the outcome.

Issues of succession

Marriage issues

Elizabeth's status as a single woman created considerable difficulties. It meant that the succession, should she die prematurely, was at the forefront of her ministers' thinking. Most were keen that she should marry to prevent the possibility of a Catholic inheriting the throne. However, the queen felt strongly that issues of marriage and succession lay within the royal prerogative and were not areas for discussion either in Parliament or round the Council table. The unwillingness of Elizabeth's councillors to acknowledge this viewpoint would cause repeated tension during her reign.

In the early years of the reign, the suitors for Elizabeth's hand included:

- **Robert Dudley**, the future Earl of Leicester (probably Elizabeth's preferred choice). However, the prospect of Elizabeth marrying Leicester horrified Sir William Cecil, whose own influence would have been seriously eroded. Furthermore, this marriage would have created many political risks, a consequence of the mysterious circumstances surrounding the death of Leicester's first wife, Amy.
- Philip II of Spain. He offered his hand in a polite gesture to Elizabeth but probably lacked serious intent partly because of his profound Catholicism.
- The archdukes Ferdinand and Charles, sons of the Emperor Ferdinand. However, both were Catholic.
- Prince Erik of Sweden, a Protestant suitor, to whom Elizabeth gave little encouragement.

CROSS-REFERENCE

Robert Dudley is profiled in Chapter 17, page 171.

A CLOSER LOOK

The death of Amy Dudley, 1560

Amy Dudley was found dead with a broken neck at the bottom of a staircase. It was immediately assumed by many that she had been murdered on the orders of her husband, which would leave him conveniently free to marry Elizabeth. In fact, it meant the opposite, for the circumstances of Amy's death made a royal marriage for Dudley politically impossible, even though the coroner's jury ruled that the death was accidental.

KEY PROFILE

Lady Catherine Grey (1540–68) was the sister of Jane Grey and therefore the granddaughter of Henry VIII's sister Mary. According to the terms of Henry VIII's will this made her Elizabeth's heir presumptive, and she was conveniently a Protestant. However, she disgraced herself through her secret marriage to the Earl of Hertford and the couple were imprisoned in the Tower by Elizabeth. The marriage was annulled in 1562.

KEY TERM

Presence Chamber: when the reigning monarch was a queen, male courtiers could not normally enter the Privy Chamber, therefore the Presence Chamber was the place where private contact could be made between monarch and courtier; the temporary banishment of Leicester and Pembroke from the Presence Chamber therefore represented a considerable punishment

KEY PROFILE

François, Duke of Alençon and then of Anjou (1555–84) was the younger brother and heir presumptive of Henry III of France.

CROSS-REFERENCE

The execution of Mary, Queen of Scots is discussed later in this chapter, on page 198.

KEY PROFILE

James VI (1566–1625) was a baby when he succeeded to the Scottish throne following the flight into England of his mother, Mary. He was brought up as a Protestant, which was a vital factor in commending his candidature for the succession to many of Elizabeth's councillors.

Marriage, the succession and Parliament

The House of Commons first raised the issue of marriage in January 1559, but Elizabeth deflected the pressure gracefully. When Parliament met again in 1563 the situation was very different: Elizabeth had been stricken with smallpox in October 1562 and for a time it seemed she might die, thereby creating a full-scale succession crisis. Councillors were perfectly aware of the disasters that might ensue should the queen die; civil war, foreign invasion and religious strife were all possible outcomes. The level of panic amongst Elizabeth's councillors when the gravity of her illness became apparent should not be underestimated.

There was no consensus as to who the successor might be. This was hardly surprising given that there were significant misgivings about each of the potential successors, the disgraced **Lady Catherine Grey** and the ardent Catholic Mary, Queen of Scots. The queen characteristically refused to commit herself. She, and the nation, had survived, but it had been a close-run thing. Elizabeth was perhaps lucky that her characteristic procrastination did not lead to disaster.

In 1566 Parliament once again pressed Elizabeth to marry. Some MPs were prompted by members of the Privy Council, including Cecil and Leicester, but their motives differed. Elizabeth reacted furiously, banishing Leicester and the Earl of Pembroke from the **Presence Chamber**, publicly rebuking other members of the Council and summoning members of both Houses of Parliament for a ferocious tongue-lashing. Elizabeth thus reasserted her view that marriage and succession were matters of the royal prerogative.

In 1579, when Elizabeth was declared capable of still bearing a child, a possible marriage to François, Duke of Anjou, brother of King Henry III of France was suggested by Burghley and Sussex. Some of her councillors and members of the public were horrified that this would lead to an infant child – under French influence – as successor. However, nothing came of the suggestion, so the crisis passed.

The final succession

Elizabeth probably took a political decision not to marry, coming to the conclusion that the disadvantages of marriage outweighed the advantages, despite the potential risks of having no direct heir of her own. The execution of her cousin, Mary, Queen of Scots, meant that Mary's son, **James VI of Scotland**, had the best hereditary claim, even though the Stuarts had been excluded from the succession in Henry VIII's will. Furthermore, James was Protestant and by 1600 already had two sons.

Since Elizabeth's councillors had a vested interest in ensuring that they remained in royal favour, once Elizabeth's successor was in place they began wooing James, even before Elizabeth's death in 1603. Essex, in particular, was in regular contact with James VI, and after Essex's death in 1601, Sir Robert Cecil kept contact with James and eventually ensured his untroubled succession, for which he received due reward.

ACTIVITY

Imagine you were an advisor to Sir Robert Cecil in 1601 to 1603. Outline the advantages and disadvantages of James VI of Scotland succeeding to the English throne.

To the very end, Elizabeth refused to name a successor and there is no conclusive proof that she accepted James's succession on her deathbed. Nevertheless, her authority had ebbed away and the arrangements for succession were already in place. Never before in English history had a change of dynasty been effected so smoothly, and much of the credit for that must be given to Cecil.

Mary, Queen of Scots

Relations between Elizabeth and Mary, Queen of Scots were inextricably linked with the issue of religion and the succession. The Catholic Mary had incurred the wrath of both the Protestant lords and the English through her marriage to the Earl of Darnley. The marriage was a disaster, with Mary being implicated in her husband's murder. A subsequent third marriage to Darnley's presumed murderer, the Earl of Bothwell, set off a brief civil war, the outcome of which saw Mary flee to England in 1567.

From the time when Mary fled south until her execution in 1587, she posed a continuous problem to Elizabeth, since some English Catholics saw her as the rightful monarch and she became the focus of plots to overthrow Elizabeth. This problem was to grow worse following the excommunication of Elizabeth in 1570, which in the eyes of the Catholic Church absolved Elizabeth's Catholic subjects from the need to obey their sovereign. This frightened Elizabeth and her Council, resulting in the tightening of the treason law. After the **excommunication**, Protestants were deemed loyalists and Catholics traitors.

KEY QUESTION

How important was the role of key individuals and groups and how were they affected by developments?

CROSS-REFERENCE

For Elizabeth's excommunication by the Pope in 1570, and the implications for English Catholics, look ahead to Chapter 23, page 229.

Mary, Queen of Scots and Catholic plots against Elizabeth

Date	Plot	Detail	Significance
1571	Ridolfi	Involved a conspiracy for Mary to marry the Duke of Norfolk and to overthrow Elizabeth.	Allowed Burghley to ensure the execution of Norfolk for treason.
1583	Throckmorton	Foreign landing in Sussex followed by overthrow of Elizabeth and her replacement by Mary. Foiled by the efficiency of **Sir Francis Walsingham**'s espionage network.	1. Led to the creation of the Bond of Association. 2. Worsened Anglo-Spanish relations. 3. Tightened conditions of Mary's captivity.
1585	Parry	Plot to assassinate the queen.	Led to the acceleration of parliamentary proceedings on a bill to ensure the queen's safety.
1586	Babington	Mary complicit in a plot to assassinate Elizabeth but exposed by Walsingham's codebreaker, Thomas Phelippes.	Enabled Burghley to secure Mary's execution.

KEY PROFILE

Sir Francis Walsingham (c1532–90) was a Cambridge-educated lawyer who began his royal career as a diplomat and was promoted to secretary in 1573, when he joined the Council. He was concerned principally with diplomacy and with espionage. He was a fervent Protestant who enjoyed close connections with many of those who shared his religious views.

ACTIVITY

How can the information about the role of Walsingham and his officials be used to support arguments concerning the quality of Elizabethan government?

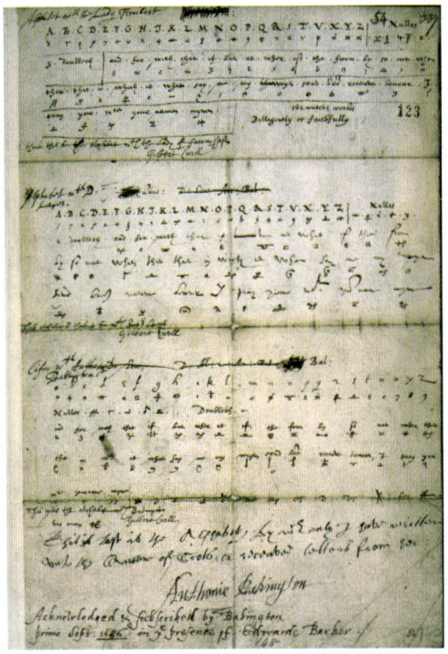

Fig. 1 *A letter in code from Mary, Queen of Scots to Anthony Babington with Babington's postscript*

Mary's trial and execution

Elizabeth was reluctant to press for the execution of another anointed monarch. Eventually, it was decided that Mary should face trial at Fotheringhay Castle in Northamptonshire where she was moved the day after Babington's execution. Privy councillors and nobles assisted by judges were ordered to try her, but several of those commissioned pleaded illness. Some feared **regicide**; others were more concerned that to condemn to death the mother of their possible future monarch might not be a particularly sensible career move. Mary was plainly guilty, but at Elizabeth's command no sentence was pronounced.

There were four months of delays during which time Elizabeth patently shrank from ordering her cousin's execution. Burghley, on the other hand, who had long held the view that Elizabeth's personal safety and the security of the Protestant State required Mary's execution, used his old tactic of parliamentary pressure to influence Elizabeth. Parliament duly petitioned Elizabeth, but she refused to sign the death warrant until 1 February 1587 and then gave contradictory orders about its despatch. Mary met her end with great dignity and composure. In the eyes of many English Catholics she had died a martyr for the Catholic faith.

A CLOSER LOOK

Elizabeth's reluctance to seek Mary's execution stemmed from her developed notions of rulership. Monarchs, even one like Mary who had lost her throne, were divinely ordained and to seek a fellow monarch's death could be seen as a challenge to divine law. At a more basic level, Elizabeth feared that the execution of Mary could undermine her own security as a monarch.

KEY TERM

regicide: the execution or murder of a monarch

Fig. 2 *The execution of Mary, Queen of Scots, as sketched by an eyewitness*

KEY PROFILE

Sir John Hawkins (1532–95) was a merchant and ship owner from Plymouth. His career benefited from marriage to the daughter of naval treasurer, Benjamin Gonson, whom he succeeded in that office. A privateer (i.e. legalised pirate) and slave trader, he also served with distinction against the Armada as Rear Admiral.

England's relations with Spain

Relations in the 1560s

Anglo-Spanish relations were usually cordial in the 1560s. However, they deteriorated towards the end of the decade because of:

1. The trading activity of **John Hawkins**. Hawkins attempted to break the Spanish trading monopoly in the Caribbean. He so infuriated Spanish interests that in September 1568 his fleet was blockaded in the Mexican port of San Juan de Ulúa and only two of his ships were able to escape.
2. The situation in the Netherlands. Philip II wanted a tighter form of political organisation in the Netherlands under more direct Spanish control, which would help to root out heresy. Elizabeth came under pressure from Protestant

councillors to aid the Dutch Protestants who feared danger. She was reluctant to take action, having suffered heavily from her French adventure, and had qualms about aiding rebels who were fighting sovereign authority.

3. The English found opportunities to harass the Spanish. For example, when, in November 1568, a storm forced several Spanish vessels, carrying 400,000 florins which was intended to pay the army of the Duke of Alba, Philip's general in the Netherlands, to seek shelter in English ports, Elizabeth impounded the money. (This led Alba to seize English ships and property in the **Netherlands**.)

Furthermore, the breakdown in Anglo-Spanish and Anglo-Dutch trade, Philip's encouragement to the Northern Rebellion in 1569 and the Ridolfi Plot in 1571, and the excommunication of Elizabeth in 1570, had all served to sour Anglo-Spanish relations by the early 1570s.

The Netherlands and declining Anglo-Spanish relations, 1570–85

In 1572, Elizabeth, possibly inadvertently, contributed significantly to the deterioration of Anglo-Spanish relations by expelling the **Sea Beggars** from English ports. They were forced to land in the Dutch port of Brielle and their occupation of the port, unchecked by the Spanish garrison there, sparked off full-scale revolt against the rule of Spain.

By 1576 all of the provinces of the Netherlands had risen against what they saw as atrocities by the Spanish army. Collectively, they produced the Pacification of Ghent, which called for the expulsion of all foreign troops and the restoration of the provinces' autonomy, a situation favoured by Elizabeth.

Fig. 3 *An illustration typical of the anti-Spanish propaganda produced by the Dutch rebels, which served to reinforce the attitude of those English Protestants who felt that Elizabeth should adopt a stronger anti-Spanish foreign policy*

CROSS-REFERENCE

You can read more about the trading activities of Sir John Hawkins in Chapter 22, pages 217–218.

A CLOSER LOOK

The Netherlands was a loose grouping of 17 provinces that historically owed allegiance to the Duke of Burgundy. Philip II had inherited the title and therefore had suzerainty over the Netherlands, which he was trying to transform into more direct political control.

CROSS-REFERENCE

For Elizabeth's problems in France look back to Chapter 17, pages 170–172.

CROSS-REFERENCE

The Northern Rebellion of 1569 is outlined in Chapter 21, pages 214–215.

Elizabeth's excommunication is discussed in Chapter 23, page 229.

KEY TERM

Sea Beggars: Dutch pirates licensed by the rebel leader William of Orange

Fig. 4 *The Netherlands*

CROSS-REFERENCE

The possibility of Elizabeth's marriage to the Duke of Anjou is discussed above, page 196.

However, the provinces quarrelled amongst themselves and the French were prepared to invade the Netherlands. This was not what Elizabeth had hoped for and she even contemplated marriage to the French Duke of Anjou to retain English influence in the Netherlands.

From an English perspective, the situation in the Netherlands simply got worse as divisions among the provinces of the Netherlands led to the emergence of two separate entities, the Union of Utrecht (largely northern and Protestant) and the Union of Arras (largely southern and Catholic). The Spanish made their peace with the Union of Arras, thereby creating the basis by which the new governor-general, the Duke of Parma, could begin his reconquest of the northern provinces. To make matters worse, in 1580, Spanish power was strengthened by the annexation of Portugal.

ACTIVITY

Produce a memorandum on behalf of the radical Protestants on the Privy Council outlining the reasons why Elizabeth should support the Dutch rebels and outlining what forms that support might take.

Elizabeth adopted a more overtly anti-Spanish position, for example by:

- supporting the Portuguese pretender, Don Antonio
- knighting Francis Drake on circumnavigating the globe (irritating the Spanish hugely in the process)
- treating the Spanish ambassador contemptuously.

Such issues, some of them trivial in themselves, served to heighten tensions between the two countries.

A CLOSER LOOK

Portugal and the claim of Don Antonio

The kingdom of Portugal, often an ally of England, had come under Spanish control in 1580 on the death of the childless King Henry. This gave Philip II control of the large Portuguese fleet and the use of major ports such as Lisbon. Don Antonio was a member of the Portuguese royal family. He was a claimant to the Portuguese throne and his claim was from time to time supported by Elizabeth, who was cynical about Don Antonio but saw him as a possible weapon to use against Spain. Don Antonio's claim was flawed in that he was illegitimate, which limited his usefulness for Elizabeth.

After 1580 the situation in the Netherlands, already bad, deteriorated seriously from an English perspective as Parma's reconquest of the north gained momentum, leaving only the provinces of Holland and Zeeland in Protestant hands. To make matters worse, the rebel leader, William of Orange, was assassinated in 1584.

Philip II and the Catholic League in France came to an agreement in the Treaty of Joinville at the end of 1584. This alarmed Elizabeth because the Guise family led the Catholic League and with the Guises as his allies, Philip II no longer had a political motive to prevent him from supporting Mary, Queen of Scots.

CROSS-REFERENCE

The relationship between Mary, Queen of Scots and the Guise family is explained in Chapter 17, page 170.

Deterioration of Anglo-Spanish relations, 1585–87

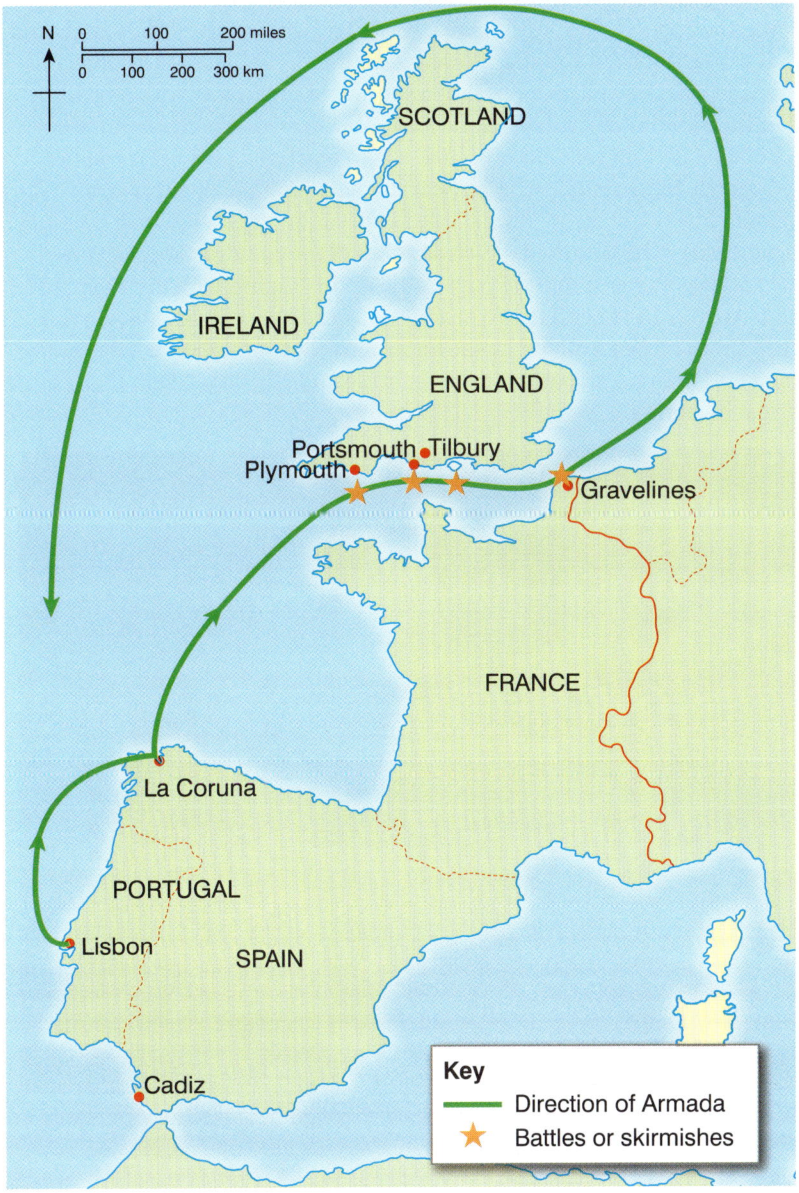

Fig. 5 *The route of the Spanish Armada*

To counteract the terms of the Treaty of Joinville, Elizabeth made an alliance with the Dutch Protestant rebels in the Treaty of Nonsuch in 1585 and sent troops to the Netherlands under the command of the Earl of Leicester. However:

- The troops, badly and irregularly paid, were so ill disciplined that they alienated the Dutch.
- The Dutch felt betrayed when two officers, William Stanley and Rowland Yorke, deserted and joined Parma.
- The English commanders quarrelled among themselves.
- Leicester quarrelled with the Dutch. (The Dutch thought Elizabeth was trying to do a deal behind their backs with Parma.)

Leicester returned to England, resigning his command in January 1588. The fiasco encouraged Philip to think that he could exploit the divisions between the English and Dutch.

The Spanish Armada

The organisation of the expedition against England was highly complex and took over two years to come to fruition. Philip had convinced himself that he was doing God's work and that he was engaged in a Catholic crusade. However, the Spanish fleet, or Armada, was huge, with many of the vessels and their crews having been commandeered from the Portuguese. The sailing of the Armada was delayed, as a result of a successful English attack on Spanish ships in the harbour at Cadiz in April 1587. The Armada finally set sail from La Coruña on 22 July 1588. Its objective was to reach the port of Gravelines, in the Spanish Netherlands, where it was intended that the Spanish army, commanded by the Duke of Parma, would board the ships so that an invasion of England might be launched. It was sighted off the coast of Cornwall on 29 July and was engaged in indecisive battle in the English Channel from 30 July to 6 August. In the end the Armada was forced because of unfavourable winds to try to return to Spain by the hazardous route of sailing north towards Scotland and then back south to the west of Ireland. This cost them many more ships, lost in storms.

A CLOSER LOOK

Why was the Armada defeated?

A number of explanations for the Armada's defeat have been suggested. The strategy which required the fleet to land in the Spanish Netherlands so that Parma's army could be taken on board was flawed; the Armada's leadership (by the Duke of Medina Sidonia) might be questioned; the English were quick to exploit the opportunities offered by the vagaries of the weather, for example by sending fireships to destroy some of the Armada while at anchor; the English also benefited from superior gunnery and manoeuvrability, and the 'Protestant wind' favoured the English.

Fig. 6 *After the defeat of the Spanish Armada, Elizabeth's triumph was depicted in a number of Armada portraits; in this version, attributed to George Gower, she demonstrates England's international triumph through the placement of her right hand on a globe of the world. The top right-hand corner shows the Armada being destroyed by the 'Protestant wind'*

The continuing war against Spain 1588–1604

The war against Spain dragged on at great expense for a further 16 years and peace was not concluded until after the deaths of both Elizabeth and Philip.

The war was fought on several fronts:

- at sea off western Europe
- in the Caribbean
- on land in France, the Netherlands and Ireland, where it was connected to a revolt against Elizabeth's rule.

Elizabeth sought national security above all other considerations. For many, however, both at court and in the armed forces, England was involved in a war for both national and religious survival against a universal Catholic conspiracy. This view was shared up to a point by Lord Burghley, who saw Spain as engaged in a war of conquest. Whatever the differences in emphasis among English policy makers, they all shared an assumption that national and/or religious considerations were paramount. However, there were strategic differences. Some took a 'minimalist' view, which in effect concentrated limited resources in the Netherlands to confront the Duke of Parma. Others such as John Hawkins favoured a more expansive naval campaign, which they argued could be self-financing, while accepting that a land campaign in the Netherlands was also necessary.

War at sea

Those who favoured a more expansive naval campaign could support their case by arguing that war in the Netherlands tended to be expensive and difficult, while England had enjoyed success with small-scale naval attacks in the Caribbean and on mainland Spain in 1585 and 1587.

From 1595 the English made three attacks on mainland Spain and its colonies. These included a spectacular but short-lived victory with the capture and occupation of Cadiz and the sinking of four galleons. However, there was no strategic follow-up. Hawkins and Drake advocated an attack on Panama, which they regarded as the weakest point in the Spanish empire, but the attack failed and both Hawkins and Drake died at sea.

The capture of Cadiz humiliated Philip II and prevented Spanish merchant vessels from sailing to the West Indies, which proved a blow to the Spanish. It also provoked Philip into an uncharacteristically incautious response. In 1596 he again ordered a fleet to invade England. However, by the time it set sail it was well into autumn and was defeated by storms. Nevertheless, the threat to England remained clear.

The Spanish also tried to exploit a rebellion in Ireland for their own ends. To prevent a possible Spanish attack on Ireland, a fleet under the Earl of Essex's command was despatched to attack the Spanish fleet in harbour in north-west Spain in 1597. Essex's fleet was driven back to Plymouth by adverse winds, and was eventually used to sail to the Azores, suggesting that the need for booty had once again superseded wider strategic considerations. The Spanish fleet succeeded in setting sail for Ireland and, but for the wind, might well have landed virtually unopposed there.

Further fear of invasion in 1599, prompted almost entirely by false intelligence, created a huge panic in England. Thereafter, naval activity was directed almost entirely by the need to prevent Spanish landings in Ireland. In the end, little had been achieved at very great cost.

War in the Netherlands

For several years after 1588, the main arena for the war on land between England and Spain remained the Netherlands. After Leicester's failures, relations between the English Crown and the Dutch improved.

In 1589 Sir Francis Vere was made commander of the English forces and proved highly capable. He forged a positive relationship with the Dutch leader,

A CLOSER LOOK

Financed partly by the Crown and partly by private investors, some of these expeditions were led by courtiers such as the Earl of Cumberland and Sir Walter Raleigh, while others were led by professional seamen such as Hawkins, Drake and Martin Frobisher. They achieved mixed levels of financial success, particularly with the capture of the Spanish treasure ship the *Madre de Dios* in 1592, but ultimately they achieved little in the way of strategic success. By deflecting resources away from the Netherlands, it could be argued, in fact, that they made the achievement of strategic success more difficult.

CROSS-REFERENCE

The Irish rebellion is discussed in Chapter 21, pages 210–212.

Maurice of Nassau. This, combined with the problems faced by the Spanish, whose troops mutinied on a regular basis and who were overcommitted in France, ensured that gradually the territories that had been lost to the Duke of Parma were recovered.

The cost to the English of maintaining a force in the Netherlands was high, but the Dutch paid a share of the running costs. By 1594 the Spanish had been expelled from all of the lands of the northern Netherlands. The Dutch revolt had proved successful and some of the credit was due to the English Crown. English strategic objectives were triumphantly achieved. The northern Netherlands became an independent state; the southern Netherlands, while remaining under Spanish sovereignty, also achieved a degree of autonomy. No major foreign power was therefore entrenched in the Netherlands.

ACTIVITY

Produce a chart relating to events in the Netherlands, indicating English involvement and significance.

Dutch event and date	English involvement	Outcome and significance

Summary

Despite its many shortcomings and its increasing expense, Elizabeth's foreign policy had proved broadly successful. She and her councillors had changed the emphasis on foreign policy away from dynastic considerations and the desire for glory to a more hard-headed approach to what might have constituted a national interest. The conflict with Spain was a long-running and expensive sore, but the English ultimately fared the better from the conflict, enhancing Elizabeth's reputation.

ACTIVITY

Refer back to the analysis by Penry Williams of the succession issue quoted at the beginning of the chapter. How successfully did Elizabeth and her councillors cope with the problems he outlined? Who should be credited most with the achievement of what appeared in 1603 to be a successful outcome?

ACTIVITY

Summary chart

Complete the following chart, evaluating England's policy towards Spain.

	Success/failure	Evidence
Maintenance of national security		
Netherlands		
Financing foreign policy		

EXTRACT 2

What made it all so exceedingly frustrating was that the war dragged on for nineteen long years and that, although victory seemed on several occasions – in 1589, in 1591, in 1596 – just around the corner, in the event it never arrived. On those three occasions victory did seem almost within sight, at least victory in the sense that Elizabeth understood it: the expulsion of Spanish troops from the Netherlands and those countries' return to the substantial measure of home rule they had enjoyed under Charles V, combined with the restoration of the French monarchy to strength and independence as an effective counterpoise to Spanish mightiness. On each occasion, however, victory slipped away. Those whose shoulders were most galled by the burdens therefore tended to blame the government, some for not making peace, quite as many for not winning the war. This happened all the more because government was getting more inbred, and court and country were beginning to grow apart. All this added up to a widespread groundswell of grumbling. It all bred a new and more critical attitude to central government.

Adapted from R.B. Wernham, *The Making of Elizabethan Foreign Policy, 1558–1603*, 1980

EXTRACT 3

From the days of Secretary Walsingham onwards, Elizabeth has been criticised for her slow, indecisive and stingy habits when dealing with overseas problems, charges to which modern historians from Froude onwards have added ill-placed reproaches at her unwillingness to promote ideals, whether as the champion of Protestantism or as the godmother of a reconstructed and liberated Netherlands. Her objectives were prosaic and local, but practicable. Her success is to be measured by the survival of the cloth-export traffic to central Europe and by the maintenance of royal credit in foreign exchanges as well as by the defeat of the Armada in 1588. Her policy, whatever its shortcomings in execution had worked. By the time of her death, the kingdom had weathered the threat of invasion.

Adapted from G.D. Ramsay, 'The foreign policy of Elizabeth I' in *The Reign of Elizabeth I*, edited by Christopher Haigh, 1996

EXTRACT 4

The key to Elizabethan conservatism remains financial, and it is on the success of its financial policies that Elizabethan government must be judged. Here, foreign policy played a central role, for the peculiar circumstances of European politics in the second half of the sixteenth century placed England in a uniquely critical position. Not only were the possibilities for military and naval intervention practically limitless, but over £1 million of Elizabeth's wartime expenditure took the form of loans and subsidies to allies. Moreover, this was a government deeply conscious of the disasters created by military over-extension in Edward VI's reign. That it was able to conduct a reasonably successful foreign policy without bankrupting the Crown, for all the failures in detail, was its great accomplishment. The danger lay in the bequest to Elizabeth's successors of the myth of a glorious foreign policy that they found impossible to live up to.

Adapted from Simon Adams, 'England and the world under the Tudors' in *The Oxford Illustrated History of Tudor and Stuart Britain*, edited by John Morrill, 1996

A LEVEL PRACTICE QUESTION

Evaluating historical extracts

Using your understanding of the historical context, assess how convincing the arguments in Extracts 2, 3 and 4 are in relation to Elizabethan foreign policy.

STUDY TIP

In answering such questions it is important to try to define what the relevant foreign policy objectives might have been. Only then can you properly measure how successful the outcomes might have been.

A LEVEL PRACTICE QUESTION

'Elizabeth I's policy towards Spain was always weak and unconvincing.' Assess the validity of this view with reference to the years 1568 to 1603.

STUDY TIP

In order to make the task more manageable, it might be helpful to think in terms of sub-periods based on key turning points, for example the deterioration of relations in 1568 and the drift to war in the period 1585 to 1588.

21 Society in Elizabethan England

EXTRACT 1

The English State was more stable in the second half of the sixteenth century than were its neighbours. France and the Low Countries were torn apart by civil war throughout the period; and Philip II faced two major rebellions. By comparison Elizabeth faced only very minor outbreaks within England itself, though Ireland was a different matter. If the low level of taxation was one reason for English stability, it was not the only one. English society was comparatively unified: English nobles did not have the privileges, especially the exemption from taxation, enjoyed by their counterparts on the continent; and as a result the tax burden, while lighter, was more evenly spread. Nor did England suffer from the major famines that struck France in the 1590s and which led to peasant uprisings. The system of poor relief limited destitution.

Adapted from Penry Williams, *The Later Tudors: England, 1547–1603*, 1995

LEARNING OBJECTIVES

In this chapter you will learn about:

- social continuity and change in Elizabethan England
- problems in the regions
- the significance of social discontent
- the extent and significance of rebellions.

KEY QUESTION

As you read this chapter, consider the following Key Question:
How did English society and economy change and with what effects?

Society: continuity and change

Fig. 1 *Burghley House, built by Lord Burghley*

ACTIVITY

Evaluating historical extracts

In Extract 1, Penry Williams attempts to link the nature of the Elizabethan State to some of the key aspects of English society at that time. List what these are. As you read through this chapter, ask yourself whether the contents support or detract from the argument which he put forward.

English society remained under aristocratic domination during the reign of Elizabeth. There were few hereditary peers. The highest peerage title, duke, carried inherent dangers in Tudor England: each of the four ducal titles that existed in England in the period from 1547 to 1572 – Somerset, Northumberland, Suffolk and Norfolk – met a bloody end with their holders suffering traitors' deaths. After 1572 Elizabeth was careful not to create any more dukes.

By Elizabeth's reign, the nobility had become more peaceable than in earlier times, and less concerned with defence. Below dukes, the other four **ranks of the peerage**, though few in number, sought to enhance their prestige through massive building projects; part of the motivation for this was to ensure that they could accommodate the queen in appropriate surroundings on royal progresses. Houses such as Burghley (then in Northamptonshire and built by Lord Burghley) and Wilton in Wiltshire (built by the Earl of Pembroke) were therefore conceived and built on a grand scale. Elizabeth herself chose not to emulate such grandeur, being inclined on cost grounds to modify some of the many building projects of her father.

CROSS-REFERENCE

The five ranks of the peerage (duke, marquess, earl, viscount and baron) are introduced in Chapter 4, page 34.

ACTIVITY

Research

Discover whether there are any Elizabethan houses in your area. What can you find out about their owners in Elizabeth's reign?

CROSS-REFERENCE

The social structure of early Tudor England is discussed in Chapter 4, pages 33–38.

Below the peerage came the gentry. This term continued to elude precise definition and embraced a wide social range – from influential knights of the shire and figures of national importance, such as Sir Christopher Hatton, to modest local landowners. Between these two extremes came the county gentlemen and esquires who dominated local government through their work as justices of the peace (JPs) and who often took on the burden of local office without receiving any tangible rewards. The gentry class increased in size during Elizabeth's reign, and the proportion who were seriously wealthy went up.

The other layers of society differed little from what they had been at the start of the century. However, the reign of Elizabeth was a period during which the gap between rich and poor widened. The period witnessed the beginnings of a consumer society amongst the prosperous members of the landed, mercantile and professional classes. Landed incomes increased, especially after about 1570. On the other hand, poorer sectors of the population found themselves vulnerable to enclosure and to the persistent decline in real wages.

CROSS-REFERENCE

Measures to help with poor relief in the 1550s and 1560s are outlined in Chapter 18, pages 176–177.

By the end of Elizabeth's reign the population was roughly 4 million. The bulk of the people still lived in the countryside. The only large city was London, whose population, much of which by now lived outside the bounds of the City, was probably as high as 150,000. London acted as a huge magnet for migrants from other parts of the country. The largest provincial cities were Norwich and Bristol, but few other cities had populations in excess of 5000.

A CLOSER LOOK

Some urban areas had developed their own systems of poor relief by the 1570s and it was a scheme developed in Norwich that provided the basis for the Elizabethan poor law legislation between 1576 and 1601.

Poverty and poor relief

The later years of Elizabeth's reign saw further measures to relieve poverty.

- An Act of 1572 established the principle that local ratepayers should be required to pay a rate for the relief of their own poor.
- The Poor Law Act of 1576 was the first act to attempt to create a national system of poor relief to be financed and administered locally. Under the Act, towns were required to make provision for the employment of the deserving poor.
- Further Acts in 1598 and 1601 completed the legislative process. Under the Elizabethan Poor Law Act of 1601, the parish became designated as the institution required to raise the rates for, and to administer, poor relief. Each parish was to appoint an overseer of the poor who was to ensure both the efficient collection of poor rates and the appropriate distribution of relief to the poor. The overseers' key responsibilities were relieving the **impotent poor**, setting the able-bodied to work and apprenticing poor children. Their activities were supervised by justices of the peace.

Thus, Elizabethan government had taken upon itself the responsibility of ensuring a minimum level of subsistence for the **deserving poor**. This was a legislative achievement that remained substantially intact until 1834.

In contrast, the treatment of the **undeserving poor** remained harsh. An extremely repressive and ultimately unenforceable Act against vagrancy had been passed in 1547. Although it was quickly repealed, the notion remained that the undeserving poor should be whipped. In 1572 an Act added branding to the range of punishments available to the authorities. During the panic of 1597, an Act was passed which laid down that first-time offenders should be whipped and then sent back to the parish of their birth; repeat offenders could be executed.

KEY TERMS

deserving or **undeserving poor:** the deserving poor were those who were actively seeking work or were too old, too young or too ill to do so; the undeserving poor described those whom society considered to be beggars or vagrants

impotent poor: a subcategory of the deserving poor, which comprised those who could not look after themselves, either because of age or infirmity or because they were orphans

EXTRACT 2

The measures of parish relief adopted in the reign of Elizabeth were probably sufficient, with the assistance of charitable bequests and indiscriminate alms-giving to keep the aged and 'impotent' poor alive at a very low level of assistance during times of normal harvests. Over most of the country these measures, combined with the government's corn policy, helped to avoid widespread starvation. But in the north people did die of hunger in bad years: a report from Newcastle in 1597 spoke of 'sundry starving and dying in our streets and in the fields for lack of bread'; and other parts of northern England were probably still worse off. But in the Midlands and the south-east disease seems to have been a more dangerous killer than hunger – though it is hardly possible to make a clear distinction between the two. How far the government's measures were responsible for this happier fate it is impossible to say.

Penry Williams, *The Tudor Regime*, 1979

EXTRACT 3

There is little evidence for a problem of rural poverty on a large scale, except during the famine crisis of 1596–98. In villages in Bedfordshire and Essex, income from the poor-rate always exceeded expenditure, and there was always enough to maintain the deserving poor, at least until the 1590s. What may be suggested as normal in the later Tudor period was that many were certainly desperately poor in all areas, but except in times of famine or economic depression the rural areas could normally support their indigenous poor, sending on their way paupers and vagrants who tried to come in from elsewhere. Where the system broke down was in the towns, especially in the larger towns and, above all, in the capital. What this might have meant is that if the countryside remained free of overwhelming poverty, it was achieved only through exporting its problems to the towns.

Adapted from David M. Palliser, *The Age of Elizabeth: England Under the Later Tudors, 1547–1603*, 1983

EXTRACT 4

The poor law could not be an ambitious blueprint for social reconstruction or major schemes for public works financed by central taxation or a new kind of slavery. Such utopian ideals were cut down to size by the realities of local government represented in Parliament by sceptical MPs. The poor law had to be applicable to small rural communities as well as major cities. It was likely to reflect the interests of those who had traditionally managed charitable distributions. It was bound therefore to be parochial if it was to be nationally uniform. Such matters as who was to be counted a vagrant had in the end to be left to local constables and justices to determine; similarly, the question of who were the impotent. A local tax for the poor was a striking achievement and one unique to England.

Adapted from Paul Slack, *The English Poor Law, 1531–1782*, 1990

A LEVEL PRACTICE QUESTION

Evaluating historical extracts

Using your understanding of the historical context, assess how convincing the arguments in Extracts 2, 3 and 4 are in relation to poor relief in Elizabethan England.

CROSS-REFERENCE

Treatment of the poor under Edward VI, including the Act against vagrancy, is outlined in Chapter 21, page 208.

The reform of the poor law in the last two parliaments of Elizabeth's reign is outlined on page 191.

For the crisis of 1597, look ahead to Chapter 22, page 221.

STUDY TIP

In applying you own contextual knowledge to this question you should demonstrate an understanding of poor relief from a national perspective, and a grasp of the local context. The latter will require an understanding of how effectively local officials responded to the responsibilities imposed upon them by national legislation.

Problems in the regions

Fig. 2 *Regional government in the sixteenth century*

England under Elizabeth I was a much more unified State than France or Spain. It was also, relatively speaking, much more peaceable. Elizabeth's reign witnessed only one serious rebellion in England – the **Northern Rebellion** of 1569 – which collapsed fairly quickly, compared with greater social disorder in Spain and outright civil war across more than three decades in France. The tendency of the aristocracy and greater gentry to abandon fortified castles and instead to build comfortable but essentially indefensible country houses suggested a confidence in social order and peace that was all the more remarkable given the limited resources of the State to enforce its power in Tudor England.

It should not be assumed, however, that the country was always peaceable. Ireland, Wales and the north of England all posed problems.

CROSS-REFERENCE

The Northern Rebellion of 1569 is discussed in detail in the next section of this chapter, pages 214–215.

Problems in Ireland

CROSS-REFERENCE

England's relations with Ireland during the reigns of Henry VII and Henry VIII are discussed in Chapter 3, pages 27–28, and Chapter 9, pages 90–91.

Elizabethan attitudes to Ireland were simple. Ireland should be subjected to a policy of 'Englishness' in both religious and secular matters. Elizabeth was proclaimed Supreme Governor of the Church of Ireland in 1560. However, she lacked the power to impose Protestantism on a population that was largely Catholic, mostly Gaelic in language and whose customary laws and landownership differed hugely from that of the English. What happened was that Ireland became, in the words of John Guy, a 'breeding ground for fortune hunters'. The 'get-rich quick' mentality of the English incomers and the frequent use of **martial law** led to bad relations with both the Gaelic Irish and the Old English – the descendants of the Normans and English who had settled in Ireland since the eleventh century.

It was no surprise, therefore, that rebellions broke out in the south against such English rule in 1569 to 1573 and 1579 to 1582, this latter rebellion being linked with a Spanish incursion into County Kerry. Anglo-Irish relations were further soured by the brutality of the response of the Lord Deputy of Ireland, Lord Grey of Wilton, to the latter rebellion.

KEY TERM

martial law: legal authority and political control exercised by military authority

Fig 3 *A woodcut showing the heads of Irish rebels on spikes above Dublin Castle*

It was the third Irish rebellion of the reign, closely linked to the Anglo-Spanish war, that proved much more difficult and expensive for the English Crown to suppress. This was centred on Ulster, where the clan chief Hugh O'Neill, created Earl of Tyrone by Elizabeth in 1585, rose up in rebellion in 1595 with the Spanish attempting to exploit the situation by including an Irish contingent in the **Armada of 1596**. This was unsuccessful, but the fact that the Spanish had so clearly signalled their intentions caused much unease among Elizabeth and her councillors, made worse when the rebels were victorious at the Battle of Yellow Ford in August 1598. As a result of this battle and its aftermath, Tyrone and his allies were in control of much of Ireland 'beyond the Pale'. It looked as if Tyrone might establish an independent and Catholic Ireland that would look to Spain for support.

It was in this context that Elizabeth, in some desperation, sent the **Earl of Essex** to Ireland as Lord Lieutenant in 1599. This proved to be an error, thanks to the readiness of Essex to disobey the queen's orders. Essex had a large force, but, instead of confronting Tyrone, he made a truce before defying the queen's orders and returning to court. As soon as the truce expired, Tyrone moved south and camped near Kinsale on the coast, to the south-west of Cork, hoping to link up with a Spanish army. This was to be the high point of his power.

CROSS-REFERENCE

The attempted invasion of England by the Spanish Armada of 1596 is covered in Chapter 20, pages 202–210.

The Earl of Essex is profiled in Chapter 19, page 187, and his significance in Elizabeth's government is outlined in Chapter 19, pages 187–188.

KEY CHRONOLOGY

Ireland

1569 Outbreak of first rebellion against English rule

1579 Outbreak of second rebellion against English rule, brutally suppressed by Lord Grey of Wilton

1595 Outbreak of third rebellion against English rule

1598 Irish triumph at Battle of Yellow Ford

1599 Earl of Essex becomes Lord Lieutenant of Ireland but makes an unauthorised return to England in September

1600 Essex relieved of his office

1601 English force under Lord Mountjoy defeat Irish rebels at Kinsale

1603 Tyrone makes peace with Mountjoy

Fig. 4 *Ireland in the 1590s*

The English, shorn of Essex's weak leadership, made significant progress under the new Lord Lieutenant, Lord Mountjoy, and Sir George Carew. Tyrone seemed saved by the landing in Kinsale of over 3000 Spanish troops during September 1601. However, the English triumphed on Christmas Eve, 1601. Tyrone retreated back to Ulster before eventually negotiating a peace with Mountjoy in March 1603. By then, unbeknown to Tyrone, Elizabeth had died, and Mountjoy appears to have offered generous terms in order to be able to leave Ireland and attend the new king, James I.

In the event, James found himself committed to returning to the policy, abandoned 70 years earlier, of entrusting rule in Ireland to the local nobility, of whom the most important was the utterly unreliable Tyrone. Meanwhile, much of Ireland had been destroyed or impoverished by continued conflict, the Crown had expended huge sums of money and the conflict had left a huge legacy of bitterness among the native population.

ACTIVITY

Produce a pamphlet from the perspective of a supporter of O'Neill's Ulster rebellion criticising the Elizabethan authorities for their treatment of Ireland.

Wales

By Elizabeth's reign, the Welsh border was no longer a problem. The integration of England and Wales had continued. Though much of Wales remained relatively poor, and although linguistic and cultural differences remained, border issues were rarely an issue for the Elizabethan State.

- The structures of border administration, most importantly the Council of Wales and the Marches, remained in operation.
- The Welsh language disappeared as a medium of government. However, it was preserved as a medium of religion with the translation of both the Book of Common Prayer and the Bible into Welsh. The publication of dictionaries and grammars in Welsh also helped to preserve the language.
- Poverty did remain endemic and although many Welsh gentry seem to have prospered under Elizabeth, the disproportionate number of Welshmen implicated in the **Essex 'rebellion'** suggests a significant level of discontent with the political situation towards the end of Elizabeth's reign.

CROSS-REFERENCE

To recap on the Council of Wales and the Marches, look back to Chapter 10, page 101.

The Essex 'rebellion' of 1601 is detailed in Chapter 19, page 188.

The north of England

The situation was rather different in the far north of England. So long as Scotland remained a separate and independent state, the possibility of border conflict remained. Moreover, the continuation on the borders of a lawless subculture which placed a large emphasis on casual violence and rustling of sheep and cattle created problems for the authorities in both countries. On the English side of the border administrative responsibility lay with the wardens of the three border marches. Traditionally, wardens had been appointed from the families of the great northern magnates such as the Percies and the Dacres. Henry VIII had signalled a move away from this policy by appointing southerners, a strategy continued by Elizabeth. The problem with this approach was that it was difficult for nobles without a local landed base to control either the northern landed families or the border clans.

CROSS-REFERENCE

Henry VIII's policies regarding the wardens of the border marches are discussed in Chapter 10, page 101.

A CLOSER LOOK

Border administration

To counteract the difficulty posed by using southerners with no local land as border wardens, Elizabeth had sometimes to resort to the appointment of wardens from the second rank of northern landowners. The most notable of these was Sir John Forster who was more successful in exploiting his office for financial gain than in maintaining border security.

Border security was an issue following the 1569 rebellion as some of the rebel leaders escaped into Scotland. Between 1578 and 1585, when the grip on power of the Protestant lords in Scotland was tenuous, the governing of the borders once again became a key issue. The murder in a border incident in 1585 of Francis Russell, son of the Earl of Bedford, looked as if it might create a long-term problem in Anglo-Scottish relations. But skilful diplomacy ensured that James VI accepted an annual pension of £4000 along with hints about his possible succession to the English throne.

Outside border administration, primary responsibility for the maintenance of order lay with the Council of the North based in York. Elizabeth certainly felt unable to grant the office of president of the Council to a member of the northern nobility, none of whom she really trusted. The alternative (awarding the post to a southern magnate) created problems.

Social discontent and rebellions

Yet for the most part the reign was a period of relative order. The one significant rebellion in the north in 1569, the Northern Rebellion, had little to do with the social and economic aspirations of the poor. Even in the mid-1590s when a perfect storm of severe harvest failure, rising prices and outbreaks of plague created a desperate situation for many, social stability broadly held up. The authorities certainly feared vagabondage and reserved severe treatment for those whom they considered to be the undeserving poor. Food riots took place in London as well as in Kent, Hampshire and Norfolk. The heavy-handed response of the authorities to the so-called 'Oxfordshire rising' of 1596 – in reality not a rising but an ill-thought-out scheme by a tiny group of four men made desperate by their experience of poverty to seize armaments and march on London – reflected a fear about social dislocation which did not reflect reality.

The Northern Rebellion, 1569–70

The only significant rebellion against Elizabeth took place mainly in Durham and the North Riding of Yorkshire in 1569, which linked to a rising in Cumberland in 1570. It was headed by the leading northern nobility, the earls of Northumberland and Westmorland, and genuine religious fervour among both leaders and ordinary participants played a part. However, the rebel leaders also had political motives. They considered themselves dishonoured by having been displaced from their traditional aristocratic role of controlling northern government. It has also been argued that the rebellion was tied in with a courtly conspiracy, at the centre of which was Westmorland's brother-in-law, the Duke of Norfolk. It was proposed that Norfolk should marry Mary, Queen of Scots, who could be restored to the Scottish throne – a plan which triggered a volcanic response from Elizabeth when she discovered it.

Fig. 5 *The area of the Northern Rebellion, 1569*

The rebellion began on 9 November. The rebels marched on Durham, seized the city on 14 November and heard Mass in the cathedral, thereby giving a clear indication of the Catholic character of the rebellion. The rebels then marched on York, camping for a time on Bramham Moor, west of the city. However, they made no attempt to capture it; neither did they march south in an attempt to pressurise the government. Instead, they moved back into the county of Durham and besieged the Crown's stronghold of Barnard Castle, which fell to the rebels on 14 December. However, when news came to the rebel leaders that a Crown force was on its way north, the earls disbanded their forces and fled over the border into Scotland. The following month, Northumberland's cousin, Leonard Dacre, restarted the rebellion in Cumberland, only for his force to be heavily defeated at Naworth, east of Carlisle, by a royal force under the command of the queen's cousin, Lord Hunsdon.

The rebellion failed for a number of reasons:

- hopeless disorganisation, with a lack of clarity concerning the rebels' objectives
- poor leadership
- lack of expected foreign support
- decisive action by the authorities.

The Crown's servants on the spot acted sensibly in difficult circumstances. At court, Cecil, in particular, spent huge amounts of time on the matter, commissioning and studying a map of Durham to help him come to decisions about appropriate courses of action. However, the rebellion revealed the London government's lack of comprehension of the differences between north and south, of the problems of managing the localities and the difficulty of raising forces to deal with potential threats. It also demonstrated the ruthlessness of Elizabethan government in punishing those who had offended it. Mass executions of rebels were ordered, although how many were carried out is difficult to say.

The rebellion was geographically limited. There were few rebels from outside Durham and the North Riding of Yorkshire. The rebel earls gained no support from the equally conservative nobility of other parts of the north and there appeared to be little enthusiasm to get rid of Elizabeth. This does not mean that there was widespread enthusiasm *for* Elizabethan government, but there was little consensus about what might possibly replace it.

A CLOSER LOOK

Northumberland was eventually executed in 1572. Westmorland, still a young man at the time of the rebellion, spent the rest of his life as a pensioner at court in the Spanish Netherlands, becoming increasingly depressed and bitter about his fate. The lands of the rebel leaders were forfeit to the Crown.

ACTIVITY

Summary

When studying History in breadth you need to be able to explore specific themes across a period of years or more. 'Rebellions' comprise one such theme, and it is important for you to be able to synthesise your responses across a number of such events. Complete the following chart to compare the rebellions that took place during the reigns of the Tudor monarchs. You will need to refer back to chapters 4, 10 and 16 and 19.

	Pilgrimage of Grace	Kett's Rebellion	Western Rebellion	Wyatt's Rebellion	Northern Rebellion	Essex Rebellion
Motives of leaders						
Motives of followers						
Political reasons						
Social reasons						
Religious reasons						
Economic reasons						
Other reasons						
Effectiveness of Crown response						
Level of threat to Crown						

To reinforce the Crown's hold on the north, the Council of the North was reconstituted in 1572 and placed under the control of the Earl of Huntingdon. Huntingdon was an outsider with no local ties who owed his influence entirely to the favour of his relative, the queen. Moreover, he had strong Puritan inclinations. This might not have been much of an advantage at court; in the north, however, where Catholics were perceived as potential enemies to the Crown, his strong commitment to the values of religious reform was seen as an advantage.

CROSS-REFERENCE

Puritanism is discussed further in Chapter 23, pages 226–229.

STUDY TIP

It is important that you clarify what might be understood as a real 'threat to the Elizabethan State'. Try to differentiate between the scale of the potential threats and those aspects of the State which were threatened. Which threatened the queen personally, compared with those which threatened the stability of the State but not necessarily the queen herself?

A LEVEL PRACTICE QUESTION

To what extent did the plots and rebellions faced by the Crown during the reign of Elizabeth pose a real threat to the stability of the Elizabethan State?

22 Economic development in Elizabethan England

EXTRACT 1

The land which had neglected oceanic exploration, while the Spanish and Portuguese had carved up the globe between them, had begun its world-wide expansion. Henry VII had patronised John and Sebastian Cabot in their explorations of the North American coast; Henry VIII had shown no interest, and Sebastian Cabot had gone to Spain instead; but in 1548 Sebastian accepted an invitation from some royal councillors to return to England. He was involved in the first expeditions to Morocco in 1551 and to Muscovy in 1553: thereafter, there was no stopping. American colonisation was first openly discussed in England in the 1550s, and attempts at settlement began in 1585. The East India Company was founded in 1600, and in the same year William Adams reached Japan. In short, England was already developing some of the advantages that were to lead to commercial supremacy.

Adapted from David M. Palliser, *The Age of Elizabeth: England under the Later Tudors, 1537–1603*, 1983

LEARNING OBJECTIVES

In this chapter you will learn about:

- the continuing importance of trade to the English economy
- exploration and colonisation
- prosperity and depression in Elizabethan England.

KEY QUESTION

As you read this chapter, consider the following Key Question:
How far did English society and economy change and with what effects?

ACTIVITY

Evaluating historical extracts

What view does David Palliser advance in this extract? Summarise his main argument in one sentence. As you read through this chapter note the evidence which might help to support or refute the argument contained in this paragraph.

Trade

The pattern of trade

The absence of reliable statistical evidence makes it difficult to be absolutely certain about the value to the economy of trading activities during the reign of Elizabeth. However, four points can be made with relative certainty:

1. The value of internal trade considerably exceeded that of foreign trade. The biggest single development in internal trade was the growth in the shipping of coal from the Tyne to the Thames to meet the growing demands of the London market, though some coal was exported across the North Sea, including a rapidly developing trade with France.
2. A wider range of foreign luxury goods came to be imported during Elizabeth's reign. This suggests that such goods were becoming affordable for a wider range of the population.
3. The cloth trade with the Netherlands, while remaining important, declined relatively as part of the economy. The Antwerp cloth market had declined from the early 1550s. In any case Sir William Cecil was anxious for political reasons to end the dependence on a single market. An alternative trade was developed, based on the north German port of Emden, but the major move was to Amsterdam, whose commercial growth came at the expense of Antwerp which remained under Spanish control.
4. Though attempts to establish new overseas markets did take place, for example in Russia, these remained economically marginal.

CROSS-REFERENCE

To look back on trade and exploration in the reign of Henry VIII, reread Chapter 11.

A CLOSER LOOK

The inventory of a shopkeeper from remote Kirkby Lonsdale in Westmorland included Spanish silk, French garters and Turkish purses.

ACTIVITY

Use a map to plot the trade routes discussed in the following section.

Attempts to expand trade

The main centre of African trade was Guinea, and it was Guinea that became used as the starting point for **John Hawkins**' move into the Americas. In the process, he invented the English slave trade. He made three expeditions

CROSS-REFERENCE

Sir John Hawkins is profiled in Chapter 20, page 198.

Fig. 1 *John Hawkins*

A CLOSER LOOK

There were several attempts to widen English trade, which began in Mary I's reign but continued under Elizabeth. For example, Mary had encouraged the foundation of the Muscovy Company in 1555, which had sponsored a trading expedition to Russia under the leadership of Richard Chancellor.

KEY TERM

joint-stock companies: businesses which are owned by their shareholders, who profit in proportion to the relative size of their shareholding

KEY PROFILE

Walter Raleigh (1552–1618) was an ambitious though unpopular and ineffective courtier. His attempt to establish a colony on the North American mainland failed, as did his attempts to find treasure in South America. He was reputed to have introduced both the potato and tobacco to Europe. He completely lost favour under James and was imprisoned and executed.

from 1562, acquiring slaves in Africa that he then transported and sold in South America. His first two expeditions proved to be financially successful, although he succeeded in irritating the Spanish authorities. By the time of the second expedition in 1564, Hawkins had secured investment from prominent courtiers including the Earl of Leicester, as well as support from the queen who supplied ships – for a price. The third expedition also attracted royal support but went disastrously wrong when Hawkins's fleet was blockaded in the Mexican port of San Juan de Ulúa, although some of the gold did get back to England. Hawkins's activities antagonised further the already strained relations between England and Spain. The fact that the queen was prepared to become involved suggests that she was willing, in return for profit, to run the risk of antagonising Philip II.

The main changes in English trading patterns in the 1580s were twofold. First, the main markets for English wool moved from the southern to the northern Netherlands and there was an increase in trade with the Ottoman (Turkish) Empire. England, however, remained, according to David Palliser, relatively backward in its exploitation of trading opportunities in Elizabeth's reign.

A number of trading companies were set up, with varying degrees of success, to widen England's trading interests.

- The Muscovy Company had been incorporated in 1555 to trade with Russia and northern Europe, though it failed in the long term to compete effectively with the Dutch.
- The Eastland Company was set up in 1579 to trade in the Baltic but had a similarly limited effect.
- The Levant Company, founded in 1581 as the Turkish Company, enjoyed success in its attempts to develop trade with the Ottoman Empire.
- The East India Company was set up in 1600 to trade with Asia, but it had less investment compared with the Dutch East India Company, and therefore found it very difficult to compete in the short term.

By the end of Elizabeth's reign these were still relatively modest organisations. However, there was a significant change in that, the Eastland Company apart, they were all **joint-stock companies** owned by their shareholders in a model of organisation which would prove essential to future capitalist development.

Exploration and colonisation

What was of little importance at the time, but assumed greater significance in the light of subsequent developments, was the extension of trade to the mainland of North America and the attempt to form a colony in Virginia. The suggestion that England should start colonising North America originated with the entrepreneur and explorer Humphrey Gilbert. The process was encouraged by Richard Hakluyt in *A Discourse of Western Planting*, published in 1584. Hakluyt, a clergyman and geographer, was closely linked to Gilbert's half-brother, **Walter Raleigh**, and, through Raleigh, presented the *Discourse* to the queen.

Raleigh gained the support of a number of prominent investors, including **Sir Francis Walsingham**, and in 1585 he received from the queen a patent to colonise what would become known as Virginia. Two expeditions eventually made land on Roanoke Island in what was to become North Carolina. Unfortunately for Raleigh's investors, and even more unfortunately for those settlers who died in the attempt, the attempts at colonisation proved to be disastrous, from a combination of poor organisation, ill luck and reluctance by the queen to give the matter priority when she was faced by war with Spain. Permanent English colonisation of Virginia had to wait until the reign of James I.

Fig. 2 *Engraved from an original by John White, this shows a Native American settlement*

Prosperity and depression

Prosperity and land

Certain broad trends can be detected. In general, landowners benefited from the economic trends present in Elizabethan England. Landed incomes rose and many landowners acquired a range of material possessions which would have been unknown to their grandparents' generation. As well as benefiting from increased income from land, in many cases large landowners had been able to profit from the generosity of Henry VIII and Edward VI when disposing for a quick profit often at knock-down prices much of the land which they had acquired through the dissolution of church property.

CROSS-REFERENCE

Sir Francis Walsingham is profiled in Chapter 20, page 197.

ACTIVITY

Research

Use oxforddnb.com to research the importance of Richard Hakluyt in promoting the urge to establish colonies in the Americas.

Fig. 3 *A woodcut illustrating a scene from Edmund Spenser's poem* The Shepherd's Calendar

CROSS-REFERENCE

The boom in country-house building that took place during the Elizabethan period is discussed in Chapter 21, page 207.

One of the consequences of this was the huge proliferation of building, not just of great houses, but of more modest though nevertheless imposing **country houses**. It seems clear that a building boom of unprecedented scale took place in Elizabeth's reign.

At more modest levels of society farmers were able to benefit from the rise in agricultural prices. The Essex clergyman William Harrison in his *Description of England*, published in 1577, noted the improvement in living standards enjoyed by farmers (or at least those based in the south-east of England). Inventories taken after an individual's death often confirmed this same pattern of improvement. There does seem to have been overall an increase in all aspects of agricultural production, though bad harvests provided interruptions to this trend.

Prosperity and trade

The relationship between trade and prosperity has been much debated by historians. One problem relating to this debate is the absence of really hard evidence, which makes it very difficult to come to a definitive conclusion. Broadly speaking, economic historians in the first half of the twentieth century tended to argue that trade was buoyant in Elizabethan England, a point reinforced by the evidence of shipbuilding which took place at the time; in the second half of the century a more pessimistic view tended to predominate, with historians emphasising what was seen as a desperate search for new markets to offset the long-term decline in the cloth trade. This pessimistic view has been reinforced by the argument that English financial institutions were much less sophisticated than their counterparts in the Netherlands, Germany and Italy.

Urban prosperity

It is impossible to generalise about this. It is clear that some old-established towns, for example Stamford and Winchester, did decline during Elizabeth's reign. Urban decay was particularly associated with corporate boroughs that had been heavily dependent on the cloth industry, as this had migrated to more rural areas. On the other hand, the condition of some other old-established towns, such as York and Norwich, continued to improve. Relatively new urban settlements, such as Manchester and Plymouth, also developed. Those towns which did well tended either to have a broad range of manufacturing industry or were unincorporated towns in which industry was able to develop without hindrance from regulation. One issue which is very difficult to resolve is the impact of the growth of London on other urban centres. It was often alleged at the time that the growth of London, both as a port and as an industrial centre, had a detrimental effect on other towns and cities. On the other hand, some places, most importantly Newcastle upon Tyne, benefited from supplying London's economic needs.

Depression

Not all shared in this prosperity. For many, real wages fell, and this was a particular problem at times of harvest failure. According to statistical evidence collated by David Palliser, 9 of the 44 harvests of the reign could be described as poor. The impact was particularly bad when there were successive bad harvests. This made the experience of 1594 to 1597, when there were four successive poor harvests, catastrophic for some people. By 1596 real wages had collapsed to less than half the level which they had been a mere nine years earlier. This provided the context for the one real subsistence crisis of Elizabeth's reign, in 1596 to 1597. While distress was common throughout the kingdom, conditions seem to have been worst in the far north with starvation the outcome both in the more remote rural areas and in the urban centre of Newcastle, which doubtless had attracted the poor and the indigent from across the region. The corporation of Newcastle reported burying 25 homeless people who were presumed to have starved.

CROSS-REFERENCE

The government's response to the crisis of 1596 to 1597 is discussed in Chapter 22, page 221.

The economic condition of the regions

It is possible to make some tentative comments on the relative levels of prosperity. It is clear from taxation records and similar sources that the wealthiest part of the country was the south-east, followed closely by Norfolk and Suffolk and the 'inner West Country' counties of Somerset, Gloucestershire and Wiltshire. The poorest counties were those to be found in the north and in the west Midlands. This tended to be reflected in income levels amongst different social groups. The evidence of inventories of goods left by labourers in Hertfordshire, for example, suggests they left goods worth almost three times as much as their counterparts in northern England. In this context, therefore, it is perhaps little wonder that the depression of the mid-1590s had such a devastating effect in the north.

EXTRACT 2

Evictions of tenants certainly occurred, especially those with the weakest sorts of tenancies; and certainly there were many disputes over rights, as landlords showed their eagerness to acquire more land, to enclose land or to jack up their rental income. Many a tenant of small resources could not afford legal redress against such pressures; or, squeezed between rising prices and inadequate land to provide a consistent saleable surplus, sold out to neighbours with larger holdings or to landlords eager to consolidate their estates. In this way, such men went down the social ladder to swell the growing number either of wholly landless agricultural labourers or that familiar stratum of the pre-industrialised society, the struggling husbandman, the small peasant with just enough land to feed his family in good times but forever at the mercy of a bad harvest and often in debt to local tradesmen.

Adapted from Donald C. Coleman, *The Economy of England, 1450–1750*, 1977

EXTRACT 3

A combination of relatively broadly spread prosperity, and only a small proportion of the population wholly dependent on wages, limited the degree of impoverishment. The evidence of inventories – which reach down to a fairly humble social level – suggests that even the better-off labourers lived better, and enjoyed more consumer goods, than their grandparents. If they were falling behind the landholders, they were still generally better off in absolute terms. It may well be that, as a result of rising prices, smallholders and the landless had to run faster to stay in the same place. Many took up additional employments to increase the family income, especially the making of consumer goods like stocking, nails, pins, soap, starch and beer. That in turn presupposes a large home demand for these goods, and does not suggest a badly impoverished society.

Adapted from David M. Palliser, *The Age of Elizabeth: England under the Later Tudors, 1547–1603*, 1983

EXTRACT 4

Industrial growth was barely sustained between 1550 and 1603. It seems that the pool of surplus labour caused by population expansion, the decline in purchasing power of wage-earners, and the fact that some two fifths of the population were on the margins of subsistence, combined to depress industrial demand and gave merchant entrepreneurs insufficient incentive to raise output, seek organisational change or technical innovation, or practise import substitution on a wide scale. Consumer demand was mainly for a restricted range of products: woollen textiles and leather goods, building materials, and agricultural and household implements.

Adapted from John Guy, *Tudor England*, 1988

STUDY TIP

Look back at Chapter 21 to help you with the social aspects of this type of question. One way of approaching this question would be to identify the main aspects of economic change which are mentioned, and then link this to those who were winners and losers as a result.

A LEVEL PRACTICE QUESTION

Evaluating historical extracts

Using your understanding of the historical context, assess how convincing the arguments in Extracts 2, 3 and 4 are in relation to Elizabethan society and the economy.

The economic record of Elizabethan government was very mixed, though it should be remembered that the concept of economic policy as such did not exist at the time. Ministers tended to react in an *ad hoc* manner to the situation as they found it at a particular time. Sometimes their response was to seek the passing of legislation, such as the **Statute of Artificers**, which quickly became redundant. Their main priority was in the maintenance of public order, which many of the political elite considered threatened by the **subsistence crisis** of the 1590s. It is evident, however, that relations between the Crown and landed elites, on the one hand, and the commercial elites of the City of London, on the other hand, became closer during the reign, especially through participation in joint-stock companies, and this helped to lay the foundation for future commercial expansion.

CROSS-REFERENCE

The Statute of Artificers is outlined in Chapter 18, page 176.

The subsistence crisis of the 1590s is covered in Chapter 24, page 238.

ACTIVITY

Summary chart

Use the material in this chapter and chapters 5, 11, 17 and 21 to evaluate economic and social change and continuity across the whole of the Tudor period.

	Continuity/change	Evidence
Landowners and the elites		
Farmers		
Labourers and the poor		
Overseas trade		
Exploration		

A LEVEL PRACTICE QUESTION

Is it true to say that by 1603 England was economically and socially more diverse than it had been at the beginning of Elizabeth's reign in 1558?

STUDY TIP

It is good practice to establish a context covering the whole period in your opening paragraph. A formula such as 'in 1558 ... by 1603' can work well. Don't forget to provide evidence on both the economy and society in your essay.

23 Religious developments and the 'Golden Age' of Elizabethan culture

EXTRACT 1

At the end of Mary's reign, Catholicism had been the religion of a large majority of English people; by the end of Elizabeth's it was the faith of a small sect. In 1603 the bishops reported to their new king that there were 2,250,765 Church of England communicants (persons attending the Communion service) and only 8596 adult **recusants**; this was a massive underestimate, and it excludes the church papists, but it indicates the scale of the Catholic community. Within two generations the Catholics had dwindled to numerical insignificance. In 1559 the Protestants had seized control of the Church, its assets and its power; unless there were further political changes, time would consolidate their victory. Those, for whom religion was what happened in their local church, went along with the new ways.

Christopher Haigh, *English Reformations: Religion, Politics and Society under the Tudors*, 1993

LEARNING OBJECTIVES

In this chapter you will learn about:

- change and continuity in religion in Elizabethan England
- the culmination of the English Renaissance and the 'Golden Age' of Elizabethan art, literature and music.

KEY TERM

recusant: term used to describe those who refused to attend the services of the Church of England

KEY QUESTION

As you read this chapter, consider the following Key Questions:

- How did intellectual and religious ideas change and develop, and with what effects?
- How important was the role of key individuals and groups and how were they affected by developments?

ACTIVITY

Evaluating historical extracts

What does Christopher Haigh tell us, in Extract 1, about the difference between the state of religion at the beginning and end of Elizabeth's reign? Roughly, what proportion of the population was Catholic by the end of the reign? According to Haigh, why was a 'Protestant' victory assured?

As you read through this chapter, consider the view put forward here by Haigh about the reasons for the decline of Catholicism.

Religious developments

From the queen's perspective the state of religion in 1563 was broadly positive. She had achieved the settlement that she largely desired. However, there was much concern among both the higher and lower clergy regarding the apparently unreformed nature of the Church. Equally, Catholics, although not subject to persecution, found it difficult to practise their faith in public. The key issue was whether the settlement was to be regarded as 'complete' or whether there was scope for further change. Against this background, **Puritanism** emerged amongst those who considered the settlement incomplete.

CROSS-REFERENCE

Religious developments in Elizabeth's reign up to 1563 are the subject of Chapter 18.

KEY TERM

Puritanism: the belief amongst godly Protestants that the Church of England needed to be purged of any remaining 'superstitious' (i.e. Catholic) practices

A CLOSER LOOK

Figure 1 depicts a father teaching his child how to sing a metrical psalm. This is significant because metrical psalms were the only form of church music favoured by more radical Protestants, and this represents one of the first depictions of behaviour that would become known as 'puritan'.

Fig. 1 *A woodcut from the frontispiece of* Tenor of the Whole Psalmes in Four Parts, *published in 1563*

ACTIVITY

Thinking point

On what grounds might Puritans have found the 1559 settlement incomplete? Before answering this question, you should refer back to Chapter 17, pages 167–171.

Puritanism

Puritanism was an important influence in the 1560s and 1570s. Puritans believed in the eradication of 'popish superstition' and their emergence can be traced back to the failure of the Convocation of Canterbury in 1563 to go further in its reform of the Church. However, some groups within the broader Puritan framework certainly posed a challenge to the Elizabethan settlement.

The Vestiarian Controversy

The emergence of tensions between the queen, who desired conformity and obedience based on complete acceptance of the settlement, and 'Puritans', who believed in the eradication of 'superstitious' practices, led to the Vestiarian Controversy. Several figures within the Church decided that they could not obey the rules on clerical dress laid down in the Act of Uniformity and royal injunctions as this specified the wearing of Catholic and therefore 'superstitious' dress.

The queen forced the issue by dismissing the prominent Oxford academic Thomas Sampson from his post at Christ Church College for his refusal to wear the required vestments.

KEY PROFILE

Archbishop Matthew Parker (1504–75), who had been chaplain to Anne Boleyn, was a Cambridge academic. He did not go into exile during Mary I's reign, choosing to live quietly in East Anglia. He was a somewhat reluctant appointee as archbishop, and he seems never to have been happy in his discharge of the political aspects of his role.

Archbishop Parker, and five bishops, issued the 'Advertisements' in March 1566 which required clergy to follow 'one uniformity of rites and manners' in the administration of the sacraments and 'one decent behaviour in their outward apparel'. Thirty-seven London clergymen refused to signify their support and were consequently deprived of their posts.

The whole business showed the extent of the queen's determination to enforce the settlement, but reforming bishops were caught between conflicting pressures: the need to obey the royal supremacy and the desire to remove the remaining vestiges of Catholic practice within the Church.

The Presbyterian movement

The Presbyterian movement was one aspect of the broader Puritan movement. Presbyterians believed that the Church of England, which was already Calvinist in its doctrine, should be further reformed in its structure and its forms of worship. Its ideas grew out of Calvin's views on Church organisation and discipline, and it emerged partly in reaction to the Vestiarian Controversy.

A CLOSER LOOK

Presbyterians and Puritans

The terms Presbyterian and Puritan are not synonymous. 'Puritan' was usually employed as a term of abuse to describe those who thought of themselves as 'godly'. Presbyterians believed specifically in the introduction of a **Calvinist** form of Church government: the office of bishop should be abolished, all ministers should be equal in status and lay elders should have a key administrative role. A crude simplification would be that all Presbyterians were Puritan but not all Puritans were Presbyterian.

CROSS-REFERENCE

Calvin and Calvinism are explained in Chapter 17, page 169.

Some Presbyterians began to question the scriptural basis for the authority of bishops and other aspects of the Church. The criticisms were voiced in two pamphlets known as the two Admonitions, whose main author was John Field.

- The first Admonition attacked the Book of Common Prayer and called for the abolition of bishops.
- The second Admonition provided a detailed description of a Presbyterian system of Church government.

There followed a pamphlet war between **Thomas Cartwright**, a Cambridge academic, and the vice-chancellor of Cambridge University, **John Whitgift**. Cartwright and the Presbyterians believed that a Church founded on 'superstitious' or 'popish' principles must be spiritually flawed and the 1559 settlement had to be modified, while Whitgift argued that the Presbyterians' attitude was destructive and would split the Church.

Although a geographically narrow movement, largely confined to London, Essex, the university of Cambridge, Suffolk and parts of the east Midlands, Presbyterianism attracted some high-ranking support. The Earl of Huntingdon, the Earl of Leicester and even Lord Burghley saw the advantages of Presbyterianism as a bulwark against the influence of Catholicism. All three of them defended clergymen who fell foul of the authorities because of their alleged sympathy for the Presbyterian movement.

The Presbyterian movement grew in the 1580s. Ideas for Church government through local assemblies and provincial and national **synods** were developed, but attempts to bring change through Parliament failed, despite the efforts of Peter Turner in 1584 and Anthony Cope in 1587.

KEY PROFILE

Thomas Cartwright (c1535–1603) was Professor of Divinity at Cambridge until he was forced out of his post by Whitgift. He was the spiritual leader of the Presbyterian movement.

CROSS-REFERENCE

John Whitgift is profiled in Chapter 19, page 193.

KEY TERM

synod: a Church council that in this context would exist outside the official Church hierarchy

A CLOSER LOOK

Both Turner and Cope introduced bills which, if enacted, would have replaced the Book of Common Prayer with a new prayer book stripped of any remaining 'popish' elements. Neither bill generated much support. Cope was imprisoned briefly, though the fact that Elizabeth knighted him five years later suggests that he quickly recovered his position.

ACTIVITY

Draw a spider diagram to indicate the key Presbyterian ideas. You should organise these around the following: ideas on theology; Church government; role and status of the clergy; relationship between Church and State.

Whitgift's Articles and the attack on Presbyterianism

The Archbishop of Canterbury, John Whitgift, was determined to destroy Presbyterianism. He issued Three Articles to which clergy had to subscribe:

1. Acknowledgement of the royal supremacy.
2. Acceptance of the prayer book as containing nothing 'contrary to the Word of God'.
3. Acceptance that the Thirty-Nine Articles conformed to the word of God.

The second Article created a crisis of conscience for many clergy, not just Presbyterians, who thought that some parts of the prayer book lacked scriptural justification. Whitgift was forced to back down under pressure from councillors such as Leicester and Walsingham. He reduced the second Article to a simple acceptance of the prayer book and most clergy were able to justify accepting this by arguing that their preaching ensured godliness within the Church.

Whitgift's campaign had some success: he forced Burghley's protégé, George Gifford, out of his post, and Cartwright was refused a licence to preach, despite Leicester's pleas. However, the Church paid a price. By treating radical and moderates alike, Whitgift caused much despair among clergymen. Moreover, while he undoubtedly had the complete support of the queen, his policies and attitudes were regarded with suspicion by many of her ministers.

By the late 1580s Presbyterianism was in decline. Very few Puritan clergy were prepared to break with the Church by refusing to accept the Three Articles, and the failure of Cope's 'Bill and Book' in 1587 showed the futility of a parliamentary approach. Presbyterianism was further weakened by the death of its key organiser, John Field, in 1589. No synod was held after 1589 and the reputation of the Presbyterian movement suffered on account of the satirical **Marprelate tracts**.

KEY TERM

Marprelate tracts: a set of scurrilous and satirical attacks written in the late 1580s about some of the bishops of the time

Radical Puritans (Separatists)

Separatism was the most extreme form of Puritanism. Indeed, most mainstream Puritans regarded Separatists with abhorrence. Its adherents wanted to separate from the Church of England altogether. Separatists regarded the Church of England as incapable of reforming itself sufficiently to root out all 'popish' or 'superstitious' practices and they wanted to create independent church congregations. They were resolutely opposed to the queen's status as Supreme Governor of the Church of England. Separatism as a movement emerged in the 1580s. Robert Browne became the leader of a significant congregation in Norwich, but his challenge soon petered out, and he went into exile in the Netherlands with some of his congregation in 1582. He later returned to England and made his peace with the authorities in 1585, aided by the good offices of his relative, Lord Burghley.

Henry Barrow and John Greenwood led Separatist movements in London, although the numbers involved were small. Nevertheless, their activities were sufficient to alarm the authorities and led to the passing of the Act against Seditious **Sectaries** in 1593. Barrow, Greenwood and John Penry were tried and executed 'for devising and circulating seditious books'. Quite why the authorities chose to adopt such harsh measures against such a numerically insignificant movement is difficult to explain, but vindictiveness on the part of Archbishop Whitgift has been put forward as an explanation. Whatever the reason, Elizabethan Separatism was destroyed.

KEY TERM

sectaries: a term used, usually with disapproval, to describe members of sects which had separated from the Church of England

The decline of Puritanism

Puritan influence declined in the late 1580s, partly because of the deaths of **Leicester, Mildmay and Walsingham**, its political supporters at court, and partly because the defeat of the Spanish Armada reduced the perceived threat of Catholicism and lessened its attractions. Furthermore, the disappearance of Presbyterianism meant that Puritan attitudes became more acceptable within the traditional Church structure. The fundamentally Calvinist beliefs of the Church of England were reaffirmed in the Lambeth Articles of 1595, which proved acceptable to Puritans and their opponents such as Whitgift alike. Furthermore, the 1559 Book of Common Prayer was accepted by both as the basis for an acceptable form of worship.

A CLOSER LOOK

Leicester died in 1588, Mildmay in 1589 and Walsingham in 1590.

A CLOSER LOOK

The Lambeth Articles were a series of nine points of doctrine, approved by Whitgift and issued under his authority, which largely reasserted the essentially Calvinist doctrine of the Elizabethan Church. (Disputes between Whitgift and his Puritan enemies had never been about the Church's doctrine.)

By the end of Elizabeth's reign, religion was no longer a serious political issue and the 'godly' Puritans were housed within the Church, although they were still hoping to purify it and others by their example.

Fig. 2 *Queen Elizabeth at prayer*

ACTIVITY

Draw a table to illustrate the different aspects of Puritanism, with some comment on the extent to which each might have posed a challenge to the Elizabethan settlement.

Context	Puritan attitude(s)	Extent of challenge
Royal supremacy		
Book of Common Prayer		
Theology		
Preaching		

Catholicism

Elizabeth is often quoted as not wishing to make 'windows into men's souls'. This has frequently led to an assumption that Elizabeth adopted an attitude of toleration towards Catholics in the early years of her reign. However, toleration of Catholics was conditional on obedience, and not all Catholic practices were tolerated.

Although the Act of Supremacy in 1559 laid down fines for those who did not attend Church services - the **recusants** - these were rarely demanded. Much energy was spent on removing Catholic imagery from parish churches and on searching out images that had been hidden away, however. Furthermore, the old religious 'mystery plays' were abolished because of their link to the feast of **Corpus Christi** and hence to the doctrine of transubstantiation.

Most English Catholics survived as 'church papists', outwardly conforming and obeying the law by attending Anglican services. However, an active minority followed the Catholic bishops, who had (except one) refused to conform to the Oath of Supremacy in 1559. While some Catholic intellectuals went into exile, most frequently to the Spanish Netherlands, rather than conform, some priests survived as private chaplains to Catholic members of the nobility who protected them or conducted secret Catholic services. Such Catholics were known as recusants.

The **Northern Rebellion** of 1569 (with its Catholic religious undertones) provoked a punitive attitude towards Catholics. To make matters worse, Pope Pius V excommunicated Elizabeth in 1570 and called on all loyal Catholics to depose her. This placed English Catholics in an impossible position, forced to choose between loyalty to their Church and loyalty to their monarch.

CROSS-REFERENCE

The feast of Corpus Christi is described in Chapter 6, page 54.

The Northern Rebellion of 1569 is discussed in Chapter 21, pages 214–215.

Fig. 3 *Saint Edmund Campion*

The penal laws against Catholics

Three progressively more severe Acts against the Catholics were passed during the 1570s and 1580s.

1. A 1571 Act made the publication of papal bulls treasonable.
2. The 1581 Act to Retain the Queen's Majesty's Subjects in their Due Obedience. This made it treason to withdraw subjects' allegiance to either the queen or the Church of England. Saying Mass became punishable by heavy fine and imprisonment and the fine for non-attendance at church was raised to the prohibitive figure of £20 per month. Although the laity were not too harshly treated, 4 Catholic priests were executed in 1581, and 11 in 1582.

CROSS-REFERENCE

The prospect of Spanish invasion, which formed the background to many of the anti-Catholic measures, is discussed in Chapter 21.

The plots against Elizabeth are outlined in Chapter 20, page 197.

Fig. 4 *The Triangular Lodge at Rushton, Northamptonshire. This was designed and built by the Catholic recusant Sir Thomas Tresham and was an expression of his commitment to Catholicism. While the lodge's emphasis on the Trinity is not in itself exclusively Catholic, it is supported by texts and symbols which demonstrated a Catholic commitment*

KEY TERM

Society of Jesus: formally recognised as a religious order in 1540, this looked actively to reconvert places which had become Protestant during the Reformation

3. The 1585 Act against Jesuits and Seminary Priests. This made it treasonable for priests ordained under the Pope's authority to enter England. This made it much easier for the courts to secure convictions for treason; 123 priests were convicted and executed under the terms of this Act from 1586 to 1603.

The penal laws were complemented by a savage increase in the financial penalties with the fine for recusancy being set at £20 per month in 1581. In 1587 the law was tightened and any recusant who defaulted on his payment of fines could have two thirds of his estate seized by the Exchequer. The persecution of recusants was at its height from 1588 to 1592.

The tightening of legislation was partly a response to the international situation and the worsening relations with the Catholic King Philip II of Spain and partly because of fear of Catholic rebellion, made worse by the onset of Catholic missions of priests intent on upholding and spreading the Catholic faith. The pressure against Catholics was reinforced by the drafting of a 'Bond of Association for the Preservation of the Queen's Majesty's Royal Person' by Burghley and Walsingham in October 1584 in response to the Throckmorton Plot. Anyone who took the oath of association was required to execute summarily [i.e. murder] anyone who attempted to usurp the Crown or make an attempt on Elizabeth's life.

The Catholic missions

In 1568 a college was founded at Douai, in the Spanish Netherlands, in order to train Catholic priests to be sent to England and to keep Catholicism alive and win new converts. By 1575, 11 of these 'seminary priests' had arrived in England, by 1580 there were about 100, and 179 arrived in England between 1580 and 1585. This was dangerous work as they had to operate, in secretive circumstances, from the country houses of Catholic gentry and aristocracy. Merely being a Catholic priest was sufficient, from 1585, to incur the death penalty.

The **Society of Jesus** began sending Jesuit priests to England in 1580. The Jesuits combined high intelligence and organisational skills with a dedication to the cause of the restoration of Catholicism to England. The first Jesuits to become involved in attempting to re-Catholicise England were Robert Parsons and Edmund Campion. (Campion was captured and executed in 1581.)

However, the success of the missions was limited. While the Catholic gentry were enabled to retain their faith, humbler Catholics were often ignored. The educated priests associated more readily with their protectors than the 'ordinary people' and often became more like household chaplains. Catholicism thus became more of a 'country-house religion' than the popular faith it had been in the 1560s. Moreover, priests themselves became divided as a result of a bitter dispute over leadership of the missionary movement, thereby weakening the Catholic mission.

A CLOSER LOOK

Because of the proximity to the Channel ports, most Catholic priests operated in the south-east of England, where the proportion of Catholics in the population was smallest. In 1580 nearly half of the priests in England were serving the relatively small population of Catholics in London, Essex and the Thames Valley. Meanwhile, there were far fewer priests in the north, where the proportion of Catholics in the population was much higher and where their ministry might have borne more fruit.

ACTIVITY

Revision

Make a spider diagram to show why the efforts to restore Catholicism in England were unsuccessful. You may need to refer back to chapters 16, 19 and 20. In establishing your reasons for the failure of the Catholic missionary movement, you will need to consider both the movement's own shortcomings and the problems which it faced in trying to undermine an anti-Catholic political and social establishment.

Fig.5 *Inscription made by George Beesley in the Lower Martin Tower, Tower of London; Beesley, a Catholic Priest, was imprisoned and executed for his faith in 1591*

EXTRACT 2

In the 1580s the powerful and organised opposition which threatened the established Church appeared at times to be so formidable that it seems remarkable that the Church managed to emerge fundamentally unchanged at the end of the decade and to be in a position to launch a vigorous counter-offensive against those who sought to change it. There were many very influential people in the 1580s who were prepared to answer 'yes' to the question asked in a Puritan petition of 1588 – 'whether the desire of a further and better reformation in the Church of England, in dutiful manner, be not warranted by the word of God and law of England'? But the fierce onslaughts were repelled, mainly, it seems, because the queen resolutely and skilfully resisted any attempts to alter the church.

Adapted from Patrick McGrath, *Papists and Puritans under Elizabeth I*, 1967

EXTRACT 3

Whitgift's Protestantism, even his Calvinism, was not in question, and on the subject of preaching he would have found it easier to agree with Grindal than with his royal mistress. But, sharing Elizabeth's dread of 'factious' nonconformity and bringing to his office a schoolmasterly testiness which was all his own, he required the entire clergy of his province to endorse by formal subscription the established doctrine, liturgy and government of the Church as entirely scriptural. Francis Bacon would later warn Whitgift and his colleagues that 'in standing so precisely upon altering nothing', they incurred much of the blame for what ensued. Hundreds of preaching ministers were silenced and placed in peril of deprivation, often on account of minor conscientious scruples. This was a tactical error which created a broad alliance of forces hostile to the Archbishop.

Adapted from Patrick Collinson, *English Puritanism*, 1983

EXTRACT 4

The state of religion in Elizabethan England fell short of the Puritan ideal. None the less, historians should not underestimate the achievements of the late Elizabethan Church: the great advance made in the conversion of the people during the second half of the reign, the improvement in the quality of the clergy and the revitalisation of the Church courts. Through the efforts of the government, bishops and Puritan laity, a new framework for Protestant worship and devotion was erected in most English parishes, which ultimately led to a major change in religious beliefs. Lay people's memory of Catholic forms of worship gradually disappeared as the external features of the old religion were eventually removed from the churches, while a regular exposure to the Elizabethan prayer book and to Protestant sermons imbued ordinary men and women with a deep anti-papalism.

Adapted from Susan Doran, *Elizabeth I and Religion, 1558–1603*, 1994

STUDY TIP

In applying your own contextual knowledge of the condition of the Church, it is important to consider not only the policies and attitudes of the Church's leadership, but also the responses of ordinary people.

A LEVEL PRACTICE QUESTION

Evaluating historical extracts

Using your understanding of the historical context, assess how convincing the arguments in these three extracts are in relation to the condition of the Church of England during the reign of Elizabeth I.

The culmination of the English Renaissance and the 'Golden Age' of art, literature and music

The reign of Elizabeth witnessed a considerable flourishing in many aspects of English culture. The 'high' culture of the well-off was transformed and a vigorous popular culture also developed. However, popular and elite culture were not necessarily mutually exclusive. One aspect of Shakespeare's distinctive appeal was his ability to appeal both to an educated elite and to the 'groundlings' who attended performances in large numbers.

A CLOSER LOOK

Hilliard, in particular, enjoyed much favour at court, portrayed the queen and many courtiers and redesigned the royal seal. His most famous portrait *Young Man among Roses*, whose sitter might well have been the Earl of Essex, is an *impresa*, a combination of portrait and motto, which was intended to depict the ideals and aspirations of the sitter.

Art

English painting, heavily influenced by Flemish models, flourished during Elizabeth's reign, with artists benefiting from a range of patrons. Formal portraiture remained important, with the queen a frequent sitter, as were courtiers, especially the Earl of Leicester, along with sitters from the gentry and mercantile classes. Formal portraiture, however, lacked an artist as skilful as Holbein had been during the reign of Henry VIII. Instead, what became culturally the most important aspect of Elizabethan painting was the portrait miniature, whose most technically gifted exponents were Nicholas Hilliard and Isaac Oliver.

It was also a golden age in architecture. The queen was very reluctant to commission new buildings, but her courtiers and other wealthy individuals made up for this lack, often being able to afford extravagant building projects because of the family acquisition of former monastic land at knock-down prices. This period saw the emergence of the first named English architect (as opposed to formerly anonymous master masons). This was Robert Smythson, who worked on Longleat in Wiltshire and Wollaton Hall in Nottinghamshire as well as on a series of other country houses.

Fig. 6 *'Young Man among Roses' by Nicholas Hilliard*

Literature

The increased educational opportunities of the sixteenth century led to the emergence of a highly literate and often quite sophisticated viewing and reading public. The viewing public was treated to plays, not just by Shakespeare, but also by significant dramatists such as Thomas Kyd and Christopher Marlowe. There was an increasingly sophisticated infrastructure for the production of plays in London. Companies of actors operated under the patronage of courtiers, most importantly the Lord Chamberlain's Men, of which Shakespeare was a member. However, the companies operated within a competitive market environment at theatres such as the Globe and the Swan. These placed an emphasis on the ability of dramatists such as Shakespeare to produce new plays on a regular basis to appeal to audiences drawn from across the social classes. Occasionally, Shakespeare's plays had direct political connotations. The most notorious was the sponsoring at the Globe Theatre by supporters of the Earl of Essex of a performance of *Richard II*, a medieval king who had been the victim of usurpation in 1399. Elizabeth was alleged to have remarked: 'I am Richard. Knowe ye not that?'

Fig. 7 *The Globe Theatre*

A CLOSER LOOK

Courtier builders included Burghley (Burghley House in Northamptonshire and Hatfield House in Hertfordshire), Sir Christopher Hatton (Holdenby House and Kirby Hall, both in Northamptonshire), and the Earl of Pembroke (Wilton House in Wiltshire).

Much prose literature tended to have a narrow readership. An exception was Foxe's 'Book of Martyrs', which had a wide readership amongst 'godly' Puritans. The two most influential writers were Sir Philip Sidney and Edmund Spenser. Sidney saw himself as a conscious moderniser of the English language through the adaptation of classical forms. He was largely responsible for

CROSS-REFERENCE

Foxe's 'Book of Martyrs' is discussed in the context of religious developments, in Chapter 16, page 155.

the revival of the sonnet in English poetry and was therefore an essential precursor of Shakespeare in that context. Despite their courtly connections, both Sidney and Spenser were political outsiders; some of their work can be seen as being highly critical of the Elizabethan court.

Music

Music flourished in a variety of forms in Elizabethan England. Elizabeth, herself a skilful musician, was responsible at the time of the settlement for saving the musical culture of English cathedrals and Oxbridge colleges which were threatened by Protestant reformers who emphasised the importance of the word of God rather than the 'beauty of holiness'. The two greatest composers of the reign, Thomas Tallis and William Byrd, wrote extensively for the Church of England. Each of them, however, was Catholic and Byrd, in particular, demonstrated the strength of his Catholicism in works composed in secrecy for his Catholic patrons.

ACTIVITY

Extension

Listen to examples of William Byrd's Catholic compositions online and conduct further research into his music. How do such works demonstrate the extent of his Catholic commitment?

Secular music making also flourished, especially at court. Renaissance convention laid down that courtiers should be skilled musically. This encouraged the development of the madrigal, a musical form which originated in Italy, as a complex part-song that could be sung by a small mixed-voice choir and whose most important composers were Thomas Morley and Thomas Weelkes. Madrigals were usually 'non-political'. However, in 1601 Morley put together a collection of 25 madrigals by 23 different composers entitled *The Triumph of Oriana* which explicitly honoured the queen. Music was therefore a means of reinforcing the 'Gloriana' myth which sustained support for the queen at a time when her reputation was slipping. More intimate music was provided by John Dowland.

At a more popular level both instrumental music and song flourished. Many towns had official bands ('waits') who performed on formal occasions and who presumably performed informally on other occasions. Broadside ballads, songs printed cheaply on a single sheet of paper, became popular. Often these were extremely bawdy; the innuendo in a popular song such as *Watkins' Ale* is unmistakable.

KEY PROFILE

John Dowland (1563–1626)

Dowland's speciality was the solo voice accompanied by lute, with an emphasis in his songs on the fashionable late-sixteenth-century theme of melancholia. This was popular in elite circles because of the link which had been made in the Renaissance between melancholia and artistic or literary pretensions.

A CLOSER LOOK

William Byrd (c1540–1623)

Byrd's Latin motets, in particular, emphasised themes such as captivity, martyrdom and liberation and offered unmistakable moral support for the Catholic missionary movement. It was only Byrd's skill as a musician, his willingness to continue to write for the established Church and his courtly connections which ensured his safety, despite his obvious sympathy for the Catholic cause. In such instances music was fulfilling a fundamental religious and political purpose, and it is no coincidence that Byrd's music for the Church of England, while being extremely well crafted, lacks the emotional intensity of his Catholic compositions.

Summary

By the end of Elizabeth's reign England had been transformed both religiously and culturally. Catholicism survived essentially as the country-house religion of a small minority. The Church of England, from its uncertain start, had become much more assured and confident, increasingly commanding the support, or at least the acceptance, of most people. In addition, by the end of the reign England demonstrated a great cultural flowering which in its range and depth would not be achieved again for several centuries.

ACTIVITY

Group work

In pairs or small groups, investigate an aspect of Elizabethan culture which interests you. Prepare an illustrated presentation for your class.

A LEVEL PRACTICE QUESTION

'The challenge posed to the Elizabethan Crown by Catholicism was never as strong as Elizabeth I and her ministers believed.'
Assess the validity of this claim.

STUDY TIP

Quotation questions ask you to weigh up the evidence for and against a statement. You could consider linking native Catholicism and the missionary movement with the Catholic plots and the threat posed by Spain. Decide on your argument, and then use supporting evidence to write your essay.

24 The last years of Elizabeth

EXTRACT 1

There were many reasons for dissatisfaction with Elizabeth's rule. In refusing to name her heir, she took enormous risks for her kingdom. All possible solutions to the problem carried with them dangers, but her course was the most dangerous of all, and only good fortune saved the country from a disputed succession. She procrastinated over matters of foreign policy and military strategy. She did little to strengthen her Church and a good deal to weaken it. She allowed royal revenues to be eroded by inflation and she sold off the lands of the Crown. She let the Cecil group take over the court, antagonising Essex and many other of the younger nobles. However, there is more to be said on the other side. Elizabeth had the great gift of choosing able ministers and of standing by them, giving her realm the stable regime that it had lacked under her father, her brother and her sister. She had a skill in public display which made her deeply admired. Thanks in part to her caution, the realm was preserved from the dissensions and calamities that beset Europe and the Crown was saved from the disasters that befell it under those two interventionist monarchs, Charles I and James II.

Adapted from Penry Williams, *The Later Tudors, 1547–1603*, 1995

LEARNING OBJECTIVES

In this chapter you will learn about:

- the political condition of England by 1603
- the economic condition of England by 1603
- the state of society in England by 1603
- the state of religion in England by 1603.

KEY QUESTION

As you read this chapter, consider the following Key Questions:

- How effectively was England governed during this period?
- How did English society and economy change and with what effects?
- How far did intellectual and religious ideas change and develop and with what effects?

ACTIVITY

Evaluating historical extracts

As you read through the chapter, look for evidence which will either support or challenge the view put forward by Williams in Extract 1 concerning Elizabeth's overall record as queen.

The political condition of England by 1603

Though England enjoyed broadly effective government during most of Elizabeth's reign, there was a decline in royal authority and the quality of administration during the 1590s. One of the reasons for this revolved around anxieties over the succession; another concerned the queen's ministers and problems in the Privy Council and between factions. The crisis involving the Earl of Essex, which culminated in his execution for treason in 1601, is indicative of the difficulties which royal authority faced.

However, despite the **Essex 'rebellion'** a broad political unity had been achieved by 1603. All English people, apart from a small minority of militant Catholics, were broadly loyal to the Crown. On the other hand, the queen had reigned too long; her reputation had been tarnished by the events of the last years of her reign, and she seemed out of touch with the aspirations of a younger generation who looked forward to the accession of a king.

CROSS-REFERENCE

The decline of government in the 1590s is outlined in Chapter 19.

For the Essex 'rebellion', look back to Chapter 19, page 188.

One of the main reasons for the apparent decline in royal authority was the issue of the succession, which is discussed in Chapter 20, pages 195–197. On the other hand, Elizabeth's 'Golden Speech' of 1601 at the final parliamentary session of her reign (see Chapter 19, page 193) moved many MPs.

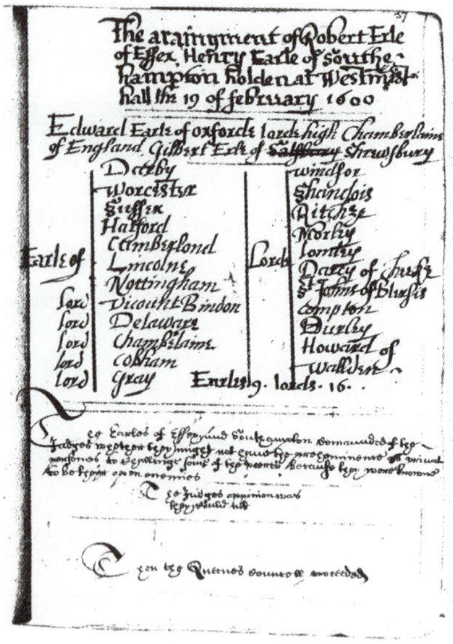
The araignment of Robert Erle of Essex, Henry Earle of Southampton holden at Westminster hall the 19 of February 1600

Edward Earle of Oxforde lorde high Chamberlaine of England Gilbert Earle of Shrewsbury

Earles of Derby, Worcester, Suffex, Hartford, Cumberland, Lincolne, Nottingham
Vicount Bindon
lord Delaware
lord Chamberlaine
lord Cobham
lord Gray

Lords Windsor, Shandois, Ritche, Morley, Lomley, Darcy of Chiche, St Johns of Bletsoe, Compton, Burley, Howard of Walden

Earles 9. lords 16.

Fig. 1 *A later transcript of the trial of the Earl of Essex*

ACTIVITY

In order to assess the political condition of England in 1603, complete the following table with appropriate and supported judgements. You should also consult Chapters 17 and 19.

	Early years, 1558–63	Mid-reign, 1563–88	Later years, 1589–1603
Importance of influence of ministers			
Importance/ influence of Privy Council			
Effectiveness of relationship between queen and Parliament			
Government's dealings with order/ disorder/ rebellion			
Dealing with issues of marriage and succession			

The economic condition of England by 1603

In some respects England had experienced considerable economic continuity during the sixteenth century. However, by the beginning of the seventeenth century it was evident that some of the economic circumstances which would later in the century lead to commercial domination were in place, even if only in an early form. For example, the setting up of trading companies to challenge the domination of the Spanish, Portuguese and Dutch and the beginnings of an interest in the Americas. Nevertheless, the importance of such factors should not be exaggerated, and the organisation of English capitalism, in particular, was crude in comparison with the commercial sophistication of the Dutch.

Regardless of this, cottage industries such as nail making, hosiery, soap manufacturing and brewing flourished, and total production clearly rose substantially during the course of the sixteenth century. This suggests that domestic demand was thriving. It was, however, only through thrift, multiple employments and hard work that many people were able to avoid poverty at the end of the sixteenth century.

The state of society in England by 1603

Though England remained a socially divided society with huge differences in living standards between the wealthy few and the poor majority, there were constraints which prevented society from breaking down completely. Crucially, perhaps, most of the time the majority of the population could be fed, and there was only one subsistence crisis in the 1590s when it is known that there were deaths from starvation. The experience of the bitter years of poverty and harvest failure from 1594 to 1597 did, however, help to shape the reform of the poor law enacted in 1598 and 1601. These limited the worst effects of poverty, at least as far as the deserving poor were concerned.

Furthermore, in contrast with many continental societies, the nobility were subject to taxation.

ACTIVITY

In order to assess continuity and change in the economic and social condition of England during the reign of Elizabeth, you should complete the following table. You will also need to consult chapters 18, 21 and 22.

	Continuity/evidence	Change/evidence
Overseas trade		
Internal trade		
Industry		
Standards of living		
Prices/inflation		
Attitudes to the poor		

The state of religion in England by 1603

By the end of her reign Elizabeth could look upon a religious situation which was favourable. Compared with the beginning of her reign the level of popular Catholicism had declined. Moreover, English Catholics were fundamentally divided between a majority who tried to accommodate conflicting loyalties to Crown and faith and a minority who identified wholeheartedly with the bull of excommunication and who sought a Catholic succession. The Church of England, on the other hand, had become an institution with which the majority could identify, albeit in a rather loose way. Puritanism as a dynamic movement had faded and the majority of Puritans had become assimilated within the Anglican mainstream. Separatism, never a numerically strong movement, had virtually disappeared. There was a broad consensus surrounding the Church of England, which ensured a substantial degree of religious unity.

ACTIVITY

Summary

In order to assess the importance of religious issues in Elizabethan England, you should complete the following table. You will need to draw on material from Chapters 18 and 23.

Context	Importance
Attitudes to royal supremacy	
Attitudes to the relationship between Church and State	
The changing condition of the Church of England	
Key aspects of doctrine/religious ideas/church services	
The nature and influence of English Catholicism	

Fig. 2 *A drawing of the queen's funeral procession*

EXTRACT 2

Queen Elizabeth did not attempt to solve problems, she simply avoided them – and then survived long enough for some to go away. The rest returned to plague her successor, James I – but that was his problem, and she had never given much attention to what would happen after her death. Her refusal to tackle the succession issue, her sale of Crown lands to finance wars, and her denial of place and reward to the Essex generation showed how limited was her concern for the future. This pragmatic approach to politics was possible because Elizabeth had a restricted conception of her role as queen. Though she spoke much of her duty to God and her care for her people, this was political rhetoric to justify her role. After the ecclesiastical settlement of 1559, she felt no public obligation to do anything more – she did not reform administration, or purify the Church or improve the lot of the poor – because she saw no reason why she should.

Adapted from Christopher Haigh, *Elizabeth I*, 1988

EXTRACT 3

Elizabeth I carefully managed her own policy. As Sir Robert Naunton later explained, 'though very capable of counsel, she was absolute enough in her own resolution. Which was apparent even to her last'. She knew her mind; her instinct to power was infallible. When her privy councillors tried to manipulate her, they were rarely successful; she would lose her temper and the matter would rest in abeyance. Yet she repeatedly postponed important decisions. Her successive ditherings drove Burghley to distraction. Thus she wavered over intervention in 1559–60 in support of the Protestant lords in Scotland; over the safety of the realm and the succession issue in the 1560s, 1570s and 1580s; over the trial and execution of Mary, Queen of Scots in 1585–87; and over what became the most vexed issue of all, whether or not to offer military assistance to the Dutch Protestants in their heroic struggle against Philip II.

Adapted from John A. Guy, 'Tudor monarchy and political culture' in *The Oxford Illustrated History of Tudor and Stuart Britain*, edited by John Morrill, 1996

A LEVEL PRACTICE QUESTION

Evaluating historical extracts

Using your understanding of the historical context, assess how convincing the arguments in Extracts 1, 2, and 3 are in relation to Elizabeth I.

STUDY TIP

In order to answer this question effectively, you would need to draw on material from all of the chapters which deal with Elizabethan politics and government. You should consider both those features of Elizabethan government which remained broadly the same across the reign and those features which experienced change.

A LEVEL PRACTICE QUESTION

'By 1603 it was clear that the English people had benefited little in social and economic terms from the rule of Elizabeth I.' Assess the validity of this view.

STUDY TIP

Remember that the term 'English people' covers all social classes, occupational groups and geographical areas. One way of approaching the question would be to organise your material into two groups: those who benefited and those who suffered. The term 'benefited' can be interpreted in a variety of ways. At its simplest level the term can relate to standards of living. However, you might also consider, for example, such issues as order and disorder and the religious framework.

Conclusion: Restoring and developing the powers of the monarchy

Fig. 1 *'An allegory of the Tudor Succession' by Lucas Heere; note that Elizabeth is accompanied by personifications of peace and prosperity*

When Henry VII acceded to the throne with a weak claim and with a number of enemies who seemed poised to bring him down at the earliest possible opportunity, it might have been difficult to envisage the successful rule which characterised much of the Tudor dynasty. Henry VII never considered himself fully secure as monarch, and this helps to explain the peculiar nature of much of his rule. Yet he was broadly successful in gaining security, restoring the Crown to financial health and giving England relative security in its relations with foreign powers. Most importantly of all, perhaps, his death was followed by the first untroubled succession in almost a century, which was a tribute to the political skill which characterised his reign, even if this was little appreciated either by his heir or by the country more widely.

At one level Henry VIII appeared to make the monarchy more powerful. His frequent resort to the execution of those who had displeased him led his rule to be characterised as tyrannical. Moreover, the break with Rome and the dissolution of the monasteries enhanced both his power and, in the short term, his riches. On the other hand, the scope of parliamentary legislation undoubtedly expanded during his reign so that sovereignty rested at times with the 'king-in-Parliament' rather than with the king as an individual.

Despite the difficulties (and potential danger) of the mid-Tudor years when the minor, Edward VI, and Catholic female, Mary I, held the throne, respect for royal authority survived. Elizabeth I's inheritance (as laid down in Henry VIII's will) went unquestioned.

KEY QUESTION

How effectively did the Tudors restore and develop the powers of the monarchy?

The power of the monarchy was maintained during the long reign of Elizabeth I, though her sex and her virginity both necessitated a distinctive approach to government which was completely different from anything which might have been undertaken by a male ruler. Though doubtless unfair, the criticisms of her which came, however obliquely, from male courtiers, contributed to a more general feeling by the start of the seventeenth century that she had ruled too long and that the time was right for the restoration of male rule. What they got, however, was the somewhat ineffectual James I (James VI of Scotland), whose rule quickly became the object of criticism. Under James I's son and successor Charles I, criticism eventually brought about a breakdown in relations, which led in 1642 to civil war between the supporters of the king and those of Parliament. The forces of Parliament proved victorious and in 1649 Charles was tried for treason, found guilty and executed. Within two generations of the death of Elizabeth, the powers of the monarchy had been destroyed and England had become a republic.

KEY QUESTION

In what ways and how effectively was England governed during this period?

The effectiveness of government

The quality of government varied during the Tudor period. Under Henry VII, government was broadly efficient, especially when it came to the collection of revenue. However, this efficiency came at the expense of popularity, and there was much rejoicing amongst the political nation when Henry VII died.

Henry VIII repudiated his father's legacy and often governed extravagantly. Moreover, he struggled to adopt a consistent approach to government. He twice sought to govern with the aid of a chief minister, in the form of Thomas Wolsey and Thomas Cromwell, each of them a remarkable man who rose from very humble origins to dominate the machinery of government. Each in the end overreached himself, lost royal favour and was brought down by members of the conservative nobility whose traditional predominance they had temporarily usurped. Henry lurched from dependence on a chief minister to operating within a conciliar framework, though with limited success. By the end of the reign his record as monarch was distinctly flawed, the benefits to the Crown of the acquisition of much of the wealth of the Church having been thrown away in pursuit of a futile foreign policy paid for by land sales and the disastrous debasement of the currency. Moreover, while he had demonstrated his power by bringing about the break with Rome of the English Church, his lack of a clear vision of what form an English Church might take caused much confusion. This placed his successors, the Protestant Edward VI and the Catholic Mary I, in much difficulty.

Fig. 2 *King James I of England*

That she was able in some measure to resolve this confusion was perhaps Elizabeth I's greatest domestic achievement. Much of her government was administratively sound; she chose her ministers, especially Lord Burghley, wisely, trusted them and most of the time even forgave them when she considered they had worked against her interests. However, Elizabeth's government had fundamental weaknesses. In particular, the failure to undertake necessary institutional reform left problems for her successor, James I, which he was never able satisfactorily to resolve.

KEY QUESTION

How did relations with foreign powers change and how was the succession secured?

Relations with foreign powers

At the start of the Tudor period, Henry VII's emphasis for most of the reign was on peaceful coexistence with his continental neighbours. This policy attitude was shaped by two fundamental factors: his reluctance to spend money on foreign wars and the primacy of his aim to maintain the security of the dynasty. In the process he irritated many members of the traditional nobility, whom he was preventing from exercising what they considered to be their traditional right to pursue glory by waging war, particularly against the French.

Thus, the nobility broadly welcomed the accession of Henry VIII, who provided them with opportunities for glory. The price for this was paid not only by the Crown, which saw its finances depleted, but also by the country more generally when the policy of debasement added to the already evident inflationary pressures. Unsuccessful and expensive military activities marred the reigns of both Edward VI and Mary I. Moreover, the proposed marriage of the latter to Philip of Spain provoked rebellion in 1554.

Elizabeth I, having intervened on behalf of Protestant co-religionists in Scotland and France in the early years of her reign, became as reluctant as her grandfather to get involved in foreign conflicts. One consequence of that reluctance was that her intervention in the Netherlands on behalf of the Dutch rebels against Philip II of Spain was probably too long delayed. Moreover, she was dragged reluctantly into outright war against Spain. The victory over the Spanish Armada enhanced the prestige of the monarchy in a way which had not occurred since the reign of Henry V (1413–22). However, this level of prestige was not maintained as the war dragged on and Elizabeth had to raise unprecedented levels of taxation in order to finance the conflict. The war did not officially come to an end until after Elizabeth's death.

Society and economy

KEY QUESTION

How did English society and economy change and with what effects?

The economy was the context in which there was, relatively speaking, least change. Internal trade continued to predominate. There was some attempt to correct the overdependence of the export market on the cloth trade to Flanders. The development of alternative markets for cloth in the northern Netherlands (Amsterdam) and north Germany (Emden) was not only economically healthy, it also coincided with the religious priorities of the Elizabethan regime, as it encouraged the exploitation of 'Protestant' markets at the expense of Catholic Flanders. The reign of Elizabeth also saw attempts to widen the export trade – to Russia and the Baltic as well as to North Africa and other parts of the Mediterranean.

Attempts at exploration, begun under Henry VII and largely ignored under Henry VIII, began again under Edward VI and Mary. At first such efforts were modest, but they became connected to attempts to widen trade and to support wider religious and foreign policies, as happened in Elizabeth's reign with Drake's circumnavigation. The first attempts at colonisation of the Americas in Elizabeth's reign were short-lived and disastrous. However, further attempts at colonisation – in Virginia from 1607 and in Massachusetts from 1620 – proved successful, and much of the eastern Americas was colonised by English settlers during the seventeenth century, thereby laying the foundations of future empire.

The social structure of England changed little during the Tudor period. The social dominance of the nobility was reinforced by the reluctance of monarchs, especially Henry VII and Elizabeth I, to create new peers. This would change under the early Stuarts. James I especially was very keen to increase the numbers of peers, though this necessarily 'diluted' the exclusivity of the nobility as a caste. Many members of the greater gentry also enjoyed great wealth. This was especially evident amongst Elizabethan ministers such as Sir Christopher Hatton and Sir Ralph Sadler. The landed gentry was not an exclusive caste, and entry to its ranks was easily accomplished, for example, by lawyers and by merchants who had prospered through trade. On the other hand, there is much evidence to suggest that the condition of many of the poor deteriorated as real wages stagnated. In this context, therefore, the reform of the poor laws in 1598 and 1601 proved to be a considerable legislative achievement which remained in force until the passing of the Poor Law Amendment Act in 1834.

KEY QUESTION

How far did intellectual and religious ideas change and develop and with what effect?

Intellectual and religious change

The Tudor period witnessed considerable intellectual and religious change. Much of this happened irrespective of the nature of the regime, but the break with Rome created a situation in which the Crown became the dominant force in religious matters in the realm.

When the Tudor age began, medieval culture and intellectual ideas remained predominant. England was still experiencing 'the age of Gothic'. The first hints of intellectual change were in the air, and humanist ideas gradually became more influential, especially during the reign of Henry VIII. In the early stages of the reign, with the encouragement of the monarch, the humanism of thinkers such as More and Erasmus became very fashionable. There was, however, no simplistic relationship between humanism and religious change. Humanists could be found on both sides of the religious divide in the 1530s – and More was willing to sacrifice his life rather than compromise his religious principles.

The hardening of religious attitudes brought about by the Reformation reduced the freer exchange of ideas which had been a characteristic of the age of humanism, and this narrowing continued during the reign of Elizabeth despite the queen's apparent nostalgia for the previous age and her suspicious attitude towards clergymen who were convinced about the correctness of their own ideas. Intellectual developments were relatively few during the reign of Elizabeth. However, the reign did witness a unique cultural flowering. Shakespeare came to the fore as a playwright in the mid-1590s, though many of his greatest dramas were written after Elizabeth's death, and the stage in general flourished. Shakespeare was not alone. In addition to the theatre, the period was also a golden age of English music, though much of this was produced as part of the Catholic counterculture associated with William Byrd.

KEY QUESTION

How important was the role of key individuals and groups and how were they affected by developments?

The role of key individuals

The Tudor age saw many exceptional individuals make their mark on the history of the period. Henry VIII and Elizabeth I are the most easily recognisable monarchs from English history in the popular mind. Each, particularly the former, had their flaws. However, their contribution, for better or for worse, to the development of English history was formidable.

A number of Crown servants were also touched with greatness and, perhaps also, notoriety. Cardinal Wolsey rose from humble origins to dominate Henry VIII's government for 15 years; Thomas Cromwell emerged from obscurity to dominate for 8 years. Each of them had an ability to work with the most difficult of royal masters, partly because of an instinctive understanding of what the king's needs might be. Lord Burghley had an easier task in serving Queen Elizabeth. Less creative than Wolsey or Cromwell, nevertheless his comprehensive grasp of political situations and his huge capacity for work ensured his indispensability. However, he stayed in power for too long and prevented the possibility of changes which might have modernised the quality of government.

At an intellectual and cultural level, the outstanding English figure in the first part of the Tudor period was Sir Thomas More. He was, perhaps, not quite the saintly figure revered by the Catholic Church, and was certainly a flawed figure as a politician. However, he stands first amongst English intellectuals of the period. Some writers, including practising politicians such as Bishop Gardiner and Sir Thomas More, wrote about the relationship between the individual and the State. At the start of Elizabeth's reign, Bishop Jewel's *Apology* asserted the continuity between the early Church and the Church established by the Elizabethan settlement. In the second half of the Tudor period, as illustrated above, the influence of individuals can be seen more in cultural than in intellectual areas.

Summary

The Tudor age was clearly a pivotal period in English history. Some of the changes experienced during this time were absolutely fundamental to the English historical experience. The most important of these was the break with Rome. Over time Catholicism, once the norm of ordinary people's religious experience, became increasingly perceived as a foreign institution to which loyal English people could hold no allegiance. The restoration of the power of the monarchy was rather less important. The fall of the monarchy and the creation of a republic which lasted from 1649 to 1660 lent a temporary feel to the restoration of monarchical power which was characteristic of the Tudor age. None of this could realistically have been anticipated in 1603. England was an ordered and secure society which had witnessed few of the extremes of violence and persecution which had characterised many parts of continental Europe in the second half of the sixteenth century, and for that the Tudors deserve much credit.

Glossary

A

Act of Attainder: declared a landowner guilty of rebelling against a monarch

Amicable Grant: ordered by Wolsey in 1525 to raise more money for war

annates: revenue paid to the Pope by a bishop or other cleric on his appointment, collected in England and sent to Rome; also known as the 'First Fruits' (*primitiae* in Latin)

anticlericalism: opposition to the Church's role in political and other non-religious matters

B

benefactor: a person who makes a charitable donation

bond: a legal document which bound an individual to another to perform an action or forfeit a specified sum of money if they failed to do so

bourgeoisie: middle-class residents of towns and cities

bull: a letter or formal declaration issued by the Pope

bureaucrat: an official in a government department, in particular one perceived as being concerned with procedural correctness at the expense of people's needs

C

Calvinism: ideas on Church doctrine and organisation put forward in Geneva by the French reformer John Calvin

caste: a class or group of people who inherit exclusive privileges or are perceived as socially distinct

Catholic reformation: the attempts of the Catholic Church across Europe to reform itself

chamber: the private areas of the Court; also a key department for the efficient collection of royal revenues

chancery: the main court of equity in the kingdom

chantries: chapels where Masses for the souls of the dead took place

chivalrous: gallant, or courteous; a code of conduct associated historically with the dutiful behaviour of medieval knights

common rights: denotes the legal right of tenants to use common land, for example for keeping animals; the exact nature of these rights varied from place to place

Corpus Christi: literally meaning the 'body of Christ', Corpus Christi is a feast of the Catholic Church which celebrates the 'blessed sacrament'

courtier: a person who attends a royal court as a companion or adviser to the monarch

D

diocese: an area under the pastoral care of a bishop in the Christian Church

Duchy of Lancaster: a significant body of property, mostly but not exclusively situated in Lancashire, which personally belonged to the king but was formally the territory of the duke

E

elites: select groups that are superior in terms of ability, birth or qualities to the rest of a group or society

Erasmianism: the body of ideas associated with Erasmus and his followers

Erastian: the view that the State should have authority over the Church

extort: obtain (something) by force, threats, or other unfair means

extraordinary revenue: money raised by the king from additional sources as one-off payments when he faced an emergency or an unforeseeable expense of government; this could be made up of parliamentary grants, loans, clerical taxes, for example

F

feudal aid: a right by which the Crown could impose a tax on their tenants for the knighting of the eldest son, the marriage of the eldest daughter or to ransom a lord

feudal system: the medieval system by which society was structured depending on relationships in which land was held in return for some form of service

fifteenths and tenths: standard form of taxation, calculated in the fourteenth century, paid by towns and boroughs to the Crown

G

Gothic: the style of architecture prevalent in Western Europe in the twelfth to sixteenth centuries, characterised by pointed arches and large windows

grace: the pure state a soul needed to be in to enter heaven

grazing rights: a legal term referring to the right of a user to allow their livestock to feed (graze) in a given area

Groom of the stool: the most intimate of an English monarch's courtiers, who became a man in whom much confidence was placed and royal secrets were shared as a matter of course

guilds and confraternities: voluntary associations of individuals created to promote works of Christian charity or devotion

H

Hanseatic League: a group of free cities originating in the thirteenth century, which came together to form a commercial union with the intention of controlling trade in the Baltic Sea; the league dominated commercial activity in northern Europe from the thirteenth to the fifteenth century

heir presumptive: the person who is first in line of succession but whose position could be displaced by a new heir with a better claim

heresy: the denial of the validity of the key doctrines of the Church

homily: a published reading which could be substituted for a sermon produced by a clergyman

household government: medieval system of governance where the head of a household, invariably an adult male, had authority over the property, labour, and mobility of everyone living on his land

huguenot: term used in the sixteenth and seventeenth centuries to denote French Protestants

Hundred Years War: conflict that lasted on-and-off from 1337 to 1453, and was fought between England and France

I

Iconoclasm: the rejection or destruction of images associated with established values and practices

Imperial jurisdiction: official powers to make legal decisions and judgements belonged to the king and could not be challenged by the Church or any other power

Intercession: the action of saying a prayer on behalf of another; in traditional Catholic thinking it was the role of the priest to intervene with God on behalf of an individual

Intercursus Malus: trade agreement from 1506; this treaty never became fully operative and by the following year trading relationships had been restored on the basis of Intercursus Magnus

Intercursus Magnus: the major commercial treaty between England and the Duchy of Burgundy which restored normal trading links between the two

K

King's Great Matter: concerned the annulment of Henry VIII's marriage to Catherine of Aragon and his desire to marry Anne Boleyn; this was a complex situation which would ultimately lead to England's break from the Catholic Church

L

laity: refers collectively to those who were neither priests nor members of a religious order

letters patent: legal instruments issued by the monarch in the exercise of his or her prerogative powers

Lord Chamberlain: also known as the Chamberlain, an experienced nobleman and member of the king's council, and a personal friend of the king; he had administrative and political duties, often speaking for the monarch in an official capacity, and was also responsible for organising court ceremonies

M

magnate: a member of the higher ranks of the nobility

marriage-by-proxy: a proxy marriage is one in which one or both of the individuals being united is not physically present, usually being represented instead by another person

martial law: legal authority and political control exercised by military authority

mercenaries: hired soldiers who offer their services to the highest bidder and have no specific commitment to the cause for which they are fighting

merchants of the staple: incorporated by royal charter in 1319, they controlled the export of wool

mixed farming: a system of farming which involves the growing of crops as well as the raising of animals as livestock

O

Oxford reformers: men such as Grocyn, Linacre and Colet who were amongst the first English scholars to adopt humanist ideas and approaches

P

papal dispensation: permission required from the Pope in order to be exempted from the laws or observances of the Church

papal legate: position of control over the English Church, superior to that of the Archbishop of Canterbury

parliamentary sanction: an official confirmation or ratification of a law given by Parliament as the acclaimed body of the State

pastoral farming: farming involving the rearing of animals – either for animal by-products such as milk, eggs or wool, or for meat

patronage: the system by which the Crown distributed favours to those that were seen as loyal

peasant: a country dweller who farmed directly on land which can be either owned or rented

peerage: group of persons who held one of the five ranks of the aristocracy (duke, marquis, earl, viscount, baron); they were usually considerable landholders, exercised considerable power in their localities and were members of the House of Lords

perpendicular style: the dominant form of church architecture in England from the later fourteenth to the early sixteenth century, so-called because of its emphasis on vertical lines

***praemunire*:** a parliamentary statute enacted in 1393 to prevent papal interference in the rights of the Crown to make appointments to Church office

prerogative rights: describes those rights or powers which the monarch could exercise without requiring the consent of Parliament

privy chamber: comprising the close personal servants of the monarch; its members had direct access to the monarch and therefore could influence him or her more directly

protectorate: term used to describe the rule of Edward Seymour, Duke of Somerset, who was in charge of the kingdom as Edward was too young to rule in his own right

purgatory: the state in which the souls of the dead were purged of their sins before they could enter the kingdom of heaven

puritanism: the belief amongst godly Protestants that the Church of England needed to be purged of any remaining 'superstitious' (i.e. Catholic) practices

R

real wages: the value of income in relation to prices of goods on the market, instead of actual money received

recognizance: a formal acknowledgement of a debt or other obligation which could be enforced by means of financial penalty

recusant: term used to describe those who refused to attend the services of the Church of England

reformation: a sixteenth-century movement opposing the Catholic Church, which resulted in the establishment of Protestant and reformed churches

regicide: the execution or murder of a monarch

Renaissance: a cultural and intellectual movement which, beginning in Italy, emphasised a revival of interest in classical learning and the arts

S

scholasticism: a system of philosophical analysis in the medieval period

sectaries: a term used, usually with disapproval, to describe members of sects which had separated from the Church of England

sectional interests: the interests of a particular group within a community or country

secular: something not connected with religious or spiritual matters

statute of uses: a law passed to prevent landed property from being turned into trusts

submission of the clergy: the formal surrender of the Church's independent law-making function

subsidy: historically, a grant issued by Parliament to the sovereign for State needs

subsistence crisis: when harvest failure raises food prices to such an extent that significant numbers of the poor die from starvation

sumptuary laws: laws that attempted to regulate how individuals should dress, depending on their social status

supplication against the ordinaries: a form of petition directed against alleged abuses of ordinary jurisdiction

suzerainty: the feudal control of one territory by another

synod: a Church council that in this context would exist outside the official Church hierarchy

T

tonnage and poundage: the right to raise revenue for the whole reign from imports and exports

transubstantiation: the Christian belief that the substance of bread and wine was completely changed into the substance of Christ's body and blood by a validly ordained priest during the consecration at Mass

W

wardship: an aspect of the feudal system which enabled the Crown to gain the profits from property held by a minor

Bibliography

Books for students

Anderson, Angela and Imperato, Tony, *Access to History: an Introduction to Tudor England, 1485–1603*, Hodder Education, 2001

Carpenter, Rebecca, *Religious Conflict and the Church in England c1529–c1570*, Oxford University Press, 2015

Ellsmore, Samantha, Hudson, David and Rogerson, David, *The Early Tudors: England, 1485–1558*, John Murray, 2001

Fellows, Nicholas, *Disorder and Rebellion in Tudor England*, Hodder Education, 2002

Guy, John A., *The Tudors: a Very Short Introduction*, Oxford University Press, 2000

Lee, Cathy, *Britain, 1483–1529*, Nelson Thornes, 2008

Mervyn, Barbara, *The Reign of Elizabeth: England, 1558–1603*, John Murray, 2001

Murphy, Derrick, Tillbrook, Michael and Walsh-Atkins, Patrick, *England, 1485–1603*, Collins Flagship History, 1999

Randell, Keith and Turvey, Roger, *Access to History: Henry VIII to Mary I: Government and Religion, 1509–1558*, Hodder Education, 2008

Turvey, Roger and Heard, Nigel, *Edward VI and Mary: a mid-Tudor Crisis?*, Hodder Education, 2006

Turvey, Roger and Rogers, Caroline, *Access to History: Henry VII*, Hodder Education, 2005

Warren, John, *Elizabeth I: Religion and Foreign Affairs*, Hodder Education, 2002

Warren, John, *Elizabeth I: Meeting the Challenge, England, 1541–1603*, Hodder Education, 2008

Books for teachers and extension

Brigden, Susan, *New Worlds, Lost Worlds: the Rule of the Tudors, 1485–1603*, Penguin, 2000

Carpenter, Caroline, *The Wars of the Roses: Politics and the Constitution in England, c1437–1509*, Cambridge University Press, 1997

Collinson, Patrick, *English Puritanism*, Historical Association, 1983

Collinson, Patrick, *The Sixteenth Century, 1485–1603*, Oxford University Press, 2000

Doran, Susan, *England and Europe, 1485–1603*, Pearson, 1992

Doran, Susan, *Elizabeth I and Religion, 1558–1603*, Routledge, 2000

Duffy, Eamon, *The Stripping of the Altars: Traditional Religion in England, 1400–1580*, Yale University Press, 1992

Elton, Geoffrey R., *Reform and Reformation: England, 1509–1558*, Arnold, 1977

Elton, Geoffrey R. (ed.), *The Tudor Constitution: Documents and Commentary*, Cambridge University Press, 1982

Fletcher, Anthony and MacCulloch, Diarmaid, *Tudor Rebellions*, Pearson, 2008

Goodman, Anthony, *The New Monarchy: England, 1471–1534*, Blackwell, 1988

Graves, Michael, *Elizabethan Parliaments, 1559–1601*, Pearson, 1996

Gunn, Steven J., *Early Tudor Government, 1485*–1558, Palgrave, 1995

Guy, John A., *Tudor England*, Oxford University Press, 1988

Guy, John A. (ed.), *The Tudor Monarchy*, Hodder Education, 1997

Haigh, Christopher, *Elizabeth I*, Pearson, 1988

Haigh, Christopher, *English Reformations*, Oxford University Press, 1993

Harper-Bill, Christopher, *The Pre-Reformation Church in England, 1400–1530*, Pearson, 1996

Hoskins, W.G., *The Age of Plunder: the England of Henry VIII, 1500–1547*, Pearson, 1976

Lander, Jack R., *Government and Community: England, 1450–1509*, Arnold, 1980

Loach, Jennifer and Tittler, Robert (eds), *The Mid-Tudor Polity*, Palgrave, 1980

Loades, David, *The Mid-Tudor Crisis, 1545–1603*, Palgrave, 1992

Loades, David, *Power in Tudor England*, Palgrave, 1996

Loades, David, *Tudor Government*, Wiley Blackwell, 1997

MacCulloch, Diarmaid, *The Later Reformation in England*, Palgrave, 2000

MacCulloch, Diarmaid, *Tudor Church Militant: Edward VI and the Protestant Reformation*, Allen Lane, 2000

O'Day, Rosemary (ed.), *The Longman Companion to the Tudor Age*, Pearson, 1995

Palliser, David, *The Age of Elizabeth: England under the later Tudors, 1547–1603*, Pearson, 1983

Scarisbrick, J.J. *The Reformation and the English People*, Blackwell, 1984

Slack, Paul, *Poverty and Policy in Tudor and Stuart England*, Pearson, 1988

Slack, Paul, *The English Poor Law, 1531–1782*, Palgrave, 1990

Slack, Paul, *Poverty and Policy in Tudor and Stuart England*, Pearson, 1988

Sheils, William, *The English Reformation, 1530–70*, Pearson, 1989

Williams, Penry, *The Tudor Regime*, Oxford University Press, 1979

Williams, Penry, *The Later Tudors, 1547–1603*, Oxford University Press, 1991

DVD

'Burning Convictions' and 'Body of a Queen', in *A History of Britain*, written and presented by Simon Schama, BBC, 2000

Online resources

Search for Professor Keith Wrightson of Yale University's lectures entitled Early Modern England on: www.youtube.com

www.oxforddnb.com (accessible through most public libraries)

www.tudors.org

www.history.ac.uk

www.british-history.ac.uk

www.historyofparliamentonline.org/research

Acknowledgements

The publisher would like to thank the following for permissions to use their photographs:

Cover: Mary Evans/Epic/Tallandier; **p1**: Apic/Getty Images; **p3**: David Lyons/Alamy; **p6**: Stefano Bianchetti/Corbis UK Ltd.; **p10**: Great Malvern Priory, Worcestershire, UK/Bridgeman Art Library; **p11**: Belvoir Castle, Leicestershire, UK/Bridgeman Art Library; **p17**: National Archives; **p23**: (l) Image Asset Management/Age Fotostock, (r) Leemage/Corbis UK Ltd.; **p25**: MPI/Getty Images; **p27**: GL Archive/Alamy; **p35**: (l) Julio Donoso/Sygma/Corbis UK Ltd., (r) Collection of the Earl of Pembroke, Wilton House, Wilts./Bridgeman Art Library; **p36**: Corpus Christi College, Oxford, UK/Bridgeman Art Library; **p37**: Image Asset Management/Age Fotostock; **p40**: Loop Images Ltd./Alamy; **p45**: British Library Board, All Rights Reserved/Bridgeman Art Library; **p46**: Interfoto/Superstock Ltd.; **p55**: Private Collection/Photo © Philip Mould Ltd, London/Bridgeman Art Library; **p57**: Frick Collection, New York/Superstock/Art Archive; **p59**: Reproduced by permission of the Provost and Fellows of Eton College/Eton College Collections; **p60**: (l) Reproduced by permission of English Heritage/Heritage-Images/Getty Images, (r) M J Perris/Alamy; **p63**: The Berger Collection at the Denver Art Museum, USA/Bridgeman Art Library; **p65**: (l) Image Asset Management/Age Fotostock, (r) The Print Collector/Heritage-Images/Getty Images; **p67**: Imagno/Austrian Archives/Getty Images; **p71**: British Library Board, All Rights Reserved/Bridgeman Art Library; **p73**: The Print Collector/Alamy; **p76**: (t) Active Museum/Alamy, (b) Universal History Archive/Getty Images; **p77**: Corbis UK Ltd.; **p81**: DeA Picture Library/J. E. Bulloz/Art Archive; **p87**: Prisma Archivo/Alamy; **p88**: Niday Picture Library/Alamy; **p89**: Leemage/Corbis UK Ltd.; **p90**: Prisma Archivo/Alamy; **p98**: Château de Blois/Gianni Dagli Orti/Art Archive; **p99**: Mary Evans Picture Library; **p102**: Wojtek Buss/Age Fotostock; **p106**: His Grace The Duke of Norfolk, Arundel Castle/Bridgeman Art Library; **p111**: (l) Mark Bolton/Corbis UK Ltd., (r) Bristol Museum and Art Gallery, UK/Bridgeman Art Library; **p116**: Angelo Hornak/Alamy; **p117**: Heritage Image Partnership Ltd./Alamy; **p118**: Private Collection/The Stapleton Collection/Bridgeman Art Library; **p121**: (t) Robert Harding Picture Library Ltd./Alamy, (b) Image Asset Management/Age Fotostock; **p125**: Royal Collection Trust © Her Majesty Queen Elizabeth II, 2015/Bridgeman Art Library; **p126**: National Trust Photographic Library/Bridgeman Art Library; **p127**: Hulton Archive/Stringer/Getty Images; **p130**: Abpixs/Alamy; **p133**: National Portrait Gallery, London, UK/Bridgeman Art Library; **p134**: Photograph courtesy of Sotheby's Picture Library; **p137**: (bl Graham Uney/Alamy, (r) Stefano Baldini/Age Fotostock; **p142**: The Print Collector/Heritage-Images/Getty Images; **p145**: Miramare Palace Trieste/A. Dagli Orti/Art Archive; **p147**: Universal History Archive/Getty Images; **p148**: Trustees of the Bedford Estate, Woburn Abbey, UK/Bridgeman Art Library; **p150**: Prisma Archivo/Alamy; **p153**: Stuart Bebb/St. John's College, Oxford University; **p156**: Private Collection/Bridgeman Art Library; **p158**: Private Collection/Bridgeman Art Library; **p160**: The National Archives, London, England/Mary Evans Picture Library; **p166**: Heritage Image Partnership Ltd./Alamy; **p167**: Active Museum/Alamy; **p169**: Andrew Baskott/Alamy; **p171**: Pictorial Press Ltd./Alamy; **p175**: Hatfield House, Hertfordshire, UK/Bridgeman Art Library; **p177**: Hoberman Collection/Corbis UK Ltd.; **p179**: Gregory R. Freeman; **p186**: Hulton Archive/Getty Images; **p188**: De Agostini Picture Library/Getty Images; **p189**: The Print Collector/Heritage-Images/Getty Images; **p192**: BL/Robana/Age Fotostock; **p198**: (l) National Archives/Mary Evans Picture Library, (r) BL/Robana/Age Fotostock; **p199**: Image Asset Management/Age Fotostock; **p202**: Archivart/Alamy; **p207**: Tim Scrivener/Alamy; **p211**: World History Archive/Age Fotostock; **p218**: DeA Picture Library/Art Archive; **p219**: Photo Researchers/Mary Evans Picture Library; **p220**: Universal History Archive/Getty Images; **p226**: Ann Ronan Pictures/Age Fotostock; **p229**: (t) Art Archive, (b) The Granger Collection/TopFoto; **p230**: Tim/Age Fotostock; **p231**: The Board of Trustees of the Armouries/TopFoto; **p233**: (l) Hulton Archive/Getty Images, (r) DeA Picture Library/Art Archive; **p238**: Microfilm reproduction courtesy of The Folger Shakespeare Library; **p240**: British Library/Robana/Rex Features; **p243**: National Museum of Wales/Getty Images; **p244**: Ann Ronan Picture Library/Heritage Images/Getty Images

We are grateful for permission to reprint from the following copyright texts:

Simon Adams: 'England and the World under the Tudors, 1485–1603' in John Morrill (ed): *Oxford Illustrated History of Tudor & Stuart Britain* (OUP, 2000), reproduced by permission of Oxford University Press; and 'Eliza Enthroned: The Court and its Politics' in Christopher Haigh (ed): *The Reign of Elizabeth 1* (Macmillan, 1984), reproduced by permission of Palgrave Macmillan; **George Bernard**: introduction to *Henry VII by* S. B. Chrimes (Yale University Press, 1999), reproduced by permission of Yale University Press; **Susan Brigden**: *New Worlds: Lost Worlds: the Rule of the Tudors, 1485–1603* (Penguin Press, 2001), copyright © Susan Brigden 2000, reproduced by permission of Penguin Books Ltd; **Christine Carpenter**: *The Wars of the Roses: Politics and the Constitution in England c1437–1509* (Cambridge University Press, 1997), reproduced by permission of the publishers; **Donald C Coleman**: *The Economy of England 1450–1750* (OUP, 1977), reproduced by permission of Oxford University Press; **Patrick Collinson**: *English Puritanism* (Historical Association, 1983), reproduced by permission of The Historical Association, London; **Susan Doran**: *England and Europe 1485–1603* (Longman, 1986, 1996), copyright © Susan Doran 1986, and *Elizabeth I and Religion* (Routledge, 1994), copyright © Susan Doran 1994, reproduced by permission of Taylor & Francis Books UK; **Eamon Duffy**: *The Stripping of the Altars: Traditional Religion in England c1400–1580* (Yale University Press, 1992), copyright © Eamon Duffy 1992, reproduced by permission of Yale University Press; **G. R. Elton**: *Henry VIII: an Essay in Revision* (Historical Association No 51, RKP, 1962), reproduced by permission of The Historical Association, London; **Steven J. Gunn**: *Early Tudor Government 1485–1558* (Palgrave Macmillan, 1995), reproduced by permission of Palgrave Macmillan; 'Henry VII' in *The Oxford Dictionary of National Biography* (2004), reproduced by permission of Oxford University Press; and 'The courtiers of Henry VII', *English Historical Review*, CVIII (426): 23–49 (1993), reproduced by permission of the author and Oxford University Press; **John Guy**: *Late Tudor England, 1547–1603: NOHE* (OUP, 1988); and 'Tudor Monarchy and Political Culture' in John Morrill (ed): *Oxford Illustrated History of Tudor & Stuart Britain* (OUP, 2000), reproduced by permission of Oxford University Press; **Christopher Haigh**: *English Reformations: religion, politics and society under the Tudors* (Clarendon Press, 1993); and 'Politics in an Age of Peace and War 1570–1630' in John Morrill (ed): *Oxford Illustrated History of Tudor & Stuart Britain* (OUP, 2000), reproduced by permission of Oxford University Press; and *Elizabeth 1* (Longman, 2001), copyright © Christopher Haigh 2001, reproduced by permission of Taylor & Francis Books UK; **R. Hoyle**: *The Pilgrimage of Grace and the Politics of the 1530s* (OUP, 2001), reproduced by permission of Oxford University Press; **Eric Ives**: 'Henry VIII' in *The Oxford Dictionary of National Biography* (2004), reproduced by permission of Oxford University Press; **Norman Jones**: *The Birth of the Elizabethan Age: England in the 1560s* (Blackwell, 1995), copyright © Norman Jones 1993, reproduced by permission of Wiley Blackwell; **David Loades**: *Tudor Government: Structures and Authority in the 16th Century* (Blackwell, 1997), copyright © David Loades 1997, reproduced by permission of Wiley Blackwell; **Wallace MacCaffrey**: 'Politics in an Age of Reformation, 1485–1585' in John Morrill (ed): *Oxford Illustrated History of Tudor & Stuart Britain* (OUP, 2000), reproduced by permission of Oxford University Press; **J. K. MacConica**: *English Humanists and Reformation Politics under Henry VIII and Edward VII* (OUP, 1965), reproduced by permission of Oxford University Press; **Christopher Morris**: *The Tudors* (Batsford, 1955), reproduced by permission of B T Barsford, part of Pavilion Books Ltd; **David M Palliser**: *The Age of Elizabeth: England under the later Tudors 1547–1603* (Longman, 1983), copyright © David M Palliser 1983, reproduced by permission of Taylor & Francis Books UK; **George D Ramsay**: 'The Foreign Policy of Elizabeth 1' in Christopher Haigh (ed): *The Reign of Elizabeth 1* (Macmillan, 1984), reproduced by permission of Palgrave Macmillan; **Paul Slack**: *The English Poor Law* (Cambridge University Press, 1995), reproduced by permission of the publishers; **Richard B Wernham**: *The Making of Elizabethan Foreign Policy 1558–1603* (Univ of Calif Press, 1980), reproduced by permission of University of California Press, via Copyright Clearance Center; **Anna Whitelock**: *Mary Tudor: England's First Queen* (Bloomsbury, 2009), copyright © Anna Whitelock 2009, reproduced by permission of Bloomsbury Publishing Plc.; **Penry Williams**: *The Tudor Regime* (OUP, 1979), and *The Later Tudors: England 1547–1603: NOHE* (Clarendon Press, 1995), reproduced by permission of Oxford University Press; **Joyce Youings**: *Sixteenth Century England* (Allen Lane, 1984), copyright © Joyce Youings 1984, reproduced by permission of Penguin Books Ltd.

We have made every effort to trace and contact all copyright holders before publication, but if notified of any errors or omissions, the publisher will be happy to rectify these at the earliest opportunity.

The author would like to thank the following people: Sally Waller, Philip Stanton, Margaret Haynes.

The publisher would like to thank the following people for offering their contribution in the development of this book: Sally Waller and Philip Stanton.

Index

Topics available from *Oxford AQA History for A Level*

Tsarist and Communist Russia 1855-1964

978 019 835467 3

Challenge and Transformation: Britain c1851-1964

978 019 835466 6

The Tudors: England 1485-1603

978 019 835460 4

Stuart Britain and the Crisis of Monarchy 1603-1702

978 019 835462 8

The Making of a Superpower: USA 1865-1975

978 019 835469 7

The Quest for Politica Stability: Germany 1871-1991

978 019 835468 0

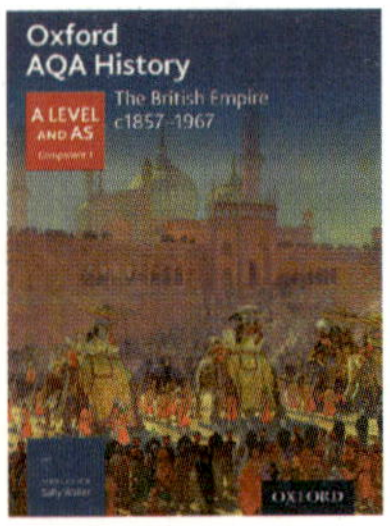

The British Empire c1857-1967

978 019 835463 5

Industrialisation and the People: Britain c1783-1885

978 019 835453 6

Wars and Welfare: Britain in Transition 1906-1957

978 019 835459 8

The Cold War c1945-1991

978 019 835461 1

Democracy and Nazism: Germany 1918-1945

978 019 835457 4

Revolution and Dictatorship: Russia 1917-1953

978 019 835458 1

Religious Conflict and the Church in England c1529-c1570

978 019 835471 0

International Relations and Global Conflict c1890-1941

978 019 835454 3

The American Dream: Reality and Illusion 1945-1980

978 019 835455 0

The Making of Modern Britain 1951-2007

978 019 835464 2

The Crisis of Communism: the USSR and the Soviet Empire 1953-2000

978 019 835465 9

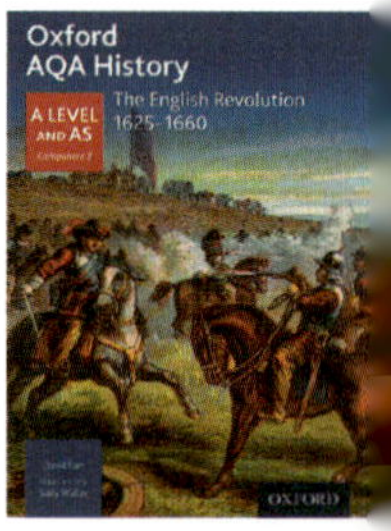

The English Revolutio 1625-1660

978 019 835472 7

France in Revolution 1774-1815

978 019 835473 4

The Transformation of China 1936-1997

978 019 835456 7

Also available in eBook format

eBook Available

Order online at **www.oxfordsecondary.co.uk/aqahistory**

OXFORD